Multicultural American Literature

MULTICULTURAL AMERICAN LITERATURE

Comparative Black, Native, Latino/a and Asian American Fictions

A. ROBERT LEE

UNIVERSITY PRESS OF MISSISSIPPI

Para Pepa una vez más

© A. Robert Lee, 2003

Edinburgh University Press Ltd
22 George Square, Edinburgh

Published in the United States of America by University Press of Mississippi, 2003

Typeset in Goudy Old Style by
Hewer Text Ltd, Edinburgh, and
printed and bound in Great Britain
by Antony Rowe Ltd, Chippenham, Wilts

ISBN 1-57806-644-1 (cloth)
ISBN 1-57806-645-X (paperback)

Library of Congress Cataloging-in-Publication Data available

The right of A. Robert Lee to be identified as
author of this work has been asserted in accordance
with the Copyright, Designs and Patents Act 1988.

Contents

Acknowledgements

However recent its commissioning, *Multicultural American Literature: Comparative Black, Native, Latino/a and Asian American Fictions*, I now realise, has had a long, not to say exhilarating, gestation. Its origins begin from when, as a British student of American culture, I first landed in a mid-1960s America of civil rights, black power, Vietnam, the counter-culture, women's and gay rights, and, most of relevance, the emerging new consciousness to do with US idioms of ethnicity.

In the decades since, and from university bases in Canterbury, England, a dozen American campuses spanning Princeton to Berkeley where it has been to my infinite advantage to hold visiting appointments and, since 1996, Nihon University (Nihon Daigaku) Tokyo, I have built up a huge array of debts. Given an academic career which, as much by chance as not, thus connects not only England, Europe and America, but also Japan and other parts of Asia, it would be impossible to overstate the support, and quite the best of critique, from friends whose own geographies, and ethnicities, have been at once wondrously discrepant yet linked the one to the other. Across the board they, quite as much as myself, should be held to account for what follows. They will understand the spirit in which I say this, an indebtedness for which I thank them profoundly.

First, it has been my utter good fortune not only to have met with, but to have enjoyed friendships with, and on occasion interviewed for the BBC and other media, a number of the writers whose work this study seeks to map or who have influenced its making. These include Gerald Vizenor, Ishmael Reed, John Wideman, John A. Williams, Betty Bell, John Yau, Kimiko Hahn, Carmen Tafolla, Lorenzo Thomas, Clarence Major, Mitsuye Yamada, Alurista, Lorna Dee Cervantes, Linda Hogan, Tino Villanueva, Gary Pak, the late Leon Forrest and Chester Himes, and Louis Owens, doyen of Native American studies, whose untimely death occurred as I was completing this study.

Within the academy, I have had the benefit of a wide range of encouragement and relevant discussion. Those from whom I have learned, and to whom I remain grateful, include Lyn Innes and Abdulrazak Gurnah of the University of Kent at Canterbury; Mary Condé of Queen Mary College, London; Clive Bush of King's College, London; Richard Gray, Colin Samson, Jacqueline Kaye and Ann Marie Acklam of Essex University where I was invited to give the annual American Studies lecture, on US Multicultural Autobiography, in 2002; David Dabydeen of the University of Warwick; Andrew Hook and Susan Castillo of Glasgow University; David Murray and Judie Newman of the University of Nottingham; and Barry Lewis, Peter Dempsey and Tony Hepburn of Sunderland University which has done me the honour of making me one of its annual visiting professors, and especially Donald MacRaild, currently of the University of Northumbria, who was good enough to get the appointment started.

In the USA, I need most especially to include the Departments of Ethnic Studies at the University of California at Berkeley and at the University of Colorado at Boulder, both of which have shown me greatest welcome. At Berkeley, that has especially meant Gerald Vizenor, in whose trickster company many of the approaches of this book were first explored, Laura Hall, Ling-chi Wang, Sau-ling Cynthia Wong, Jean Molesky-Poz, Gary Strankman, Dorothy Wang, now of Northwestern University, Matt Wray, who gave me invaluable suggestions as to whiteness studies, and Joe Lockard, now of Arizona State University, who has long been a friend and co-worker in this terrain. At Colorado, it has meant Evelyn Hu-DeHart, recently moved to Brown University, Lane Hirabayashi, Marilyn Alquizola, Ward Churchill and Annette Dula, and from an earlier time Cordelia Candelaria, now of Arizona State University, and the late Salvador Rodríguez del Pino. Others of long standing who have helped me steer my way through multicultural America include Harold Cruse of the University of Michigan, Werner Sollors of Harvard University, Barbara Fields of Columbia University, Nell Irwin Painter of Princeton University, Joseph Skerrett of the University of Massachusetts at Amherst, Amritjit Singh of Rhode Island College, John Halcón of California State University San Marcos, María de la Luz Reyes, formerly of the University of Colorado, Epifanio San Juan Jr, recently of Washington State University, John G. Cawelti, formerly of the University of Kentucky, Arnold Krupat of Sarah Lawrence College, Alan Velie of the University of Oklahoma, Russell Leong of UCLA, Seiwoong Oh of Rider University, Marco Portales of Texas A. and M. University, William New of the University of British Columbia, who will perhaps indulge me in including him in a North American listing, and Avis Kuwahara Payne of the Multiethnic Literature of the United States Association (MELUS).

In Europe, my debts, equally, continue to multiply. They include Hans Bak of the University of Nijmegen, Theo D'Haen of Leuven University, Mario Maffi of the University of Milan, William Boelhower of the University of Padua, Franco LaPolla of the University of Bologna, Elizabetta Marino of the University of Rome, Ole Moen of the University of Oslo, Gunther Lenz and Susanne Opfermann of the University of Frankfurt, Helmbrecht Breinig and Wolfgang Binder of the University of Erlangen, Rocío Davis of the University of Navarra, Begoña Simal González of the University of Coruña, Basia Ozieblo of the University of Málaga, Angel-Luis Pujante and Juan Antonio Suárez of the University of Murcia, and the Open University of Spain (UNED) which on different occasions has invited me to video-record lectures on US multicultural literature. It has also been a bonus to have played a part in the creation of the Society for Multi-Ethnic Studies: Europe and America (MESEA), and not least to have been invited to give a plenary lecture, 'Ethnics Behaving Badly: US Multicultural Narratives' at the Orléans conference, in June 2000. I thank all of its stalwarts, but especially Alfred Hornung of the University of Mainz as President, again Rocío Davis as Secretary, and Cathy Waegner of the University of Siegen, Dorothea Fischer-Hornung of the University of Heidelberg, and Heike Raphael-Hernandez and Alison Goeller of the University of Maryland in Heidelberg.

In Japan, it has been my good fortune to have Takeshi Onodera for a departmental colleague at Nihon University, along with Ichitaro Toma, Kimitaka Hara, Takeshi Sekiya, Yuko Noro, Tomoko Kanda and Stephen Harding. I also owe related debts to Yuji Nakata of Konan Women's University, Arimichi Makino of Meiji University, Hideyo Sengoku of Rikkyo University, and Teruyo Ueki of the Asian American Literature Association (AALA). Among my *gaijin* circle, I need to list David Ewick of Chuo University and Susan Anicad of Sophia University for their friendship and frequent bibliographical help, William Gater and Sandra Lucore of the University of Tokyo, and Dorsey Kleitz of Tokyo Woman's Christian University. Terry Caesar of Mukogawa University, James Vardaman of Waseda University and Nicholas Williams of Saitama Institute of Technology generously took time out to read various chapter drafts. Their suggestions have been invaluable. Asia has afforded me yet other forums for which I especially thank Vicki Ooi of Hong Kong University, Iping Liang and Jung Su of National Taiwan Normal University, Taipei, and So-Hee Lee of Hangyan's Women's University, Seoul, and Sooyoung Chon and Min Jung Kim of Ewha Woman's University, Seoul. To all: *arigato gozaimashita, xie-xie/mgoi, gamsahamnida.*

Another kind of help has presented itself in university and conference invitations where I have been able to air much of the analysis contained here. My gratitude to various bodies for the opportunity, across the years, in seeking to evolve perspectives on US and other multiculturalism and its writings, remains considerable: the British Association of American Studies (BAAS); the European Association of American Studies (EAAS); the Institute of US Studies, London; the Norwegian Association of American Studies (NAAS); the Spanish Association of American Studies (SAAS); the Japanese Association of Asian American Studies (JAAS); the American Studies Association of Korea (ASAK); the International Society for the Study of the Chinese Overseas (ISSCO) at their Hong Kong, Taiwan and various San Francisco conferences; the Roosevelt Center, Middelburg, the Netherlands; the National Association of Chicano Studies (NACS), where I had the privilege of conversations with Don Luis Leal; the University of California at Riverside Research Seminar in Native Studies; the Taiwan Normal University Literary Research Seminar; along with the forums afforded by MELUS and MESEA. I should also mention how useful it has been, these past several years, to contribute an annual section on the scholarship of US multicultural literature to the *Year's Work in English Studies.* My thanks go to the various editors, and the English Association, for the opportunity.

Not least are my debts to students in England, Europe, America and Asia. I acknowledge them without reservation.

Nicola Carr at Edinburgh University Press has been a veritable editorial Griselda. I thank her, and all the team in George Square, for keeping faith with the project.

In Josefa Vivancos Hernández I am lucky to have a rarest *compañera*, an ongoing gift of life and Spain. *Gracias por todo.*

America and the Multicultural Word

Legacies, Maps, Vistas, Theory

I began to realize that being black or Chicano or Native American, you are forced to see and become aware of disparate cultures. We had to become multicultural, and I think this will be a major factor in determining who finally survives in this country. It's like evolution – if you have a limited viewpoint you are at a disadvantage. Those who have incorporated other perspectives and allowed their vision to embrace other ways of looking at the world have a better chance of surviving. (Ishmael Reed)[1]

But does this mean that faced with the multiple anchorages that ethnicity provides, learning from Japanese Americans, Chinese Americans, Filipino Americans, Mexican Americans, Jewish Americans, Native Americans, and yes, Indian Americans, I can juggle and toss and shift and slide, words, thoughts, actions, symbols, much as a poor conjuror I once saw in the half darkness of the Columbus Circle subway stop? Can I become just what I want? So is this the land of opportunity, the America of dreams? (Meena Alexander)[2]

I

Multicultural American Literature. The phrase might almost be thought redundant. How can America, or its literature, and from the puritans to the postmoderns, in any accurate sense ever have been thought other than multicultural? Who, indeed, doubts Reed's 'disparate cultures', Alexander's 'multiple anchorages'? Yet, given past habits of interpretation, the response has to be: not a few. For whether as a history, or for more immediate purposes a line of authorship, America, long, and almost by automatic custom, has been projected as a mainstream nothing if not overwhelmingly Eurocentric, Atlantic, east to west, and white-male in its unfolding.

Given the hold of this perspective, and always granting the exception, others in the drama of nation until recently for the most part were to be thought margins, a species of ethnic outrider. Native America, the tribes, had become so by historic evisceration, and dispersal, and whether on or off reservation. Afro-America, south and north, could be visible yet somehow not, an 'other' America of colour-line and ghetto and to be associated with its own subcultures of language, crime, music or dress. A whole realm of Spanish-speakers, notably Chicano/a, Puerto Rican and Cuban-Floridian, their axis either south–north or island to mainland, likewise existed as an America elsewhere – Hispanic, brown and usually poor. Asian America had arisen out of Pacific migrancy that was anything but the pageant of Anglo-America's Pilgrim Fathers, obscure by language and custom, even, as in latter-day accusations against the Los Alamos nuclear scientist, Wen Ho Lee, to be thought still caught up in Yellow Peril conspiracy.

The call, however, especially in the light of the identity politics of the 1960s and in which civil rights became a beacon, would increasingly go up for a massive change of perception and redress. It is not that the diversities of American culture, literary or otherwise, and from pre-Columbian to present times, had gone unremarked. How, in truth, could they? The issue, rather, turns upon the presiding, if erroneous, sense of their forever supposed being located at the edges of a white canonical America, a vernacular, sometimes picturesque or exotic, sub-peopling within the national realm. In this context, the 'minority' within minority ethnic population slips into the apparently self-evident confirmation of a lesser order of literary-cultural interest and achievement. This invites every kind of challenge.[3]

The term 'fiction', to this end, likewise also requires its own kind of loosening, a working latitude. It is meant to embrace novels, novellas, stories and story-cycles, autobiography as implicated in its own kind of fictionality, even a number of verse chronicles, and at a larger reach American culture-myths, all, and however different the one from the other, *ficciones* in the spirit of Jorge Luis Borges. For the aim, nothing less, from within the range of US multicultural narrative of the last half-century, and in no way to exclude that of white-ethnic America, is to map, and compare, the arising literary fictions of Afro-America, Native America, Latino/a America and Asian America.

Multicultural American Literature opens with a re-examination of a number of recent landmark novels, and of the imaginative fashioning they give to the four legacies in play, by Ralph Ellison, Scott Momaday, Rudolfo Anaya and Maxine Hong Kingston. The account of ethnic autobiography which follows, and of related notions of autoethnicity and autofiction, looks equally to the canniness of imagination which lies behind the self in view. As to the chapters which address the literary-ethnic tracks involved, Black, Native, Latino/a and Asian American, each is intended both to situate authorship and fiction within its own due context of history, locale, politics, and popular culture alongside high forms, and in working through a spectrum of texts to call up at the same time parallels and interconnections, tacit or explicit, between each.

The ensuing chapters offer analysis in matching spirit: comparative fictions of ethnic site drawn from topographies of Indian Country, Asiatown (to include one Asian Canadian novel), Harlem as centrifugal black city, and a *chicanismo* of borderland, migrancy and *barrio*; novels and stories of multiethnic America which turn on the notion of Atlantic and Pacific island as literal hemispheric geo-history, and yet, always, the trope of inner personal body of life and experience; and a gallery of literary fictions which, at whatever risk of seeming unexpectedness, can best be defined as the ethnic postmodern. By way of rounding out, and as cultural ideology, whiteness and a sampler of its fictions comes under scrutiny, the not-so-secret sharer in the setting of terms whereby almost all American literary ethnicity has been construed.

II

If, since the 1960s, there has been little short of a rebirth of Black, Native, Latino/a and Asian American writing, to embrace poetry, theatre, discursive work, performance art and popular culture, along with all the working varieties of literary fiction, that is anything but to deny prior lineage or embattled ground. Quite the busiest pulls of allegiance continue to arise, an ongoing and liveliest exchange of claim and counter-claim.

Inevitably, these also arise from, and reflect back upon, America's larger political and ideological debates about multiculturalism and ethnicity. Are such, in the first instance, to be thought the codes of a better understanding of America's cultural diversity, the opening of the American mind as Lawrence W. Levine calls it? Or, in Arthur M. Schlesinger Jr's phrase, do they amount to the disuniting of America? One camp speaks of bywords for cultural democracy, a more plural canon; the other of balkanisation, the subjugation of self to category, a wearying political correctness.[4]

To complicate matters yet further, Right and Left equally have their own in-house divisions. The former are by no means agreed on what kind of 'one America' they advocate. Should it be economically *and* socially conservative, and if to create a national order beyond classification by ethnicity leave as is, or better recognise and dismantle, racial privilege? The latter, likewise, are of different stripes. A number of neo-Marxists see multiculturalism as gestural or boutique cultural politics, a cover-up for deeper divisions of class, the exploitation of migrant and other cheap labour, and an evasion of each continuing and unresolved subterfuge of racism. Yet other liberal-leftists back a multicultural ethos to the hilt as the very ground-condition of all future American politics, as important to the shaping of the nation's power arrangements as class, gender or region. In this sense, ethnicity is to be understood as live human dynamic, busy in contradiction, contestatory as need be, anything but inert category.

Ilan Stavans, Mexican Jewish, American by choice, and consciously emulating James Baldwin in *The Fire Next Time* (1963), concludes his *The Hispanic Condition: Reflections on Culture and Identity in America* (1995) with a 'Letter to My Child'. Having spoken of heritages which give a hemispheric bridge to George Washington and Simón Bolívar and, in his own immediate case, to Mexico and America and its 'encounter between Anglos and Hispanics' (p. 19), he offers the following prospectus:

My son, you will certainly live in an age in which the fruits of multiculturalism will be flavorful. Although some, like the Australian critic Robert Hughes, author of *Barcelona*, believe the climate has given way to a culture of complaint

. . . multicultualism, I've no doubt, is a benign weapon. It is my belief that multiculturalism will be an entrance door to a more humane world. (pp. 198–9)

As to race itself, everyday shorthand or not, is there not always somewhere the echo of eugenics, the notion of supremacism in IQ, or blood, or colour, each, on abundant past evidence, tied into the grain of slavery, colonialism, and Nazi and other fatal ideology?[5] In the case of America, especially, a further complication comes into play. DNA and a whole slew of new genetic excavation suggests that about 30 per cent of American whites, more than 50 million people, have at least one black ancestor, and the average African American is approximately one sixth white. It has become a commonplace of research biology that, in fact, there is no gene for race.

Black–Native mix, like white-Native mix, has been a long-time fact. White-Asian and Black-Asian interracialism, marriage and offspring, has more than doubled in the last decade. *Mestizaje* lies at the very heart of Latino/a lineage. Even 'mixed race' hardly covers matters. Is not, in, of, and for itself, almost another kind of 'ethnic' meta-identity in play? Little wonder that the 2000 census, for the first time, gave Americans the opportunity to designate themselves, and their children, as being of more than any one ethnic-racial stock. This is anything but to deny that race maintains its grip as a term both of offence and defence, or that it does not imply, almost always, hierarchy by colour.

That, moreover, is not to pass over the fact of how 'race', within much of America, has been a term too often fixed at the assumed white–black divides. In his spirited account of 'color politics', *Yellow: Race in America Beyond Black and White* (2002), Frank H. Wu not only decries model-minority notions of Asian America, its 'honorary whiteness' (p. 18), he argues for an end to the one usual, if always selective, binary:

People speak of 'American' as if it means 'white' and 'minority' as if it means 'black'. In that semantic formula, Asian Americans, neither black nor white, consequently are neither American nor minority. (p. 20)

Authorship, inevitably, at once embodies, and explores, so hugely various a demography. A poet like AI (Florence Anthony), born of a Japanese father and a mother black, Choctaw and Irish, and whose collection, *Cruelty* (1973), opened a career of monologue-poems, appears in both African American and Asian American references. Leading modern names in the African American novel have long drawn from their Native as well as black lineage, whether in the form of the Georgia-Cherokee subplots in Alice Walker's civil rights classic, *Meridian* (1976), and her womanist *The Color Purple* (1982), or the multi-tapestried use of both Cherokee and Zuni materials in Clarence Major's *Such was the Season* (1987) and *Painted Turtle: Woman with a Guitar* (1988).

Alurista (Alberto Baltazar Urista Heredia), Chicano poet and activist, and whose *Floricanto en Aztlán* (1971) remains a benchmark of Chicano consciousness, uses legacies at once Mexican, Nahuatl and US-Chicano, to write verse full of hybrid allusion and code-switching. Most of Native fiction's current figures, Scott Momaday, Leslie Marmon Silko, James Welch, Louise Erdrich, Gerald Vizenor or Sherman Alexie, do anything but deny themselves resort to histories both indigenous and European, and in their meeting, as in their fissures and contraflows, an arising complexity of personal cross-history.

For each of these writers, however usually identified under any one category of birth, ethnicity in reality has always meant an eclecticism of family ancestry, a cross of line and home, often itself the very subject of their work. It has even been mooted that, in writing 'mixed-race' literature, they imply an America headed into post-ethnicity. If so, an ironic convergence might look to be in prospect. It would involve, unlikely as it might appear, the overlap between those who endorse a national literature (albeit according to its Eurocentric canon), and those who believe that ethnic eclecticism and complementarity will eventually lead to an end to all preferential cultural ancestry.[6]

As to the latter prospect, David Palumbo-Liu, in the Introduction to the essays collected in *The Ethnic Canon: Histories, Institutions, and Interventions* (1995), argues that complementarity does not mean co-option, some mere token diversity which once taken note of can safely be incorporated and so disarmed. Advocating a critical multiculturalism which by no means overlooks both past and present exclusion in the construction of US 'nationalist narrative', not to say the intersections of class, ethnicity, gender and ideology within constructs like 'mainstream' and 'minority', he writes:

> the goal is to resist the essentializing and stratifying modes of reading ethnic literature that make it ripe for canonization and co-option.[7]

Each ethnic text, in other words, carries its own unique dislocatory force, a resistance to being thought 'representative', given a nod of recognition, and then simply absorbed into the more or less same-as-usual American canon.[8]

Given all these contributing lights, how far, then, are the fictions designated multicultural, or ethnic, genuinely to be allowed to challenge, not to say reconfigure, the usual received notions of America's literary canon, if not, indeed, the very notion of canonicity itself? How, in consequence, is America, and American literature, best to be identified?

III

To begin addressing these and related literary counts, first with a chapter-heading quotation by Ishmael Reed, storyteller, metafictionist, poet and essayist, and for good reason recognised as one of Afro-America's best wits, and then with a follow-up observation by Meena Alexander, born in India, Manhattanite, poet, novelist, and the autobiographer of the compelling transcontinental life she unravels in *Fault Lines* (1993), could not be more apt. Both speak not only to the always changing dynamic of America as ethnic-cultural regime but also to a profound sense of the literary consequence.

Can there, should there, indeed, any longer be the one master narrative, the one agreed canonical America with its one agreed literary canon? Who else, and with what implication, has given imaginative weight and form to America's multicultural ply, its huge, diverse funds of human story? Multicultural authorship, stirringly, not to say quite inevitably, contests the notion of an Our America whose *Mayflower*-birthing bequeaths a dispensation ever self-privilegingly white-Anglo and, in keeping, ethnic nowhere but at the margins. Only of late has Anglo-ism begun to win understanding as itself endemically, rootedly ethnic.

Reed's contention in his 1989 interview that Americans have 'a better chance of surviving' the more they become aware of their plural legacies offers a well-taken tease. He argues that according ethnic America better recognition, and in all its history and diversity of voice, is not to be thought a source of division. The effect, rather, and no doubt ironically, can be to help usher in an ever more textured, and so ever more durable, national identity. That is, in literature as in life, multiculturalism operates as a kind of Darwinism, an ongoing evolutionary route which, if intelligently seized upon, promises stronger, not weaker, health.

Acknowledging the controversies entailed, in which he has played a leading participant-observer role, he entitles a recent anthology under his editorship *Multi-America: Essays on Cultural Wars and Cultural Peace* (1997).[9] Reed's essay-work, in fact, has been pledged from the outset to counter precisely those he terms mono-culturists and America as Common Culture monolith. His Introduction to the essays in *MultiAmerica*, full of customary sharpshooter edge, offers a prospectus. Accuracy, he suggests, if nothing else, should bear out how selective most main-stream versions of America have been:

> The McIntellectuals and their black and brown Talented Tenth auxiliary insist that we embrace a common culture, and their consensus seems to be that this culture is Yankee, or Anglo . . . Though frictions do exist within the multi-cultural community, the thing that unites these various factions is an opposition to white supremacy and to the one-sided discussion of ethnicity and multiculturalism by the national media. These monoculturists must feel right at home when they appear on networks to engage in sound-bite dismissals of multiculturalists as engaging in political correctness, or disuniting and balkanizing the country . . . I think that a new definition of a common culture is possible, and that because of their own ethnic status, Latinos, African Americans and Asian Americans with knowledge of their own ethnic histories and cultures as well as those of European cultures are able to contribute to the formation of a new, inclusive definition. (pp. xvi–xvii)

These remarks also give a reminder of how, along with the Nuyorriqueño poet Victor Hernández Cruz, the Chicano novelist Rudolfo Anaya and the Chinese American author Shawn Wong, Reed established the Before Columbus Foundation in 1976. A glance at the prizegiving of the Josephine Miles Award by its house journal, *The Before Columbus Review*, might almost be a roster of the best-known names and achievements in the field. With the issue of the two collections, *The Before Columbus Foundation Fiction Anthology* and *The Before Columbus Foundation Poetry Anthology*, in 1992, and its ongoing conferences pledged to 'this country's multicultural, multiethnic, and multiracial diversity', it became clear that the Foundation sought nothing less than to realign American writing, less a decanonisation than an end to the one, all-determining canonicity.[10]

It also became clear that Reed and his fellow editors intended a literary multiculturalism that meant anything but counter-exclusions. In 'The Ocean of American Literature', which acts as Preface to both volumes, Reed gives special emphasis to inclusion, the array of co-voicing:

> We meant Irish Americans and Italian Americans, as well as Asian Americans, African Americans and Native Americans . . . American literature in the last decade of this century is more than a mainstream . . . a dominant mother culture with an array of subcultures tagging along. (pp. xxiv–xxv)

Almost any selection of Reed's own essays adds illustration and lustre. His title piece in *Shrovetide in Old New Orleans* (1978) explores New Orleans as the very paradigm of a lived city multiculturalism. Vodoun, Africanism, offers one vein, not least in the person of Marie Laveau as turn-of-the-century conjure-woman, its Hoodoo Queen, along with jazz, blues, each and every black anthem and marching song. Spain adds its weight in placenames, house and balcony designs, and the colourful local *azulejos* or tiles. Mardi Gras as a transposed French Canadian or *arcadien* Catholic festival, with interfusions of *santería*, becomes 'a bright moment on the American death calendar' (p. 31). Foodways bring their taste and variety from Cajun gumbo to Delta oyster to Native maize. Old-style Dixie, in contrast, is accusingly remembered through the Confederate Flag as 'America's swastika' (p. 15). Overall, this is a *topos* of the American city as living syncretism, with, in Reed's styling, essay-chronicle to match. The touch, to be sure, is full of irreverent squibs and comic shots, but always to serious and well-taken purpose and born of a formidable controlling intelligence.

Writin' is Fightin': Thirty-Seven Years of Boxing on Paper (1988), its title borrowed from a rap throwaway by Muhammad Ali, reprints 'America: The Multinational Society', another of Reed's best-celebrated essays. Pitched in what Reed, as always with an ironic sting, insists is his working-class style, it indicts Hitler as 'the archetypal monoculturist' (p. 54), speaks of the Puritans as 'a daring lot, but they had a mean streak' (p. 55), chastises received versions of Early America as a 'Zion Wilderness' (p. 55), reminds his readers that the US system of government owes debts to the Iroquois, and looks to the nation's 'exciting destiny' (p. 56) as residing in a better-understood and relished 'crisscross' (p. 56) of its contributing cultures.

'The world is here' (p. 56) ends the piece. Some leftist commentary has taken after him in this as avoiding an oppressive economics of colour-line or class and capitalist exploitation. Reed would readily answer that his is anything but mere interethnic good feeling and that he wholly recognises, whether in the case of black domestic worker, Filipino fieldhand, Chicano migrant labourer, or even a white-poor stratum, the need for remediation in issues of wealth and power-structure inequalities. That lies implicit as a challenge in any serious move towards a just American multicultural order.[11]

Airing Dirty Laundry (1993) yields 'Black Irishman', a vintage autobiographical account and a striking vindication of Reed's view of America as a 'land of distant cousins', anything but 'separate bloodlines' ('Distant Cousins', p. 273). Invited by his friend, the San Francisco poet and publisher, Bob Callahan, to San Francisco's Irish Cultural Center, he gives witness over stew and dumplings to the long interaction of Black and Irish life. The point is made about the overlap of British slaveholding with its colonial rule in Ireland and Marcus Garvey's telegram of congratulation to the founders of the Irish Free State. He sees links in both civil rights movements, not least in how the marches in Londonderry and Belfast call up those of 1960s Dixie like Selma and Montgomery, or in how the hunger-strike protests of Bobby Sands and the IRA blanket detainees, even in their fierceness, shadow the Christian-pacifist politics of Martin Luther King.

These lead him to contemplation of his own literal, yet also figurative, black Irishness through surname and family mix of origins. He thinks back upon his grandmother's recall of her immigrant Irish father, a blue-collar union organiser, and a supposed renegade from his own whiteness for having married a Chattanooga, Tennessee black woman. In this genealogy, along with his own Native bloodline, and as in literary argument and practice, Ishmael Reed gives memorably personal witness to the more inclusive phenomenon: the facts, and the fictions, and at all levels of class and gender, of America as multicultural estate.

Meena Alexander offers another, yet wholly complementary, bearing. In *The Shock of Arrival: Reflections on Postcolonial Experience* (1996), looking back on a life which bridges the India of Allahabad and Kerala, the Sudan, England, and New York City, she speaks to her own Indo-American identity as both a prior, and yet ongoing, dynamic of shapings:

> In our multiple ethnicities as Asian Americans, we are constantly making alliances, both within and outside our many communities. In order to make up my ethnic identity as an Indian American, I learn from Japanese Americans, Korean Americans, Chinese Americans, African Americans, Native Americans, Hispanic Americans, Jewish Americans, Arab Americans. And these images that slip and slide out of my own mind jostle against a larger shared truth. And my artwork refracts these lines of sense, these multiple anchorages. (p. 128)

The repeated phrase, 'multiple anchorages', like 'multiple ethnicities', once more perfectly applies: no one *grand récit*, no single pre-emptive minority fable, no essentialist signature.

For American ethnic identity, and the literary work to which it gives rise, almost of necessity involves multifarious kinds and degrees of voice, reflective of cultures as much implicated in debate with themselves as synchronicity with a supposedly agreed America at large. Essentialist ground rules, or protocols, moreover, apply even less as America's demography becomes the yet greater cross-hatch. Alexander's own authorship from the outset reflects these processes as well as any, the interacting mix and plurality, the abrasions and even fissures, of America's multiculturalism as the very grain of 'artwork', whether her own, or that of her fellow ethnic writers. Ethnic categories may well signify communal history but not at the expense of individual contrariety.

Afro-America, however singular its own history from slavery to the cities, has thus also been tied into the Black Atlantic, an interconnecting, and massively various, weave of Africa, Europe, the Caribbean and South America. Blackness as sign invites recognition of every nuance of geography, speech or memory. Native America, increasingly, has come to be construed as much through mixedblood or crossblood populations as through any supposed fullblood quantum. Its writings, in consequence, have always, and matchingly, been multivocal, sited in the city as well as the land, open to American mass culture as well as to traditional tribal influence.

America as Latino/a dispensation has increasingly meant not only Chicano/a, Puerto Rican or Cuban American dispensations, but others of, say, Dominican, Colombian, Peruvian or Salvadorean origin. Besides Spanish, or every kind of Creole, theirs, too, has been a resort to yet other languages of the Americas, whether Brazilian Portuguese, Caribbean French, or a raft of indigenous tongues from Mayan to Nahuatl. They each convey not only the heteroglossia of the USA but of the Americas at large, a hemispheric and mosaical order of word and literature. Asian America, ongoingly migrant, and as diverse in class as geographical origins whether a mainland Asia of China or Korea and Indo-Pakistan, or Japan, or the island Pacific like the Philippines and Hawai'i, looks to regimes themselves previously already shaped by the energies of their own multiculturalism.

The challenge, overall, becomes one of making ethnicity neither too prescriptive, nor yet so porous as to curb usable definition. The grand sweep risks losing particularity. Too particular a focus risks losing genuine overlap and linkage.

IV

Implicit in these same histories has to be recognition of a similar diversity of discursive space, traditions of debate, be they spoken or written, which, through time, have borne each and all cultural variation within both group and self-identity. The representative literary voice, however understandable the temptation to believe otherwise, can itself never be other than yet one more species of fiction.[12]

William Apess, born in 1792 a mixedblood Pequot (evidence gathers also of a black inheritance), saw himself a convert to Christian piety and yet an unyielding Native dissenter. In *A Son of the Forest* (1829), he is to be heard, characteristically, through an observation like 'I could not find the word "Indian" in the Bible and therefore concluded it was a word imported for the purpose of degrading us'. Subsequently, in his 'Eulogy on King Philip' (1837), he suggests that the anniversary of the Pilgrim Landing, 22 December, would better be thought a Native Day of Mourning. If Apess is to be thought an ethnic voice (Native? Mixedblood? Black-Native?), there can be no mistaking the individual inflection within.[13]

Frederick Douglass (1818–95), son of a white slaveholder father and black slave mother (in a reverse of Apess, it emerges he may have been of part-Native background), gives his *Narrative* (1845) a plain style which yields a similar play of ambiguity. In the always greatly freighted formulation of 'written by himself', he seeks to counter the anonymity of his birth, absentee parentage, and slaveholding's requirement of illiteracy, not to mention the custom of using a white intermediary (usually an abolitionist) in telling slave stories. Douglass, in fact, could not manifest greater self-complexity, the composite of historic escapee across the Chesapeake Bay from Maryland to Boston, abolitionist speaker, and, however obliquely, *auteur*, who, having fashioned his own name, might be thought to half-taunt in his closing phrase 'I subscribe myself . . . FREDERICK DOUGLASS'.[14]

Neither Apess nor Douglas, and without the slightest diminution of their historic importance, can be thought representative without the most careful negotiation of the term. Nor, in their wake, and despite claims to the contrary, has ethnic writing ever submerged its necessary differences into one ideological or even literary standard, be the author African American, Native, Latino/a or Asian American.

Zora Neale Hurston, always 'bodacious', to use a favoured adjective of her own, affords a voice closer to our own time, yet, if anything, still less given to speaking for others than for herself. Her autobiography, *Dust Tracks on a Road* (1942), for all its companionable ease, could not at the same time more insist on its own no-holds-barred rights of contrary opinion. In looking back with unashamed affection to Eatonville, the all-black Florida township in which she was raised, and to its fund of community memory and talk, for instance, she can also excoriate in 'Seeing the World as it Is' any one-note 'Negro' category. 'There is no *The Negro* here', runs one of her typical pronouncements. 'Why', she goes on to ask in a smack at the comfort of stock formula, 'should Negroes be united? Nobody else is in the United States' (p. 251). In these kinds of comments, and whether or not (as is often alleged) the book plays down historic white racism in order to palliate her likely majority readership, there has been no shortage of grounds for controversy. Ralph Ellison would add his own shot in alleging, for all her feminist heroisation, that her writing too easily edges towards burlesque.

Gerald Vizenor, mixedblood Anishinaabe (or Chippewa/Ojibway) novelist, poet and Berkeley professor, and one of the most prolific authors in Native American tradition, equally decries the representative status. He has long, and boldly, satirised mainstream reductions of America's indigenous peoples into 'the Indian' as a hopeless conflation of diverse tribes, languages and tradition. In the essay-collection *Crossbloods: Bone Courts, Bingo, and Other Reports* (1990), he leaves no doubt of his resistance to any, or all, projections of the one Native collectivity of voice:

The use of the word 'Indian' is postmodern, a navigational conception, a colonial invention, a simulation in sound and transcription. Tribal cultures became nominal, diversities were twisted to the core, and oral stories were set in written languages, the translations of discoveries . . . Native American Indians are burdened with colonial pantribal names, and with imposed surnames translated by missionaries and federal agents. More than a hundred million people, and hundreds of distinct tribal cultures were simulated as Indians; an invented pantribal name, one sound, bears treaties, statutes, and seasons, but no tribal culture, language, religion, or landscape.[15]

At the same time, he has shown anything but reluctance to take on the American Indian Movement (AIM) as having colluded in the problem. However theatrically attractive to the media, do not many of the leading names, unelected and so unaccountable, time and again play anachronistic or radical chic 'Indians'? Although this has put him in several kinds of firing line at the same time, he has made one of his hallmark words that of *postindian*, the teasing, and yet always wholly serious, rejection of 'Indian' as misconceived from the start, erroneous in both geography and history. For him, moreover, to write postindianly has of necessity meant to write postmodernly.

A US bilingual heritage might almost be guaranteed to ensure writing, a literature, rich not only in an overlap of the languages involved but also in code-switches, amalgams, a play of registers. Sandra Cisneros, the acclaimed Chicana storyteller of *The House on Mango Street* (1983) and *Woman Hollering Creek and Other Stories* (1991) and, against stereotype, raised in Chicago, offers a first-hand perspective:

> As a young writer . . . I was aware I had to find my voice, but how was I to know it would be the voice I used at home, the one I acquired as a result of one English-speaking mother and one Spanish-speaking father? My mother's English was learned in the Mexican/Italian neighborhood she grew up in on Chicago's near south side, an English learned from playmates and school, since her own parents spoke Spanish exclusively. My father, on the other hand, spoke to us in a Spanish of grandmothers and children, a language embroidered with the diminutive . . . These two voices at odds with each other – my mother's punch-you-in-the-nose English and my father's powdered-sugar Spanish – curiously are the voices that surface in my writing. What I'm specially aware of lately is how the Spanish syntax and word choice occurs in my work even though I write in English.[16]

The lecture from which these remarks are taken, delivered in 1986 at Indiana University under the title 'Ghosts and Voices: Writing from Obsession', looks to a family upbringing not only of paired languages, or of language within language, but also of the differing pulls and counter-pulls of idioms bound into gender, age, and a city neighbourhood of overlapping ethnic diversity.

In 'Mother Tongue' (1990), a kindred act of literary reflection, Amy Tan also ponders different registers, in her case English, Chinese, and the Chinese-English between, which she impressively first put to use in *The Joy Luck Club* (1989). She thinks back on the simultaneous kinds of English she grew up with, each in itself a source of story and inherited meaning and history:

> I began to write stories using all the Englishes I grew up with: the English I spoke to my mother, which for lack of a better term might be described as 'simple'; the English she used with me, which for lack of a better term might be described as 'broken'; my translation of her Chinese if she could use perfect English, her internal language, and for that I sought to preserve the essence, but neither an English nor a Chinese structure. I wanted to capture what language ability tests never reveal: her intent, her passion, her imagery, the rhythms of her speech and the nature of her thoughts.[17]

If, throughout *The Joy Luck Club*, the mah jong table acts as a kind of exchange bureau for each mother-daughter life story, it does so, equally, in the idioms listed in 'Mother Tongue'. The China ferried into America is told, heard as it were, in voices at once winningly dissonant yet also complementary.

For in these, and fellow ethnic writers, the representative voice once again does not, and actually cannot, exist. Theirs are ethnicities drawn from lives, sites, memories, transformations of past into present, all, assuredly, drawn from shared community reference: no one suggests that any given ethnicity does not have its own codes and reflexes. Yet at the same time, and always, the writings – the fictions – remain as wholly and necessarily particular as each author's power to shape, and so sustain that ethnicity, and as occasion requires to draw upon its crossply with all other factors which have gone into individual make-up.

V

'"Did you ever hear of Christopher Columbus?" "*Bien sûr!* He invented America; a very great man"'[18] Henry James could little have anticipated how this exchange in the Louvre between the copyist Mlle Nioche and Christopher Newman in his early novel, *The American* (1877), would foreshadow a present-day call to arms. For few historic names have more been enlisted in the exchanges of polemic to do with America's national identity than that of Columbus. The quincentenary of 1992, especially, became a staging ground, a contest of rival claim and interpretation, in truth a latest debate about multicultural America itself. It is a controversy which recurs every 12 October. The Columbus Day debate (the only other federal 'name' holidays are for George Washington and Martin Luther King) affords yet another bearing on the literary fictions under consideration.

The one version, typified in Samuel Eliot Morison's long-standard *Admiral of the Ocean Sea* (1942), proposes the Atlantic visionary, the utopian and pathfinder into a Brave New World.[19] The other, as argued in a study like Kirkpatrick Sale's *The Conquest of Paradise* (1990), sees a malign Euro-colonialist, the begetter of a history of dispossession, human property, racist cruelty and privilege.[20]

The Federation of Italian American Organizations, as drawn from groups like the Sons of Italy or the Saint Anthony's Society, looks to a champion, a hero of the fifteenth-century merchant city of Genoa who became *Vice-Almirante* of Spain's *Reyes Católicos*. Native Americans, and many Latinos, by contrast, see in him little to celebrate or admire. South Dakota, with its considerable Sioux population, actually opted to rename Columbus Day 'American Indian Day', and the Treaty Council, a branch of AIM, staged a mock trial of Columbus, along with Cortés and de Soto. In Denver, Colorado, other protest takes the form of the Four Directions march.[21]

As 1992 took its course, Columbus as a network of cultural naming came under scrutiny – the countless high schools, towns, streets, businesses, clubs, diners and sports teams, not to mention Meena Alexander's Columbus Circle subway stop. Whether Columbia University as Ivy League bastion, or Columbus, Ohio as industrial steel and auto city, or Oregon's Columbus River Project (one of the largest electricity-generating systems in the world), voices were raised. The US postal service found itself a target on account of its Columbus Day special issues. Literary work from Mathew Carey's *The Columbian Magazine* (1786–92) to Washington Irving's three-volume *Life and Voyages* (1828), and from Hart Crane's sweeping, imagist *The Bridge* (1930) to Philip Roth's *Goodbye Columbus* (1959) as a site of Jewish-goyim courtship and manners, won new attention as a genealogy.

Other Columbus symbolism became just as provocative or controversial: the naming of NASA's space shuttle Columbus; the broadcast of a popular TV detective series under the name Columbo the title figure played by Peter Falk, an actor Jewish and one eyed; or the fact that Columbus Day actually began as a quasi-masonic celebration in 1792 and the result less of any national patriotism than of Tammany Hall politicking.

That much remains unknown about Columbus himself not a little compounds the controversies. What language, for instance, was Columbus supposed to have thought his own? Genoese, Italian, Spanish, Catalan, Arabic, even Hebrew, or more plausibly *castellano aportuguesado*? Do we read authentic Columbus in his Logs and Journals, or the highly edited transcriptions of Fray Bartolomé de las Casas, himself a later witness for indictment of Spain's *encomienda* system of Native slavery on the basis of his *Obra Indigenista* which first appeared in Seville in 1552–3? Were his first Caribbean landfalls actually the Discovery of America, whether Watling Island in the Bahamas (which he named San Salvador) or Samana Cay as is now thought and whose people were the Guanahani, or Cuba which followed, or, most of all, Hispaniola (another Columbus naming derived from Española) and today's Haiti and Dominican Republic?

There remains, furthermore, the plait of signatures available in Columbus's own lifetime of 1451–1506. They include the Cristoforo (or Cristoforus) Colombo of Genoese; the Cristóbal Colón of Castillian; the Cristóvão Colón of the Portuguese he spoke during his eight-year stay in Lisbon seeking the patronage of Dom João Segundo and learning the Atlantic wind-cycles; the Juan Colom sometimes attributed to him as a possible Jewish *converso* or *marrano*; the Colonus used for him by his son; and the Xρο FERENS, the Christ BEARER, as enciphered in his own headily messianic Greek-Latin amalgam.[22]

Sorting out these puzzles, as Columbus's marriage, exhumation and possible reburial in the Dominican Republic, might well have been a spur to pause and caution. Little so, it would seem. To admirers, Columbus remains the Renaissance quester whose four Atlantic voyages of 1492–3, 1493–6, 1498–1500 and 1502–4 align him with Amerigo Vespucci, Giovanni da Verrazano, Bartolomeu Diaz, Vasco da Gama, Vasco Núñez de Balboa and Ferdinand Magellan in the epic discovery of the Americas. His detractors see a first supremacist. The exploitation of the 'gentle' Amerindian Arawaks, as he called them, the Taino people of *Española*, gives a preview of the decimations, all the vexed and winding turns of racist and colonial oppression.

If the Admiral has featured mightily in American mainstream literary writing and myth, so, too, he has recurred within multicultural fictions. Max Yeh's *The Beginning of The East* (1992) supplies a Chinese American bead, a story-meditation on Columbus as cartographer and thus the imperialist inventor as much as the discoverer of the New World. Yeh's feat is to invent a counter-Columbus, Chistopher Ng, who sets himself to map the modern global-economy world and its politics and cultural power systems his Genoese forebear has bequeathed. Native America looks to *The Crown of Columbus* (1991), co-written by Louise Erdrich and Michael Dorris, high-paced and full of wry speculation, and Gerald Vizenor's *The Heirs of Columbus* (1991), a soaring pastiche in which Columbus becomes, of all things, a returnee mixedblood whose casino and other 'heirs' reflexively exploit a cyber-age America still enravelled as much in the fictions as the facts of 'the Indian'.

Colombo, Colón, Colom, Colonus, and out of them, Columbus. The competing versions of history built into this nomenclature supply a perfect refraction for the current debates. Was 12 October 1992, like each other Columbus Day, a celebration of nation, an America forged from diversity into one? Was it, on the other hand, the triumphalism of a Euro-mainstream at the expense of a far more inclusive ethnicity? For no less than Columbus, America itself has become the subject of vying interpretations to embrace ideology, politics, demography and, quite as dramatically, the ever-enlarging archive of multicultural literary-imaginative fiction.

VI

Relevant theorisation of American multiculturalism and ethnicity, and of the literature written under their ticket, has been busy and, as often as not, once again highly disputatious. Issues of canon-formation, mainstream–minority divide, who defines whom, not to say examination of the one or another ideology behind appraisal of America as civilisation, have all entered the fray.

The gain has been distinctive. It has led to better scrutiny of the codes of cultural-historical discourse in play. Ethnicity is to be seen for its own historic frame and yet, at a myriad of cultural levels, as an interacting dialectic, shaped by, even as it gives shape to, the rest of American life. If, too, it draws from its own profoundest sediments of cultural reference, it has also, and equally, in Werner Sollors's phrase, always been self-inventing.[23] Yet here, too, there have been risks. Prime among them, and raised by authors from Toni Morrison to Scott Momaday, has been concern at insufficient individuation of the imagining to hand, texts, literary fictions, made into case-study, or sample, rather than conscientiously recognised for their own terms and reach.

But if any one convergence point can be said to derive from conceptualised overviews of ethnicity, and multiculturalism at large, it has turned upon self-inscription, or put otherwise, the uninscription of, and contesting of, so-called American master narratives. In this, postcolonial theory has much counted, the analysis of Eurocentrism in general, and of the structures and languages of power within the European empires of Africa, Asia, the Middle East, and the Americas of the Caribbean and Pacific in particular, as pointers both to America's global culture-imperialism and its history of internal colonialism.

The latter, inevitably, calls up the ascendancy which created African American slavery and the colour line of segregation and ghetto, or the Indian Wars with subsequent Native relocation and the reservation, or the takeover of a Mexican-Chicano southwest and of Puerto Rico and the subsequent displacements of the *barrio* and population migrancy, or Asian exclusion and internment. At the same time, however, it has also led to better analysis of the subtler, internal workings of the cultural psychology of supremacism and racialisation as much upon those most with, as without, access to the levers of power. This, however, is by no means to doubt, as the present book's consideration of the postmodern turn especially confirms, that American ethnic authorship has not ever more increasingly taken imaginative control of its own past-into-present, its own geographies of word.

Edward Said's *Orientalism* (1978), with its celebrated taxonomy of Arab-Islamic exoticism under western eyes, is accordingly also to be seen as offering a pathway into analysis of American forms of ethnic othering. Gayatri Spivak's *In Other Worlds: Essays in Cultural Politics* (1987), in delineating subalternism and the footfall of the British Raj, has similarly been brought to bear, the political-economic hierarchy of one imperialism as the forerunner of another. Homi Bhabha's *The Location of Culture* (1994), for all the stultifying coagulation of style, tracks the very dialectic of 'otherness' as it operates within nation and narrative. It finds scholarly companion-ship in studies which analyse most ethnicities of colour, and their disempowerment and tokenisation, in relation to white-establishmentarian American identity.

The lexicon has become familiar, both in general terms and in US-centred literary-cultural theory and critique: hegemony, identity-formation, essentialism, alterity, indigenism, subject positionality, subalternism, or notions of Baudrillardian simulation. The effect, since the 1960s, and the ushering in of an Age of Theory, has indeed been to change the figuration by which multiculturalism and ethnicity in literature and the other arts, as in life, has been construed. Rarely can it be said to have taken on greater self-absorption than in the United States. Controversy, again, has been to the fore, in the one view due and corrective enquiry into governing assumptions about the national culture, in the other view minority special pleading to do with entitlement and grievance. Four symptomatic readings give more explicit localisation to these considerations.

Henry Louis Gates Jr's *The Signifying Monkey: A Theory of Afro-American Literary Criticism* (1988) argues for 'signifying' as a wholly distinctive black trope, the black text as given to its own literary self-reflexivity with roots in Yoruba and other West African oral rhetoric, and given dynamic in Afro-America's own cultural strategies of word as survival. Gerald Vizenor's *Fugitive Poses: Native American Indian Scenes of Absence and Presence* (1998) looks to the fabrication of 'Indians' from travel and captivity narrative onwards, whether as daguerreotype, canvas, Cody circus warrior, museum exhibit, movie figure, or TV healer. Each, it suggests, amounts to a variety of savagism, set-piece Nobility or Devil, victim or eco-messiah. *Postindian* understanding pitches against simulation, not least as given in anthropology, and for a perception of Native people and culture as live, enactive, an evolving continuance of story.

Ramón Saldívar's *Chicano Narrative: The Dialectics of Difference* (1990) delineates both the multiple-register plurality of literary and popular culture forms within Chicano/a voice and, at the same time, its ever more endemic hybridity with, and shaping of, a wider multicultural America. Sau-ling Wong's *Reading Asian American Literature: From Necessity to Extravagance* (1993) posits a literature framed by a body of keynote motifs, alimentation, doubling, social and cultural mobility and forms of play, the transition from Asian into Asian American cultural style.[24]

These kinds of analysis lie utterly enseamed within my own discussions, even if, at whatever risk of rebuke, this will not at every turn appear to be an explictly theory-driven and referenced account. I would want to see theory demonstrably flow from the primary texts under analysis rather, as has so often been the case, than the other way round. Such, in part, has also to do with an emphasis derived from Cultural Studies/American Studies auspices.

To this end, I have not hesitated to bring to bear political and language history, or the popular culture of film, TV, sport, music, or even foodways. The plentiful allusion to American fictions of all these kinds, and whether construed as mainstream or ethnic or, in fact, both, is meant in Clifford Geertz's term to 'thicken' a sense of context. I have also sought to recognise how the issues have nowhere near concluded. US multicultural literature, as category and roll-call, remains contested ground and subject to yet larger ideological debate.

The trick, if I have it anywhere near right, is to situate each text within multiple contexts of US culture and ethnicity, both high and broad, and yet indeed to give recognition to particularity, a self-fashioning force of invention. The chapters that follow, thereby, aim not only to map, and compare, four domains from within the last half-century's overall body of ethnic narrative texts, but also to recognise an American literary terrain as challenging in its stylings as in its human widths and depths. The one fiction is so aligned with the other, if a spectrum then also a continuum.

No one could be more conscious that, in keeping with this plenty, my coverage has been busy even to a fault, But, to repeat, it seeks throughout to remain locally attentive, close in its readings. In these several and linking aspects, and quite as emphatically, I also hope that *Multicultural American Literature: Comparative Black, Native, Latino/a and Asian American Fictions* goes a considerable way in conveying my own pleasure in, not to say long-time indebtedness to, the authorship to hand.

NOTES

1. Ishmael Reed (1989), Interview with Mel Watkins, in James Olney (ed.), *Afro-American Writing Today*, Anniversary Issue of *Southern Review*, Baton Rouge in, LA: University of Louisiana Press, pp. 26–7.
2. Meena Alexander (1993), *Fault Lines: A Memoir*, New York: The Feminist Press at the City University of New York, p. 202.
3. Relevant contextual historical and political scholarship includes Stephen Thernston (ed.) (1980), *Harvard Encyclopedia of American Ethnic Groups*, Cambridge, MA: The Belknap Press of Harvard University Press; John D. Buenker and Lorman A. Ratner (eds) (1992), *Multiculturalism in the United States: A Comparative Guide to Acculturation and Ethnicity*, Westport, CT: Greenwood Press; Judy Galens, Anna Sheets and Robyn V. Young, with Rudolph Vecoli (eds) (1995), *Gale Encyclopedia of Multicultural America*, vols 1 and 2, Detroit, MI: Gale Research Inc.; Alpana Sharma Knippling (ed.) (1996), *New Immigrant Literatures in the United States: A Sourcebook to Our Multicultural Heritage*, Westport, CT: Greenwood Press; Cheryl Russell (1998), *Racial and Ethnic Diversity: Asians, Blacks, Hispanics, Native Americans and Whites*, Ithaca, NY: New Strategist Publications; and Elliott Robert Barkan (ed.) (1999), *A Nation of Peoples: A Sourcebook on America's Multicultural Heritage*, Westport, CT: Greenwood Press.
4. Lawrence W. Levine (1996), *The Opening of the American Mind: Canons, Culture and History*, Boston, MA: Beacon Press. Levine's arguments were pitched to counter those of Allan Bloom (1987) in *The Closing of the American Mind*, New York: Simon and Schuster. Others who have entered the fray include Arthur M. Schlesinger Jr (1992), whose *The Disuniting of America: Reflections on a Multicultural Society* (New York: W. W. Norton) seemed to many to betray vintage Kennedy-style liberalism. Yet more alarmist are accounts like John J. Miller (1998), *The Unmaking of Americans: How Multiculturalism has Undermined the Assimilationist Ethic*, New York: Free Press, and Alvin J. Schmidt (1997), *The Menace of Multiculturalism: Trojan Horse in America*, Westport, CT: Praeger Publishers.
5. In *Dust Tracks on a Road* (1942, restored text New York: HarperPerennial, 1996), Zora Neale Hurston gives a typically bracing dismissal of 'race' as a way of assigning achievement or its lack: 'the word "race" is a loose classification of physical characteristics. It tells nothing about the insides of a people. Pointing at achievements tells nothing either. Races have never done anything. What seems race achievement is the work of individuals. The white race did not go into a laboratory and invent the incandescent light. That was Edison. The Jews did not work out Relativity. That was Einstein. The Negroes did not find out the inner secrets of peanuts and sweet potatoes, nor the secret of the developments of the egg. That was Carver and Just. If you are under the impression that every white man is an Edison, just look around a bit. If you have the idea that every Negro is a Carver, you had better take off plenty of time to do your searching' (p. 249).
6. A timely essay-collection is to be found in Jonathan Brennan (ed.) (2002), *Mixed Race Literature*, Palo Alto, CA: Stanford University Press.
7. 'Introduction', p. 17, David Palumbo-Liu (ed.) (1995), *The Ethnic Canon: Histories, Institutions, and Interventions*, Minneapolis, MN: University of Minnesota Press. For an account of the social and educational implications of critical multiculturalism, see

Stephen May (ed.) (1995), *Critical Multiculturalism: Rethinking Multicultural and Antiracist Education*, London: Falmer Press.

8. Cherrié Moraga (1983), in *Loving in the War Years: lo que nunca pasó por sus labios*, Boston, MA: South End Press, adds a gender perspective to the question of writing under a 'representative' guise as both a lesbian and a chicana. In a reflexive aside in her Introduction, she observes: 'Riding on the train with another friend, I ramble on about the difficulty of finishing this book, feeling like I am being asked by all sides to be a "representative" of the race, the sex, the sexuality – or at all costs to avoid that' (p. vi).

9. Ishmael Reed (ed.) (1997), *MultiAmerica: Essays on Cultural Wars and Cultural Peace*, New York: Viking Penguin.

10. Ishmael Reed, Kathryn Trueblood and Shawn Wong (eds) (1992), *The Before Columbus Foundation Fiction Anthology: Selections from the American Book Awards 1980–1990*, New York and London: W. W. Norton, and J. J. Phillips, Ishmael Reed, Gundar Strads and Shawn Wong (eds) (1992), *The Before Columbus Foundation Poetry Anthology: Selections from the American Book Awards 1980–1990*, New York and London: W. W. Norton. I have sought to give recognition to these anthologies in A. Robert Lee (1994), 'Afro-America: The Before Columbus Foundation and the Literary Multiculturalization of America', *Journal of American Studies*, 433–50 28: 3 (December); Reed has also been the general editor of the four-part HarperCollins Literary Mosaic Series: Al Young (ed.) (1995), *African American Literature: A Brief Introduction and Anthology*, New York: HarperCollins; Gerald Vizenor (ed.) (1995), *Native American Literature: A Brief Introduction and Anthology*, New York: HarperCollins; Nicolas Kanellos (ed.) (1995), *Hispanic American Literature: A Brief Introduction and Anthology*, New York: HarperCollins; and Shawn Wong (ed.) (1995), *Asian American Literature: A Brief Introduction and Anthology*, New York: HarperCollins. Other anthologies, for sure, reflect the changes, most notably Paul Lauter (gen. ed.) (1990), *The Heath Anthology of American Literature*, Lexington, MA: D. C. Heath.

11. Few have been tougher than a neo-Marxist cultural analyst like E. San Juan Jr (2002) in *Racism and Cultural Studies: Critiques of Multiculturalist Ideology and the Politics of Difference*, Durham, NC: Duke University Press.

12. Considerations which address the issue of discursive space, plurality of definition and voice include Paul Gilroy, 'Cultural Studies and Ethnic Absolutism', in Lawrence Grossberg et al (eds) (1992), *Cultural Studies*, New York: Routledge, and Gilroy (1993), *The Black Atlantic: Modernity and Double Consciousness*, Cambridge, MA: Harvard University Press; Gerald Vizenor, Interview, in Wolfgang Binder and Helmbrecht Breinig (1995), *American Contradictions: Interviews with Nine American Writers*, Hanover, NH: and London: Wesleyan University Press/University Press of New England, pp. 145–65; José David Saldívar (1991), *The Dialectics of Our America: Genealogy, Cultural Critique, and Literary History*, Durham, NC: Duke University Press; and Sau-ling C. Wong, 'Denationalization Reconsidered: Asian American Cultural Criticism at a Theoretical Crossroads', reprinted with introduction in Amritjit Singh and Peter Schmidt (eds). (2000), *Postcolonial Theory and the United States Race, Ethnicity, and Literature*, Jackson, MS: University Press of Mississippi, pp. 122–48.

13. William Apess (1829), *A Son of the Forest: The Experience of William Apess, a Native of the Forest, Comprising a Notice of the Pequod Tribe of Indians*, New York: author. Republished (1831) as *A Son of the Forest: The Experience of William Apess, a Native of the Forest*, 2nd edn, revised and corrected, New York: author.

14. This aspect of Douglass I examine (1998) in *Designs of Blackness: Mappings in the Literature and Culture of Afro-America*, London: Pluto Press, pp. 25–30.

15. Gerald Vizenor (1990a), *Crossbloods: Bone Courts, Bingo, and Other Reports*, Minneapolis, MN: University of Minnesota Press, Introduction, pp. xxiii–xxiv.

16. Sandra Cisneros (1978), 'Ghosts and Voices: Writing from Obsession', *The Americas Review*, Spring: 1. Reprinted in Nicolas Kanellos (ed.) (1995), *Hispanic American Literature*, New York: HarperCollins, pp. 47–8.

17. Amy Tan (1990), 'Mother Tongue', *The Threepenny Review*. Reprinted in Joyce Carol Oates (ed.) (1991), *The Best American Essays 1991*, New York: Tickner and Fields, pp. 196–202.

18. Henry James (1877), *The American*, Chapter 1. For a modern reference (1981), see *The American*, New York: Penguin, p. 39.

19. Samuel Eliot Morison (1942), *Admiral of the Ocean Sea: A Life of Christopher Columbus*, Boston, MA: Little, Brown.

20. Kirkpatrick Sale (1990), *The Conquest of Paradise: Christopher Columbus and the Columbian Legacy*, New York: Knopf.

21. Other quincentenary histories of note include Felipe Fernández-Armesto (1991), *Columbus*, London and New York: Oxford University Press; Jeffrey Burton Russell (1991), *Inventing the Flat Earth: Columbus and Modern Historians*, New York: Praeger; Stephen Greenblatt (1991), *Marvellous Possessions: The Wonder of the New World*, Chicago, IL: University of Chicago Press; Paolo Emilio Traviani (1991), *Columbus: The Great Adventure: His Life, Times and Voyages*, New York: Orion Books; John Noble Wilford (1971), *The Mysterious History of Columbus: An Exploration of the Man, the Myth, the Legacy*, New York: knopf; Zvi Dor-Ner (1991), *Columbus and the Age of Discovery*, New York: Morrow – the companion volume to the seven-part PBS series (1991); and William D. Phillips Jr and Carla Rahn Phillips (1992), *The Worlds of Christopher Columbus*, Cambridge and New York: Cambridge University Press. For a Native American re-estimation of Columbianism, see M. Annette Jaimes (1992), (ed.), *The State of Native America: Genocide, Colonization, and Resistance*, Boston, MA: South End Press.

22. For a Columbus under Jewish auspices (1992) see Rabbi Marc D. Angel (1992), 'A Chance to Learn', *Hassadah*, 73: 5 (January), 10–11; also (1991) his *Voices in Exile: A Study in Sephardic Intellectual History*, New York: Ktav.

23. Werner Sollers (ed.) (1989), *The Invention of Ethnicity*, New York: Oxford University Press.

24. These are all listed in the secondary bibliography. I offer a full analysis of Gerald Vizenor's *Manifest Manners* in 'The Only Good Indian is a Postindian?: Controversialist Vizenor and *Manifest Manners*', in A. Robert Lee (2000), *Loosening the Seams: Interpretations of Gerald Vizenor*, Bowling Green, OH: Bowling Green State University Popular Press, pp. 263–78.

CHAPTER ONE

Landmarks

Ellison, Momaday, Anaya, Kingston

We are what we imagine. Our very existence consists in our imagination of ourselves. Our best destiny is to imagine, at least, completely, who and what, and that we are. The greatest tragedy that can befall us is to go unimagined. (N. Scott Momaday)[1]

I

Four American storytellers. Four 'ethnic' voices. The literary fiction of recent multicultural America can hardly look to a more consequential quartet than Ralph Ellison, Scott Momaday, Rudolfo Anaya and Maxine Hong Kingston. Along with other best multicultural authorship – a matching circuit might as easily list, say, Toni Morrison, Louise Erdrich, Rolando Hinojosa and Amy Tan – theirs have become prime names, each the author of fictions indeed unique in the 'imagination of ourselves', and yet, stirringly, of America's always larger human passage.

For as much as, respectively, they draw from the Afro-America of Dixie and Harlem, the Native America of Jemez Pueblo reservation, the *chicanismo* of New Mexico, and the 'Gold Mountain' Chinese America of San Francisco, their different fictions display a virtuosity which carries the local towards an emphatically more inclusive ambit. Little wonder their writings have become an admired gallery, at once a prompt to celebration and yet challenge. Cavils, even so, have arisen, a reminder that whatever the acclaim, it indeed takes place amid critical debate and contestation.

Ellison could be acknowledged to have written a masterwork in *Invisible Man* (1952), a novel whose inspired envisioning of the American racial psyche, not to say tricksterly riffs of language and each organising intertextual echo, led to the National Book Award and a host of other awards and prizes. Yet he would long continue to arouse sniping as an alleged cultural conservative in refusing separatist Black Power allegiance in the 1960s. His unyielding, and often expressed, belief in the dense human interaction, not to say fusion, of black and white in the making of America, and which he also makes a major strand in his posthumous novel, *Juneteenth* (1999), accusingly put him outside the loop of clenched-fist politics, the call for cultural nationalism and the 'revolution now' of Black Power. Was he not too loftily high-conservative, above the fray, an African American version of Matthew Arnold?

Momaday, however quickly he became a touchstone for modern Native literary achievement on the basis of *House Made of Dawn* (1968), also faced murmurs. Few doubted his insider's familiarity with Kiowa, Laguna and Navajo history, or tribal creation story, or Sun and Peyote cosmology. Nor was his story of Abel, Second World War damaged Laguna mixedblood, and the slow, arduous recovery from self-loss inside a Native context of pueblo rite and healing, to be thought other than deeply affecting. The charge, not a little perversely, and even patronisingly, was rather of a novel somehow too consciously literary in design. Momaday allegedly had traded the advantages of the performative immediacy, the improvisation, of oral Native tradition for an obscuring modernism.

Anaya, likewise, in *Bless Me, Ultima* (1972), had written a rich, intimate novel of *chicanismo*, a pageant of first-person memory. Its summoning of a 1940s New Mexico as much figural as actual, not to say shaped by the dual legacies of English and Spanish, Catholicism and *curandería*, and Mexico and America as two border histories joined and yet not, amounted to hugely important fare. The southwest, its landscape, funds of vernacular myth, and magic of feel, had found new expression. Agreement was widespread that, as the boy Antonio Márez becomes heir to Ultima's ancient wisdom, Anaya had shaped his version of a Chicano Portrait of the Artist. None of this, however, altogether quietened suspicions of sentimentality, too fond or indulgent an account.

Kingston's two chronicles of Chinese American life, *The Woman Warrior: Memoirs of a Girlhood among Ghosts* (1977) and *China Men* (1980), met with immediate success, an inspired blend, as it seemed, of myth, gender and history in the mapping of Asia-in-America. Even so, according to a fellow writer like Frank Chin, this popularity owed as much to the relentless bad image she had given to Chinamen, along with her misuse, as he would allege, of the Fa Mu Lan 'woman warrior' tradition. Wittingly or not, Kingston had transposed China, and Chinese America in its wake, into an ongoing fiefdom of misogyny, and so added to vintage western orientalism. The affrays quickly grew animated. Did Chin's critique mean that China lore, its warrior, monkey and trickster legend, was to be thought ever fixed or sacrosanct? If right only in part, what premium attaches to freedom of invention, Kingston's or anyone else's?

'Our fate is to become one, and yet many – This is not prophecy, but description' (p. 499), reads a celebrated sentence in the Epilogue to *Invisible Man*. Ellison's narrator, it hardly needs stressing, speaks as the novel's invented and confessional voice, and one hedged in canniest double-talk and subterfuge. But it is a view, in fact, Ellison himself frequently espoused in essay and interview, namely to yield nothing to the version of America, in life or literature, as given to any one exclusive ethnic ascendancy or encampment.

This 'one and yet many' focus, however each time differently pitched and angled, carries into the body of American multicultural fiction. If modern US writing has burgeoned, it does so, in considerable degree, for how it extends, and cross-refers, the voicing of the culture's ethnic plurality. Those fictions given explicit tagging as multicultural, or ethnic, of necessity have been part of that endeavour. But their achievement, in fact, goes further. They have been to the forefront in gifting America with some of the most compelling markers of its overall imaginative estate.

II

The publication of Ellison's *Juneteenth*, a half-century on from *Invisible Man* and fortuitously as may be, supplies a near-perfect chronological framing, 1952 to 1999, for the present study. Both books serve, as it were, as also bookends, within whose dates of appearance the span of America's new literary-multicultural dispensation can almost exactly be situated.

What, first, to re-emphasise in the achievement of *Invisible Man*? There can be little doubting its impact as a novel of African American rite of passage, a major feat of telling as deftly seamed in myth as history. Ellison had managed a kind of transhistoric update both of slave-escape and of the Great Migration. In the one, the implications are existential, self-identity denied, recovered, and then given free word. In the latter, they are odyssean, those of flight with its recent echo of escape from slaveholding, the transfer of over a million blacks from postbellum Dixie into the cities of the north. Each phase in the narrator's trajectory, from the opening Battle Royal with its shadow of bloodstock slave pugilism through to the politics of the Brotherhood and of Ras and the riot as the shadow of Harlem's explosion in 1943, portrays an Afro-America, an America, if keyed to the postwar present, then also, and inextricably, steeped in the footfalls of the past.

In this respect, intertextuality in *Invisible Man* could not more count, whether the variety of Afro-America's own music, talk, art, and different kinds of script, or whether that of the western High Canon. Both legacies, however, Ellison makes subject to his own novel's laws of motion, its governing patterns of voice and image.

Black tradition clearly affords Ellison one set of registers, whether back-country vernacular as in Trueblood or the street jive of B. P. Rinehart and his Harlem brethren. Luminaries from Frederick Douglass to Booker T. Washington to Marcus Garvey make re-embodied appearances. Jazz, blues, Satchmo (an Armstrong refrain like 'What did I do to be so black and blue' echoes throughout), scat, the dozens, Afro-folklore to embrace Brer Rabbit, Jack the Bear, High John the Conqueror, Peter Wheatstraw and Shine, not to mention black foodways from chitterlings to yams, all lie shrewdly embedded in the text. Not the least, too, of the novel's bravura of first-person voice, derives from Ellison's command of black preachment both religious and secular, Afro-America's unique strategies of call and response and signifying.

Equally, Ellison is not to be denied his careful self-availing of other litanies, Graeco-Roman as in the allusions to Homer, a Europeanism to call up Dante, Dostoevsky, André Malraux or Thomas Mann, a body of England reference spanning Lord Raglan on heroism to H. G. Wells's invisible man to the T. S. Eliot of 'The Waste Land', the America of Poe, Melville and Twain, and a political-historic line to embrace Jefferson, Franklin, Abraham Lincoln and Horatio Alger. Whatever else, *Invisible Man* lays claim to distinguished literary forebears.

'So why do I write, torturing myself to put it down?' (p. 501) asks Ellison's unnamed narrator, reflexively conscious of how his own black on white of the page challenges, even as it re-imprints, an America itself racially written in black and white. Irradiated into visibility by the 1,369 bulbs each 'illegally' running on electricity stolen from Monopolated Light & Power, he offers his text as would-be matching illumination, a Book of Revelation in which truth vies with lie, one version of America with another. Told as though from 'border area' Harlem and a 'basement that was shut off and forgotten during the nineteenth century' (p. 9), *Invisible Man*, rightly, has been taken to subvert almost all the long-historic perceptual 'fictions' by which blackness has been reduced to stereotypic shadow, one-note coloration.

In its own words, the novel acts as 'confession' (p. 7), that of the narrator's life as the memory index of an enclosing, larger black American history. 'Keep this Nigger-Boy Running' (p. 35), his dream tells him, is the message within the mountain of America's white paper promises. 'Live with your head in the lion's mouth. I want you to overcome 'em with yeses, undermine 'em with grins, agree 'em to death and destruction' (pp. 19–20) is the counter-tactic advised by his dying grandfather. This learning of offence out of defence, self-meaning wrested from a Dixie, even a Harlem, where meaning has so often been denied, becomes a veritable Pilgrim's Progress for the narrator. Each phase of the novel, to include his own 'authorial' self-positioning in the Prologue and Epilogue, and his negotiation as much of, as with, the reader, gives confirmation.

Battle Royal, which opens the novel, with its small black boys obliged to fight before the town's white business clique, supplies a near-perfect Dixie colour-line iconography. The boys are forced to play incipient warrior-studs, provoked and yet hexed by white American womanhood in the form of the stripper tattooed with the stars and stripes, herself at once a figuration of desire and yet exploitation. They, in turn, fight blind, unsighted, the shock from the electrified rug as they collect prize money a further trope of all-too-literal power over powerlessness. The narrator's speech of thanks for the scholarship to the black college, itself a surreal Tuskegee or Fisk situated parodically as though in some bucolic paradise, is likewise made with literal yet also psychosomatic blood in the throat. That image runs over into the name of its President, Dr A. Herbert Bledsoe, a 'double' at once the all compliant Booker T. Washington ('Old Bucket-head' in a dig at a celebrated Washington speech) and black despot. This game of black within white and vice versa, of harlequinry as existential politics, becomes richly launched, one in a whole pattern of doublings throughout *Invisible Man*.

The narrator's encounter with Mr Norton, Boston banker-philanthropist who believes his 'fate' to be 'bound up with the Negro', continues the charade: the North's liberal white patron yet the fool and dupe of Bledsoe. This same play of seeing and unseeing takes yet further immediate turns. In the Trueblood encounter, the transgressive spectacle of the black sharecropper who has fathered children on both his wife and his daughter, and yet who tells his story almost as though comic-trickster parable, becomes a prompt, a counter-confusion, for the white banker's own incestuous hankerings.

Norton's subsequent collapse strikes the narrator as 'formless white death' (p. 79). His removal to the Golden Day, in which Louis Mumford's historic phrase has ironically become the name of a brothel used by black patients from the local psychiatric hospital, yields more distortion. These black war veterans embody the very middle class urged on the narrator, lawyers, medics, teachers and the like, yet who have become literally unhinged, wards, also, of Supercargo as emblematic nurse-keeper. In their euphoria, they become a chorus of taunt, fantasising Norton as a whiteness blended of Jefferson, John D. Rockefeller and 'the Messiah' (p. 73), and the narrator's blackness as that of a 'walking zombie' (p. 86). The clocks, in confirmation of these perceptual double-takes, appropriately are said to be 'all set back' (p. 82).

No less a world turned upside down comes into consideration when he goes on to listen to the Rev. Homer A. Barbee. The black Chicago churchman's sermon might be as Emersonian, or Franklinesque, as Mr Norton could wish, yet it is also delivered from behind 'sightless eyes' (p. 120). In the aftermath of these 'blind' words, a mockingbird is heard to sing. It amounts to apt irony when the narrator duly finds himself expelled by Bledsoe for allowing Norton 'white' sight of a 'black' reality quite beyond his Bostonian comprehension. The ensuing letters given him by Bledsoe, after an interview which causes him to speak of 'a mad surreal whirl' (p. 130) and 'my distorted vision' (p. 131), ensure his migration north to Harlem but again only on terms in which the seemingly true plays false.

Optics again rule, an America white and black, and yet somehow not, ever, and at the same time, realms or lines of vision which collide to the confusion of both seer and seen. The effect of these latest papers, thereby, is still to keep the narrator 'running'. Their revealed bad faith when opened by the son of yet another supposed benefactor, another Mr Emerson, leads directly into the next tableau: the factory making Optic White, 'the Right White' (p. 190) under the slogan KEEP AMERICA PURE WITH LIBERTY PAINTS (p. 192). The formulation speaks trenchantly to mainstream America as self-perpetuating white grid or rubric, a state of things to which the narrator responds as paint-maker by pouring 'concentrated remover' (p. 178) into the mix. His upbraiding by the foreman speaks its own volumes: 'What the hell, you trying to sabotage the company?' (p. 178). Moved to the basement under the furtive Brockway, a name to call up the badger, and his Wellsian tangle of pipes and valves, then left near-catatonic by the factory explosion, he emerges 'reborn' as a latest identity after ECT treatment and ready for a new 'field of vision' (p. 216). He will now see as he has never seen before, Harlem, Manhattan, America-at-large, the actual as indeed live phantasmagoria.

Each of the narrator's own guises serves him as the apprentice to revelation. In the elderly black couple's eviction, he sees history on the very sidewalk, among other items musical 'knocking bones', ribs used to beat a rhythm, a curling iron, a small Ethiopian flag, a tintype of Lincoln. In the Brotherhood, he becomes a member, and eventual heretic, under the leadership of the 'one-eyed', and so half-sighted, Jack, and a neophyte believer in politics as Marxian 'scientific explanation' (p. 266). Few more phantasmagoric episodes occur than when Jack's false eye plops into the glass, buttermilk, unreal, detached, and leaving only a red, a red-Marxist, socket.

In Ras the Destroyer, he witnesses rogue Garveyism, a quixotic Caribbean-Harlem knighthood of sword and lance. As mentor to the prophetically named Tod Clifton, the black youth leader driven to selling parodic Sambo dolls and who will die by the bullet, he learns both hope and limits. If, in Mary, he finds a welcoming black matriarch, he can also become the fantasy sexual primitive to a rich white Sister when assigned to 'The Woman Question' (p. 358). As Bliss Proteus Rinehart, a name to convey inner and outer identity, an elasticity of mask, he graduates into the Mr Cool with eyes hidden behind shades, the lover, the conman minister, the numbers man and politician, in each the stylish hustler. Identity becomes cynical parade, a repertoire of exploitative fast-changes.

The Harlem riot acts as ending, and yet beginning, the narrator's discard of past roles as entry into new self-authoring. Having taken cover in his manhole, he burns all his papers and impedimenta – the college scroll, one of Tod's dolls, the anonymous letter in the Brotherhood accusing him of treachery, and his Brotherhood name. The ensuing dream, a castration, 'bleeds' him of each illusory past naming, his composite othering as self. It marks, also, the beginning of the end to his underground hibernation. 'Bad air' (p. 502) is to be expelled, 'the old skin' (p. 502) excised. Resurfacing implies the challenge of self-custody of life and word. The novel, throughout, and to best effect, revels in this spin of disclosure out of concealment, seeing out of unseeing.

The cultural politics of Invisible Man, even so, still can arouse reservation. Do Matty Lou and Kate as rural-southern women, or Mary as Harlem mothering spirit, get beyond ciphers? What ideological critique should attach to Ellison, especially on the basis of the Tod-Ras episodes? Justified, or not, these doubts have by no means reduced the novel's overall stamp. It continues to hold its place as modernist writ, commandingly self-aware in language as in overall fashioning, visionary fiction in quite every sense.

Almost since it was known to be under way, Juneteenth aroused speculation. Given, in Ellison's own rueful phrase, the Long Wait, what across three decades of composition was its state of progress? How close did the posthumously published version come to his own final intention? The nearly 360 pages of manuscript destroyed in a fire at his summer house in Plainfield, Massachusetts in 1967 he had heroically rewritten. He was well known to have worried about whether the eventual 2,000 pages should become one or three volumes, about the balance of Hickman and Bliss as the principal disclosing voices, and about transitions and the amount of interior monologue. Yet whatever the misgivings, and based on the text arrived at under John F. Callahan's scrupulous editorship as Ellison's literary executor, there can never have been any doubt of the novel's ambition.

Views, nonetheless, have yet to settle. Admirers insist upon Ellison's conception of America, in a manner even beyond Invisible Man, as hall of mirrors, its cultural-ethnic identity no less real for its resort to masquerade, impersonation. The feats of style, each stream of memorial consciousness, the sermons and colloquia, the itinerary sweep through time and across the regions, are to be thought to compete with, if not indeed to outbid, those of Faulkner. The less persuaded continue to speak of strain, too willed a resolve to write epic. Afro-America might well amount to a mythical kingdom as encompassing as Yoknapatawpha. But had *Juneteenth* given it definitive realisation?[2]

In the story of Bliss, the seeming white-born child raised as a black preacher by his mentor-father, the Reverend A. Z. Hickman, to redeem an America crossed, at times nearly broken, by its race phobias and fissures, yet who becomes the racist Senator Adam Sunraider of Vermont, Ellison subjects 'black and white' to every kind of interrogation – hue, religion, language, politics. The span runs from Oklahoma to New England, Dixie to Washington DC, and from slavery-time to a present day. Whatever the debate about its powers, *Juneteenth* could not be thought other than to have put ethnicity inextricably at the very centre of American history, its unyielding, if so often contradictory, play of truth and untruth.

Ellison works the detail of his story with a keenest touch. The opening delegation of 'a chartered planeload of Southern Negroes' (p. 3), Hickman's old-time congregation come to warn Bliss of an impending plot against him even as they lay claim to his allegiance as one of their own, are said, emblematically, to be 'like people embarked upon a difficult journey who were already beyond the point of no return' (p. 5). Each best-known Washington DC icon, to include the Lincoln Memorial, the Great Seal and its eagle, and the motto of E PLURIBUS UNUM (p. 21), is called into play as context not only for the Bliss-Hickman saga but for the America which has bound them one into the other. In Bliss's Senate Chamber assassination, runs the implication, American history again mistakes shadow for substance. On the one hand, 'colour' has been made to bear the shadow of division and death. On the other, and as unentangled in Bliss's hospital reveries and each colloquium, present or from the past, with Hickman, it can also act as saving juncture.

This interplay, throughout *Juneteenth*, is given in shaping rolls of memory, narrative made up of flashback, riff, dream, remembered sermon and folk talk. Episodes both contrast and link. The early revivalist camp-meetings and Bliss's fake Lazarus-like miracle resurrections play into the film-making episode in Oklahoma, another would-be fakery and in which Ellison looks to *camera obscura* and the screen as a source of optic metaphor for black-white, white-black, perceptions of human identity. If Bliss indeed is of mixed origins, or has hitherto been thought black even if white, his awakening first love affair, appropriately, takes place with a mixedblood Native girl. Hickman's transformation from bluesman into the preacher affectionately known as 'God's Trombone' matches Bliss's passage from 'black' boy evangelist to 'white' white-racist senator. The effect is one of America, and its competing arenas and reversals of identity, indeed told as though the equivalent of jazz, a line of plot released through voice and counter-voice, each instrumental play of idiom.

'There's a heap of mystery about us people' (p. 183) says Sister Georgia, one of Hickman's early women parishioners. It makes a point heavy in southern memory, black, spoken, blues-like. But it also carries a necessary implication for the novel as a whole. For Ellison's ventriloquy in *Juneteenth*, unfinished though the novel may have been, works to orchestrate precisely his sense of the 'heap of mystery' of Afro-America as, of necessity, and no small irony, also its own species of unfinished American narrative.

III

'He had lost his place. He had been long ago at the center, had known where he was, had lost his way, had wandered to the end of the earth, was even now reeling at the edge of the void' (p. 104). On appearance, Scott Momaday's *House Made of Dawn* seemed for many the definitive portrait of worlds in collision, Native and Euro-American, Laguna New Mexico and modern California, with the Second World War Pacific and Pueblo 'Indian Country' juxtaposed as two kinds of American war zone. But if Abel indeed could be said to embody 'Indian history', a casualty of conflict both outer and inner, was there not a risk of casebook victimry, sentimentality? Nothing could have done greater injustice. For Momaday had put on offer a larger power of vision, and at every turn an interior workmanship, as wholly unique in conception as design.

In one way, the story of Abel, in his lost alcoholic displacement, gives grounds to be thought linear, chronological and western. The trajectory involves his unknown father and the deaths of his mother and brother Vidal of TB, his battle trauma from the Second World War, the return to Jemez Pueblo (Walatowa or Village of the Bear as originally called), and the drinking, prison sentence for murder, drift and injury in Los Angeles, and final return to the pueblo. The novel even goes so far as to date its sections, 1945 through to 1952, a time-present which at the same time folds back into time-past for Abel, his grandfather, Francisco, and his Los Angeles friends, the Navajo Ben Benally, and the white social worker Milly. For Father Olguin, who lives in the pueblo, it is chronology which plays into the nineteenth century through the journal of his clerical predecessor Father Nicolás and, unclerically, father to Francisco.

This same trajectory, however, Momaday puts under the auspices signalled in the Laguna Pueblo words *Dypaloh* and *Qtsedaba* for a beginning and end of story as based in the oral nexus of speaker and listener. In this, Abel's disequilibrium, and his slow-won advance into recovery, is given in terms at once circular, spatial and Native-ceremonial, and which avail themselves not only of Laguna but also, intertribally, of Navajo and Kiowa tradition. It is also in this respect that the opening and final scenes of running, the 'house of dawn' mythology itself, the linked pollen, kiva, katsina and corn allusion, hold greatest importance, the signatures of a Native centring of the world. *House Made of Dawn*, thereby, transforms into the very thing of its own plotline, a fiction about, and yet at the same time itself the enactment of, Abel's healing. Throughout each of the novel's four sections, Momaday keeps this weave marvellously in play.

In 'The Longhair', Francisco, ailing in leg as may be, embodies a lived contrast to his grandson, at one with his multiple heritages of ethnicity (Laguna-Navajo-

Tanoan-white), belief (he believes the solar as well as the Catholic calendar), land ('an intricate patchwork of arbors and gardens', p. 5), and language (he chants Laguna and Spanish en route to the bus to collect Abel), as against Abel's self-fissure, his drunken return. Abel's flashback to the eagle-catching ceremony, and his unceremonial killing of the female bird, presages his own severance. In the relationship with Angela St John, he is reduced to sex-primitive, silenced 'other' and 'non-being' (p. 37). The 'old rhythm of the tongue' (p. 58) eludes him. He can make no creation song, no 'right words' (p. 59). It is in this state of verbal, as much as existential, dispossession that he kills the albino, a figure of scaled lips and writhing tongue: this is a bar fight in one way, yet, and as Father Olguin equally recognises, Abel's vision of witchery, whiteness as Melvilleian evil and blank.

'The Priest of the Sun' and 'The Night Chanter' work likewise. Abel, newly released from prison, cannot hold down a job, has his hands and body nearly broken by the cop Martinez, finds himself caught amid different kinds of Indianness. In John Big Bluff Tosamah, he encounters an urban trickster and cynic and yet also Kiowa fond memorialist of Rainy Mountain. If witness to a peyote cult, a circle of real and false believers, he also wins new strength from Benally's 'Beautyway' and 'Night Chant' as songs of Navajo/Diné healing. Where the albino embodies whiteness as male malignancy, Milly gives him whiteness as love, an affirming feminine presence.

Abel is put to negotiate competing worlds, a remembered Laguna order of festival, deity, ceremony, as against, typically, a law-court as the instrument of white America ('Word by word these men were disposing of him in language', p. 102). The stasis of his drinking contrasts with the ceremony of running, his broken hands with the repaired body, his whitened prison cell with the multicolour of Jemez Pueblo and its surrounds. In a Second World War battlefield, in the face of guns, noise and an oncoming tank, he has danced a Native dance of disorder. In the Pueblo, however slow his rewakening, he re-enters the dance of Laguna time-space and health. This contrapuntal movement, one of unbalance played against balance, gives *House Made of Dawn* its unique dynamic, the fine-spun energy of its drama.

'The Dawn Runner' draws these seemingly divergent or contradictory lines into a circular, dynamic whole. Francisco dies, Abel inherits his spirit. The grandfather's deathbed words, again an overlap of Spanish and Laguna, balance against Abel's 'nothing to say' (p. 195). '*The great organic calendar*' (p. 198) reassumes its place: Abel takes care to provide Francisco with both a Native and Christian burial. Father Olguin, as if in shock, broaches understanding of Abel's double world. Abel's last act of running, his body ritualised by ash, his mind singing '*House made of pollen, house made of dawn*' (p. 212), and amid 'canyon, mountains and the sky' (p. 212), supplies the novel's perfect 'ending'. The dancer becomes the dance. Motion leads no longer away from, but towards, centredness.

IV

'Some time in the future I would have to build my own dream of those things which were so much a part of my childhood' (p. 248). So Antonio Márez, Rudolfo Anaya's narrator in *Bless Me, Ultima* (1972), looks back reflexively to the pending *cuentista* or storyteller he has now become and who will write that childhood into being. The note is typical, one of memory, retrospect, the novel as an unfolding series of panels in which time-past seams utterly into time-present, the actual into the imaginary, the teller into his own tale.

'Time stood still, and it shared with me all that had been, and all that was to come . . .' (p. 1) says Antonio at the outset. He repositions himself as the seven-year-old raised in Spanish-speaking New Mexico who finds himself pulled between the *vaquero* or herdsman Márez clan on his father's side and the farmer-cultivator Luna clan on his mother's. But he also acknowledges the writer-in-waiting who will learn to appropriate into the art of word the shamanism, the *brujería*, of Ultima as *anciana* or *curandera* invited by his parents to spend her last days with the family.

The novel, throughout, enravels this play of literal event into a drama of inner fantasy and imagining. If the two family dynasties are caught in history between a Mexican past and US future, so, in Ultima, whose shaman's skills protect and educate Antonio, the story takes on otherliness, the sheen of fantasy. New Mexico can be invoked as modern border state yet also magical, in which, as Antonio testifies, 'new experience and dreams strangely mixed in me' (p. 26). The upshot makes the effect of *Bless Me, Ultima* not a little Proustian, a childhood given specific time and place yet also, and at the same time, sacral and steeped in its own contemplative intimacy.

In the one trajectory, experience for the boy takes the form of his adult recollection of his ill-matched parents, his sisters Deborah and Theresa, and the three absentee GI brothers with their eventual disruptive return from the wars in Europe and Japan and drift into the easy pleasures of Las Vegas. It looks back to the Spanish of home, the English of school, the latter which anglicises him from Antonio to Tony. It summons backs to him his parents' competing hopes for him: his father's dream of a new beginning in California and his mother's hope that he will enter the priesthood. He sees, too, as he could not have in childhood, the irony of his father as one-time horseman and cattle-driver in the *llanos* (flatlands) now asphalting the New Mexico highways as if to seal in, to inhume, the very *tierra* his family once proudly herded.

The other trajectory remembers the dreamer child within, drawn to the *indio* myths of earth and mountain. These come together in the legend of Golden Carp, creation and fertility myth, 'miraculous' (p. 105), invisible to ordinary fishermen's eyes, and in which Antonio comes to believe under the tutelage of his friends Samson and Cisco. The terms are oral-formulaic, parabular, the carp as protector-god against drought:

> he went to the other gods and told them that he chose to be turned into a carp and swim in the river where he could take care of the people. The gods agreed. But because he was a god they made him very big and colored him the color of gold. And they made him the lord of all the waters of the valley. (p. 74)

The centre of all these memories, however, has to be Ultima. 'I knew she held the secrets to my destiny' (p. 11), he confirms at the outset. As her name implies, she is a Last One, midwife at his birth, explainer of his *pesadillas* or nightmares, teacher of herbs and flora, and martyr who at the cost of her own death brings down the murderer Tenorio Trementina. Antonio thus finds himself irresistibly drawn back to her bag of potions, the deific owl with its links to Christly dove and Aztec eagle, and her very aroma. It is the owl whose each successive cry heralds a major turn not only in her life but his own: the attack on Tenorio in his first attempt to kill Ultima in which he loses an eye; its accompaniment of Ultima on her every mission; and its death as a foreshadowing of Ultima's.

A Catholic believer, Ultima nonetheless incarnates a oneness with a yet prior knowledge, the spirituality of the natural order. Hers is Antonio's bulwark against an adult world often crudified into swearword and curse – *chingada* or *puta madre* (p. 103) and the like. But if she signifies for him guardian, the very anima of *chicanismo*, he for his part becomes the perfect apprentice, the eventual word-maker with his own style of magic. She is able to call out these rising creative-imaginative sympathies, the artist's ability to see both the Márez-Luna world yet also that of *curandera*, carp and owl, each literal contour of New Mexico landscape yet also memory's inner landscape, and all without the slightest undue contradiction.

This interaction, precisely, of experience and dream determines all the linking parts of the novel. Antonio thinks back to the deaths he has witnessed: Lupito, unhinged by his Asian war experiences, who shoots at Chávez, the sheriff, only to invite his own destruction; Narciso, the town's basically harmless drunk, killed by Tenorio Trementina, who wrongly believes Ultima a *bruja* or witch responsible for the death of his daughter but for whom Narciso had only gratitude and love; Florence, the drowned boyhood friend with whom he strikes up a bond of private friendship and ritual and who first guides him to the Golden Carp; and Ultima herself who teaches him that death can be continuity and restoration as well as separation. He likewise undergoes a cycle of childhood fevers and cure as when he re-sees as dream the Lupito killing, imagines himself assailed by the avenging Tenorio astride his horse, or is present as Ultima ministers with her secret herbs to a member of the Téllez family. Each happens, or happened; but each, equally, goes on happening in his own chambers of memory, to await transcription by the memoirist he will, and has, become.

A similar back-and-forth of memory also encloses 'Jasón's Indian' (p. 9), the unspeaking sentinel to a pre-conquistador past. Like the carp and owl, his is the embodiment of a tribal and vernacular past as against the Holy Weeks, Communions and Masses of the parish church under the Irish-named Father Byrne. Antonio re-dreams his own birth and Ultima as 'the old woman' who delivers him. He dreams several times of the brothers who strike out in directions he comes to realise he cannot follow. He dreams of Tenorio's dead daughter ('*my dream-fate drew me to the coffin*'), a vision with its own Macbethian overtones of witchery. Ultima's grave, whose celebrant he becomes, also passes into dream, a figuration of past and future, legacy and destiny.

A shared membrane of remembrance settles, too, over the novel's placenames, notably Los Alamos as atomic test-site. Anaya has his text recall its Spanish meaning as 'The Poplars' and one of the most beauteous pine and desert landscapes in America. More domestically, for Antonio, 'El Puerto' ('refuge', 'harbour') as the home of the Lunas and 'Las Pasturas' ('pasture') as that of the Márez family resonate to equal effect even as they pass into time past. Memory, in other words, in all its overlapping and coalescing kinds, yields mixed fare for the narrator-memoirist, pain yet warmth, breakage yet love.

But 'build my own dream' *Bless Me, Ultima* does, a portrait of childhood's dream itself told as dream. The force of the dream derives, overwhelmingly, from Ultima, her spirit carried by the narrator from first associations to written word. For the memory of her, as of his family, of his land, and of all the voices and myths that have made up the *chicanismo* of his life, cannot be thought other than Antonio Márez's memory – and memorialisation – of himself.

No account of *Bless Me, Ultima* can pass over lightly Anaya's passionate sense of New Mexico as a necessary storehouse of Chicano identity. In interview, he has spoken explicitly of its hold for him in this respect:

> [The] landscape plays a major role in the literature that I write. In the beginning, it is an empty, desolate, bare stage; then, if one looks closely, one sees life – people gather to tell stories, to do their work, to love, to die. In the old days the sheep and cattle ranchers gathered in that small village, which had a train station, watering station for the old coal-burning trains. It was prosperous; they were good times. Then after the visit or the business at hand is done, the people disappear back into the landscape and you're left as if alone, with the memories, dreams, stories, and whatever joys and tragedies they have brought to you.[3]

Manifestly, *Bless Me, Ultima* arises out of this store of 'memories, dreams [and] stories'. The same can be said of his subsequent novels. *Heart of Aztlán* (1976) deals with the generational transition of a rural family into the urban *barrio* of Barelas in Albuquerque. *Tortuga* (1979) offers magic realist drama, a crippled boy's path into recovery and self-independence (*tortuga*, tortoise, refers to his hospital plaster cast) within a New Mexico landscape as hallucinatory as real. *Albuquerque* (1992) aggregates the cultures of the Río Grande into New Mexico's main city as a site of evolving habitation and cultural mix. *Shaman Winter* (1999) offers a Sonny Baca 'mystery', urban-contemporary in every way yet also dream fiction with its seventeenth-century cast of indigenous prophets and warlocks. The bead, undoubtedly, may differ. But all these fictions of memory add to Anaya's clear conviction in *Bless Me, Ultima* of *chicanismo*, and the southwest, as a present drawn always from, and to, its own plurality as past.

V

The very locution 'Chinese American', as Maxine Hong Kingston vividly attests in *The Woman Warrior: Memoirs of a Girlhood among Ghosts* and *China Men*, hinges always on a double paradox, East inside West, West inside East. Kingston herself, born of parents who, almost mock-archetypally, owned a California laundry, would find herself at the working juncture, and often enough disjuncture, of both. Maybe, too, her tease of genre, autobiography or novel, even, and intermediatingly, autobiographical novel, adds its own comment.

The China of the one East ranks as Ancient Regime whose ideograph signifies the centre of things and in which ancestral gods required daily cognisance and assuagement. In the other East, the original Gum Sahn or Gold Mountain has become the Asian America of the 1960s, a new global imperium with successor western gods and a here-and-now California. Yellow-white gaps, as she calls them, also overlap, be it the realness of reality, time and space, family and gender, or eating and even the loudness of talk. Her two volumes, pairings of myth, essay, calendar and talkstory (*gong gu tsai*), exhilaratingly fold both these dispensations into each other, East and West as discrete yet continuous, realms of fact yet fiction.

The vantage point she sets up in *The Woman Warrior* begins, perhaps understandably, on a note of interrogation:

> Those of us in the first American generations have had to figure out how the invisible world the emigrants built around our childhoods fits in solid America.
>
> The emigrants confused the gods by diverting their curses, misleading them with crooked streets and false names. They must try to confuse their offspring as well, who, I suppose, threaten them in similar ways – always trying to get things straight, always trying to name the unspeakable. The Chinese I know hide their names; sojourners take new names when their lives change and guard their real names with silence.
>
> Chinese-Americans, when you try to understand what things in you are Chinese, how do you separate what is peculiar to childhood, to poverty, insanities, one family, your mother who marked your growing with stories, from what is Chinese? What is Chinese tradition and what is the movies? (p. 5)

'Trying to name the unspeakable' in every way applies. Kingston's role is one of excavation, 'figuring out', whether of China as first source, of Chineseness in America, and of who and what she is herself. This latter involves not only history and ethnicity, however, but gender.

Five female personae preside: No Name Woman, her 'drowned-in-the-well' aunt; Fa Mu Lan, legendary woman warrior who replaces her father in the Imperial Army; Brave Orchid, her mother and one-time Chinese midwife; Moon Orchid, the Chinese aunt who comes to America to reclaim her bigamous husband but whose unhingement leads to the California State mental asylum; and Ts'ai Ten, poet, exile, ambassador. In the figures of these five, Kingston creates a composite mantle, a collective 'I' which incorporates both the plurality of female selves within her prior ancestry and those of her own self.

'No Name Woman' invokes 'my aunt, my forerunner', a woman who, in having plotted her own sexual destiny, had a child, and been hounded to death by her Chinese village as an adulteress and shaming disrupter of the established order, in revenge drowns herself in the communal drinking water. She thereby becomes one of the most powerful of ghosts in the Chinese firmament, a water ghost. She also, decades later, comes to haunt, to inspirit, her niece: woman-relation, outlaw, pioneer, undefeated if not unpunished warrior, and above all, writer.

'White Tigers', which follows, tells, in adopted voice, the complementary myth of My Lan, swordswoman and 'female avenger' (p. 43) who rids her land of foreign usurpation. She, too, serves as a presence Kingston hopes to incorporate into herself ('I would have to grow up a warrior woman', p. 20). But so resolved, and in a nice time-switch to the 1960s as America's supposedly most liberated decade, Kingston offers ironic recognition that the old curbs and dispensations still cling: 'I went away to college – Berkeley in the sixties – and I studied, and I marched to change the world, but I did not turn into a boy . . .' (p. 47).

She even speaks with some envy of Japanese immigrants who can find unchanging role models in the samurai and geishas. For her, living among American ghosts as her parents designate them, she must find new ways of being a swordswoman. She must, as it were, enword her own 'Chineseness', somewhere between Han China and Anglo-America. To do that, too, she has no option but to combat the racism and ignorance which surround her, 'the nigger yellow' attributed to her by one employer and the dehumanisations implied in language like 'gook' and 'chink'.

'Shaman' calls up her mother's life as a trained midwife in China, especially the memory of her medical certificate ('When I open it, the smell of China flies out . . .', p. 57). She looks back to how her mother, Brave Orchid, became for her village patients not only a trafficker in pills and bandages but also a magician, an exorcist of bad ghosts. 'The students at the To Keung School of Midwifery', Kingston recalls, 'were new women, scientists who changed the rituals' (p. 75). On leaving China in 1939 in the aftermath of the Japanese invasion and Nanking, Brave Orchid finds new ghosts to confront, the America of Taxi Ghosts, Bus Ghosts, Police Ghosts, and, some years later, Urban Renewal Ghosts. Americans, she comes to think, are all Work Ghosts, with 'no time for acrobatics' (p. 104). Her life, like that of her daughter after her, becomes that of the laundry; and, with the sale of the original village land in China, she has 'no more China to go home to' (p. 106). Whatever thus ensues, it will have to ensue in America, Brave Orchid as both emigrant and immigrant, and Kingston in her wake as the author both of her mother's story and of her own.

In 'At the Western Palace', the perspective broadens to include the saga of Brave Orchid's sister, Moon Orchid, who at the age of 68 and having travelled through Hong Kong brings still more 'Chinese business' (p. 151) into Kingston's life. Having waited nearly fifteen years, Moon Orchid seeks her long-emigrated and now remarried husband ('He looked and smelled like an American', p. 152), begins to deteriorate mentally under the stress of her husband's repudiation and her own foreignness (she 'misplaces herself in space', as Brave Orchid calls it), and ends up in an all-woman asylum deludedly but contentedly believing on the grounds that they never depart that her fellow inmates are none other than her own 'daughters'. Two worlds have this time not fused, except in dementia, a disjuncture at once sad but ultimately benign.

'A Song for a Barbarian Reed Pipe', which rounds out the volume, opens with Brave Orchid cutting her daughter's tongue 'so that you would not be tongue-tied' (p. 164), a prophetic act for the two-language speaker and writer her daughter Maxine will become. The girl, released from the speech restraints of her childhood, warms to California's other diversities of voice: 'I liked the Negro students (Black Ghosts) best because they talked the loudest and talked to me because I was a daring talker too' (p. 166). Vexatious, feisty, noisy where her own sister exists in intimidated silence, her will to voice finds its trope in the contrasting calligraphies of Chinese and English:

> I could not understand 'I'. The Chinese 'I' has seven strokes, intricacies. How could the American 'I', assuredly wearing a hat like the Chinese, have only three strokes, the middle so straight? (p. 166)

She ponders, relatedly, the auditory impression of Chinese speech on English-only Americans and American speech on Chinese-only immigrants. To American ears, she thinks Chinese sounds 'chingchong ugly' (p. 171), whereas in reverse 'the Chinese can't hear American at all; the language is too soft' (p. 172). Other fissures equally trouble her: between being as she calls it 'Chinese-feminine' and 'American-feminine' ('American Chinese girls have to whisper to make ourselves American-feminine', p. 172); between the general openness of manner of Americans and 'the secrecy of the Chinese' ('"Don't tell," said my parents', p. 183); and between the 'vampire nightmares' (p. 190) of her ravening Chinese past and the matching fear of becoming the 'our crazy one' (p. 190) of her American present.

Over time, however, the cut-tongued, and thereby unsilenced, talker and writer grows to the point where, even as a schoolgirl, and amid the hiss and steam of the laundry, she can vaunt her writerliness to her mother with 'if they say write ten pages, I can write fifteen' (p. 201). Linkingly, the final myth she alludes to has to do with the 'song' of Wai Yen, a second-century poetess, who has been captured by barbarians, had two children by the chieftain, neither of whom grows up speaking Chinese, and who has learned that the barbarians's 'reed music' about 'for ever wandering' she must learn to attend to, and respect, as much as her own original culture.

The fable bears utterly on the China which shadows Kingston's America, a China, moreover, itself neither the one thing nor the other ('Soon I want to go to China and find out who's lying – the communists who say they have food and jobs for everybody or the relatives who write that they have not the money to buy salt',

p. 205). Her odyssey through time, through a Babel of warring languages and yet silence, through acts of past dynastic daring yet also feints and cunning, and from Han country to Hong Kong to San Francisco, leads 'Maxine', reflexively, to her own eventual legibility as Chinese American writer. It is that eclectic tale, and its eclectically genred telling, which she also so spiritedly makes over into *The Woman Warrior*.

The impulse to excavate in no way diminishes in *China Men*:

> I'd like to go to China if I can get a visa and – more difficult – permission from my family, who are afraid that applying for a visa would call attention to us: the relatives in China would get in trouble for having American capitalist connections, and we Americans would be put in relocation camps during the next witch hunt for Communists. Should I be able to convince my family about the good will of normalization, it's not the Great Wall I want to see but my ancestral village. I want to talk to Cantonese, who have always been revolutionaries, nonconformists, people who invented the Gold Mountain. I want to discern what it is that makes people go West and turn into Americans. I want to compare China, a country I made up, with what country is really out there. (p. 84)

Whether indeed a China ancestral or overseas, actual or 'made up', the pursuit is indefatigable, a process of dramatic rediscovery. In giving her focus, this time, to the China Men within her own lineage, she both uses 'real' history and hypothesis, live and invented memory. The upshot is narrative genealogy, Kingston's Chinese American equivalent of, and at the same time alternative to, the founding Anglo-American mythus of Plymouth Rock, Jamestown and the Pilgrim Fathers. Hers, however, delineates the transition not from Europe to America but from Han Mountain to Gold Mountain, the Chinese settling of America by acts both illegal (being smuggled aboard ships, using forged credentials, impersonating others as paper sons) and legal (being processed respectively at Angel Island on the West Coast and Ellis Island in New York).

The result becomes an unfolding scroll of cultural patrimony, America as possessed by the Chinese American descendants of those 'three great mandarins' who sailed into the Bay of Manila in 1603 to the amazement of the Filipinos, and, even, of their possible, perhaps mythical, ocean-faring predecessors who vie with the Bering Strait journeyers, the Vikings, and the Celts, as America's possible first discoverers.

Her China Men she invokes as a sequence: Great-Grandfather Bak Goong, who worked the Hawaiian sugar plantations and returned to Han country with a new wife; Grandfather Ah Goong, who dug the land for the Central Pacific Railroad and took part in the bitter strike of 1867 ('He had built a railway out of sweat', p. 149); her own 'American father' Ba-Ba, laundryman, born in San Francisco in 1903; and her unnamed brother who fights in Vietnam only to return home a veteran unhonoured by his natal America. These lives she sets within, and against, the sorry history of the

1892 Exclusion Act and other anti-Chinese legislation as embodied in bills like the Burlingame Treaty, the Scott Act and the Geary Act, a Chinese American right to residency won against Yellow Peril and the nativist phobias which have so marked Asian entrance into America.

The binding thread throughout *The Woman Warrior* and *China Men* is one of survival and continuity. For Kingston, a clear, abundant vindication is to be found in the 'million or more' Chinese Americans spread from Hawai'i to California to New York, not to mention an Overseas China of quite global proportions. In her own fashioning, Chinese America offers the very sign, or hallmark, of unfinished human transformation, a western East, an eastern West, and a United States in its cultural negotiation of both, anything but yet concluded.

VI

Kingston's fictions, like those by Ellison, Momaday and Anaya, could not better embody 'our imagination of ourselves'. The kinds of controversy they have aroused, if muted over time, to a degree still persist, whether *Invisible Man* as politically mandarin, *House Made of Dawn* as too caught up in a modernist spiral, *Bless Me, Ultima* as self-indulgent, or Kingston's *The Woman Warrior* and *China Men* as drawing upon flawed gender mythologies. But a discerning readership can be under no obligation to let them go unrefuted. All of these fictions, in more durable ways, speak to, even as they write into being, an America given over to the stir, the human complexity and yeast, of its own multicultural energies, and be they at different times of gain or loss, within the making of its own identity.

NOTES

1. N. Scott Momaday, 'The Man Made of Words', in Rupert Cosco (ed.) (1970), *Indian Voices: The First Convocation of American Indian Scholars*, San Francisco, CA: Indian Historian Press, pp. 49–84.
2. For a judicious account of strengths and weaknesses, see Richard King (2000), 'The Uncreated Conscience of My Race/The Uncreated Features of His Face', *Journal of American Studies*, 34:2 (August), 303–10.
3. Juan Bruce-Novoa (ed.) (1980), *Chicano Authors: Inquiry by Interview*, Austin, TX: University of Texas Press, pp. 184–5.

CHAPTER TWO

Selves

Autobiography, Autoethnicity, Autofiction

I can't say who I am
unless you agree I'm real.
  (LeRoi Jones/Imamu Amiri Baraka)[1]

For centuries our stories were passed in oral tradition . . . With written language came the task of learning how to hammer the voice onto the page with these little nails called 'alphabet'. For many Native Americans it's only been a matter now of two generations. (Diane Glancy)[2]

I want to say simply that they lived, through everything – poor uneducated 'Meskins', my people – heroic, brown, tragic and beautiful; they lived with hope because to have given up would have been against God, against life . . . Now, in all their violence and sorrow, they live on, tied right here to me. I need to say, finally, this is where it all began, and I can put it all to rest. (Olivia Castellano)[3]

as I sought for ways to live agreeably in Anglo-American society, my memories of Manzanar, for many years, lived far below the surface. When we finally started to talk about making a trip to visit the ruins of the camp, something would inevitably get in the way of our plans. Mainly my own doubts, my fears. I half-suspected the place did not exist. So few people I met in those years had even heard of it, and those who had knew so little about it, sometime I imagined I had made the whole thing up, dreamed it. Even among my brothers and sisters, we seldom discussed internment. If we spoke of it at all, we joked. (Jeanne Wakatsuki Houston)[4]

I

Autobiography, virtually from its modern outset, has invited a generous elasticity of definition. It embraces the would-be portraiture in the round, the memoir, the reminiscence, the 'life and times' account, even, as in Gertrude Stein's *The Autobiography of Alice B. Toklas* (1933), the self-acknowledging guise of the one life for another. In these, as in other variations, can it be doubted that autobiography works always as its own species of fiction, persona as much as person, conjuration as much as actuality? It is in this respect that a coining like 'autofiction', usually dated from the appearance of Roland Barthes's *roland BARTHES par roland barthes* (1975), has been advanced, less the life than the *vraisemblance* of a life, a theatre of self whose reflexive manoeuvres and play of mirrors help to give the more multi-aspected portrait.[5]

US ethnic autobiography, so-called, cannot but also fall within these considerations yet always with any number of differences. A term like 'autoethnicity' has thus entered the reckoning. Drawing on analogies with ethnopoetics and ethnomusicology, autoethnicity acknowledges the one life within a specific or shared genesis of community, locale, history and language. Synecdoche, along with autoethnography, has become companion usage, part for whole, the telling of any given life as somehow the telling of a contextual ethnic lineage.[6]

Yet these versions, in their turn, have also met with doubts, especially from those who hold that self-fictions, ethnic or otherwise, always elude category, some too-readily surmised unity of interest or kind. Is ethnic autobiography somehow predeterminedly testimonial, my life as evidence? Many, in fact, read almost in defiance of expected ethnic lines, or piety, each loaded up in its own kind of contrariety of viewpoint and word.

Whatever the case, and whether or not so acknowledged in recent theory, ethnic autobiography – ethnic fictions of self – are not to be denied their own kind of challenge to the fuller understanding of America's 'first person singular', Ralph Waldo Emerson's lustrous term in his Journal for January–February 1827. They do so, moreover, and as the roster which follows abundantly gives evidence, to wholly enlivening effect. It is also to this end that texts from the four traditions are juxtaposed, a sequence of self-writings which invite their own connection and comparison.[7]

II

In general my narrative is an autobiographical account. Specifically it is an act of imagination. When I turn my mind to my early life, it is the imaginative part of it that comes first and irresistibly into reach, and of that part I take hold. This is one way to tell a story. In this instance it is my way, and it is the way of my people. (Scott Momaday)[8]

Momaday's construing of his own autobiography as 'an act of imagination', like the dictum that 'We are what we imagine' in his essay 'The Man Made of Words', no doubt can be said to provide a sightline for autobiography in general. Is not autobiography, to an extent, always the weave of fiction into fact, the given life as much self-performance as self-history? This emphasis on imagining, however, when attributed to Native autobiography, takes on even greater implication.[9]

First it underlines that these are lives free of the custodianship of any interlocutor.

Momaday likely has in mind the many 'as told to' past transcriptions, not to say mistranscriptions, whether by missionary or anthropologist, folklore-collector or language-interpreter. How, too, to counter-imagine Native lives against a quite stunning array of stereotype of savagism, ancient and modern, European and American? Wholly in keeping, he gives emphasis to the literary properties of Native autobiography, the uses of pattern, image, and, crucially, the spoken within the written. In this latter respect, Momaday has shown himself to be aware of the need to transcend possible fissure between tribal and western notions of using the self as story: the oral as against the scriptural, the immodest elevation of the individual over the community. The point, in all his writing, has been to cross any supposed gap.

For Patricia Penn Hilden, however, Berkeley historian raised in Los Angeles, heir both to Nez Percé-Wallowa origins and a Quaker line traceable to William Penn, the dividing lines amount to near-insurmountable obstacles. In *When Nickels Were Indians: An Urban Mixed-Blood Story* (1995), she offers the following view:

> Writing autobiography, an art that flies in the face of most Native American tradition, pushes this dilemma in one's face. On the white, European side, the heir to modernist self-examination plunges into such inspections of memory with some enthusiasm and recklessness. On the other, however, the utter reticence of Native America blocks not remembering, but rather the telling of it to outsiders.
> A dilemma.[10]

For Gerald Vizenor, by contrast, this could not be more flat wrong. Citing the power of individual vision quests, styles of bearing and dress, and specifically the use of tribal nicknames not one in a lifetime but many and each with its story, he counters:

> Indians, tribal people, are more individual than contemporary whites . . . [As to] this idea that so many interpreters of Indian life story and autobiography have, and that is that Indians are communal, that they couldn't write autobiography because it is antithetical to their being of essential communal experience. Now, what rubbish![11]

As to why Momaday's *The Names*, along with the earlier *The Way to Rainy Mountain* (1969), continues to win admiration, that, precisely, can be said to lie in his unique reflexive deployment both of the tactics of 'western' literary autobiography and of Native oral legacy. If, in truth, there has been reticence about keeping sacred, communal, certain memory, it has not inhibited hybridity, un-reticence, in all the best-known Native first-person lives.[12]

Founding autobiographies, whether by Samson Occom, Mohegan crossblood convert and author of 'A Short Narrative of My Life' (1762), or by William Apess, Pequot Presbyterian minister and author of *A Son of the Forest: The Experience of William Apess* (1829), both blend memories of tribal custom into an acquired New

England Calvinism. Massachusetts serves as quintessential Anglo-America yet, true to the indigeneity of its name, a Native inheritance of clan, forest and belief system. Wholly also to the point, these texts convey an early endeavour to situate the oral within the written world, a recognition of the spoken life having been made scriptural.

The subsequent litany has been plentiful. Sarah Winnemucca's evidentiary account of her Paiute origins, family, child-raising, and tribal time-space, is given in her *Life among the Piutes [sic]: Their Wrongs and Claims* (1883). Charles Alexander Eastman, Ohiyesa by his Santee Sioux name, as the first-ever Native medical doctor, discloses the trauma of treating Wounded Knee survivors in *Indian Boyhood* (1922). An Oglala Sioux Holy Man's memoir like *Black Elk Speaks* (1932), given all the editorial midwifery of John G. Neihardt, serves to remind quite how consequential was Native oratory. Luther Standing Bear's *My People, the Sioux* (1928) and *My Indian Boyhood* (1931) include his recollections of stepping east as one of the first tribal enrollees (he was Ponca Sioux) in the Indian School at Carlisle, Pennsylvania, and a life lived as bilingual author, Buffalo Bill Cody circus performer and movie actor. Each bears witness to history's transitions, to speech into print, at once gap and yet conjuncture.

In her autobiographical chapbook, *Claiming Breath* (1992), Diane Glancy, who describes herself as of 'Arkansas backhill culture mixed with Cherokee heritage' (p. 22), gives an update to this interplay of Euro-American and Native identity:

> I want to explore my memories & their relational aspects to the present. I was born between 2 heritages & I want to explore that empty space, that place-between-two-places, that walk-in-2-worlds. I want to do it in a new way. (p. 4)

This is not to underplay harsher tellings of mixedblood history. Among those which carry an unbenign force of memory, few read more uncompromisingly than Maria Campbell's *Halfbreed* (1973), a Canadian Cree-Metis life of drift and addiction whose tribal-historical roots lie in Louis Riel's rebellion of 1884 and the 'Indian' history of Manitoba and Saskatchewan, or Janet Campbell Hale's *Bloodlines* (1993), a modern urban Californian life with its beginnings in Skitswish tribal history and equally marked by setbacks of drift, drugs and imprisonment.

Were confirmation of either the variety of first-person Native voice or the resources of image and memory available, it can readily be found in a contemporary anthology like *I Tell You Now: Autobiographical Essays by Native American Writers* (1987). Its eighteen contributors run from Mary TallMountain, whose Alaska origins as Koyukon Athabascan ('that ancient nomadic life', p. 3) give the most vivid sense of human origins behind her verse, to Joy Harjo, poet, musician and film-maker and born in Oklahoma of a European and Creek-Cherokee family ('I . . . know that it is only an illusion that any of the worlds are separate', p. 266).

This, and similar anthologies, also gives context to three landmark autobiographies: Scott Momaday's *The Names* (1976) as a winding New Mexico mixed Native and white family genealogy and sense of place; Leslie Marmon Silko's *Storyteller*

(1981), whose horizontal book-format in itself might be taken to point to a Laguna conception of space-time, land and family; and Gerald Vizenor's *Interior Landscapes: Autobiographical Myths and Metaphors* (1990) as a 'crossblood remembrance' reaching from Chippewa White Earth Reservation, to Minneapolis, to Japan and, finally, to California.

In *The Way to Rainy Mountain* (1969), Momaday offers a first portrait of origins, his own life-journey highlighted against the migration of the Kiowa people from Montana to Oklahoma, and told as a series of twenty-four triads: personal and family history, calendar history and tribal-mythic history. The effect is one of contending, yet brilliantly complementary, narratives. Something of the same, if less explicit, holds also for *The Names*, the Momaday born of Kiowa father and part-Cherokee mother, raised on Navajo and Jemez Pueblo reservations where his parents were teachers, and the eventual Stanford Ph.D. with a dissertation written under the direction of Yvor Winters on the New England poet Frederick Goddard Tuckerman and, by his own acknowledgement, an abiding interest in the strategies of voice and image of Emily Dickinson.

Imagining, or 'reflections' (p. 161) as he calls them, takes on a quite special force throughout *The Names*. However literal the sweep of New Mexico, Oklahoma, Arizona and the Dakotas as 'Indian Country', or of the lives and family played out within their sound and sight, he could not more insist on, for him, their inwardly memorial and visionary resonance. He speaks of his closing journey to Tsoai, the myth-laden natural tower of the Black Hills, as implicating him in a double response: 'I saw with my own eyes and with the eyes of my own mind' (p. 167). This quite especially holds as to lineage and to landscape.

First there is the summoning of his mixed genealogy. For his paternal Kiowa people, he begins from their creation-myth as the Kwuda who emerged from a hollow log, itself to become a motif also at the close of *The Names* – 'a fallen tree, the hollow log there in the thin crust of ice' (p. 167). The remembrance to follow includes his naming ceremony as Tsoai-talee by Pohd-lohk, step-great-grandfather and one-time member of the Seventh Cavalry; the life of Mammedaty, his horseman grandfather buried at Rainy Mountain Cemetery; and his father Huan-toa or Alfred Morris Mammedaty, caught on the cusp of prior tribal and modern 1920s life, wanderer, watercolourist, teacher. As to his maternal Cherokee-white line, he invokes that through his beauteous mother Natachee, her grandmother Natachee and the marriage into the Galyan-Scott-McMillan dynasty with its different roots in Anglo and Celtic Appalachia and Cajun Louisiana.

This signifies family as literal mosaic, fragment and photograph, yet also, and more fugitively, as fictions of, and in, memory. It leads him to call up the last Kiowa sun dance in 1887; life in Navajo country or *Dine bikeyah* in the 1930s; his white grandfather, Theodore Scott, photographed at Fort Sam Houston playing the banjo of his hill forebears; or Jemez Day School as among his 'most vivid and deeply cherished memories' (pp. 117–18). Each, along with the references back to Kiowa tribal devastation brought on by smallpox in 1839–40 and measles in 1892, or his childhood sense of query to the point of near-bafflement as to 'how to be a Kiowa

Indian' (p. 101), or his first horse with its harking back to the Kiowa as a horse culture and its change of visual line for him ('I had a different view of the world', p. 155), provokes a reach into fact but also a call to imagination ('I lay the page aside, I imagine', p. 93).

Landscape, equally, is made subject to these double auspices, a southwest at once actuality and yet vision, the one given time and yet always a species of meta-time. Whether Jemez Pueblo, or Gallup in New Mexico with its nearby iconic Route 66, or Rainy Mountain and its cemetery or, en route to the Kiowa homeland, Tsoai or Devil's Mountain, the literal topography takes on its own imagist wrap, an implied immanence to township, mesa, desert and horizon. The account of Monument Valley works typically, landscape if in shape and timeline best accommodated in Navajo then whose perfect linguistic fit Momaday seeks to emulate in his own prose:

> The valley is vast. When you look out over it, it does not occur to you that there is an end to it. You see the monoliths that stand in space, and you imagine that you have come upon eternity. They do not appear to exist in time. You think: I see that time comes to an end on this side of the rock, and on the other side there is nothing forever. I believe that only in *dine bizaad*, the Navajo language, which is endless, can this place be described, or even indicated in its true character. Just there is the center of an intricate geology, a whole and unique landscape which includes Utah, Colorado, Arizona, and New Mexico. The most brilliant colors in the earth are there, I believe, and the most extraordinary land forms – and surely the coldest, clearest air, which is run through with pure light. (pp. 68–9)

The sustained imagining of the southwest's geology, its time, air and light, as of the lineages it has hosted and which are shown to have been bound into, and around, the name Navarre Scott Momaday, gives *The Names* its distinction. It makes for autobiography simply luminous in the telling.

In a 1986 interview, Leslie Marmon Silko gives her version of the place of story in Laguna community life and tradition:

> The key to understanding storytellers and storytelling at Laguna Pueblo is to realize that you grow up not just being aware of narrative and making a story or seeing a story in what happens to you and what goes on all around you all the time, but just being appreciative and delighted in narrative exchanges.[13]

If the observation holds for spoken storytelling, that of live mouth and ear, so it can be said to have been adapted to modern, and even postmodern, Native autobiography. *Storyteller*, certainly, itself could not better be thought an endeavour to shadow these spoken 'narrative exchanges', the text as enactive, at once celebration and mural, story-cycle and text-and-image collage.

Silko acknowledges at the outset her own paradox of writing oral heritage through the figure of Aunt Susie, protectress, Carlisle-educated teacher, and archivist of Laguna life and family:

> This is the way Aunt Susie told the story.
> She had certain phrases, certain distinctive words
> she used in her telling.
> I write when I still hear
> her voice as she tells the story. (p. 7)

Oral-written, the speaking voice overheard as it were, makes a perfect point of entry. Each component text within a text, to include the unfolding photography, speaks in equal weight with the other, the effect one of a longitudinal or simultaneous voice, none unduly more privileged than the other.

The pattern is established at the outset. Aunt Susie herself, and Great-Grandma A'mooh and Grandpa Hank, speak as though live, a continuum, to which she supplies a species of gloss in interlocutions like 'Storyteller' (pp. 17–32) and 'Storytelling' (pp. 94–8). The point is made explicit in 'The Storyteller's Escape' (pp. 247–53):

> With these stories of ours
> we can escape almost anything
> with these stories we will survive . . .

Silko's white Marmon family is given equal play alongside her Laguna family, rarely more touchingly than in the story of Grandpa Marmon's refusal to bow to anti-Indian prejudice in an Albuquerque hotel ('These are my sons', he tells the manager in a proud show of paternity, p. 17).

Real-life history weaves into poem-chronicle or legend throughout. Aunt Susie's story of the drowned children who become butterflies (pp. 7–15) offers an opening instance. The Yellow Woman episode (pp. 54–62) gives a story of present-day love told as coyote myth. The episode of the golden-feathered rooster which Silko unfolds in a letter to the poet James Wright develops into a wonderfully Aesopian story (pp. 226–7); likewise the comic-absurd story 'Uncle Tony's Goat' (pp. 171–6) as retold from the Acoma poet Simon Ortiz.

The actual includes references back into history ('Grandpa Stagner had a wagon and team and water drilling rig. He traveled all over New Mexico drilling wells', p. 88); or into the near-contemporary like the police encounter and death in 'Tony's Story' (pp. 123–9); or into personal memory as when the author remembers an encounter with a bear ('When I was thirteen I carried an old .30-30 we borrowed from George Pearl', pp. 77–8). The mythic can be a Pueblo creation story ('The world was already complete/even without white people./There was everything/including witchery', p. 130); a vignette of tricksterism ('One time/Old Woman Ck'o'yo's/son came in/from Redleaf town . . . He asked the people/"You people want to learn some magic?"', pp. 111–21); a Mexican-Pueblo courtship told as coyote fable

('Coyote holds a full house in his hand', pp. 257–65); a corn fertility parable ('The Go-Wa-Peu-Zi Song', p. 158); or a Spider Woman sexual drama of love and fate ('Estoy-eh-Muut and the Kunideeyahs', pp. 140–54).

Silko also extends her range beyond the pueblo ('The Hills and mesas around Laguna/were a second home to my father', p. 160) or, as she writes in a letter to Lawson F. Inada in September 1975, 'The purple asters are growing in wide fields around the rocks past Mesita clear to the Sedillo Grant' (p. 170). Centred on Laguna pueblo life as may be, *Storyteller* also has no shortage of allusion to Hopi, Navajo, Sioux and Apache culture, typically the opening image of 'a tall Hopi basket' with its inlaid woven grasshopper or Hummingbird Man (p. 1) and 'A Geronimo Story' (pp. 212–23) as the near-mythic cavalry pursuit and escape version of the legendary Apache fighter yet also magical and holy deer-man.

Throughout, Silko keeps her reader-listener aware of the protocols in play. Introducing a Laguna-Keres myth to do with Acoma place, she issues a reminder of how story, tribally, is by necessity a shared circle and consent:

> The Laguna People
> always begin their stories
> with 'humma-hah':
> that means 'long ago.'
> And the ones who are listening
> say 'aaaa-eh' (p. 38)

Yet, equally, she reserves her own margin to adapt, transform, collate, as imaginative form requires and as, in fact, oral tradition itself has always allowed:

> I know Aunt Susie and Aunt Alice would tell me stories they had told me before but with changes in details or descriptions. The story was the important thing and little changes here and there were really part of the story. There were even stories about the different versions of the stories and how they imagined these differing versions came to be. (p. 227)

This could virtually also serve as *Storyteller*'s prospectus, Silko's authorial guidance as to the interaction of oral and written, Native-spoken and Native-scriptural, in the delivery of her own self-telling.

The opening, full-page, black-and-white photograph in Gerald Vizenor's *Interior Landscapes: Autobiographical Myths and Metaphors* offers 'Clement Vizenor and son Gerald, in Minneapolis, 1936'. As an image of parent-and-child affection, it looks replete. Smiling, open-shirted, a father in fedora holds his two-year-old in protective arms. The boy, bright-eyed, wrapped, although the subject of the camera, appears to be monitoring its very action. Behind them lie piled-up bricks and two stern, crumbling houses, one with a curtained window. The picture, however, contains more than a few dark hints of prophecy.

First, Clement Vizenor, 'crane descendant' (p. 3) and 'reservation-born mixedblood in dark clothes' (p. 22), Chippewa house-painter and feckless ladies' man from White Earth, Minnesota, within a year would be found murdered with his throat cut in another Minneapolis street. Police left the murder an 'unsolved', a brawl perhaps, or a jilted husband's revenge, at any rate one more 'Indian' who had got himself killed and bequeathed himself only in name.

Fatherless, his son would be quickly deposited with relatives, or fostered out, by his unavailing yet eventually thrice-married Swedish American mother, Laverne Lydia Peterson. It was a young life without protection, despite the benign intervention of his feisty, irascible Anishinaabe grandmother, Alice Beaulieu, herself, in trickster fashion, to enlist his aid in persuading a blind younger man of her enduring physical beauty and to become her husband. Vizenor's self-authoring, in life, as later in script, becomes as much necessity as calling.

That finds its life shape as he evolves from Minneapolis 'mixedblood fosterling' to leading Native American writer-professor presently at Berkeley, from the Boy Scout who camps on grounds 'stolen from tribal people by the federal government' (p. 62) to adult enrolled member of the Chippewa White Earth Reservation. Throughout all of *Interior Landscapes*, he emphasises yet further paradox: the GI sent to Korea, and by chance of having a name at the end of the alphabet assigned to a unit in Camp Chitose, Japan, transmutes from soldier into author ('Mount Fuji over my typewriter . . . my liberation was the military in Japan', p. 128); the mixedblood Native American who fantasises a new life as a reincarnated Lafcadio Hearn; and the returnee soldier who, on demobilisation, studies for a technical qualification at New York University but who, after Asian-areas studies at Minnesota University, becomes successively city activist, journalist, professor at Oklahoma and Santa Cruz and Berkeley, and, again, among the most published writers in the Native canon.

The other kind of self-authoring finds its shape in the 'Vizenor' of his books. The classroom Minnesota youngster who dreamed up 'Erdubbs MacChurbbs' as his *alter ego* storyteller, and an early manifestation of his taste for baroque naming, has become one of the most international and voluble of Native authors. A literary output of over thirty volumes accrues to his name. This, and each other paradox, *Interior Landscapes* makes into the one narrative spectrum, a present of interacting pasts. The span runs from 'Families of the Crane', with its allusion to Anishinaabe clan systems, through to 'Honor Your Partners', partly a credo of Vizenor's own postmodern improvisations and tactics, and partly an account of the violent, and anything but communitarian, threats against him from AIM members for having dared criticise their politics of Red Power as radical chic. The twenty-nine 'auto-biographical myths and metaphors', or first-person fictions, each dated yet gapped one from another, serve as interfoliations within, discrete yet at the same time complementary panels of memory.

Not inappropriately, he sees himself early on in the 'earthdiver' role of Anishinaabe creation-myth, a postmodern earthdiver, however, as likely to call upon a Eudora Welty, Michel Tournier, Primo Levi, William Scheick or Michel Foucault all of whom supply prefatory quotations as upon tribal legends of Naanabozho, generic begetter of the Anishinaabe. This tribal-cum-postmodern blend, in fact, becomes the very hallmark of *Interior Landscapes*.

A reference to Ishi, last of the Yahi, eventually the maker of museum artefacts in San Francisco, links to his own academic tenure at Berkeley. Anishinaabe legacies of Nature, pictographs carved on bark, he connects to his lifelong taste for the dynamic stillness of haiku and for Matsuo Basho as master of the form. He ponders another kind of connection between Hollywood and 'the Indian' in recalling that his mother, a frequenter of Depression-era movies, fell for his handsome mixedblood father because he resembled George Raft. His father's death likewise calls up an overlap of two worlds: 'Clement William must have misremembered that tribal web of protection when he moved to the cities from White Earth Reservation' (p. 26).

One-time classroom daydreaming finds its army counterpart when he tells a none-too-interested officer in Japan 'I want to be a writer' (p. 126). As he moves into authorship, he finds himself more and more authored by his own truest subject: Native America in all its historic mixedblood windings. Patronising white school or city authorities metamorphose into 'the new fur traders' (p. 185), a nice reference back to an ancestry which calls up his own *métis* or French Canadian Chippewa family, the Vezinas, whose name was mistranscribed into Vizenor by the then Indian Agent. Vizenor's own 'trickster signature' (p. 263) as storyteller, two centuries on, might well be thought a textual making good. In the National Guard, he thinks himself 'a mixedblood featherweight' (p. 80), his boxing that of a kind of shadow tribal warrior. 'Death Song for a Rodent', a vignette of his remorse on shooting a squirrel, again suggests a linkage between past and present, the modern hunter in disregard of Anishinaabe woodland etiquette.

As journalist, his purview widens to include reporting the suicide of a twelve-year-old Dakota Sioux boy, Dane White, also inadequately parented, and then detained in a prison cell for school truancy to quite disastrous effect; the murder trial of Thomas James White Hawk, a killer for sure yet, on Vizenor's long-held reckoning, also a victim of 'cultural schizophrenia' (p. 289); and, in 'Avengers at Wounded Knee', his keen understanding of the Seventh US Cavalry's massacre of Big Foot and his Minneconjou Sioux (nearly 300 in all) at South Dakota's Wounded Knee Creek in 1890, and yet, at the same time, his unpious take on the Dennis Banks style of warrior bravura during the 1973 protest with its drugs, guns and even limousine service as what he calls 'a revolutionary tribal caravan' (p. 237). He remembers his own haunting by skinwalkers or tribal poltergeists, in a Santa Fe room where, previously unknown to him, there have been painful deaths. He also recalls an article he once wrote for the *Minneapolis Tribune* which indicts a University of Minneapolis archaeological dig as 'tribal desecration'. With just the right working blend of seriousness, yet trickster provocation, he proposes a 'federal bone court to hear the natural rights of buried human bones' (p. 258).

These interfolding domains of Native and white, city and reservation, America and Japan, street and campus, amount to a life remembered always as simultaneity and yet contradiction. In this, they take their cue from an observation by N. Scott Momaday, his greatly admired co-spirit: 'Story-telling', he quotes from Momaday's address to the First Convocation of American Indian Scholars, is 'a process in which man invests and preserves himself in the context of ideas'.[14] The point holds exactly for Vizenor's own 'survival trickeries on the border' (p. 73). He indicts fixed categories of 'Indian' as Hollywood or TV silhouette, or as social-science case-study, or, perhaps above all, as prime exhibit in the annals of victimry. *Interior Landscapes* unravels a life full of contradance: Native modernity from out of Native ancestralism, city from reservation, Indian, in the term he has made quite his own, as postindian.

Not the least accompaniment to Vizenor's challenge to stereotypic fictions of 'The Indian' lies in ventriloquy to match. *Interior Landscapes* both remembers, and monitors its remembering, be the auspices Anishinaabe trickster talk or Baudrillardian theory of representation. In 'Crows Written on the Poplars: Autocritical Autobiographies' (1987), 'a mixedblood causerie' as he calls it in a phrase nicely also summoning of French Canadian fur-trader origins, he offers the following manifesto:

> Gerald Vizenor believes that autobiographies are imaginative histories; a remembrance past the barriers; wild pastimes over the pronouns . . . mixedbloods loosen the seams in the shrouds of identities. Institutional time, he contends, belies our personal memories, imagination, and consciousness.[15]

The effect of his own autobiography, certainly, could not be more to 'loosen the seams', a challenge to fixed borders both in Native identity and in autobiography as but one of many available genres for its expression.

III

Afro-America's 'written by himself/herself' as the recurrent half-title of so much slave narrative might almost have become a mantra, the signal of de-enslavement from denial of ownership of the word in equal part with the body. Frederick Douglass's *Narrative* (1845) and Harriet Jacobs's *Incidents in the Life of a Slave Girl* (1861), as two best-known writings, make the point insistently. Both draw into themselves the further unshackling drama, the relish, of actually 'making', or in Momaday's sense, imagining, the self within and upon the page. This memory of an 'I' once so arbitrarily dispossessed, and then, albeit still against odds, able to seize and recognise its own literate – and literary – scriptural re-formation, gives a quite special resonance to almost all African American autobiography.

Black first-person writing in slavery's aftermath looks first to the tier which includes Booker T. Washington and W. E. B. DuBois, Southerner and Yankee respectively, and long taken to embody contrasting politics of acquiescence or activism. The litany of 1920s-sponsored 'New Negro' classics which follows carry their own insistent differences and variety, whether James Weldon Johnson's stately, even mandarin *Along This Way* (1933), Claude McKay's feisty, often self-conflicted memory of Jamaican origins and a 1920s life in Harlem in *A Long Way from Home* (1937), Langston Hughes's always greatly resolute yet seemingly *flâneur* life as given in *The Big Sea* (1940) and *I Wonder as I Wander* (1956), or Zora Neale Hurston's model of vernacular yet, even so, for some racially evasive memory in *Dust Tracks on a Road* (1942).

Contrariety carries forward as a hallmark throughout. Richard Wright's *Black Boy* (1945) centres on Dixie as both substance and shadow, a remembrance of white segregation and yet also of broken black family, a recall of beginnings and at the same time of leave-takings. James Baldwin's *Notes of a Native Son* (1955), as in the essay-work which follow, honours even as it carries its own disaffiliation from Wright and moves into a unique body of evidentiary witness to Harlem and iconographies of race and identity far beyond. Malcolm X's *Autobiography* (1965) may have been dictated on the move, always improvisationally, to Alex Haley, yet it would achieve fixture both in its own literary right and as a text at the very epicentre of 1960s militancy. Audre Lorde's *Zami: A New Spelling of My Name* (1982) has signified a new marker in gender writing, a 'biomythography' of black lesbian life.

Others in the lineage invite like cognisance, each at once parts of a continuum yet always singular in matching life to style. Chester Himes in *The Quality of Hurt* (1972) and *My Life of Absurdity* (1976) not only addresses, but gives narrative embodiment to, 'the eccentricities of my creativity'. Maya Angelou's five-volume Life beginning with *I Know Why the Caged Bird Sings* (1969) eventuates out of, and then orders, her 'assembly of strivings'. June Jordan's *Civil Wars* (1981) delineates a self-making as Bedford-Stuyvesant child, Harlemite, single mother, writer, urban planner, bisexual, ongoing activist. *The Autobiography of LeRoi Jones/Amiri Baraka* (1984) delivers a writer-ideologue's rite of passage from within America's 'maze of light and darkness'. A formidable prison archive looks to Eldridge Cleaver's *Soul on Ice* (1968) as urging a new political virility, George Jackson's *Soledad Brother* (1970) as an autodidact's Gramscian challenge to America as penitentiary, and Angela Davis's *An Autobiography* (1974) as Marxist, or more precisely Marcusean, dissent. The belated recognition of this span, and voicing, of Afro-America's first-person texts has led to a still gathering re-evaluation, a tradition whose full depth has only lately begun to be recognised.

The two autobiographies which do duty, John Edgar Wideman's *Brothers and Keepers* (1984) and Lorene Cary's *Black Ice* (1991), have not been free of controversy. The one takes the form of a double-story in which Wideman overlaps himself as professional novelist with his street brother, Robby, sentenced without parole as an accessory to murder. Was he at risk, as he acknowledges, of exploiting his brother's life as an *exercice de style*? The other, in all its own play of contradiction, offers the self-account of a black education inside a historic white New Hampshire boarding school. Was this the would-be model life or self-justifying privilege?

Wideman leaves no doubt of his own challenge in telling two lives in one, not to mention his awareness of losing the rough-edged unpredictability of actual life inside the well-made fiction:

> Even as I manufactured fiction from the events of my brother's life, from the history of the family that had nurtured us both, I knew something of a different order remained to be extricated. The fiction writer was also a man

with a real brother behind real bars. I continued to feel caged by my
bewilderment, by my inability to see clearly, accurately, not only the last
visit to my brother, but the whole skein of our lives together and apart. This
attempt to break out, to knock down the walls. (p. 18)

He sets himself a self-denying ordinance – 'I would have to root my fiction-writing
self out of our exchanges' (p. 77). This sense of scruple, of the likely dubious morality
of converting the hard edge of both his own and his brother's life into literary
consumer goods, pursues him: 'Do I write to escape, to make a fiction of my own life?
If I can't be trusted with the story of my own life, how could I ask my brother to trust
me with his?' (p. 78).

The life drama, for sure, beckons and dazzles: November 1975 and Robby's part in
a botched robbery (a TV scam, a killing, in Robby's words 'heavy business', p. 149);
the cross-country flight to Wideman's then University of Wyoming home ('the two
thousand miles between Laramie . . . and Pittsburgh, Pennsylvania . . . Robby was
inside me', p. 4); the capture and arraignment at the Colorado courthouse of Fort
Collins ('that citadel of whiteness', p. 20); and the imprisonment at Western State
Penitentiary, Pennsylvania ('a giant wart', p. 42) and within it the prison status
'P3468 Robert Wideman' (p. 49).

This frame, in its different time-shifts and alternations of voice, Wideman fills with
notation of family genealogy, grandparental origins in South Carolina and migration north, life in black Homewood, prison as black fact and metaphor, and always
the two connected but divergent sibling histories. In John the impulse is to the
written word, study, books, university, and a settled marriage across the colour-line
to his Jewish wife Judy and children. In Robby it lies in a fever of inner-city hustle,
drugs, rap, women, theft. Wideman's achievement is to account for that linkage and
yet severance ('His story freeing me, because it forces me to tell my own', p. 98), the
two trajectories which, interactingly, have credentialled himself as author-custodian
and Robby as member of America's 'inmate nation' (p. 188).

For both, he borrows from written and spoken register, letter-exchanges, talk,
sibling memories shared and yet not. Place features especially, whether the grandfather Harry Wideman's northward move to Pittsburgh ('a raw, dirty, double-dealing
city', p. 22, and 'Steeltown, U.S.A.', p. 40), South Street in Philadelphia as 'home'
(p. 32), the 'Homewood' Wideman makes his own mythical kingdom in his fiction
(a 'close-knit, homogenous community', p. 73) and Wideman's Wyoming prairie
outpost, where he teaches at the university, with its snow, space, distance. In terms
of Robby's life, by contrast, almost everything is enclosure – street, car, house, even
the Philadelphia Black Power protests which give him a temporary sense of efficacy,
his own body as held and run by drugs. To these can be added his movement
through the Detroit of the Projects, into the white-run courtroom and white-
dispensed sentence ('Murder One is life', p. 174) and, eventually, into life in a
Western Penitentiary cell ('When a convicted criminal enters prison, he is first
stripped of the clothing that connects him to the outside world', p. 187).

Wideman's awareness of the challenge within his own writer's space to try to imagine the self of his own freedom and the self of Robby's incarceration, a not one but double autobiography, becomes the very dialectic of the text. His visits to the prison, notepad jottings, mutual and family encounters in the primly mock-respectable 'visiting lounge' (p. 222), each coded exchange of word or past, is keyed to this interplay of freedom and incarceration. He offers an overall gloss in the following: 'If you're born black in America you must quickly teach yourself to recognize the invisible barriers disciplining the space in which you may move' (p. 221). *Brothers and Keepers* holds this condition to the light, a two-act life told within the one act of life-writing.

To move on to Lorene Cary's *Black Ice*, evidently, is to move into contrastive, almost opposite, terrain: a black scholarship girl's entry into St Paul's School in bucolic New England from her 'Main Line' Philadelphia beginnings in the suburb of Yeadon. This could not be more black Middle America, one a professional cadre, high SAT (Scholastic Aptitude Test) scores, family support and general all-round achievement. Even so, Cary acknowledges at the outset the immediate arising question: 'Were we black kids a social experiment?' (p. 5).

Her response is to lay out a credo of sorts, autobiography as dialogic remembrance of her own as but one kind of black life among many:

> I began writing about St Paul's School when I stopped thinking of my prep-school experience as an aberration from the common run of black life in America. . . . The narratives that helped me, that kept me company, along with the living, breathing people in my life, were those that talked honestly about growing up black in America. They burst into my silence, and in my head, they shouted and chattered and whispered and sang together. I am writing this book to become part of that unruly conversation . . . (p. 6)

Within each phase of the story, whether her father's judo as 'a vision of power' (p. 11), her mother's efficacy as raconteur and her 'dramatic maternity' (p. 54), or her own 'class of 1974' (p. 35) arrival and eventual 'Rector's Medal' (p. 219) as star alumna, the rite of passage is one not only of education as inward change and growth but also an ethnic politics of access.

That does not obscure set backs, even shock: the feeling of 'utter aloneness' (p. 47) in her white New Hampshire fastness, her own stereotype of her Japanese friend Yumiko ('I felt ashamed for having thought of her as a geisha girl', p. 66), the recall of racist 'nigger' ditties (p. 78), her abrupt sexual initiation (p. 107), and the contrast of the sequestered school with her summer waitress job at the Hearthglow DeVille restaurant which restores her 'back to black and white America' (p. 156). Yet, when Vernon Jordan visits the school, he speaks of the lack of a 'blueprint', 'uncharted water', for the next phase of black advance and leaves no doubt of her role ahead – ' "We're going to need every one of you" ' (p. 203).

Cary has every reason to insist on her story as one wholly and also to be included in the reckoning of Afro-America. She resolves that St Paul's will be her school as of everyday process rather than as the favouring of a select band of 'ethnic alumni'

(p. 232). In this spirit she recalls friendships, her classes in English, Spanish and a vexatious algebra, not to mention the school's Anglicanism and British nomenclature (sixth forms and the like), along with an African American summoning of Sojourner Truth, Martin Luther King, Malcolm X and Toni Morrison. This resolve not to be denied, or to be spoken of as being situated only at the privileged margins of black life, is impressive. She will not have her life story, if no drama of inner-city or prison, made the lesser for taking place where, and as, it does.

That *Black Ice* takes on a retrospect in the form of her own return as a teacher, then as a regent, with mention of marriages, a divorce and children, adds its own continuity to her observation that 'I audit the layers of reminiscences' (p. 127). But Cary also gives a striking twist to notions of typicality. Unmistakably, she is heir to African-American culture and history at large. But she also recognises herself as a new kind of participant in the story. The life she tells, a First as may be, she looks to see become as typical as any other, black entry into all and anything America offers. In this respect, hers may be autobiography in quieter measure, the lowered voice. But this far from diminishes its radical implications.

IV

Recent Latino/a autobiography, in English or Spanish, offers its respective plenty. The span extends from Piri Thomas's *Down These Mean Streets* (1967), Nuyorican classic of street-level Manhattan gang and drug existence, to Ray Gonzalez's *Memory Fever* (1993), Tex-Mex portrait of a border of mind as much as history, or from Gloria Anzaldúa's *Borderlands/La Frontera: The New Mestiza* (1987), lesbian-*chicana* record of 'my proccupations with the inner life of the Self', through to US Puerto Rican personal narratives like Edward Rivera's *Family Installments: Memories of Growing Up Hispanic* (1983) and Judith Ortiz Cofer's *Silent Dancing: A Partial Remembrance of a Puerto Rican Childhood* (1990) – the one a New York father-and-son story and the other a portrait of island origin and immigration to New Jersey. In Richard Rodriguez's *Hunger of Memory: The Education of Richard Rodriguez* (1982) and Esmeralda Santiago's *When I was Puerto Rican/Cuando Era Puertorriqueña* (1993, 1994), the dialectic of leave-taking and arrival becomes all, the one a west coast of 'Mexican' Sacramento, the other an east coast of 'Puerto Rican' Brooklyn.

Rodriguez could not have managed a more controversial bow. To admirers, often of the political right, he offers a vindication of the virtues of assimilation whatever the pains of cutting free from family and ethnic-cultural intimacy. To detractors, notably among Chicano activists, his opposition to affirmative action, bilingual education, even vernacular Catholicism, signalled a *trahison des clercs*, a Life whose refusal of any or all minority status continues to smack of self-absorption, too great a pondering of his own face in the mirror.

Little, however, could he, or anyone else, have foreseen how 'this intellectual autobiography' (p. 175), as he terms *Hunger of Memory*, together with *Days of Obligation: An Argument with My Mexican Father* (1992), and each *Time, American Scholar* and PBS McNeil-Lehrer *News Hour* essay, would make him the media conservative favourite he has become. For there can be little doubt of his bravura, the willingness to play mainstream cat among the ethnic pigeons and with an eloquence as ready as his stance of end-of-history melancholy. In this, his auto-biography can be compared to great advantage with, say, Linda Chavez's *Out of the Barrio: Towards a New Politics of Hispanic Assimilation* (1991), like-minded in assimilationist outlook but wholly workaday in style.

As six 'essays impersonating an autobiography . . . chapters of sad, fugue-like repetition' (p. 7), *Hunger of Memory* thus gives a new imaginative turn to *latino* autobiography. The effect, depending on ideological viewpoint, is to be applauded or decried. Is Rodriguez simply affirming America's promise of the sovereign self, for all the talk of loss, parental and community severance, a necessary, for some exemplary, process of self-realisation? Is he guilty of mainstreaming, as it has been called, an over-ready willingness to cede the importance of his Mexican American origins to what he dubs public America? Whichever holds, there can be no doubting Rodriguez's willingness to speak against the grain of ethno-piety and to take his polemical chances.

Each essay proffers both witness and challenge. In 'Aria', he insists that 'bilingu-alists simplistically scorn the value and necessity of assimilation' (p. 26), as if to have done once and for all with the special pleading, the self-ghettoisation, he believes perpetuated by a carried-over insistence on *barrio* or family Spanish – 'a private language' (p. 5) – in a larger American culture whose prime tongue is English. The opening terms of reference are, in keeping, high-literary, and to his detractors not a little pretentious – 'I have taken Caliban's advice. I have stolen their books. I will have some run of this isle' (p. 3). If he seeks to anticipate denigration as 'Tom Brown' or 'the brown Uncle Tom' (p. 4), he also has his boldness, a self-stance which offers no concession to the easy show of ethnicity: 'Aztec ruins hold no special interest for me. I do not search Mexican graveyards for unnameable ancestors . . .' (p. 5). He celebrates a life of books, study, and which has one culminating expression in his Fulbright year in the British Museum Reading Room as preparation for a Berkeley thesis on Renaissance literature, even as he asserts how greatly he rues leaving behind parents who 'have never heard of García Lorca and García Márquez' (p. 5). Is this, again, special pleading, self-indulgence, or a show of fierce honesty?

'The Achievement of Desire' casts him as the 'scholarship boy' (p. 46), à la Richard Hoggart, and who, again, 'cannot afford to admire his parents' (p. 49) if he is to enter America's public domain. 'Credo' has him arguing for a return to Latin for 'the high ceremony' of the Mass as a signifier of universalism and necessary bulwark against the 'ghetto Catholic' church (p. 79) with its Spanish or other ethnic-language religious services.

'Complexion' turns upon the contemplation of his own Aztec features, over which he lingers at, for some, all too narcissistic a length. His dark complexion and skin tone have caused him to feel 'mysteriously marked' (p. 125), a 'divorce from my body' (p. 125), but now exorcised by his plunge into a larger (and within it an unstatedly Gay?) world. In 'Profession', he looks back to his time doing graduate work in the English Department at Berkeley when he became, in a term he repeats with some scorn, a celebrity 'minority student' (p. 142), believing himself favoured, and so demeaned, by a process which has put category above self. Finally, in 'Mr Secrets', and with a dip back into his resoluteness to be a book-reader in a home where manual work set the standard, he returns to the need to enter, to exist in, and to turn to his own working advantage, America's public language, namely English as against the provincialising US Spanish of his ancestral migrant-Catholic family culture.

Little wonder *Hunger of Memory* was, and remains, a jousting-ground for notions of cultural centre and periphery, the canonical as against the ethnic self. Rodriguez, in his own phrase, 'languages' himself, the Chicano-who-was articulating the American-who-is and who speaks of ever hoping to 'form new versions of myself' (p. 190). Articulacy, and the education which produced it, undoubtedly reigns, a rise to word, consciousness, book, literature, media, the world. In his follow-up volume, *Days of Obligation: An Argument with My Mexican Father* (1992), and in a remembrance of his young life in Sacramento, California, he speaks of his own eclectic making, his pathway into an America beyond any one ethnicity:

> Asians rounded the world for me. I was a Mexican teenager in America who had become an Irish Catholic. When I was growing up in the 1960s, I heard Americans describing their nation as simply bipartite: black and white. When black and white argued I felt I was overhearing some family quarrel that didn't include me. Korean and Chinese and Japanese faces rescued me from the simplicities of black and white America. (p. 166)

Even so, the jury remains out as to any absolute or final balance of gains and losses. Has the public life sought in this way, and found, and for all his talk of loss, been at a cost under-recognised even on his own part?

Esmeralda Santiago's *When I was Puerto Rican*, which has a follow-up in *Almost a Woman* (1999), operates at quite another pitch. Together they amount to a life, first island-based then Manhattan-based, and which as she says in the Spanish-language version has been 'vivida en español, pero . . . inicialmente escrita en inglés' ('lived in Spanish but . . . initially written in English', p. xv). For just as America shadows Puerto Rico, so English shadows Spanish, the author's access not only to a dual historical but dual linguistic-imaginative citizenship.

'We call them *gringos*, they call us spiks' (p. 73), explains Papi, wayward father to Esmeralda or Negi (from 'Negrita' on account of her dark hair), as he scratches out a living amid the poverty of Macún in rural Puerto Rico. The stark contrast of these two Americas lies in her childhood as *jíbara*, or 'Puerto Rican country dweller' (p. 12), who 'had my last guava the day we left Puerto Rico' (p. 4) as against the first days of young girlhood in Brooklyn where 'all our time was spent indoors' (p. 252). In chronicling the life in between, Santiago in fact delineates her transition from Puertorriqueña to Nuyorriqueña, the girl learning her letters in a back-country schoolroom to the Performing Arts scholarship student who goes to Harvard.

Within lies the rising curve of Esmeralda's consciousness, the inner self which is witness to her parents's fights and yet love-making and column of children, and to her grandfather's '*jíbaro* tales of phantasms, talking animals, and enchanted guava trees' (p. 49) even as the mainland New York to which her grandmother has emigrated and of which 'I'd never heard mention of a Rockefela' (p. 56) slowly encroaches on her awareness. 'Being American is not just a language' (p. 73) her father also tells her, as if conscious always that his own hardscrub life, his *sinverguenzas* or misbehaviours, along with his denunciations of 1898 and the USA's 'imperialist' takeover, little suffice as preparation for the move of his common-law wife and her children to the world Esmeralda calls the 'Juniper States' (p. 64).

What in fact she imports is a whole 'Borinquén' of memory, its fauna and foodways, the tapeworms which infest her and her siblings in childhood as though emissaries of the family's poverty, the Catholicism merged with the *santería*, the US food and diet programmes, hurricanes, local politicking, her mother's breaking taboo by taking a factory job, the scare of a ritual in which she is required to close the eyes of a dead child, and her 'teenayer' initiation both on the island and in New York. 'I had no idea where I was. . . . I wished I had a map so I could place myself in relation to Puerto Rico' (p. 223), she says on landing in Brooklyn. *When I was Puerto Rican*, in truth, serves as that map, a life told as time in equal part with place, the one consciousness a bridge across two Americas.

V

Whatever the plaudits won by Maxine Hong Kingston's *The Woman Warrior* and *China Men*, the effect was also to win new attention for a larger first-person Asian America as literary regime. The roster, in fact, has been considerable, whether Carlos Bulosan's *America is in the Heart* (1946), the classic Filipino autobiography of a lifetime's worker activism both for political freedom in his homeland and decency of pay and conditions in the agriculture and industry on the west coast, or Mary Paik Lee's *Quiet Odyssey* (1990), a Korean and then Korean American life, or a Canadian-Japanese memoir of wartime internment, silence and survival like Joy Ogawa's *Obasan* (1988), or David Mura's expatriate, self-mirroring American year in Japan as told in *Turning Japanese: Memoirs of a Sansei* (1991). Four yet other lives, derived in turn from Japan, China and India, augment still further the accent, and chronology, of this roster of Asian America told in the first person.

The baseline for the 'Monica Sone' remembered in *Nisei Daughter* (1953, 1979) bespeaks a first and necessary accusing memory: the 1942 in which 120,000 Japanese Americans were sent to relocation camps, 'a time', as she says, 'when they became prisoners of their own government, without charges, without trials' (p. 122). Even more graphically, in the light of Pearl Harbor, she recalls reading window signs saying 'We kill rats and Japs here' (p. 160). Yet, for all that Executive Order 9066 would lead directly to internment, she does not doubt herself American, a citizen of double origins yet always an American: a stance which has sometimes opened her to charges of too ready a compromise or forgiveness, even self-denial.

This dual sense of herself she first locates in her 1930s waterfront Seattle growing up, a world of fondly reinvoked Japanese newspapers, tea sets, gossip, family lore, yet all of it lived in close proximity to a white Euro-America as expressed in the local Teamsters Office, burlesque houses, cafés and the Salvation Army. She leaves little doubt, even so, of the potential for self-division, a fissure of allegiance: 'I didn't see how I could be both a Yankee and Japanese at the same time. It was like being born with two heads. It sounded freakish and a lot of trouble' (p. 19).

In striving to calm, and at best overcome, this two-way pull, she calls to mind the everyday and small things of her coexistent worlds. She lingers over the Japanese Garden in Seattle given by the people of Yokohama in recognition for help after the 1923 earthquake ('a bit of Oriental heaven which the Seattle Japanese had helped to create', p. 60). 'In our family,' she elsewhere recalls, 'we ate both Western and Oriental dishes' (p. 13). The Carollton Hotel taken over by her father becomes a home for both Asians and white Americans. She lives amid not only two languages but also two calendars, on the one hand 'Lincoln's Birthday, Washington's Birthday, Memorial Day, the Fourth of July, Labor Day, Thanksgiving, Christmas and New Year's' (p. 66), and on the other, a calendar which celebrates Tenchosetsu, the Emperor's Birthday. If she listens to American radio, to crooners or the big bands, she also hears her parents at Nippon Kan Hall singing *naniwa bushi*, 'old Japan . . . a kind of ballad singing' (p. 77). She compares American eating styles with the formal refusals necessary in Japanese etiquette ('*Arigato*, I have plenty thank you', p. 86). In all, as she tells it, her existence before internment becomes a balancing act, an inspired equilibrium.

This is underscored the other way round in her first youthful visit from America to 'old Japan', 'a strange land of bicycles' (p. 90) in which 'people stared at our foreign clothes and I felt self-conscious' (p. 91). She meets her grandfather with his Japanese dream of America, is struck by the silences of Japanese culture as against the volubility and noise of America, and collects a kind of mini-museum of Japan to take back to America – a toy samurai sword, a kimono, Japanese stockings, her mother's scroll, and a host of exquisite small sculptures and silk and other designs.

All of these, however, she and her family must hide when forced to de-Japanise their American home in the wake of Pearl Harbor. To be American in this case means to eviscerate origins, to erase rather than celebrate ethnic-cultural legacy. The effort, inevitably, is to no avail. Yet when her parents are sent to their camp, her mother, almost as though viscerally, not to say ancestrally, insists on taking 'a gallon of soy sauce' (p. 168). Winning as that has to be, the questions which then arise, given in what sounds as though a faux-naïf voice, admit of little assuagement:

What was I doing behind a fence like a criminal? Maybe I wasn't considered an American anymore. My citizenship wasn't real after all. Then what was I?. . . . I was certainly not a citizen of Japan as my parents were. . . . One thing was sure. The wire fence was real . . . (p. 177)

To compound these ironies, she also recalls the formation of the Nisei combat unit, an Americanisation truly freighted in double identity.

Her self-reckoning is benign. On return with her family after the war from Camp

Minidoka in Idaho, she muses: 'To be born in two cultures is like getting a real bargain in life, two for the price of one' (p. 236). She argues the advantages of being nisei over issei, and even the camps as a way of 'educating' her fellow Americans as to the returns on ethnic pluralism. To doubters, she remains self-deluding. To those more favourably disposed, she writes ahead of her time – her life, her story, the means to 'a deeper, stronger, pulse in the American scene' (p. 238). Either way, *Nisei Daughter* does important service, imaginative Japanese American autobiography born of literal American history.

In Garrett Hongo's *Volcano* (1995a), nisei gives way to sansei, the Second World War and camp internment to a 1990s journey of Japanese American genealogy, and Seattle to Hawai'i. For Hongo himself, it marks the transition from the poet of *Yellow Light* (1982) and *The River of Heaven* (1988) to autobiographer and memoirist. In his Introduction to the collection, *Under Western Eyes: Personal Essays from Asian America* (1995b), he leaves little doubt of his governing impetus:

> As a child of the Asian diaspora, I felt that the master narratives of America were not open to me . . . would not easily incorporate stories that I knew except as addenda to the grander tales of Manifest Destiny, white settlement of the West, and the idea of 'civilization' being brought to Hawai'i by Christian missionaries and planters. For most of my adolescence and early adult life, I felt that there was no literary matrix in which I could address the histories of the imagination and plantation experience in Hawai'i, and my own stories were completely untold . . . I needed to repossess my own childhood, my own ethnic background.[16]

Volcano, as Hongo expresses it, deals in 'a universe of associations' (p. 46) centred on his Hawaiian birthplace, the HONGO STORE of his ancestors within the island township of Volcano. The store he thinks of as 'a kind of faith . . . a preserve of identity and consciousness' (p. 287), its iconic resonance that of hearthstone, talk-place, a timeline of family within a timeless Pacific ocean domain. Each surrounding fauna, fern, rock, trail and laval formation supplies the contextual topography, family and island an inextricable source of genesis. Volcano, place and store, become for him a call to excavation:

> I thought I might turn my family losses around – the store that has passed out of our care, the broken promise of its inheritance, the life we'd been sundered from becoming as familiar with this extraordinary place and its various histories as a Hasid is with his chosen text, as a Buddhist monk might be with his puzzling koan and regimen of meditation. Because I did not grow up here. Because I did not understand my father – so much *of* Hawai'i and another time – though I loved him. I wanted to know the place and I wanted to tie my name to it, to deliver out of the contact a kind of sacred book – a book of origins. (pp. 26–7)

The analogy between the island's physical becoming and his own American, or Japanese American, becoming holds throughout. He speaks of molten lava as making him feel 'as though wrapped inside his own brittle shroud of birthing', and of the double implication of its 'heat', 'flow', 'radiance' (p. 112). His seizure of word, the will to self-articulation, becomes even greater when he sets it against internment and its accompanying community effect of 'public disgrace', 'silence' and 'deep prohibitions' (p. 221). The stance becomes transgressive. As he goes on to say of a taboo first love with the white girl Regina in his California high school, 'I was acting outside history. I could cross history' (p. 221).

The 'beguilement that would be lifelong' (p. 256) takes the form of linked incursions into time and place: Hawai'i itself ('its first human settlers called it Hava-iti . . . or, more simply, "Paradise"', p. 3); the Japan brought across the Pacific ('My grandfather had sold liquor and prepared food (mostly Japanese things like beef *teriyaki* and shrimp *tempura*', p. 10); and a Japanese America which causes him to ponder ethnicity itself ('there is a world of feeling and specificities among the vast and monolithic Other of race in America', p. 227).

Each detail builds into a gathering drama of association and recall. His wife Cynthia's *yukata* calls up Japanese dress code. The local *minka* roof designs suggest a migrancy of architecture. Pondered-over foodways (*kinako* or soybean flour, *tempura*) give an alimentary imagery to the text. His father Albert is remembered as having attended Tokyo High in Honolulu. Each Hongo family history adds to this pathway of dynasty – the paternal grandfather Torau's love affairs, the flight of his first wife Yukiko, the marriage to the one-time stockgirl Eveline. Above all stands the HONGO STORE as memorial icon: at once a registry of family (Albert's vexed succession as merchant-proprietor, his move to California, Eveline's accession of the store, the presence of the two half-sister aunts Charlotte and Lily); of culture (Yukiko or Grandmother Katayama performing to *shamisen* at more than eighty years of age and in modern Honolulu the stylised dance of her *geisha* youth); and of an ongoing daily round of mealtimes, income and shelf stock, even the label whereby Hongo discovers himself to have been named after a brand of muscatel.

In the same sweep, and as born out in the portrait of his silent, wistful maternal grandfather, Kubota, who comes under wartime investigation by the FBI, Hongo does not sidestep the rankle of larger Japanese American history. Kubota remains unreconciled to America yet unwilling to return to Japan, dying of Alzheimer's, of all ironic dates, on 'Pearl Harbor Day, December 7, 1983' (p. 277). Hongo imagines his legacy as one of ceremonial lanterns, each lit and strung across the sea with 'the silvery names of all our dead' (p. 278). Both grandfathers he locates against a history of *issei* labour and Hawai'i's sugar-cane plantations, 7 December and Pearl Harbor, '9066' and the 'relocation' camps, and the ongoing court cases to gain restitution of rights and property.

Hawai'i, however, he insists is no unicultural realm. He thinks back to growing up amid 'lagoons of syntax' (p. x) in which 'Mainland English' (p. x) acts as but one register along with his own Hawaiian pidgin and each Portuguese and Cantonese loanword and intonation. That leads him to emphasise co-existent other archives of island memory, of the native *kanaka*, of the *haole* mainlanders, of an Asian diversity to include Chinese and Filipino residents.

If he can think of the literary education which leads him to the western canon, *The Iliad* to Shakespeare, Kafka to Naipaul, he also summons a Japanese virtuosity – *The Tale of Genji*, Basho's *haiku*, the theatre of noh, bunraku and kabuki, and the postwar fiction of Yukio Mishima and Kenzaburo Oe. He equally links himself to fellow Asian Americans, Frank Chin among others, and, touchingly, to Wakako Yamauchi as one-time camp internee and the author of the story and later play 'And the Soul Shall Dance'. Mainstream popular culture (*I Love Lucy* to *Star Trek*, Roy Orbison to Janis Joplin) overlaps with that both of Hawai'i (poi and papaya as foodways, hula, ukelele, 'Portuguese *chang-a-lang*' (p. 129) as music) and of migrant Japan ('Shina no Yoru' as 1930s hit song to *manga* and Godzilla and *yakusa* films).

It is a Hawai'i also full of its own locals, whether Paul Rodrigues as Portuguese American plumbing contractor, Gabby Pahinui as Hawaiian jazz guitarist, the local postwoman (not lost on Hongo as another kind of deliverer of 'the word') eased in her grief at a daughter's death of leukaemia by reading one of his poems on a Japanese graveyard or, like some *magus* or jester spirit of place, 'Old Weird Harold', the transvestite hitchhiker on Volcano Highway. These, together with the island's volcanologists, geophysicists and biologists, Hongo fondly situates as 'searchers, odd ducks, misfits, and derelicts' (p. 312).

At the same time, Hongo calls up his own self-memory, the trajectory of his life as boy, student and writer in latter-day America. In 'Self-Portrait', he invokes un-modern parents hard put to find a right family balance in hyper-modern California (his mother 'indignant at my dreaminess', p. 184, his father still outdoor-Hawaiian in metropolitan Los Angeles). He thinks of schooldays in which he and others were derided as 'sansei *kotonks*' (p. 215) – the name full of insult, a Japanese American neither sufficiently Japanese nor sufficiently American. Regina comes back into memory as the white girlfriend 'out of bounds' (p. 220). At Pomona college, he is taught by a Jewish professor, Bert Meyers, who explains the 1940s Japanese American deportations as shadowing those of European Jews. He invokes his gap year in Kyoto and Hofukuji, Okayama amid stern temple masters who reveal his spiritual shortcomings. At an opposite reach, he recalls running a Seattle theatre group he had hoped to call 'The Asian Exclusion Act' (p. 198) and his interlude as a would-be Hollywood comic scriptwriter (to be told '*you* ain't *funny*, kid . . . You might as well do poetry', p. 207).

But this, too, is Hawai'i as 'a world of faery and imagination' (p. 16). Much as Volcano township marks his birth in the backroom kitchen of the general store 'my grandfather built on the Volcano Road' (p. 3), its surrounds embody 'a big chunk of the sublime' (p. 4), his Yeatsian 'Ben Bulben' (p. 26). Sequences like 'Natal' and 'Ghost', or his two kinds of *envoi*, 'Colonial' and 'Mendocino Rose', pursue genealogy as 'dragon tail' (p. 59), 'the fog of thirty-five years' (p. 141), a past whose memory lies inhumed in the Volcano's ancestral forests, greenery and rock and often as apparently unreal as real.

In no greater respect is this true than in the four beautifully expressive sequences

Hongo designates 'Volcanology'. In '*Ugetsu*', the opening chapter, he writes of Volcano as 'craters and ancient firepit and huge black seas of hardened lava, the rain forest lush with all varieties of ferns, orchids, exotic gingers, and wild lilies, the constant rain and sun-showers . . .' (p. 4). He summons up 'steam devils' (p. 24), 'lantern ferns' (p. 71), the 'pythonlike' *uluhe* fern, and tubed black lava to suggest 'the carcass of a gigantic slug' (p. 111). Another giant fern, the *hapu'u*, becomes for him the spirit of the place, an idiom of botany yet also of music and birthing:

> The standing trunk is actually a bundle of fibrous stalks, radiating upward in successive growth-rays around a phloemlike core surrounded by an absorbent, spongy matting . . . As you walk through a strand of them, you can imagine hearing the fronds thump and snacker with the bass thrummings of birth, a silent jazz and a uteral rending going on both at once. (pp. 72–3)

Likewise the burn of the lava flow, vivid enough in its own terms, can call up Hongo's inner creative fire – a 'grinding sound', 'the joy of feeling something new' (p. 112), 'slick red gutters of fast-moving streams' (p. 233). Watching Mount Kilauea erupt 'as if from ten thousand firecrackers' (p. 284), he says, self-referringly, 'I stood on the shores of pure creation' (p. 285). The island's topography, in all its shaping energy, fuses with his own history, the upshot being Hongo's 'something new' in the literary form of *Volcano: A Memoir of Hawai'i*.

Li-Young Lee's *The Winged Seed: A Remembrance* (1995) opens its China memoir with an invitation into reverie, a text of dreams: 'In my dream my father came back, dressed in clothes we'd buried him in, carrying a jar of blood in one hand, his suit pockets lined with black seeds' (p. 11). The effect is imagist, irreal, one of self-haunting yet also exorcism. 'A jar of blood', and the ongoing 'seed' metaphor, call up his American way of taking possession of his Chinese dispossession, the resolving of a diaspora of fragmented family, lost siblings and shifting homelands. Exile emerges, in fact, as its own species of centre.

For as the acclaimed lyric poet of *The City in which I Love You* (1990), and the son of the Reverend Lee, Chinese Christian, one-time physician to Mao Zedong, persecuted minority leader in Sukarno's Indonesia, and eventual minister to a small-town Pennsylvania congregation, the challenge is to find a means, a language, to bridge the 'feudal hierarchy' (p. 18) of mainland Chinese origins to 'the sidewalks of North American cities and bridges' (p. 11). Thus the China of Tientsin, Hong Kong and Macau, or the Indonesia of Jakarta and Java, or the America of Seattle, Chicago and the township of Vandergrift in western Pennsylvania, all become as much symbolic as actual itinerary, a landscape of 'memory', 'clues', 'voices' (p. 88).

These Lee writes into being with quite stirring delicacy. His mother, Jiaying, in China has her feet 'twisted to fit into tiny hoof-shaped shoes of brocade' (p. 20). His father's meticulous, origami-style paper house becomes the very emblem of itinerant dynasty. 'Ba's Temple of Solomon' (p. 38), foldable, boxed, a container of seeds, is 'carried across borders, barriers . . . as language to language, landscape to landscape' (p. 38). Memories of his mother's taste for lychee as she flees China, or of his father's 'black cashmere coat' (p. 87) and his accordion-playing in the journey from 'China to Java and Java to Hong Kong' (p. 87), co-exist with Indonesian imprisonment in 1960–1 and the move to America. There, Chinese in America, his Baptist father who goes on to study at Pittsburgh Theological Seminary takes on nomenclature from yet another diaspora; he becomes known as The Rabbi (p. 192).

Within all this circuit of family (his father's name meaning 'Perfect Courage', his mother's 'House of Courage'), of politics (be it the China of before or after the Revolution, War Administration Macau, or the military Indonesia which accuses his father of being a spy), and of place (the Java of village servants and magic or the Pennsylvania of parishioners like the deranged Mona Cook with her 'I see the lamb', p. 81), Lee also unfolds, and closely monitors, his own inner will to language. The process takes him from childhood silence amid 'the traffic of talk' (p. 184), to his acquired Chinese brushstrokes, and to English. He speaks of the fear that the history within him risks erasure. 'Each memory I own is like a photo being eaten away from the edges towards the center' (p. 88), he says at one point. 'Here, as in childhood, I grow old before the empty pages' (p. 147), he says at another. Yet the passion for words, Chinese or American, becomes for him their own resuscitative drama, lexical seedbeds for a life whose 'silence' (p. 186) and 'missing pages' (p. 205) *The Winged Seed* both seeks and redeems.

India supplies an organising family point of departure to Meena Alexander's *Fault Lines* (1993) – yet, appropriately, the book first appeared in an American-published Cross-Cultural Memoir Series. Its span of country, religion, history, migration, and above all language, carries the almost perfect multicultural insignia. She could not be more explicit about her will to have her own divides meet, to join her past with her present: 'In Manhattan, I am a fissured thing, a body crossed by fault lines. Where is my past? What is my past to me, here, now at the edge of Broadway? Is America a place without memory?' (p. 182). These queries, those of an heir to colonialism though herself postcolonial, lead into a text she variously designates 'memoir' (p. 1), 'map' (p. 2), a 'broken geography' (p. 2), in all, and in a well-chosen Indian phrase, a 'katha' or 'story of my life' (p. 5).

It is a life, moreover, as plural in its languages as in its time and place. Malayalam she inherits from her summer and other visits to the family's ancestral Kerala. Hindi, and behind it Sanskrit, is the language of her childhood in Uttar Pradesh and the north. Arabic, which she remembers in shards, she acquires in the Sudan where her father works as a meteorologist under an arrangement with the Indian government and where she enters university. There is French, and a composite English blended, respectively, of India, England, and the full-time move to Manhattan with her Jewish American husband, the historian David Lelyveld, along with the language of her mothering of their two children. 'I was fascinated by the corrosive magic of the first person singular,' she witnesses, 'its exuberant flights, its sheer falls into despair' (p. 120). Given Alexander's eclecticism, it makes for appropriate comment.

Lines run independently and yet converge. Appa, the Malalayam for father, and Amma, for mother, point back to India, whether the greenery and backwaters of Kerala, her grandfather Ilya's *History of the Mar Thoma Church* and its Syrian rite, a stone-eating girl as an image of Indian womanhood, or the one-time fear of arranged marriage and 'the burning horror of clitoridectomy' (p. 111), then to Khartoum ('parched as a shed snakeskin', p. 71), with a return to Delhi as a world of metropolitan energy. Her inner personal course evolves from childhood compositions to a doctoral year in Nottingham where she researches Romanticism, from a breakdown and then a love affair with a Czech to a teaching position at Hyderabad and, eventually, on to the move to New York even as it alternates with her visits back to family in India. The whole at once bespeaks 'my discrepant otherness', (p. 73), and yet, as she cites Wallace Stevens, to be given its 'unlocking' as 'alphabets', a 'life in letters' (p. 200).

To get her grip on America, she also invokes Frank O'Hara's injunction to 'live as variously as possible' (p. 193). Her homes in India and elsewhere she thinks each in itself 'various, multiple' (p. 53). Her own name, when changed from the Mary Elizabeth of her passport to Meena, she thinks of as a species of conjugation ('The name means fish in Sanskrit, enamel work or jeweling in Urdu, port in Arabic', p. 74). A concluding chapter recalls a conference at Cornell on 'Writing, Ethnicity, being "Other" in New York' – 'all the stuff that drives you up the wall till you realize that you are the wall you are driven up' (p. 190).

This snappy sense of paradox is typical, a style in kind for the American autobiography of an Indian author written from the credo of 'an ethnicity that breeds in the perpetual present, that never will be wholly spelt out' (p. 202).

VI

To turn from ethnic autobiography to ethnic autofiction is to meet the first-person under familiar, yet slightly changed, auspices. This is self, and story, as consciously embodied fiction, real but offered as though collusively and under licence of narrative invention. Few more striking instances have come to hand than Oscar Zeta Acosta's *The Autobiography of a Brown Buffalo* (1972) and *The Revolt of the Cockroach People* (1973), life-writing, ethnicity, made over into carnivalesque.

Acosta in typical voice is to be met with in a letter to Willie L. Brown's campaign for the California House of Representatives in 1970:

When you speak of civil rights, civil liberties, etc. you think of black vs. white. When there's talk of investigation of these rights, of federal grants for education, of cheap housing, in other words, discrimination, you speak of Negroes. At the Chinese banquet when all the big whigs [sic] got up to talk, they mentioned the Negroes, and, second the Chinese . . . And that's the way it goes. All America is divided into three parts, white, black and yellow. . . . How about me?[17]

The Brown Buffalo. La Cucaracha. On Hunter Thompson's New Journalism reckoning in *Fear and Loathing in Las Vegas* (1972) the 300-pound 'Samoan' Dr Gonzo. Under any or all of these soubriquets, Oscar Zeta Acosta supplies a stirring, if often marginal, name in the making of 1960s counter-culture. Each remembered version of Acosta hovers intriguingly between fact and legend.

There is Acosta the anarcho-libertarian raised in California's Riverbank-Modesto who makes his name as a legal-aid lawyer in Oakland and Los Angeles after qualifying in San Francisco in 1966. There is the Airforce enlistee who, on being sent to Panama, becomes a Pentecostal convert and missionary there (1949–52) before opting for apostasy and a return to California. There is the jailee in Ciudad Juárez, Mexico, in 1968, forced to argue in local court for his own interest in uncertain street Spanish or *caló* after a spat with a hotelkeeper. As notably as any, there is the Oscar of the barricades, whether the battling lawyer of the St Basil's protest for better high schools or the *Raza Unida* independent candidate for Sheriff of Los Angeles in 1970 who regularly affirms his allegiance by signing himself 'Oscar Zeta Acosta, Chicano lawyer' and who finally leaves for Mexico in despair, madness even, at the internal divisions in Chicano politics.

To these, always, have to be added the rumbustious tequila-drinker and druggie ten years in therapy, the hugely overweight ulcer-sufferer who spat blood, the twice-over divorcee, and the eventual *desaparecido* in 1974 aged thirty-nine who was last seen in Mazatlán, Mexico, and whose end has long been shrouded in mystery. Was he drug-running or gun-running, a Chicano Ambrose Bierce who created his own exit from history, or a victim of kidnap or other foul play? Above all, there has to be Acosta as first-person singular author of his two notorious autofictions.

The 'I' persona assumed by Acosta in *The Autobiography of a Brown Buffalo* bows in with a suitable gesture of self-exposure: 'I stand naked before the mirror'. His unassuaging reflection shows him 'brown belly', 'extra flesh', 'two large hunks of brown tit' (p. 11). Evacuation becomes a bathroom opera of heave, colour, the moilings of fast-food leftovers. Hallucinatory colloquies open up with 'Old Bogey', Cagney and Edward G. Robinson. In their wake, he speaks in imagination to 'my Jewish shrink', Dr Serbin, the therapist as accuser, and whose voice, throughout, echoes like some monster Freud. Glut rules, a build-up of 'booze and Mexican food', Chinese pork and chickens, his ulcers, pills for dyspepsia, and shower-room tumescence and betraying fantasy coitus with Alice, the Minnesota leggy, blonde partner of his friend Ted Casey about to return from overseas war duty in Okinawa.

This is opening ventriloquy busy and comic in its own right, at once self-serious yet self-mocking. A touch of on-the-road Beat patois enters. Acosta plunges 'headlong' in his green Plymouth into San Francisco morning traffic. 'I'm splitting' (p. 33), he writes to his office-mate. Procol Harum sings 'A Whiter Shade of Pale' on the radio. He buys drink from a liquor store opposite City Lights Bookshop, Beat sanctuary but also to him, un-unpiously, 'a hangout for sniveling intellectuals' (p. 36). He throws in a reference to Herb Caen long celebrated for his Yiddish coining, however facetiously, of 'beatnik'. Memories of marijuana and his first LSD come to mind. He roars drunk into Dr Serbin's in the guise of 'another wild Indian gone amok' (p. 42). Acosta monitors 'Acosta'. The one text patrols the other.

At Trader JJ's, watering-hole talk-shop, he self-accusingly gives vent to bar-room and wholly un-pc macho talk about 'chinks and fags' (p. 43). The Beatles's 'Help' spills its plaintiveness into his hearing on Polk Street. A returned Ted Casey tempts him with mescaline. 'Powdered mayonnaise' (p. 67), heroin, appears at a Mafia-run restaurant where he is eating. Women, his ex-lover June MacAdoo, Ted Casey's Alice again and her friend Mary, all weave into his sexual fantasies even as, with reason, he frets about his own male prowess. The diorama is motleyed, a near-comic-cuts weave of illusion and fact. So it is, too, that on 1 July 1967 he announces himself as indeed 'The Samoan', hulk, ethnic transvestite, harlequin. 'I've been mistaken for American Indian, Spanish, Filipino, Hawaiian, Samoan, and Arabian', he witnesses, adding, in rueful defiance of any pc standard, 'No one has ever asked me if I'm a spic or greaser' (p. 68).

Acosta as up-from-the-ranks Chicano activist and yet Sixties drop-out with a love of Bob Dylan both compete and collude. On the one hand, he looks back to his Riverbank childhood with its gang allegiance and fights against then Okies ('I grew up a fat, dark Mexican – a Brown Buffalo – and my enemies called me a nigger', p. 86), along with his fantasy war-games, peach-picking, clarinet-playing and early first loves. On the other hand, he heads into the Pacific Northwest with the hitchhiker Karin Wilmington, a journey busy in allusion to Tim Leary, Jerry Garcia and the Grateful Dead, and yet more faux-Indian pose in the Hemingway country of Ketchum, Idaho. Early and later Acosta circle into each other in the remembrance of his Panama years, his one-time bid to serve as 'a Mexican Billy Graham' (p. 132).

Overdoses, bad LSD trips, blackouts, a succession of women, writer alcoholics like Al Mathews, car crashes, and odd jobs in Vail, Colorado offer a time-present. They play against his memory of time-past in Juarez jail amid 'the ugliest pirates I ever saw' (p. 192) and his need to prove to a US border official his American identity as if in a parody of formula migrant script – 'You don't *look* like an American you know', he is told (p. 195). As he makes his way back into contemporary Los Angeles along the iconic Route 66, and having told the waitress Bobbi that 'My family is the Last of the Aztecs' (p. 140) and proclaimed himself a 'vato loco' (p. 199), he speaks of rebirth, a time to come when he will take Zeta as his middle name from the last letter of the Spanish alphabet and the name of the hero in the movie *Las Cucarachas*. His route into becoming Oscar Zeta Acosta, author, can be seen to have its foreshadow in playing *auteur* in real life. As a kind of composite certificate of identity, he offers the following:

> What I see now, on this rainy day in January, 1968, what is clear to me after this sojourn is that I am neither a Mexican nor an American. I am neither a Catholic nor a Protestant. I am a Chicano by ancestry and a Brown Buffalo by choice. (p. 199)

The Revolt of the Cockroach People shows no let-up as to the revels at hand or his own designated actorly part in them:

> I stand and observe them all. I who have been running around with my head hanging for so long. I who have been lost in my own excesses, drowned

in my own confusion. A faded beatnik, a flower vato, an aspiring writer, a thirty-three-year old kid full of buffalo chips is supposed to defend these bastards. (p. 53)

So, in antic pose and with a name-card which reads 'Buffalo Z. Brown, Chicano Lawyer, Belmont Hotel, LA' (p. 48), the 'Oscar' of this second text positions himself in relation to the Chicano militants involved in the local high-school strikes of 1968. The authorial 'I' again gives off a beguiling, and greatly tactical, interplay of self and persona, the participant as observer.

On the one hand, the text yields an actual Acosta of barricade and courtroom, lawyer in school protest, counsel in the Saint Basil Cathedral protest and in the East Los Angeles 13 trials, would-be legal sleuth in exposing the truth of the Robert Fernandez and 'Roland Zanzibar' deaths, conferee with César Chávez and Corky Gonzalez, and political hopeful in the election for Sheriff of Los Angeles County. On the other, it proffers Acosta as always the writer-*semblable* who sees his own silhouette in the Aztec warrior founder god Huitzilopochtli (p. 11), speaks of himself as 'Vato Numero Uno' (p. 13), and uses the court to give a fantasticalised story of *chicanismo* with due reference to Quetzacoatl, Moctezuma, Cortés and la Malinche through to 1848 and the Anglo appropriation of the southwest.

Both again veer into each other when he summons himself as both first and third person in the bombing of the Safeway store and Bank of America branch, and, in its wake, the protest against the LA Cathedral built by the autocratic and Vietnam-supporting Cardinal McIntire almost as a deliberate insult to the Chicano poor. In the former, he sees himself as both his own first-person author and yet the *carnal* (brother or dude), self-possessed lawyer and yet a man edging into madness at the spies and fifth columnists with Chicano activism.

In the text's hallucinatory telling, the cathedral protesters transpose into a 'gang of cockroaches' (p. 11) replete with one Gloria Chavez, golfclub-swinging heroine. A 'religious war' (p. 14) erupts. The whole suggests near-comic opera, a politics of the real and the near-surreal, and for which each rallying placard sets the tone: 'YANKEES OUT OF AZTLAN' (p. 2), or during the fracas over the schools 'MENUDO EVERYDAY' (p. 41), or in the author's own rise to fame 'VIVA EL ZETA!' (p. 164). 'Oscar', in keeping, envisions himself as at once his own familiar and his own stranger: ' "Come on," our lawyer exhorts. I, strange fate, am this lawyer' (p. 14).

Questing, as he says, for 'my Chicano soul' (p. 47), fact and fantasy again vie. To the one side, he thinks of his court work and flurry of contempt imprisonments (citing himself as prisoner 'Zeta-Brown, 4889'). To the other, he gives himself to heady flights of phantasmagoria in proclamations like 'We are the Viet Cong of America' (p. 198). The two frequently play into each other. His sexual life, aided by an ingestion of Quaalude-400s, takes the form of a would-be Sheik of Araby scenario with three girl followers and yet also a gentle love-tryst with the black juror Jean Fisher. His court life can be literal depositions and briefs but also, in his mind's eye, having the entire California judicial bench indicted on grounds of historic racism.

Two sequences especially underline this dual play of narrative. First, Acosta offers the arrest, self-hanging and, above all, autopsy of Robert Fernandez, the corpse ('just another expendable Cockroach', p. 101) anatomically sliced and jarred under the guidance of Dr Thomas A. Naguchi, LA County Coroner. With just the right exoticism, Naguchi is invoked as, in fact, 'Coroner to the stars'. The autopsy he performs on Fernandez, evidently, is also meant to refract Acosta's own textual autopsy on the larger abused body of *chicanismo*. The same holds for the police shooting of 'Roland Zanzibar', based on the death of Rubén Salazar, the *Los Angeles Times* reporter and broadcaster-activist of Station KMEX. Acosta does nothing to hide his view that an iconographic drama has been under way, the yet further silencing of unwanted *chicanismo*. 'Someone still has to answer for Robert Fernandez and Roland Zanzibar' (p. 258), he writes, a memorial yet also a would-be prompt to redress.

Acosta thereby enters his text as lawyer and meta-lawyer, a historian of one timeline yet also of another far older, a doubling borne out in each reeling, absurdist exchange with Judge Alacran during the Chicano Militants trials. The courtroom to hand becomes a courtroom of history. Each of the time's prime figures equally plays double: César Chávez and Corky Gonzalez become Aztec secret sharers with Emiliano Zapata and Pancho Villa. Mayor Sam Yorty plays Janus, smiling sympathiser yet *agent provocateur* who in bad faith advises Chicano revolution. A crazed Charlie Manson, 'acid fascist' (p. 98), hovers as the presiding spirit of a Los Angeles Acosta terms 'the most detestable city on earth' (p. 23). Gene McCarthy features as both mainstream and alternative politician. Robert Kennedy enters and exits as both Democratic Party heir-apparent and yet *campesino* supporting martyr, to be killed by Sirhan Sirhan as California local and yet 'mysterious Arab' (p. 98). Support for Acosta's own campaign for sheriff is given by 'hidden' Chicanos like Anthony Quinn and Vicki Carr. Acosta gives to each an air of mask, players in America as a world here but ever elsewhere.

Fittingly, Hunter Thompson, acclaimed New Journalist, makes his appearance as the invented figure of Stonewall, one more literal yet also virtual identity. He makes a perfect shadow to Acosta himself. For like Thompson, and throughout *The Revolt of the Cockroach People* and *The Autobiography of a Brown Buffalo*, Acosta writes as the one and the other self, a canny and working compositional double.

The upshot is autobiography but not quite, a self locked into actual time and place yet also a self always deftly aware of its own fictionalisation. Queries may arise as to whether autobiography, or autoethnicity, or autofiction, best applies. But both of Acosta's volumes share at least one property with each other first-person text in this account: their resistance to the single version, fact or fiction, in the telling of ethnic selfhood in America.

Notes

1. LeRoi Jones/Imamu Amiri Baraka (1969), 'Numbers, Letters', *Black Magic: Collected Poetry, 1961–1967*, Indianapolis, IN: Bobbs-Merrill.

2. Diane Glancy (1992), *Claiming Breath*, Lincoln, NB: University of Nebraska Press.

3. Olivia Castellano (1993), 'The Comstock Journals', extracted in Tiffamy Ana López (ed.), *Growing up Chicano/a*, New York: Morrow.

4. Jeanne Wakatsuki Houston (1973), *Farewell to Manzanar*, Boston, MA: Houghton, Mifflin.

5. The term 'autofiction' is usually accredited to Serge Doubrovsky, author of *Fils* (1977) and co-editor, with Jacques Lecarme and Philippe Lejeune, of *Autofictions & Cie* (1993), Nanterre: Université de Paris X. See also the entries for Autofiction and Autoethnography in Margaretta Jolly (ed.) (2001), *Encyclopaedia of Life Writing: Autobiographical and Biographical Forms*, London and Chicago, IL: Fitzroy Dearborn.

6. A relevant collection of essays would be Deborah Reed-Danahay (ed.) (1997), *Auto/ethnography: Rewriting the Self and the Social*, Oxford and New York: Berg.

7. The contrariety of voice is considerable, not least in those autobiographies and first-person texts which depart from expected group identity. Something of the flair this has involved lies behind my pamphlet – A. Robert Lee (2001), *Ethnics Behaving Badly: US Multicultural Narratives*, Pullman, WA: Working Papers Series in Cultural Studies, Ethnicity and Race Relations.

8. This is taken from Momaday's italicised frontispiece to *The Names: A Memoirs* (1976), New York: Harper and Row.

9. N. Scott Momaday, 'The Man Made of Words', in Rupert Cosco (ed.) (1970), *Indian Voices: The First Convocation of American Indian Scholars*, San Francisco, CA: Indian Historian Press, pp. 49–84.

10. Patricia Penn Hilden (1995), *When Nickels Were Indians: An Urban Mixed-Blood Story*, Washington, DC: Smithsonian Institution Press, p. 2.

11. Interview, Wolfgang Binder and Helmbrecht Breinig (1995), *American Contradictions: Interviews with Nine American Writers*, Hanover, NH: Wesleyan University Press, p. 156.

12. Momaday has delivered himself at length of interplay of the spoken and written in Native texts. See, especially, his essay-collection *The Man Made of Words: Essays, Stories, Passages*, New York: St Martin's Press.

13. Kim Barnes (1986), 'A Leslie Marmon Silko Interview', *Journal of Ethnic Studies*, 13 (Winter), 83–105.

14. Scott Momaday (1970), in *Indian Voices*.

15. Gerald Vizenor, 'Crows Written on the Poplars: Autocritical Autobiographies', in Brian Swann and Arnold Krupat (eds) (1987), *I Tell You Now: Autobiographical Essays by Native American Writers*, Lincoln NB: University of Nebraska Press, pp. 101–9.

16. Garrett Hongo (ed.) (1995), 'Introduction', *Under Western Eyes: Personal Essays from Asian America*, New York: Anchor-Doubleday, pp. 13–14.

17. Oscar Zeta Acosta (1996), 'Letter to Willie L. Brown Jr', reprinted in *Oscar 'Zeta' Acosta: The Uncollected Works*, ed. Ilan Stevans, Houston, TX: Arte Público Press.

CHAPTER THREE

Afro-America

Styling Modern and Contemporary Fictions

No one says the novel has to be one thing. It can be anything it wants to be, a vaudeville show, the six o'clock news, the rumblings of wild men saddled by demons. (Ishmael Reed)[1]

I

For Afro-America, and by refraction America at large, it would be hard to doubt that any era since Emancipation has been more transformative in issues of race and ethnicity than the 1960s. When, in 'Many Thousands Gone' (1951), James Baldwin wrote that 'Negroes are Americans and their destiny is the country's destiny', he was as much looking forward as backward.[2] In this essay, as in the others which make up the echoing, Bible-cadenced trilogy of *Notes of a Native Son* (1955), *Nobody Knows My Name* (1961) and *The Fire Next Time* (1963), the sign had been given of a changing dispensation. His ranks among the enduring calls to America, and indeed the western order, truly to confront the spirals of fever, hex and division, built into received notions of black and white, not to say each related other variety of colour ideology.[3]

Civil Rights. Black Power. Martin Luther King and Malcolm X. The Birmingham bombings in 1963. The March on Washington and 'I Have a Dream' in 1963. The Selma March and the Watts Riots in 1965. Black is Beautiful. Let My People Go. Long Hot Summers. Eldridge Cleaver. Cassius Clay into Muhammad Ali. Congress-woman Barbara Jordan of Texas. Afros and dashikis. Motown and Soul Food. Whether the tempestuous politics of protest for which 'We Shall Overcome' provides the anthem, or the key chain of events and their *dramatis personae*, or a newly emergent black popular culture of word, dress and music, the King–Malcolm years have become an American memorial litany, a passed-down but still live archive of reference.

Yet, however much the 1960s are said to constitute a defining decade, that has meant no absence of contesting interpretation. Did it truly liberate America from Cold War deadlock and domestic white-collar conformism? How best to play Vietnam, Watergate, LBJ, Nixon, or the rise of Gay, feminist, campus and drug counter-culture, not to mention conservative reaction and distaste, into the one mix? Perhaps still more to the point, and for all that the 1960s were America's most *black* years, a period when eviction notice was served upon segregation and the colour-line whether through activist black nationalism or the more gradualist but no less persistent Civil Rights mainstream, has the legacy been sufficient?[4]

Footfalls, undoubtedly, there have been, spanning a half-century, and both political and cultural. The political names run from Stokely Carmichael to Colin Powell and Angela Davis to Condoleezza Rice. In legal terms they encompass Thurgood Marshall and Clarence Thomas. The literary arts look to a rallying black nationalist anthology of the era like *Black Fire* (1968), under the editorship of LeRoi Jones/Imamu Amiri Baraka and Larry Neal, and move on nearly a half-century to the Nobel Prize for Toni Morrison in 1993. Alice Walker's womanist credo, in life as in literature, undoubtedly has made for new awareness of black gendering and the disallowing of feminism as exclusive white prerogative. From Baldwin's essays or Ellison's *Invisible Man* onwards, the era extends to the Pulitzer Prize for drama won by Suzan-Lori Parks in 2002 for her *Top Dog Underdog*, the first ever for an African American woman playwright and a canny re-enactment of the Lincoln–John Wilkes Booth legacy in the lives of two modern black impersonators.

Other residues include the overall impetus to re-estimate America as founded in, and shadowed by, slave history. This came to something of a head in the effort to make Martin Luther King's birthday, 15 January, into a national holiday. In the lobbying begun as early as 1968 by Rep. John Conyers, given Ronald Reagan's belated presidential signature in 1983, and formally inaugurated in 1986, many felt a symbolic vindication, the recognition of what the civil rights movement, and the slavery from which it originally derives, had embodied. Even so, opinion as to gains and losses still divides.

To the one side, the years since the 1960s carry the ongoing accusation of city ghetto, drugs, gang culture, and a black prison population as disproportionate as was black frontline soldiery in Vietnam. Black rural poverty, in Mississippi as in the rest of the Deep South, remains fact. Rankles persist over discrimination, and the always contentious issues of affirmative action, quotas, school buses or college admittance, or what, with an eye to police racism, laconically has been called 'driving while black' and which had its best-known recent apotheosis in the Rodney King beating and the ensuing 1992 Los Angeles riot (55 dead, 2,000 injured and 1,200 arrested). This perspective, with its echo, if not quite replay, of the 'burn, baby, burn' riots and shoot-outs of the mid-1960s, whether Harlem, Chicago and Bedford-Stuyvesant in 1964, Watts not only in 1965 but also in 1962, Detroit in 1967, or the nearly 200 cities in all, and taken in the round, sees little easement.[5]

To the other side, recognition is invited of how a substantive black Middle America has arisen, suburban as not, and with it access not only to an economics of well-being but also to an increasingly readier use of legal and legislative resort to challenge racist practice, and spanning education, employment, housing and the military. Colored Only signs have been consigned to history. Reparation for slavery, in fact, has been an issue taken up by black-led law and academic groups. Where George Bush Sr, a beacon of WASP America, notoriously espoused the doctrine of

Benign Neglect, Bill Clinton, Arkansas homeboy and his successor, symbolically becomes America's 'black' president. His liberalism was reflected in his apology to the survivors of the Tuskegee Syphilis Experiment study, formally revealed in 1972 as a glaring instance of racism in medicine, and has carried over into his move to a post-presidency office in Harlem. For many all, or any part, of these, economics to culture, historical awareness to gender issues, imply the upward turn, the improving scenario.

Allowing, in fact, that both versions have their claim, how best to measure the changes from 1960s radicalism to the Clinton and Bush Jr presidencies and for which a figure like Jesse Jackson, King aide, Chicago-based founder of People United to Save Humanity (PUSH) and the Rainbow Coalition, and presidential candidate, acts as a best known connecting voice? Re-estimation continues of the true impact of the Student Non-Violent Coordinating Committee (SNCC), the Congress of Racial Equality (CORE), the Black Panthers (at its height estimated to be a party of 2,000 members and 40 chapters) and the Nation of Islam (founded in 1930 by Elijah Muhammad but revived in the person of Malcolm X). Likewise it is asked if King's Southern Christian Leadership Conference (SCLC) was a creature only of the 1960s or of more enduring force. The voluble black voice is still to be heard, New York's Al Sharpton as minister-radical and presidential contender or the Black Muslims' Louis Farrakhan. But, for others, the continuing gauge remains the incremental politics of the National Association for the Advancement of Colored People (NAACP), the Urban League, the different black mayorships and the Congressional black caucus.

This mixed-fare report card can look to any amount of expression. King's Nobel Prize in 1964, a tribute as much to the politics of peaceful redress as to the man, became TV headlines. His son's succession to the SCLC presidency in 1997 merits hardly a mention. Jesse Jackson, ghetto killing, or the politics of black AIDS and rap 'violence' can still become a news item. There has, however, also been talk of normalisation, Afro-America brought into line with concerns less seemingly race-specific than economic, the likes of jobs, housing or education. Race fatigue, even impatience, can get touted, the agenda having become debates over tax cuts, private health care or, latterly, homeland security. Yet black issues, as race and ethnicity in general, in fact have anything but gone missing.

II

Popular culture supplies its own accompanying curve of styles and comment. The 1960s lead directly into the TV version of Alex Haley's *Roots* (1977, to be followed by *Roots: The Next Generations*, 1979), the then hitherto most viewed series in American media history for all that some quarters thought it a confection. Was this a stir to consciousness, not to say conscience, or simply good commercial timing? From the late 1960s to the 1990s, the successive incarnations of the Bill Cosby Show (first aired in 1969 but reworked in the series begun in 1984) make him one of the most visible black figures on TV: comic, actor, mentor-father in the middle-class Huxtable family in which, no doubt aptly, he plays an MD specialising in gynaecology. Admirers applaud the attempt to portray black life beyond the ghetto, one of everyday parenthood, professional career, and children for whom 'race' is but an incidental. The less enchanted issue cavils about dismaying self-absorption, a merely consumerist black middle class.

Rap assumes musical sway, the 1990s of Ice Cube or Sister Souljah for the 1960s of Chuck Berry or Diana Ross. But if this represents the update of a vernacular eloquence begun in Africa, and brought to the Americas under slavery, and now modern performance art, there has also been discomfort at the alleged misogyny, an idiom often edged in violence. Muhammad Ali, once condescended to as the Louisville Lip, Kentucky's own bawling man-child, but long transformed into a revered black cultural icon, gives way in turn to a new sports pantheon from Mike Tyson to Venus and Serena Williams, Tiger Woods to Marion Jones. In each of Ali's successors, if such they be, the implication is that 'race politics' have become muted. Oprah Winfrey emerges into the dominant black TV talk-show celebrity with her own greatly influential monthly book club an added factor. Opinion again divides. To some, her visibility is that of positive role model. Others see an overpaid, fake 'caring' studio host.[6]

Maya Angelou reads her 'On the Pulse of the Morning' at the Clinton inaugural of 1993. What was of greater import – the poem itself, even if one not universally admired, or that it should feature at a national occasion? Spike Lee, the black screen's best-known 'adversary' name as the director of *She's Gotta Have It* (1986), with its portrait of a woman and her three lovers, and *Do the Right Thing* (1989), his Brooklyn-set meditation on Malcolm or King as pathways to combat racism, takes all, or most, before him. It is asked if acceptance has blunted his edge.

Another symptomatic and public testing-ground has been the Academy Awards. Denzel Washington and Halle Berry, three decades on from Sidney Poitier, win the 2002 Oscars. Berry's stirring words to the effect that 'It's for every nameless, faceless woman who now has a chance because this door tonight has been opened' gains all the more from the irony that her mother, Judith, is a blonde white woman. But how far do these awards assuage past omissions, the symptomatic lack of Hollywood celebration of black (or Native or Latino/a or Asian American) acting talent in the years in between?

III

However these post-1960s developments are best construed, the original era itself remains sharp as a black literary-cultural watermark, whether the Black Arts movement, the emergence of committed black theatre, the spate of new black anthologies and journals (the changeover of *Negro Digest* to *Black World* was symptomatic), the tough, if not acid, comic stand-up of Dick Gregory or Richard Pryor, or the rise in the academy and high schools of Black Studies departments. LeRoi Jones/Amiri Baraka's play, *Dutchman* (1964), became notorious for how it imaged America as Dantean racial underground, a circling 'metro' of warring hate. The temper finds expression in Clay, his protagonist-victim – 'Crazy niggers turning their backs on sanity. When all it needs is that simple act. Murder. Just murder!

Would make us all sane.' This was Black Power to be acted not only inside, but also beyond, theatre.[7]

Malcolm X's *Autobiography* (1965), along with the writings of Eldridge Cleaver, Stokely Carmichael, George Jackson, Huey Newton, Bobbie Seale or Rap Brown, bespeak an end to assimilationist patience and gradualism. The poetry of Etheridge Knight, Gill Scott-Heron or Sonia Sanchez opens up its own Black Power vista, heavy in street and spoken rap idiom and keen in its accusations of the status quo. Ebonics, black English, is advanced by the linguist William Stewart and others as a wholly distinctive American usage and word stock. A blackness of the word, in fact, at the time seemed everywhere, clenched-fist, nationalist, nothing if not ready to dismantle the racial status quo.

One measure of the change since then can be felt in comparing 1960s writing with, say, Cornel West's *Keeping Faith: Philosophy and Race in America* (1993) and *Race Matters* (1994), at once fullest acknowledgement of the causes behind the earlier militancy and yet a prospectus for a next stage of debate about black–white power relations and about the emergence of what has come to be termed critical multi-culturalism.[8] The 1960s duly also see the rise of the Black Aesthetic as a kind of literary-ideological High Command, literature to be about the business of disman-tling a racist state, remedial, and centred in and for America's black communities. So, at least, ran the advocacy of best-known proponents like Hoyt Fuller and Addison Gayle. New Criticism as prevailing literary-critical practice, and with its roots in southern cultural whiteness, was to be repudiated, and replaced by, an Afrocentric, an African American, value system. Here was a right 'black' standard with maverick slackers, Ralph Ellison and Ishmael Reed if for different reasons notably among them, called to task.[9]

Discourse, however, would again move on. Theory and interpretation in the hands of a Henry Louis Gates or Houston Baker argues for a wholly subtler deconstruction of black signifying, the cultural in-house blackness and historicity in the very shaping of African American word, myth and genre. Blackness, it is suggested, involves social and cultural constructedness, and in literary work as in life: it requires its own deconstructive etiquette with due attention to be paid to identifying tropes and figures. Feminist critique, of the kind advanced by Barbara Christian and Hazel Carby, has opened routes into the depiction of sexual role and power, the very language of woman-authored literary fiction. In aggregate the effect has been profound, Afro-America's literature as subtler, always cagier, than implied in the one-time argot of social realism or 'social protest' ('Negro protest' was a variant) and the like.[10]

In few respects, however, would the 1960s show itself more a begetting era of black word and text than in literary fiction. Ellison and Baldwin continue well beyond *Invisible Man* (1952) and *Go Tell It on the Mountain* (1953). A neo-realist line, with Richard Wright still an active influence, runs from Ann Petry's tenement and club Harlem of *The Street* (1946) through a meticulous Pacific war fiction like John O. Killens's *And Then We Heard the Thunder* (1963) to an international conspiracy saga like John A. Williams's *The Man Who Cried I Am* (1967). An autobiographical novel as experimental as Jones/Baraka's *The System of Dante's Hell* (1965) points to black postmodernism, to include Ishmael Reed, as much as it does to the author's status as all-rounder and bridge figure from the 1960s into the present century. In Walter Mosley's Los Angeles-situated Easy Rawlins series, begun with *Devil in a Blue Dress* (1990), many look to a successor series to Chester Himes's 'Harlem domestic tales'.

Alice Walker famously embodies her own womanist ethos in *The Color Purple* (1982), the lives of Celie and Shug Avery and their eventual extended family a model of black sorority. Toni Morrison's *Beloved* (1987) supplies an elegy to the inerasable, accusing 'haint' of slavery, both the reality and ghost of human ownership as stain, accusation, and yet, in Sethe, heroic survival. Morrison has not been alone in looking to storytelling company in names like Alice Childress, Paule Marshall, Kristin Hunter, Gayl Jones, Rosa Guy and Carlene Hatcher Polite.

The fictions summoned as new stylings at once extend, and vary, those above, almost inviting an emphasis on particularity of design, innovations of voice and telling. In the short stories by John Wideman and Toni Bambara, a contrast of two histories, slavery-time as against the time-present city, ancestral South and modern North, comes into play. In Ernest Gaines's *The Autobiography of Miss Jane Pittman* (1971), the historical novel undergoes transformation, a tape-recorded voice of the black south ferrying past into present, speech into script. Epic finds its mark in Leon Forrest's last novel, *Divine Days* (1992), history as black and white genealogical odyssey, a massive chorus of voice, with its operative focus in Chicago's South Side.

Black magical realism has a prime exemplar in Gloria Naylor's *Mama Day* (1988), its intertext Shakespeare's *The Tempest* and its title figure a latter-day conjure woman descended from a first slave matriarch, who presides over her South Carolina barrier island with Prospero-like command. Successor-generation womanist writing looks to A. J. Verdelle's *The Good Negress* (1995), the portrait of a young girl's meeting of her own rise to consciousness. Few black middlebrow fictions better step beyond formula and invite their own kind of recognition and enquiry, be it in terms of professional-womanly aloneness or man trouble, than Terry McMillan's *Waiting to Exhale* (1992).

The novel self-referentially under the guise of autobiography takes on new impetus in Darryl Pinckney's *High Cotton* (1992). Trey Ellis has aroused controversy with his talk of writing New Black Aesthetic fiction as developed in a novel like *Platitudes* (1988), set in computer-age Manhattan and with its satiric-reflexive aim at black literary gender wars. James Alan McPherson's *Hue and Cry* (1969) gives new energy to the black story-cycle, a species of evidentiary fiction as much by command of organising register as theme.

Situating these fictions within the one or another genre, however, is not to assume too ready or incorporating a fixity of categorisation. Rather, as borne out in their respective stylings, not the least of matters derives from the bravura of authorship working at the limits of recognisable genre. To this end, and allowing that they represent but one shelf of texts, it is a choice meant also to confirm an achievement which, with a backward glance to the 1920s New Negro and Harlem literary flowering, was early and fairly recognised as developing into Afro-America's second

Black Renaissance.[11] At a more inclusive reach, they can be said to extend yet further the literary variety, and depth, of American literature as multicultural order.

IV

In John Wideman's 'Damballah', the title story from his Homewood-Philadelphia trilogy of *Damballah* (1981), *Hiding Place* (1981) and *Sent for You Yesterday* (1983), and in Toni Cade Bambara's 'Raymond's Run', from her *Gorilla, My Love* (1972), the age can lay claim to two of its keystone stories. The former, set in 1850s slavery, and the latter, in contemporary childhood Harlem, bridge an earliest with a latest era, points of departure and arrival in Afro-America's evolving time-line. Plantation Dixie foreshadows New York metropolis, ancient river today's street. Each, in turn, achieves a rare efficacy as idiom, as loaded up in historic silence as speech.

'Damballah' amounts to a stunning headstone to slave-America, beckoningly actual yet at the same time parabular. In its imagining of the life and death of the slave Orion, known to his owner as Ryan, the story makes live the accusing juncture of Africa with America, freedom with ownership. Orion's initial immersion into the river and then silent-spoken prayer to Damballah as Vodoun presiding godhead, his attack on the overseer, and his subsequent castration and beheading in reprisal, become ritual. For the young slave-boy who, at the start, sees Orion standing mid-river, and who eventually will cast his severed head to the river, his will be a legacy of passed-on witness ('The boy could learn the story and tell it again').

Other voices enter, in turn those of Aunt Lissy as slave convert to Christianity yet who sees the ghost rise from Orion's butchered corpse, Primus who reports the brute, knifing punishment, and the Master who writes of Orion's 'utter lack of soul' and demands reparation from the original vendor. But the presiding voice, not unlike Melville's Babo in 'Benito Cereno', is Orion's. He has refused any word of English, spoken only the name of Damballah, and engaged in a willed refusal to enter into any kind of word, historic, moral, or existential, with a world which denies him the word of his own being. Only the boy hears, and is destined to pass on, Orion's ghost words, his life-over-death 'stories' as the text calls them.

'All I have to do in life is mind my brother Raymond, which is enough'. So Bambara's girl narrator in 'Raymond's Run', nicknamed Squeaky, presents herself at the outset: feisty protectress to her Down's or like-afflicted brother, school sprint champion, and 'high-prancer' intimate of Harlem's 134th and 151st Streets, Lenox and Amsterdam. Ostensibly the story pivots on the annual May Day sports meet, and the fifty-yard dash, in which Squeaky, full name Hazel Elizabeth Deborah Parker, has installed herself as champion. She even wins again, defeating Gretchen Lewis, nothing if not all athletic assurance, a girl leader. But the true 'run' is 'ole Raymond's', who hollers from the sideline, endeavours to sprint alongside his sister, and manages an effort which belies disability and advances him into his own hard-won realm of grace.

The risk, in this co-current of story, evidently could be that of a call to sentimentality, Raymond's condition as victim, his sister's care as all-too-dutiful do-goodism. In fact that is shrewdly, and at every turn, avoided in the very idiom of the story's telling, the girl's savvy, even immodest, disclosure – her boasts about her spelling prowess, her pending stardom at the piano should she so choose, and her 'roomful of ribbons and medals'. 'I have a big rep as the baddest thing around' she affirms in schoolyard black vernacular. The upshot, to Bambara's credit as her chronicler, is the sense of given sibling lives, her own and Raymond's, and of the Harlem around it, of no special pleas or deals.

V

Ernest Gaines's The Autobiography of Miss Jane Pittman also looks to the historical canvas, Civil War to civil rights, but in an unfolding of dynasty as voluminous as assuredly deft. Himself raised on a plantation in Oscar, Louisiana, Gaines's unique creation has been St Raphael Parish, a world of black, Cajun, Creole and other mixed-race communities with, always near to hand, New Orleans and the bayou country. His other novels all draw upon this shared reference: Catherine Carmier (1964) as the cross-racial love of Jackson Bradley and the novel's heroine; Of Love and Dust (1967) as the plantation heritage told across tabooed race lines with their fatal accusations; Bloodline (1968) as five contrasting first-person narratives of black selfhood; In My Father's House (1978) as the south's intergenerational black politics; and A Gathering of Old Men (1983) and A Lesson Before Dying (1993) as workings of further Louisiana black–white lineage.

No novel, however, more deservingly has won Gaines his reputation than The Autobiography of Miss Jane Pittman. Told as though in the tape-recorded voice of the centenarian Jane Pittman in the early 1960s, that of a one-time slave still living on a Louisiana plantation and who marches for civil rights at the novel's conclusion, it unspools a history, a south, from cotton slavery and the War of Secession to the era of Rosa Parks and Martin Luther King with greatest sureness. Not surprisingly, it led to an acclaimed TV version of 1974 starring Cicely Tyson. Gaines himself, in a 1978 interview with Callaloo, speaks with just the right inside appeal, and affection, when he says of the fictional Jane Pittman:

> You have seen Miss Jane, too. She is that old lady who lives up the block, who comes out every Sunday to go to church when the rheumatism does not keep her in . . . She sits on a screened-in porch fanning herself in the summer, and in the winter she sits by the heater or the stove and thinks about the dead . . . She knows much – she has lived long. Sometimes she's impatient, but most times she is just the opposite. Truth is what she remembers. Truth to me is what people like Miss Jane remember . . . (p. 37)[12]

To Jane's friend, Mary Hedges, the book's 'editor' explains: 'I teach history . . . I'm sure [Jane's] life story can help explain things to my students'. Mary's response is to ask 'What's wrong with them books you already got?', to which is answered 'Miss Jane is not in them' (p. x). As she calls up the cross-hatch of people who have entered her life, black, white, creole, cajun or mulatto, and all the Louisiana history they bear, Jane, in fact, assumes her own kind of griot voice. The one-time slave-girl, escapee, wife and mother, and eventual community historian, however, remains a black southerner, a witness to the region as both time and place. 'Miss Jane's story is all of their stories, and their stories are Miss Jane's' (p. x).

She can be as spontaneous, and at times as discontinuous, as each volte-face in her history, and aging memory, requires. These nicely intersect in the editor's further, and not a little Faulknerian, observation that 'This is what Mary and Miss Jane meant when they said you could not tie all the ends together in one direction' (p. x). Built as a quartet, 'The War Years', 'Reconstruction', 'The Plantation' and 'The Quarters', and as much seemingly spoken as written, the novel becomes a tale of the south inextricable from its telling. 'I'm headed for Ohio' (p. 14), says Jane in childhood in the aftermath of the south's defeat. But as her companions are killed by renegades from the 'Secesh' forces, in fact, she walks not out of the south but right back into it, a voice of accusation and yet celebration. Each section bears witness.

In 'The War Years', as Jane and Ned, the son of Big Laura who has been killed in the escape from the plantation, seek to escape northward from the patrollers, they also find their route into literacy and the discard of slave-naming. Jane abandons Ticey, her slave name. Ned calls himself after Frederick Douglass:

> We must have been two dozens of us there, and now everybody started changing names like you change hats. Nobody was keeping the name Old Master had given them. This one would say, 'My new name Cam Lincoln.' That one would say: 'My new name Ace Freeman' . . . Another one standing by a tree would say, 'My new name Bill Moses. No more Rufus.' (pp. 17–18)

Gaines leaves little doubt for the black south of the connection between freedom and name, the twin de-enslavement of body and word.

'And that was the deal: the Secesh got their land, but the Yankees lend the money' (p. 69). So, in 'Reconstruction', Jane cites a contemporary, the era in which she has married the warm, devoted horsebreaker, Joe Pittman (even though, in slave fashion, they have 'jumped the broom') and the return of Ned. In this surrogate son, Gaines offers a local version of Douglass, also a teacher-orator but whose challenge to postbellum white ascendancy leads to his murder by the cajun Albert Cluveau. Ned has died for refusing the south's terms ('America is for red, white and black men', p. 109). But he dies facing his killer, his blood, like that of black generations before him, sedimented into the southern soil ('For years and years, even after they had graveled the road, you could see little black spots where the blood had dripped', p. 116).

In 'The Plantation', actually the Samson plantation where Jane spends the early part of the twentieth century, she witnesses a latest twist in the drama of mulatto-dom. In the love of white Tee Bob Samson for Mary Agnes Lefabre, a creole woman 'tainted' by the merest increment of black ancestry, the most ancient of southern race taboos is broached. The affair, beautifully told as a courtship, a lost hope, ends in disaster but not melodrama. Jane's is the monitoring voice, against a backdrop of the Klan and the rise of Governor Huey Long. She remembers the sympathetic cajun, Jules Raynard, first on Tee Bob ('he thought love was stronger than one drop of African blood', p. 192), and then on the challenge to transform an old south, and its taboos, into a new south ('The past and the present got all mixed up', p. 192).

As to 'The Quarters', the section centres on Jimmy Washington, the only son of Jane's friend Lena Washington, an early civil-rights activist who challenges the pre-ordained racial order by using a whites-only water faucet. He meets his death at the hands of a white Dixie posse. Jane transforms the account of the event she acquires from Robert Samson, the latest scion of the plantation dynasty, into a kind of talking blues, literal and yet emblematic execution. 'They shot him at eight o'clock this morning' (p. 243), she intones.

Survivor of a past as cruel as any in American history, she could not be better placed to understand Jimmy's sacrifice as she puts her own body, and authority, into the march for civil rights. She does so from the 'march' as much of history as of any one southern protest or place. 'Me and Robert looked at each other there for a long time,' she says, 'then I went by him' (p. 244). On this measure, *The Autobiography of Miss Jane Pittman* has its title figure 'go by' not simply one more white southerner but the white south at large. Gaines offers her as legacy to the future, a fiction as much keyed to time-to-come as each shaping time-past.

VI

In Leon Forrest's *Divine Days*, the Dublin Juneday of 1904 in James Joyce's *Ulysses* becomes the South Side Chicago week of 16–23 February 1966. As told by Joubert Antoine Jones, playwright, newly back from military service in Germany, and heir to his aunt-stepmother Eloise Jones Hickles, proprietor of the Night Light Lounge and columnist for the *Forest County Dispatch*, this is Afro-America as indeed Epic and in length and width of narrative to do justice.

For Forrest is out to write black myth, a map of inner history, Chicago seen, and told, at once as though from a street-level perspective and yet as also the massive iconography of an odyssey begun in Africa and made American in Dixie and the cities. In the novel's portraits of lineage, a black south transformed into a black north, memories have indeed turned inward and become the very turn and wit of story. Given, also, a geography not only of 'Forest County' as citied and Lakeside Chicago, but also of its counterpoint of 'Forrest County' as the Mississippi of the Bloodworths with its slave origins, mixed lines of family descent, Bible-fundament-alism and reach into Creole-Catholic New Orleans, Forrest's own opting for narrative size, and density, could not be more requisite.

The recurrent metaphor throughout *Divine Days* turns upon dynasty and orphaning, slave heritage as loss and severance, and yet also human triumph, its remembrance to be found in Afro-America's arts of music, physical grace and, above all, word. The effect is a furtherance of Forrest's earlier Witherspoon-Bloodworth trilogy of *There is a Tree More Ancient than Eden* (1973) as Nathaniel Witherspoon's rite of passage from his mother's death into his own writer-artist manhood, *The Bloodworth Orphans* (1977) as a kind of Genesis text of the original dynasty, and *Two Wings to Veil My Face* (1984) as Great-Momma Sweetie Reed's spoken testimony to Nathaniel's riddled Chicago-Mississippi legacy. *Divine Days*, however, uses a still larger frame, its intersections and peopling to run to over 1,100 pages.[13]

In this, Joubert ('I've been hearing voices all my life', p. 10) finds himself possessed by two main presences, that of Sugar Groove Bloodworth, Mississippi son of a white slave-owner father, William Bloodworth, and his slave mistress Sarah Belle, and W. A. D. Fard, 'serial hermaphrodite' (p. 10), the religious trickster-prophet and warlock known as Fatah, a survivor cynic in whom mask rules always over reality. Their final mountaintop battle, good- as against bad-faith survival, again implies Afro-America as Homeric or Biblical ground. Sugar Groove is left eyeless, his spirit left to wander. Fard disappears. Both actualise the sense of epic, Forrest's turning spiral throughout *Divine Days* of first and last things, God and Satan, light and dark.

Within their respective magnetic pulls, Joubert seeks some principle to give pattern, a rationale, to the lives which gather, or are remembered, in his aunt's Night Light Lounge, originally named Divine Days as Fard's temple. The Lounge, where Joubert works as bar-tender and manager, serves as both hearthstone and 'a kind of large and roomy closet for drifters' (p. 76). It is the voices of those who gather there, and of those within their stories, as of Sugar Groove and Fard and yet others who have been Joubert's own making, which he finds himself called upon to write into the play he has entitled, in a further reflexive twist, *Divine Days*. If it calls up Joyce's Dublin, so Joubert's Chicago does Faulkner's Yoknapatawpha and Ellison's Harlem, American worlds also full of history, yet equally, and consciously, 'textual'.

Forrest undoubtedly can be thought unsparing, given to a force of style which insists on its own signifying at every turn. Loops of flashback work in and out of the narrative. Sermons, those of preachers from the sexually predatory Honeywood 'Sweet Briar' Cox to the 'grandiose' and devil-like Elder Tutwiler, or from the more balanced and fine-mannered Rev. Maurice Roper through to Prayer Mother Rachel Carpenter Flowers, add necessary touchstones. Theirs are the rhetorics of a creativity which ranges from the uplifting to the devious. The five barmaids, Molly Savage, Gracie Rae Gooden, Viola Hill, La Dorrestine Conway and Estella Church, each weave their own knot of South Side stories into the unfolding whole. The barbershop doyen, Oscar Williemain, brings witness both to Sugar Groove's Mississippi origins and his connection to Fard and to Joubert's own Tobias family lineage. They all, within the continuum of the novel's storying at large, share in what Joubert glosses as Afro-America's 'fabulous impulse to invent' (p. 1,128).

These storylines, moreover, often enough cross, whether that of the beauteous De Loretto Holloday, known as Imani, with whom Joubert is smitten, but whose paintings of Chicago street-bloods in hopes of finding an 'African' healing pride leads to despair, suicide and a drug scam, or of Cinderella Lilybridge, Imani's welfare client impregnated by her own father, yet one more orphan. Likewise the cast extends to the scholarly Allerton Jamesway, a believer in the black-chosen and in white-devilry like the Muslim Wingate 13 X Boswell, the Africa-fixated Fulton

Armstead, the mixed child Hans Henson Hamilton harrowingly murdered by white GIs and Germans, the hardbitten Officer Eddie Egglestone, and the warring, and baroque, Miss Frankie Foxworth and her on-off beau Daddy Bridges (the *Forest County Dispatch* speaks of their 'nod of royalty', p. 512). Not only is Forrest's cast in *Divine Days* as full, not to say dramatic, as any in Faulkner or Ellison, his novel likewise aspires to a roll-call of word, narrative as mosaic.

The dozens, bar-room scatology, diaries to include Lucia 'Big Moma' Rivers's *Clearinghouse Book* and that of De Loretto Holloday, ditties, memories of musicianship to embrace Charlie Parker, Nat King Cole and Lady Day, and a spectrum of politics from Martin Luther King to the Black Muslims whom Joubert terms 'Elijah's form of Afro-Zionism, a racist-Allah's chosen people' (p. 652), and even the gossip columns of Aunt Eloise and other reportage, build the dynamic yet further. For some, the result can be crowding, too inflated an idiom. Others, however, see that as the necessary register for an Afro-America given not only to tragedy but also to tragic wisdom.

Forrest, at the same time, is not to be denied his own busy seams of comedy, a choric and always saving irony. Williemain's barbershop telling of 'Sugar Groove Goes to Heaven', fuelled by copious drink and full of back-and-forth improvisation on black and white angels, broken wings and harps, has St Peter being heard to say 'We don't speak Black English in Heaven' (p. 103). At the very end of the novel, Joubert returns to this vignette, or rap, and has St Peter further complain of not being able to find words 'to express the meaning of all your carryings on . . .' (p. 1,135). Joubert's own retort, that of writer-playwright, runs 'No, St Peter you can't . . . That's my job' (p. 1,135).

As a Book of Voices ('I'm telling you these voices come to me and hit me at the damnedest times', p. 478), and in its every incantatory riff and counterpoint, *Divine Days* can be thought to act on that impulse from start to finish. For Afro-America as literary epic, and in styling if wholly recondite also no stranger to down-home colloquialism, has had few rarer, or more ambitious, incarnations.

VII

'A true conjure woman: satin black, biscuit cream, red as Georgia clay: depending upon which of us takes a mind to her' (p. 3). So inviting a menu of options in Gloria Naylor's *Mama Day* for Sapphira Wade, slave progenitor of the Day line of women of Willow Springs, weaves just the right ambiguity of myth into fact. For in the example of her life, as in those of Miranda/Mama Day, her sister Miss Abigail, and their grand-niece Ophelia, known as Cocoa, Naylor speaks to worlds at once the wholly plausible island juncture of South Carolina and Georgia, and yet also off any map, a realm to be reached by plane or a ferry across the Sound yet also of tempest and magic light and dark.

The novel sets itself to depict gynocracy, a line of enduring black womanhood to bridge Sapphira in 1823, mother of seven sons to her owner-master Bascombe Wade and also his assassin, with Cocoa, writing in August 1999, and widow to the exacting but loving and literally weak-at-heart George Andrews, raised in a New York 'State Shelter for Boys', with whose ghost voice she holds memorial colloquy. Sapphira as antebellum matriarch, who finagled the bequeathal of Willow Springs to her slave and post-slave offspring, is generationally reborn in Miranda and Abigail, and in turn, finds her reincarnation in Cocoa, off-islander yet also islander, a figure of contemporary black womanhood yet also heir to ancient haints and rites. Naylor writes of each with a marvellously keen ear to history as echo, sound, footfall, the narrative play and alternation of idioms.

'1823', like '124 Bluestone Road' in Toni Morrison's *Beloved*, serves throughout as private sign (the anthropologist son of Reema, a Willow Springs neighbour, gets himself wonderfully social-science befuddled in seeking its meaning), at once a literal date in history, yet also, and always, mnemonic and touchstone of womanly survival. It carries Sapphira's uprising, the 'extreme mischief' and 'witchcraft' of her bill of sale to Bascombe Wade. It passes into the life of Mama Day, midwife, island *curandera* and herbalist-spiritualist, canny, not to say quirky, wisewoman, and ultimately Prospero-like maker of the destiny in which she will save Cocoa from life-threatening brain fever at the expense of George's life. It also, finally, passes to Cocoa herself, approaching forty-seven at the novel's close, remarried and with two sons, another survivor full of her own latest and enghosted story.

As Cocoa and George dance their way into love, albeit often enough warring love, the novel directs them more and more southward, from Cocoa's Manhattan and George's Staten Island and Brooklyn to South Carolina/Georgia and Willow Springs. If this is to be thought a barrier physical universe, one of Atlantic Ocean and Woodlands, Mama Day's Trailer as against the original Wade plantation which has become The Other Place, it also serves as one equally full of inward and moral human barrier. Around it run Nature's own currents of fire and earth, wind and water, an animism understood by none on the island more than Mama Day.

Ambush and Bernice Duvall, long guiltily childless and despite Bernice's ovarian cysts first diagnosed by Mama Day, will lose their doted-over child, 'Little Caesar', in the warning violence of an ocean storm. Dr Buzzard, Hoo-Doo 'roots' man, reveals himself, if benignly, the conman, card-sharp, and ex-vaudevilleian whose real name is Rainbow Simpson. The love triangle, which will lead from the obese Ruby, her paramour and eventual husband Junior Lee ('more than a woman he's marrying himself an event', p. 134) and her rival Frances, to the jealous hair-poisoning of Cocoa and her near-fatal welts and fever, will bring calamity and yet a healing.

For Willow Springs as locale to the story being played out in the one time and yet the several is neither Brave New World pastoral nor Caliban's prison. The novel, rather, looks to a dialectic of forces, Mama Day's herbs and conjuration alongside Dr Smithfield's book medicine, Nature's storm and lightning alongside the turbulence, and eventual infection, within Cocoa. Cathartically, and at Mama Day's arranging, George's fierce hencoop death will balance against Ophelia/Cocoa's recovery of life and future. 'Your maps were no good here' (p. 177), Naylor has Cocoa say at one point to George when they first enter the island together, clear and certain signpointing as may be but to a world itself in fact anything but clear and certain.

The novel's winning feat is to weave whole seams of image and motif into this eventfulness, African slave history in the person of Sapphira Wade, African American roots and wisdom in Mama Day, a world of modernity in Cocoa. These are to be played into Mama Day's own wedding-gift quilting with its implication of historical stitch and weave, the Candle Walk island ceremony as light amid dark, and, as she tends her eggs, hens, plants and cuisine, her powers to preside over the cycle of conception, menstruation, death and re-rebirth. *Mama Day*, throughout, calls up revisionist Shakespeare, a reconstrued and deftly re-imagined *The Tempest*. But, at every turn of Naylor's telling, it does so as keyed to a lineage of womanhood unmistakably and memorably never other than Afro-America's own.

VIII

'My name Deneese Palms an I come up from Fuhginia' (p. 40). Newly arrived from 'country' Patuskie, near Richmond, and from her grandmother Dambridge's care and religiosity, Neesey so introduces herself to her Detroit classmates in A. J. Verdelle's *The Good Negress* (1995). Her 'down-home' folk-southern idiom carries about it not just the stamp of region but also of beginning girlhood, an identity which will find its evolving shape inside the south-to-north 1960s black family of Margarete, her widowed mother now remarried to Big Jim Starks, her two brothers David and Luke Edward (given as Luke edward throughout), and, in due course, Baby Clara.

Verdelle is about portraiture, a selfhood in first person positioned between 'shards of recollection' (p. 150) and 'this endlessness' (p. 299), the phrase Neesey uses at the novel's close when heading off with Luke who is wanted for robbing a petrol-station till. Literally as much as figuratively, and with great sustaining nuance, Neesey is shown to move ever more surely into a 'right use of the English language' (p. 124), as Miss Pearson, her classroom teacher, will call it, but 'right' as much to life as to grammar. For language itself, as voice, the power to name, lies at the very centre of the novel, Neesey's own increasingly self-aware inscription not only of family (to include her own railwayman father dead of a stroke too early in his forties) but of the larger worlds of rural and city blackness from which she, and they, draw their very shaping.

Verdelle manages the genuine feat of giving interiority to the girl's life. On initially being deposited with her grandmother in a Virginia of 'no blocks or corners or streets' (p. 3), she suffers a disbelief which 'can blind your eyes and block your ear canals' (p. 3). Her grandmother ('large, and busy like groceries', p. 54) helps her incorporate rudimentary etiquette (' "You ain't got nothin else to say this mornin, Baby Sister?" "How you, Granma'am?" "I'm jes fine, thank you for askin" ' p. 5). This southern domestic round, 'the tremor of the country' (p. 49), whether manners, cooking, paring pumpkin, seeing hams cured and preserved, church, the death of the boy Lonts Owens in a train accident and his mother's 'mama-grief' (p. 17), her grandmother's skin which 'flirts with her age' (p. 67) together with her remembrance of Gibraltar Jones as Welsh-named slave ancestor (pp. 112–13), or the beating she administers to Luke edward for stealing from the Watkins store, become, for Neesey, and like the oils her grandmother sends to Margarete, the very 'language' she carries north.

In Detroit, she becomes 'doctor to the flat' (p. 21), workhorse cleaner, cook, a willing domestic ('The kitchen is . . . where I know everything is going on', p. 184). But the imagination which has long operated inside her comes under new stimulus. School geography enlarges her sense of horizon, the Mason-Dixon line, each southern state, America's oceans. History, she avers, 'complicates things I think' (p. 107). Sixties music, bobby socks and other dress style, learning to dance, menstruation, a first sex encounter with her classmate Josephus, Afro-hair as her mother takes her for a bob, and family change when David marries Serena, Big Jim temporarily walks out in anger at Luke edward's indolence and her mother gives birth to Clara, all are given as though in equal part a drama of consciousness as a line of external event.

These, each, Neesey holds within an ever surer sense of her own language. Miss Pearson teaches her grammatical Rules of Agreement, better phonetics, a formal English both for and for beyond the classroom. This pedagogy comes with an enjoined respect for DuBois and African American inheritance and for a call to ambition beyond working, even part-time, in Hudson's Store as 'a good little negress' (p. 209). At thirteen, Neesey writes compulsively in her Composition Book, a novel, no less, in the form of diary, confessions, letters, all pitched as if to subdue world to word.

No image better captures this writerly impulse, from inside her black family order and its shaping geographies of north and south, than in her singsong acquisition of the Greek alphabet, the lexicon, she realises, of a further human map. The novel neither unduly heroises nor sentimentalises Neesey. Hers, nonetheless, and even as she comes up sharp against the boundaries of self and family, is language, a girl-woman's language, at once about freedom and yet in its own every energy and impulse itself a necessary freeing ('I smile about all those many discoveries, new worlds', p. 299).

IX

'Readers can . . . view Terry McMillan as the Frank Yerby of the 1990s' reads a recent reference-book entry.[14] The comment bears its own ambiguity, at once praise and, by intention or not, faint praise. Yerby, after all, and despite a number of late 'black consciousness' novels, long held sway as one of the most successful doyens of southern costume romance. Admirers were just about able to see, amid the white-centred magnolia and plantation intrigue, a coded critique of Dixie. Yet detractors would have none of it, pulp-genre writing given over to a pulp version of history.

In *Waiting to Exhale*, as in bestsellers like *Disappearing Acts* (1990) and *How Stella Got Her Groove Back* (1995), McMillan's own winning popular touch has not been open to doubt. But equivocation again arises. Is this popular fiction going about its business with genuine dispatch, the lives of four thirtyish contemporary black women in Phoenix, Arizona told in commendably accessible idiom and with pace and zest? Or is it, irrecoverably, middlebrow terrain, the readerly equivalent of 'easy listening' suitably prefaced by a line from a Celine Dion song ('If there was any other way . . . Don't you think I would have tried to find it . . .?'), and ever the script awaiting the Hollywood treatment it duly received in 1995 starring Whitney Houston and Angela Bassett? Whichever best applies, it delivers yet another styling, another turn, in the evolution of African American fiction.

In alternating each story of her quartet of Robin Stokes, Bernadine Harris, Gloria Matthews and Savannah Jackson, McMillan assumes a ready vernacular intimacy ('They say love is a two-way street . . . the one I've been on for the last two years was a dirt road', p. 39). The fare is black woman-talk, sisterhood as family, and if, to be sure, taken up with men, or the shopping mall, then also with identity, career, motherhood or not, a sense of self-place. None is dominated by race.

Each permutation, in fact, bespeaks a world intractably 'professional', whether Robin's insurance job, flings, and eventual pregnancy in the on-off relationship with Russell, or Bernadine's divorce, weight problems, move into a likely new marriage and catering business, or Gloria's world of the beauty parlour she has named 'Oasis', single-mothering of her teenage son, Tarik, and near-fatal heart attack, or Savannah's city-hopping, PR media position and uncertain run of beaux. In a nice ironic touch, they even gather at a BWOTM, or Black Women on the Move, party.

What McMillan is tapping into is a kind of black postfeminism, a circuit of friendship (few white people make any appearance) in which to sound out the current balance of gain as against anxiety. These deal in so-called 1990s New Men, single-parenting and marriage, sexual adventuring and etiquette, body image, care of ageing parents, and a hinterland of Alzheimer's and AIDS.

Those, again, who hold *Waiting to Exhale* and McMillan's other fiction in high regard applaud a sense of life-flow in which these, and each life situation and girl-talk colloquy and mutual reassurance, enter as practicality, matters arising. The less persuaded see an uncritically purveyed 'me-generation' friendship, life run, not to say formulaically told, as black Middle America consumer maze and time. Either way, McMillan, assuredly, is not to be denied.

X

On appearance, Darryl Pinckney's *High Cotton* aroused not a few kinds of consternation. Its 1950s-born author had irreverently lowered the satiric boom on DuBois's Talented Tenth, whom the novel dubs The Also Chosen, yet in whose ranks he self-teasingly also counts himself. As a portrait of black Middle America, and against long-hallowed assumptions, he had dared to vaunt the suggestion that *black* writing needs to move on from slave-legacy or the colour-line or the ghetto. 'No one sat me down and told I was a Negro' (p. 3), runs an opening line as if to set in place the maverick temper of the account to follow. High cotton, an old-south black term meaning the one head above the others, a black person who has become conspicuous, would apply in plenty.

What kind of text, furthermore, exactly had Pinckney written? Was this auto-biography real or fictional, a novel impersonating an autobiography, another autofiction, in all its own kind of spoof? Commentary found itself calling up other black genre-bending, from the fiction of Ishmael Reed to that of Trey Ellis among contemporaries, but also earlier figures and two in particular. James Weldon Johnson's *The Autobiography of an Ex-Colored Man* (1912, 1927), with its deep ironic vein of harlequinry and black-white passing along with its tease of genre, was thought to provide a precedent. George Schuyler's *Black No More* (1931), with its wheeling satiric fantasy of American skin-colour change at the hands of a rogue geneticist, also came into view. *High Cotton* was thought to belong in kind, comic-irreverent yet full of its own serious aim.

Pinckney's narrator retells his pathway through black-bourgeois life as though a mix of couldn't-help-it privilege and indictment: suburbia, NAACP-supporting parents, Columbia University and 1960s black-chic radicalism. A Harlem interlude brings his own un-ideology into direct contrast with the ideologically right-on Sister Egba. He becomes an African American connoisseur of European travel. As black Secretary to Djuna Barnes, he learns the ways of a New York and Village white literary coterie.

At the same time, he also begins to comprehend the mask of his Grandfather Eustace as South Carolina old-timer yet also Harvard and Brown graduate. Piety of all kinds falls under scrutiny, not least blackness as a form of negative privilege: 'The great thing about finding out I was a Negro was that I could look forward to going places in the by and by that I would not have been asked to as a white boy' (p. 3). Of the South as the Old Country, site of heroic black struggle and where his grand-parental line began in a town called Promised Land, he can observe with a like ironic lowering of eye:

> The Old Country became a sort of generalized stuffy room, no matter how many reunions of old-timers I attended. It wasn't safe to explore the South. The old-timers themselves discouraged too much curiosity about what lay beyond the gate. It was a place of secrets, of what black people knew and what white people didn't. No old-timer said openly that Rosa Parks had been secretary of her NAACP branch and a student of interstate commerce rulings and the Equal Accommodations Law of 1948 before she decided she was too tired to move. (p. 49)

A shared writ holds for the 1960s and for the supposed coming of Black Revolution:

> Then came the Revolution, that loss of meridian, brought to the suburbs by elder siblings on Easter break. The Revolution drove up in Day-Glo vans, electric Kool-Aid Volkswagens, and souped-up convertibles. One of my sisters could be counted on to bring home the longhairs, the other sister to drag in the militants . . . Never mind that the Revolution was tardy and hollow, had come late to the suburbs, like foreign films, certain music, bell-bottoms, and

pot. Revolutionary defiance was expected of me, and white and blacks agreed in my case, long overdue. My best friend, Hans Hansen, admitted: 'I used to think your people were lazy. Now I understand. It's sickle cell.' (p. 108)

Of his own call to arms as writer, Pinckney, or his persona, implies lassitude, a near-comic weariness at the desideratum of being ever about acts of high commitment and purpose. He engages in a mock-heroic vow to answer in literary kind the racial 'sins of Western literature' (p. 204) and runs up a rich catalogue of indictment of the racist imaging of blacks from Hemingway to Dinesen, Fitzgerald to Chopin. But with a well-taken tilt at boredom, or excuse-making, he also confesses that 'by noon, thanks to hypoglycemia, I wasn't sure it mattered that in 1925 Virginia Woolf had come across a black man, spiffy in swallowtail and bowler, whose hand reminded her of a monkey's' (pp. 204–5).

The self-guying is endemic. 'Who hadn't heard of James Baldwin? I'd even driven down 125th Street once' (p. 123), he reveals in a joust at both filo-piety and, again, himself. His closing goes yet further. Afro-America, he cannot but know himself to be aware, has been heroism itself, tough, savvy endurance from slavery to deseg-regation, Dixie to the ghettoes. But, even as he acknowledges his own resulting privilege, he owns up to feeling the clash between 'piety and resentment' (p. 304), a sense of historic debt and yet the wish to live racially off-duty as it were.

The consequence, exact to a fault in its irony, leaves him contrarily positioned, actively immobile:

Perhaps the old-timers were right to insist that we, the Also Chosen, live wholly in the future and, like early Christians, preserve only detached sayings and a wagonful of miracles from the past. The facts were many, too many. If I'd sat where they'd sat, my trousers would still be burning. (p. 304)

The upshot is his negotiation of a world still racial, or ethnic, yet also having edged complicatedly beyond either-or equations of black and white. In the narrator's rite of passage, amid 'sociological heat' (p. 305), his own Manhattan can be both black Harlem and white Columbia, his music both Ray Charles and the Beatles, his reading both Booker T. Washington and the *Times Literary Supplement*.

In tackling 'minority business' (p. 265), 'this race thing' (p. 304), he can speak reverently of 'barbershop wisdom' (p. 123) and yet give vent to irreverence ('I minded the strict rules of conduct and the tribal code that said that I, as a black, had a responsibility to help my people, honor the race', p. 306). This pull and counter-pull gives *High Cotton* its distinctiveness, life and literary genre in their styles of equivocation each the winning reflection of the other.

XI

Trey Ellis, whether his novels *Platitudes* (1988) and *Home Repairs* (1993), or an inter-ethnic tongue-in-cheek story like 'Guess Who's Coming to Seder' (1989), has likewise been a controversial entrant into black literary ranks. His talk of pursuing the New Black Aesthetic, fiction told unapologetically from perspectives as cross-racial as black and given over to an unghettoed Manhattan or San Francisco, has not everywhere endeared him. Subjecting black gender and other literary wars to pastiche, furthermore, whether in the form of inventories of middle-class consumer, high-school and TV America or the novel's own narrative self-reference, would seem to have compounded his sins. Yet a first novel like *Platitudes*, in fact, steps past all these cavils, witty, a genuinely assured ventriloquy.

The juxtaposition of Dewayne Wellington, thirtyish, divorced, a flailing author, and Ishee Ayam, rising womanist literary star, brought together over the Internet as he endeavours to find a right direction for his blocked meta-novel of generational modern identity, sets up the frame. He opts for experimentalism, the postmodern, she for woman-of-colour feminism. Within lies the ongoing, several-versioned story of Earle and Dorothy, for Dewayne two teenage black Manhattanites, but for Ishee, as she takes it up, a fable of black gynocentric strength set in red-clay Georgia.

These two stylings of the fictional novel, both models of excess, Ellis makes over into their own comedy of error, fake sex-and-daring in the one, a killing feminist righteousness in the other. The irony deepens, moreover, in how both kinds of authorship serve as 'life' refractions of the Earle–Dorothy liaison, not to say the competing fictionality by which their desire is to be rendered. To that end, and explicitly taking off from Brian O'Nolan's dictum that 'the modern novel should be largely a work of reference', the novel cheerfully, teasingly, yet always orderingly, brings every manner of compositional bric-a-brac to bear.

Actual photography of Manhattan doubles as verisimilitude for the novel's Manhattan, images of 'Earle's mother's apartment in the Upper West Side' (p. 89) through to 'Barnard College' (p. 92). Mock pop-music lyrics like those of 'The Copa' (p. 7) set a teenage, club and hit-parade context. TV listings and ads enter, and mock, Earle's life as though they were literal messages. His mother, a widow, flighty, full of appetite, goes on her several dates – Jewish, black, like some ongoing teenager. Earle himself, one of a high-school trio of friends, lives two 'authorial' lives, in Dewayne's urban version a would-be high-stepping city lover-man, in Ishee's down-home deep southern alternative a country boy, the update of a Richard Wright 'Native Son'.

Funnily ingenious menus, awful-actual film previews, and mock-SAT examinations and sex surveys play into the imagined text. Dewayne's divorce and settlement, along with Ishee's book-launches, a Barnard literary lecture, and her relationship with a leading black expatriate author, play into the 'real' text. The two authors edge closer towards each other as much in their lives as styles of storytelling. Ellis manages the ironies built into both with a fine touch.

The text, suitably enough for a high-tech era, draws into itself intricate computer-programming reference, whether Dewayne literally at the keyboard or Earle as a high-school IT star. The same high school spills out to Coney Island revels, partying in Upper Manhattan's to politicking in Harlem (Earle's ruse to get closer to Dorothy). Perhaps most engaging of all has to be Ellis's flights of parody. Ishee upbraids Dwayne, in phrasing its own self-parody, for his 'postmodernist, semio-logical sophism' (p. 79). Earle, for her, could not be figure more burdened by his own self-awareness whether in the form of would-be gallantry or sex-fantasy. Dewayne, on the other hand, is faced with Ishee's Landes County Earle, a figure caught up in the syrup of titles like *Chillun o' de Lawd*, and in her use of echoes from Richard Wright, Faulkner back-country lingo and Alice Walker-style 'Nubian Queen' matriarchy (p. 19).

As the two negotiate their way towards each other, cybernetically and then in life, Ellis takes his own authorial leave in a scene of them as lovers even as Dewayne sneaks out of the bedroom to complete, or likelier semi-complete, Earle's love for Dorothy. Given the black ideological gender wars, masculinism as against feminism, chauvinism as against man-hating, what ending, what reconciliation, asks the novel, best holds for an incoming black literary era? In sending up these schisms, not to say the novel form as both text and text-in-progress, Trey Ellis's *Platitudes* offers its own kind of bid for new imaginative fare, timely new conjure.

XII

The applause won by James Alan McPherson for *Hue and Cry*, and then for its successor *Elbow Room* (1977), did not altogether silence misgivings. If there was command, an agility of composition, the suggestion was also to be heard of too clinical a disposition, each story a case-file. None of that held for Ralph Ellison, who spoke unstintingly of sympathy, insight, not to say craft.[15]

Quite what does McPherson manage story for story in *Hue and Cry* as his first collection? Can they be said to add up to a cycle, the connecting round? Each indeed draws upon an evidentiary, even lawyerly voice (McPherson, in biographical fact, wrote a number of them when still at Harvard Law School). The effect, never other than unintrudingly managed, is to give off a sense of experience always in process of being weighed, along with, and in equal part, an invitation to the reader to take measure, to arrive at matching judgement. It is this very judiciousness, as style, a tone, which, overall, gives the organising linkage to *Hue and Cry*.

'A Matter of Vocabulary', the opening piece, sets a perfect marker. 'Things about life had always come to Thomas Brown by listening and being quiet' (p. 8). Adolescent, brother to Edward, he almost monitors his everyday acquisition of sight and sound. Three purloining elders at the Southern Baptist Church prompt doubts as to his mother's heaven-and-hell surety about an eventual Judgement Day ('the Good on the Right and Bad on the Left', p. 11). The neighbourhood drunks with whom he finds a vernacular camaraderie give him a glimpse of shared vocabulary. The next-door embalmer, Billy Herbs, embodies the link of life to death. The Caribbean-Voodoo lady, Mrs Quick, taunts his left-handedness as devilry, along with her daily colloquist, the Crab Lady. Above all, the Barefoot Lady, a demented scavenger who nightly and hauntingly repeats cry of '*Mr. Jones! I love you Mr. Jones!*', acts as the embodied ghost of his own aloneness.

In working as a potato-bagger at the Feinberg Super Market, he finds both strength and limit: an after-school position, cash, a window through which to contemplate human face, size and temperament, and yet at the same time the reminder of his distance from high-school completion and access to worlds elsewhere. The closing return of the Barefoot Lady, her banshee lamentation, catches perfectly his own sense of misery at not knowing, in truth, just what his own Great Expectations might be. McPherson's portrait could not be more detailed, and yet at the same time more spare, witness for, and yet against, a boyhood lost to itself.

McPherson's two Pullman stories, 'On Trains' and 'A Solo Song: For Doc', address legendary terrain, the etiquette of black old-time service aboard the railways of the Midwest and Pacific Northwest. Both give dramatic summary to porterage, dining-car lore, a history. The former subjects the colour-line to contrasting vistas, the 'Dearborn lady' (p. 33) who won't allow a black porter to keep watch in the outside corridor as she sleeps, and the 'woman with the Dutch bob' (p. 33) who sets up an assignation with the black barman, John Perry. The latter, told as though by 'a Waiter's Waiter' (p. 39) to a 'youngblood' writer (p. 39), portrays how the veteran Doc is finagled into retirement and a drunken death by new company rules, Pullman life as a lodge or brotherhood possessed of its own sustaining dignity of ritual yet also the epilogue to an era.

Subsequent stories work with like precision, the discreet, meticulous presentation of why, and where, hue and cry, 'should be raised', to quote McPherson quoting a standard law text as Preface. 'Gold Coast', Harvard life seen not as Ivy League glitz but janitorial lower depth, is told, in two voices, as though story-deposition. 'Of Cabbages and Kings', a story-colloquy between the narrator and his friend, Claude Sheats, does an ironic riff on the 'secrets' of American race and sex relations, white and black as encryption, one language for another. 'An Act of Prostitution', its principals the whore Philomena Brown, the black GI Vietnam veteran Willie Smith, and an Italian youth-defendant Angelo Carbone, uses a quite explicit legal setting to explore colour-coding in counsel and court tactics as, again, but symptoms of an altogether larger order of human connivance.

'Hue and Cry', as title story, the portrait of Quaker-raised New Englander Eric Carney and Margot Payne, and their cross-race love affair begun at the time of voter registration, civil rights and 1960s alternative politics, yields an anatomy of never-quite-right relationship. Race, inevitably, exerts sway, but in a manner well short of being everything. Eric risks confusing love with some kind of white-liberal stewardship. Margot, intelligence her calling card, moves from him to other lovers, none any more sustaining. Fitfully, then needfully, she becomes lover to the dull Charles Wright, black co-worker in federally funded programmes in the inner city. Charles, however, uses the very confidence she gives him to take on other relationships, its ironic aftermath to be seen as she gives herself emptily to Jerry, Eric's former room-mate, a man whose mulatto sexual vanity is his only style.

This scenario in 'Hue and Cry' of unmet need, flawed and alternating human liaison, and which McPherson even makes the subject of an intervening meta-colloquy, does specific enough duty. But it also carries the signature of the unfolding whole as constituted, each in turn, of his story-collection's other and equally memorable courtrooms of life.

XIII

Shared history, even shared consciousness, there may be. But this is an Afro-America seen, and told, through its own energetic plurality of voice. The one selection of writings, moreover, necessarily implies others, the still more various continuum.

The latter-day black novel of region can look to a ribald back-country Georgia novel like Raymond Andrews's *Appalachee Red* (1978) or to a Delta Hoodoo story like A. R. Flowers's *De Mojo Blues* (1986). The historical genre takes on yet other reflexive shapings in David Bradley's *The Chaneyville Incident* (1981), as contemporary south-to-north slave excavation, and in Sherley Anne Williams's *Dessa Rose* (1986), a vivid itinerary account of enslavement and escape along with the unslaving of the word as much as the body. A novel of African American lives at the urban lower depths, centred in crack-cocaine, and told in italicised verse form, is to be found in Ray Shell's *Iced* (1993).

A Gay dispensation opens in Randall Kenan's *A Visitation of the Spirits* (1989), with its North Carolina portrait of the breakdown of Horace Creek under Calvinist-Lutheran sexual prohibitions, Melvin Dixon's *Trouble The Water* (1989) as a parable of sexual self-loss and revenge set also in rural North Carolina, and Audre Lorde's autobiography-novel *Zami: A New Spelling of My Name* (1982) with its rallying lesbian-feminism and portrait of mother–daughter relationship. If black fiction has created its own postmodern turn, Jones/Baraka to Reed, it has also carried its science-fiction imprimatur. Speculative writing, futurism, under a space and planetary wrap, and given over to the intersections of race, ethnicity and gender, can look to few bolder or cannier sequences of storytelling than Samuel R. Delany's *Return to Neveryon* quartet (1979–87) and Octavia Butler's *Patternmaster* (1976) and its sequels.

It was sometimes feared that the 1960s, by their very momentum, might lead if not to a becalming then to a reduced energy within subsequent African American narrative. The evidence abundantly suggests otherwise. Whether modern or contemporary, or indeed postmodern, the fictions to hand assume stylings full of yet newer impetus and edge. In this, and in kind with a yet wider literary-multicultural regime, theirs continues the rewriting, and so the re-envisioning, of America.

NOTES

1. Ishmael Reed (1969), *Yellow Back Radio Broke-Down*, New York: Doubleday, p. 40.
2. James Baldwin (1951), 'Many Thousands Gone', *Partisan Review*, 18 (November-December). Reprinted in (1955), *Notes of a Native Son*, New York: Dial.
3. For full references, see the Primary Bibliography.
4. Best accounts of the 'black' 1960s include Thomas R. Brooks (1974), *Walls Come Tumbling Down, 1940–70*, Englewood Cliffs, NJ: Prentice-Hall; Sar A. Levitan et al (eds) (1975), *Still a Dream: The Changing Status of Blacks since 1960*, Cambridge, MA: Harvard University Press; August Meier and Elliot Rudwick (1976), *Along the Color Line*, Urbana IL: Illinois University Press; Harvey Sitkoff (1981), *The Struggle for Black Equality, 1945–80*, New

York: Hill and Wang; and Juan Williams (1987), *Eyes on the Prize: America's Civil Rights Years, 1954–1965*, New York: Viking Penguin.

5. The King affray and its larger implications are explored in Robin Gooding-Williams (ed.) (1993), *Reading Rodney King: Reading Urban Uprising*, New York: Routledge.

6. For a detailed and well-taken study of the Oprah phenomenon and its impact, see Vicki Abt and Leonard Mustazza (1993), *Coming after Oprah: Cultural Fallout in the Age of the TV Talk Show*, Bowling Green, OH: Bowling Green State University Popular Press.

7. Originally published as LeRoi Jones/Amiri Baraka (1964), *Dutchman* and *The Slave*, New York: William Morrow.

8. Cornel West has been a greatly influential, and controversial, figure in this debate, a role which continues in his support for the Presidential candidacy of the Rev. Al Sharpton and his contretemps with the President of Yale as to his making of a rap record.

9. For the range of the Black Aesthetic debate, see Addison Gayle (ed.) (1969), *Black Expression: Essays by and about Black Americans in the Creative Arts*, New York: Weybright and Talley; Mercer Cook and Stephen E. Henderson (eds) (1986), *The Militant Writer in Africa and the United States*, Madison, WI: University of Wisconsin Press; Addison Gayle Jr (ed.) (1971), *The Black Aesthetic*, New York: Anchor-Doubleday; John A. Williams and Charles F. Harris (eds) (1970), *Amistad 1: Writings on Black History and Culture*, New York: Vintage Books, and *Amistad 2: Writings on Black History and Culture*, New York: Vintage Books; George Kent (1972), *Blackness and the Adventure of Western Culture*, Chicago, IL: Third World Publishing; and Addison Gayle Jr (1975), *The Way of the New World: The Black Novel in America*, New York: Doubleday.

10. These and related texts are given in the Secondary Bibliography.

11. Early to use this term was C. W. E. Bigsby (1980) in *The Second Black Renaissance: Essays in Black Literature*, Westport, CT: Greenwood Press.

12. Ernest Gaines (1978), 'Miss Jane and I', *Callaloo*, 3:1 (May), 23–38.

13. This trilogy I have analysed as 'Equilibrium out of their chaos': Ordered Unorder in the Witherspoon-Bloodworth Trilogy of Leon Forrest', in John G. Cawelti (ed.) (1997), *Leon Forrest: Introductions and Interpretations*, Bowling Green, OH: Bowling Green State University Popular Press, pp. 97–114.

14. Wanda Macon, 'Terry McMillan', in William L. Andrews, Frances Smith Foster and Trudier Harris (eds) (1997), *The Oxford Companion to African American Literature*, New York: Oxford University Press, p. 493.

15. Ralph Ellison, cover note, James Alan McPherson (1969), *Hue and Cry*, Boston, MA: Little, Brown.

CHAPTER FOUR

'I Am Your Worst Nightmare: I Am an Indian with a Pen'

Fictions of the Indian, Native Fictions

to be an Indian in modern society is in a very real sense to be unreal and ahistorical. (Vine Deloria)[1]

[Aunt Susie] must have realized
that the atmosphere and conditions
which had maintained this oral tradition in Laguna culture
had been irrevocably altered by the European intrusion –
principally by the practice of taking the children
away from Laguna to Indian schools,
taking the children away from the tellers who had
in all past generations told
the children an entire culture, an entire identity of a people.
    (Leslie Marmon Silko)[2]

The Indian was an occidental invention that became a bankable simulation; the word has no referent in tribal languages or cultures . . . Native American Indians have endured the envies of missionaries of manifest manners for five centuries. The Boy Scouts of America, the wild simulations of tribal misnomers used for football teams, automobiles and other products, Western movies, and the heroic adventures in novels by James Fenimore Cooper, Frederick Manfred, Karl May, and others are but a few examples of the manifold envies that have become manifest manners in the literatures of dominance. (Gerald Vizenor)[3]

I

'Unreal and ahistorical.' 'Irrevocably altered.' 'A simulation.' Each phrase speaks to, not to say against, one of America's, one of the world's, most enduring fictions. Their shared animus, looking back to a timeline of well before Columbus's landing, is to disrupt, not to say face down, the best-known figurations of America's Native peoples. Indigenes as otherness may well date from antiquity or cross every border. But few have attracted fantasy quite so insistent, or lavishly popular and beguiling, as that of the Indian.

Fictions seize the popular imagination even as they contest one with another. Noble Savage vies with Devil's Child. Adamic innocent alternates with malign Caliban. Images of wilderness, the tomahawk, scalping, lie deeply embedded within the American, and indeed the larger western, historic psyche. Shorthand takes over, familiarly, and endlessly, to repeat itself. Cowboys and Indians. Gun versus arrow. Captivity and escape. The Only Good Indian is a Dead Indian. War Parties. Noble Chiefs. Squaws. Pocahontas. Hiawatha and Minnehaha. Sitting Bull. Custer's Last Stand. Geronimo. Vanishing Americans.

From their shoreline, or forest, first encounters with Euro-America in the seventeenth century, to the cavalry and homesteader battles of the Plains and beyond in the nineteenth, to life on the Reservations and in the cities, tribal peoples are to be denied time, access to change, and, for sure, modernity. Theirs belongs to a past folder of American history, or at best, its downward slope. The massacre at Wounded Knee in 1890 becomes endgame with an Epilogue of drift and poverty. No one could overlook the reduction of numbers, or contemporary joblessness, welfare poverty, drink and violence. Yet how to account for the ongoing Native presence of more than 300 federally recognised tribes, an estimated overall 4,100,000 people on and off reservation, and, however sparingly, important pockets of economic upturn, along with an ongoing, and to be sure sometimes re-found, sense of cultural vitality?

Native politics from the 1960s on finds reanimation through Tribal Councils, community groups, the American Indian Movement (AIM) and Native American Rights Fund (NARF) and, against stereotype, city activism. Sovereignty and land claims have been busy, along with legal action over mineral holdings, family and adoption rights, and issues of schooling and language. From Connecticut to Minnesota to Nevada, there has been the spectacular rise of Native casino economies. The assumption that Native America, Indians, somehow bowed out after Wounded Knee, to be kept alive only in the *simulacra* of daguerreotype, canvas, photograph, screen or comic strip, has always been illusion. In every tribal and mixedblood variety, they remain not only unerased, but as much among the living as other Americans. Native authorship cannot be said not to have kept pace.[4]

Vine Deloria, veteran Sioux lawyer and teacher at the University of Colorado, has made a name inveighing against this out-of-time, harlequin imaging of 'Indians' in US history. Leslie Marmon Silko, Laguna Pueblo author, in *Storyteller* as beyond, has long given herself to the politics of indigeneity, to embrace a sacral earth, a coming redress. Gerald Vizenor, Berkeley-based, and with origins in both Chippewa-Ojibway (or Anishinaabe) White Earth Reservation and inner-city Minneapolis, adds *Fugitive Poses: Native American Indian Scenes of Absence and Presence* (1998) and *Postindian Conversations* (1999) to his previous ironic undermining of essentialist fictions of 'The Indian', the making over of tribal culture into savagism, ideal or malign, or of nearly equal frequency, an 'archive of victimry'.[5]

The Native-written novel, with Scott Momaday's *House Made of Dawn* (1969) a spur and landmark, gives companion reckoning. Two intergenerational tiers especially count. The one, selectively, calls up novels by James Welch (Blackfeet/Gros Ventre), Leslie Marmon Silko (Laguna) and Louise Erdrich (Turtle Mountain Chippewa). The other can be located in five first novels by, respectively, Thomas King (Cherokee), Linda Hogan (Chickasaw), Louis Owens (Choctaw-Cherokee), Sherman Alexie (Spokane-Coeur d'Alene), and Betty Louise Bell (Cherokee).

In them, as in Vizenor's own voluminous storyings from his pilgrim novel and satyricon, *Bearheart* (1978, revised 1990), through his 'mind monkey' Anishinaabe-cum-Asia fantasia, *Griever: An American Monkey King in China* (1987), and on to his recent pastiche of the museumisation of the tribes, *Chancers* (2000), and in a spectrum which extends from Elizabeth Cook-Lynn (Crow Creek Sioux) to Michael Dorris (Modoc), Paula Gunn Allen (Laguna-Sioux) to Martin Cruz Smith (Senecu del Sur-Yaqui), Native fiction finds its own yet further continuity of invention.[6]

II

A sense of contextual lineage, and of the best-known contributions to 'the fiction of the Indian', amounts to a working prerequisite. Has not a truly tribal mix of cultures and languages, histories and beliefs, stretching across all the Americas from the Bering Strait to Tierra del Fuego and from the Caribbean to the South Seas, been rendered down into the single trope or glyph? Actual geography, Pequot Massachusetts, or the New Mexico pueblos, or the Sioux Great Plains, Black Hills and North and South Dakota, largely transposes into tourist itinerary, out-of-time backdrop or romance. Little short of a diorama of cliché has come into being, ahistoric when not actually anti-historic.[7]

Placenames, from Chicago to Manitoba, Connecticut to Seattle, the latter named after the Duwamish Salish leader Sealth, serve as merest word-shadows of the intricate tribal life histories behind them. Dime novels like *Stella Delorme, or The Comanche's Dream* (1860) by Ned Buntline, the pen name of E. Z. C. Judson, through to latter-day bestsellers like *Guns of the Timberland* (1955) by Louis L'Amour, author of more than 100 Westerns, serve up white triumph and Indian killing and vanishment according to requirement. It is in this connection that Elizabeth Cook-Lynn, long-time editor of *Wicazo sa review* and the novelist of *From the River's Edge* (1991) with its busy portrait of Sioux community, took aim at so admired a doyen of Western fiction as Wallace Stegner. In *Why I Can't Read Wallace Stegner and Other Essays: A Tribal Voice* (1996), she berates him for his talk of the tribes' 'glorious demise', his fantasy Indians, and his allegation that the Native West somehow ended with Wounded Knee ('I argue with Stegner's reality. The culture I have known . . . exists in communities all over the region, in language and myth, and in the memories of people who know who they are and where they come from').[8]

Buffalo Bill Cody, a name contrived by Buntline, and whose Wild West circuses begin in 1883, requires his own special mention. It falls to him to have re-invented the West as entertainment, a white cavalry and 'Indian warrior' spectacle. His genius lay in concocting a quite dazzling commercial simulation, US troopers and

scout-heroes set against war-painted cohorts, together with charging battle forma-
tions, whoops and bugles, and Sitting Bull, Gall, Yellow Hand and Black Elk
actually employed to enter the ring playing themselves.

The process unabates, whether Red Man chewing tobacco, the Indian Head
nickel, barbershop manikins, paratroopers with their Geronimo shouts, or Boy
Scout troop names. Pontiac (1720–69), one-time leader of the Ottawa people and
Algonquin federalist, becomes the appropriated name for a bestselling car, with Jeep
Cherokees and Winnebago motorhomes also in the line-up (Winnebagos are
variously eastern Sioux and Chippewa bad spirits). Mutual of Omaha, one of
America's largest insurance companies, vaunts a celebrated war-bonnet logo by
which Omaha's Dakota Sioux have become reduced to an advertising token. Sports
teams unashamedly assume names like the Atlanta Braves, with an echo of savagism
in the Tomahawk Chop of their fans, or the Cleveland Indians, the Kansas City
Chiefs or, as egregiously as any, the Washington Redskins.

TV has long conjured into being its own Indian Country, for recent times a series
like *Cheyenne* (1955–63), with its frontier scout Bodie, or *Dr Quinn, Medicine Woman*
(1993–), with its buckskin Florence Nightingale heroine among picture-book Cheyenne, or *Northern Exposure* (1990–), with its New York Jewish hero and Alaska
Athabascan 'Indians' like Marilyn Whirlwind and Ed Chiglia. Latterly counter-
culture hippy Indians, punk Mohawks and New Age religionists and self-appointed
TV hotline healers with their 'Indian' crystals and feathers, add nothing if not a
touch of carnival. Not a few Native authors have been moved to ask whose Indians,
whose Indian fictions, these are to be thought.

As to the view of the tribes as a parade gone by, it can look to the very founding of
the American Republic. The Boston Tea Party of 1773, with New Englanders in
assumed Mohawk garb and headgear, acts out an 'Indian' masquerade as though
from an *already* previous era. In the 1920s, one of the best-known images of Calvin
Coolidge, Vermonter, has him seated in a three-piece business suit and wearing a full
Sioux chieftain bonnet. Together they bridge the ongoing fiction: stereotypic
paleface elided into stereotypic Indian.[9]

The case of Ishi, last of the California Yahi (a division of the Yana people), who
was 'discovered' in turn-of-the-century California and, at the behest of the Berkeley
anthropologist Alfred Kroeber, lived out his days in San Francisco assiduously
making artefacts for display, gives another turn to events. For some, Ishi embodied
the romance of a last 'stone-age' man untrammelled by civilisation. For others, he
served as the very instance of the Vanishing American bequeathing burial-trophies,
as it were, to a culture he himself had once lived. In fact, in his things unsaid, his art,
and even his role in a range of Native literary treatment, he has proved elusive of
both. Wrangles about the return to tribal custody of bones, tools, and every manner
of artefact, have been increasingly frequent, not to say passionate.[10] An oblique
commentary is to be found in a best-loved text like J. D. Salinger's *The Catcher in the
Rye* (1952). At Manhattan's 'Museum of Natural History', Holden Caulfield gazes
admiringly at 'the Indian stuff' with its ever-fixed manikin fire-makers and 'squaws'
displayed under a 'big glass case'.[11]

From early canvas and photography through to Hollywood and TV, a similar visual fictionalisation operates. George Catlin's sketches, notably 'Comanche Feats of Horsemanship' in his *Manners of the North American Indians* (1841), gives expression to the heroic mould. Charles Bird King's mid-century 'Pawnee Warriors', for all their feathers and tattoo, look not only deliberately grouped, and courtly, but suspiciously Caucasian in looks. Thomas Moran's 'The Spirit of the Indian' (1869), its figures also stately to a fault, suggests, however, the tribute of farewell. Frederic Remington's *Frontier Sketches* (1898), or his oil painting 'The Last of His Race' (1908) with its warrior gazing from his bluff as much into past time as place, or any of his rearing-horse sculptures, supplies a West of Native romance for an eastern audience. Edward S. Curtis's twenty volumes of sepia photographic stills, done between 1907 and 1930, might be almost remnant pageantry, Native icons of inertia. Recent Native art has both sought to be independent of, yet been obliged to negotiate, this imagery. The Santa Fe-based artist, David Bradley, for instance, in canvases like 'Sleeping Indian' (1994), depicts a mythic Indian Country in terms of a dormant bow-and-arrows warrior and tourist trading-post, a mountain lion and mechanical earth-digger. The ironies of each contrast could not be better taken.[12]

D. W. Griffith comes into the frame, literally, with two-reelers like *The Redman and Child* (1908), *The Squaw's Love Story* (1911) and *Battle of Elderbush Gulch* (1914), the latter a rabid, savagist portraiture of 'Indians' as dog-eaters and gratuitous killers and which, in redface as against blackface, did for Natives what *The Birth of a Nation* (1915) did for African Americans. They became creatures of forest and night, a dark, skulking, indigenist conspiracy. Griffith, that is, Southern-raised film pioneer, invents his own 'ethnic' fictions, the more compelling on account of his overall visual genius.

The radio series of *The Lone Ranger*, first broadcast in 1933 on the Mutual Radio Network, then screened as ABC's 1949–58 TV series with a run of cinema versions to follow, perhaps offers the most hugely winning fiction. In these, Jay Silverheels played one of the most controversial of all Indian roles, that of Tonto as *alter ego* to Clayton Moore's white lawman replete with mask and identifying cry of 'Hi-ho Silver!' Was not this Man Friday, loyal, unswerving, duly buckskinned and all monosyllabic Indian-talk, not least 'You Kemo Sabe' meaning 'You Trust Scout'? This is not to overlook the precedent, however ambiguous, of Silverheels as Native screen actor, early in a line to include Chief Dan George in *Little Big Man* (1970) and *The Outlaw Josey Wales* (1976), Larry Littlebird as Abel in the film of *House Made of Dawn* (1972), Will Sampson as Chief Bromden in *One Flew Over the Cuckoo's Nest* (1975) and Gary Farmer in *Powwow Highway* (1992).[13]

In movie terms, 'Indian' legacy, the fiction made more glamorous by the screen's transition from black and white into colour, also takes on well-known figurations. Jeff Chandler as Cochise in the Apache-settler conflict of *Broken Arrow* (1950), or Richard Harris as the British aristocrat Lord Morgan, transformed, through the Sun Dance ritual, into adoptee Dakota Sioux in *A Man Called Horse* (1970), supply Noble Indian fare, warrior aristocracy. A movie like Robert Mulligan's *The Stalking Moon* (1968) suggests in its Apache stalker an update of the indigene as ongoing unseen threat.

John Ford, the best-known cinematographer of the West, equally perpetuates the ambiguity inherent in these 'Indian' representations. If a cavalry trilogy like *Fort Apache* (1948), *She Wore a Yellow Ribbon* (1949) and *Rio Grande* (1950), with John Wayne at the helm, and backdrops of Monument Valley, Arizona – actually Navajo heartland, is to be thought a *tour de force*, how far is the price the stylisation of Native peoples as bonneted chiefs, daemon kidnappers, healer elders and doe-eyed tribal women? Perhaps *The Searchers* (1956), with its reworking of 'Indian captivity' and the Western's codings of white–red genetics and blood, signalled Ford's recognition of his own complicity. Arthur Penn's *Little Big Man* (1970), taken from Thomas Berger's 1964 novel, can also be thought rare in offering a degree of Native viewpoint of the West. Behind the comedy entertainment of 111-year-old Jack Crabb as one-time white into Cheyenne foundling, and each absurdist zigzag from sole survivor of Custer's last stand to adopted son of a preacher, is there not also unease, a sense of one American history having too often been told at the expense of another?[14]

Yet more recent Hollywood, whether Kevin Costner's *Dances with Wolves* (1990), with its Sioux actors and subtitles, or Michael Apted's *Thunderheart* (1992), with its Oglala Sioux setting and based on the Pine Ridge shoot-out of the 1970s, may well suggest a changing dispensation. But whatever Costner's liberal good intent, or attempts at 'Native' landscape, *Dances with Wolves* cannot resist a white frontier adventure, captivity romance, laid-on Sioux wolf symbolism, and a regulation Vanishing American ending. Apted's *Thunderheart*, within its murder-investigation format, shows an evident sympathy about the abuse of Native land and mineral rights. The Ghost Dance, however, whatever its profound revivalist implications in the 1890s under the Paiute medicine man, Wovoka, known as Jack Wilson, and after the death of Sitting Bull, simply blurs into a background silhouette of dancing and chanting 'Indian'.[15] A Disney cartoon like *Pocahontas* (1995), replete in pastoral and love song, and however winning the animation, says little of Virginia's Powhatan Confederacy, the Tidewater battles (1622–44), John Smith, or the appropriation in a term like 'princess' for her actual status and tribal beliefs before Christian conversion and life and death in England.[16]

Native cinema faces the same challenge as Native fiction. How to 'unfilm' inherited fictions? Irony, a species of trickster screening, would seem to have been one way, as in the Hopi film-maker Victor Masayesva's *Imagining Indians* (1992), with its fantasy of a Native visit to the dentist as an imagined extraction of 'Indians' as stereotypes of sweatlodge and dream-catcher chic. Jonathan Wacks's *Powwow Highway* offers a witty reverse captivity story which begins from Northern Cheyenne's Dull Knife Reservation, itself named after a leader who once sought to lead the Cheyenne back to their homelands. In *Smoke Signals* (1997), the Cheyenne-Arapaho director, Chris Eyre, transfers the bittersweet stories of Sherman Alexie's *The Lone Ranger and Tonto Fistfight in Heaven* (1993), involving Spokane tribal figures like Victor Joseph and Thomas Builds-the-Fire, from page to screen with a right measure of wit.

To both can be added Gerald Vizenor's *Harold of Orange* (1983), a trickster short feature in which he has Indians not so much play Indians as play at playing Indians.

He draws on a phenomenon of long standing. Geronimo's appearances, at small-town parades and rodeo, in the role of 'captured Indian' almost perfectly anticipates Iron Eyes Cody, tear in eye, paddling a canoe against a polluted industrial backdrop, as part of the Keep American Beautiful Campaign first aired on TV in 1971. Is the latter fair use or more Indian fiction, one not only steeped in eco-sentimentality but hypocrisy given past historic seizure of Native lands?

TV itself can even be said to supply its own revisionist version of 'Indians'. Commentary has not been far off the mark in suggesting that an unprecedentedly successful series like Gene Roddenberry's *Star Trek* (1966–9), or the sequels *The Next Generation*, *Deep Space Nine* and *Voyager*, offer in figures like the Vulcan Mr Spock, the android Data or the black commander Tuvok a reworking of the American indigene. Each, at least, is suitably other, impassive, spiritual, arcane, marked by colour or visage, and, true to James Fenimore Cooper's formula of Chinachgook and Natty Bumpo, mainstays to James Kirk, Jean-Luc Picard or Kathryn Janeway as white leader-captain.

The potency of western culture's co-option of Native America equally makes its way into language. For just as the Columbian conquest began a seizure of land and body, so the principal colonizing idioms of English, Spanish, French, Portuguese and Dutch seized, and in an always vexing term *translated*, 'the Indian' each into its own pre-emptive writ. Indian/savage, indio/piel roja, peau-rouge/sauvage: these, and their like, became the lexical-pair bondings of Euro-colonialism, an othering, a binary, by linguistic fiat. As freighted as any has been 'squaw', initially an Algonquin word for a married woman, but long tied into primitivist nomenclature. A placename like California's Squaw Valley continues to be a source of provocation.

As to tribal languages themselves, they at first could indeed be construed by New England's Puritans as the Devil's Tongue, or, just as exotically, and a frequent assumption, some diasporic Lost Tribe's Hebrew. Translation led into every kind of impasse, literal misunderstandings to be sure, but also, as in the case of many missionary syllabaries and lexicons, vernacular and especially sexual usages either changed or, frequently, censored. As the first 'Indian' texts began to appear in print, themselves often twice or even three times made over from oral sources or adapted from pictomyth, histories that once had been delivered in performance, full of live improvisation, became scriptural and linear, a fixity all too reassuringly western.[17]

The story of Longfellow's *The Song of Hiawatha* (1855), set on the shores of Gitchee-Gummee, anglicised Anishinaabe phrasing for Lake Michigan but usually taken for child-talk, could not be more to the point. Initially it came to attention as an Anishinaabe/Chippewa/Ojibway oral myth centred on the trickster deity Manabozho or, among other spellings, Naanabozo or Nanapush, and collected by the one-time New York entrepreneur and eventual Indian Agent, Henry Rowe Schoolcraft, in *Algic Researches: Comprising Inquiries Respecting the Mental Character-istics of the North American Indian: First Series: Indian Tales and Legends* (2 vols, 1839). In Longfellow's fashioning, impossibly conflated with the sixteenth-century Mohawk-Iroquois leader Hiawatha, it emerges as classic American Indian romance. No poem of 'the Indian' has more taken hold. Cast, ponderously, in a trochee-form derived from the Finnish folk epic *The Kalevala* (Longfellow, after all, was holder of the Smith Chair of Languages at Harvard), it has been translated into over eighty languages and quite innumerable plays, operas, pageants and children's and other editions. One of them, in a perfect ironic turn of the wheel, has been Anishinaabe-Chippewa.

This reinforces the view not only that little or no Native literature preceded the 1960s but also that other tribal arts, because ascriptural, do not harbour their own literary significance. Spoken creation story, chant or the dance narratives of the powwow therefore win lesser attention. A whole dimension of narrative is over-looked within Anasazi clay and wall design, Ojibway bark pictographs, Osage and Tlingit blankets, Pueblo pottery, Hopi basketwork, Zuni or Hopi katchina carvings, or Navajo sand paintings, silverwork, and turquoise and coral jewellery. All of these imply Native worlds, a cosmos, being 'told', created, memorialised.

What recognition is to be accorded the Cherokee savant Sequoyah (1770–1843), known as George Guest, who created the first written form of Cherokee ('I thought that would be like catching a wild animal and taming it')? Nor should the literary inclusions of Native journalism be bypassed, from a founding journal like the *Cherokee Phoenix* (1828–34) through to contemporary publications like the Lakota *Indian Country Today*, New Mexico's *Gallup Independent*, Minnesota's *Native American Press/Ojibwe News* or Washington's *Yakima Nation Review*. Native word has never been in short supply.

For many in Euro-America, the supposed want of a world of word and text was to be situated within social-Darwinian destiny, the inability of the tribes to evolve and adapt. It is a formula long complicit in the stupendous, white-contrived loss of Native landholdings, the impact of gun and Bible, the importation of disease, and the view of indigenous peoples as both wayward and infantile. It is also a view which, notoriously, underwrites the issue of 'Indian drinking'. The assumption has become widespread that alcoholism, from illicit whiskey as firewater through to the recent controversies about Fetal Alcohol Syndrome (FAS) for which Michael Dorris's *The Broken Cord* (1989) became a controversial marker, somehow afflicts tribal America in a degree uniquely greater than any other population in America.

Similarly, the issues of removal always require consideration, whether the sending of young tribespeople to the Indian Boarding Schools of Pennsylvania like that at Carlisle, the unremitting use of Oklahoma as arbitrarily assigned homeland or, to give a notorious instance, the dispatch of a chained, prisoner-of-war Geronimo and his Chiricahua (and other) Apaches to a distant Fort Pickens, Pensacola, Florida, in 1886, even after their voluntary surrender. It takes no undue ironist to note that, in proportion to evisceration, the Indian became an ever greater candidate for Euro-American myth and fantasy. What 'education' as to American history could best have applied? What version of Indians would a Native authorship be disposed to create?

Recognising the fuller human idiom of civilisations like those of the Olmecs, Mayans and Aztecs, or, in more subsequent western experience, of the Algonquins, Navajo, Chippewa-Ojibway, Laguna and Acoma Pueblo, Sioux, Cherokee,

Comanches, Arapaho, Hopi, Apache (whether Mescalero, White Mountain, Jicarilla or San Carlos), Chickasaw, Osage, Zuni, Blackfeet, Salish, Nez Percé, Seminoles, and each myriad other clan and grouping, makes for a necessary point of departure. One can begin, for instance, with tribal self-naming, often enough simply 'the people', as against extraneous, and often wildly prejudicial, nomenclature. That embraces the *Diné*, the Navajo word for themselves, *Numa* for the Paiutes, *Apsaloka* for the Crow, *Tsis-tas* for the Cheyenne, and *Oceti Sakowin* (or Seven Fireplaces) as the different branches of the Sioux know themselves. Each tradition invites a due sense of lived time-space and calendar, creation and vision-myth, art, dance, wordplay and humour, cedar-burning, child-rearing, and foodways, whether wild rice, cornmeal, maize, game or fish cooked over mesquite.[18]

How, accordingly, to 'read' shamanism, or the animism of bear, crow, raven, turtle and otter, or each legend-bearing Tlingit totem pole, or the powwow and wealth-redistributing potlatch, or the spirituality of the sweatlodge, kiva, katsina, or Ghost, Sun and Peyote cosmology? Along with each has to be the utterly compendious trickster lore, the Coyote of the Navajo, Spiderwoman for the Pueblos, Weesageechak for the Cree. Do all Native philosophies, moreover, settle into shared wheel, circle or hoop, with the earth, for all its centrality, as gynocentric mother? Above all, how to come even close to the 'translation', let alone the scripturalisation, of the sumptuous, and simply inescapable, oral legacy of Native America, each ceremony and story?

A further selective tendency has been that of victimry, 'Indians' as one-time slain warrior-hunter or tragic squaw, or, of late, drinker or foodstamp mother. This denies the survival wisdom, and irony, brought on by having had to negotiate Euro-America's will to dominance, not to mention the complex dimensionality of place and time in all Native tradition. Assigning to others only the one-note role of victim has never been helpful, as survivors of the Nazi and Armenian holocausts have been at pains to attest. But 'the Indian', however much a fiction from the start, actually enters a double curve as *both* victimiser and victim.

Nor can the issue be said to have been reliably advanced by expertise begun with missionaries and explorers, added to by photographers and folklorists, and, from the late nineteenth century onwards, given the stamp of science by anthropology. How far can the arising accounts reliably be thought to have articulated 'Indian' reality? Why, as a first consideration, should tribal informants ever have revealed all or anything like all to outsiders, especially in matters sacred? Do not the taxonomies of missionary religion, or of different explorer accounts, or for sure of anthropological social science, more reflect categoriser rather than categoried?

Anthropology in particular has come in for satiric treatment, fact parodied not only as, but in, fiction, typically Gerald Vizenor's *The Trickster of Liberty: Tribal Heirs to a Wild Baronage* (1988), with its Berkeley-style campus, purloined 'Indian relics' and shy at the academism as against trickster lives, and Michael Dorris's story 'Shining Agate', in his collection *Working Men* (1993), as the retelling of an Athabascan ice-fishing prank at the expense of its social-science investigators.

How, in other words, to meet in its historicity, and every variety, a Native

America enrolled and unenrolled, fullblood and crossblood, and, not the least of it, contemporary? In the latter respect, one also looks to the vast concourse of *mestizos* (Native-Spanish), *métis* (French-Canadian-Native) and, at just the slightest remove, America's Chicano and other Latino populations as born of Aztec-Castillian and related crossovers. In this, too, there cannot be overlooked Black-Native, Asian-Native, or even Jewish-Native mixedbloods, each a continuing part of the New World's pervasive *mestizaje* across Canada, the United States and Latin America. As the Mexican-Chicano performance artist Guillermo Gómez-Peña observes with considerable pertinence: 'How can the five hundred million *mestizos* who inhabit the Americas go on being called a "minority"?'[19]

Pope Julius II could decree in 1512 that Indians were to be thought descendants of Adam and Eve, the conferring of a Christian soul. But it did little to inhibit the Euro-American need to figure Native peoples as the 'other' of threat, rape, phantom death and, always, the obstacle to America's winning of the west. The latter phrase, in common with Manifest Destiny, could not more smack of civilisation over savagery.

Such, for long, conveniently kept out of sight the actual historic ravage and injustice, whether New England's treatment of the Pequots, or the forced removals of the Cherokee from Georgia to Oklahoma in 1835 after the discovery of gold on their land and now known as the Trail of Tears, or the killing of 500 or so Shoshone by Federal troops in 1863 at Bear River, Idaho, or the murder of the Cheyenne in the Battle of Wazita at Sand Creek, Colorado in 1864, or the unprovoked army attack on the Blackfeet at Marias River in 1870, or the culminatingly memorial massacre of Wounded Knee in 1890 which Gerald Vizenor has not been alone in calling the My Lai of American history. In this respect, the ignominious role of Oklahoma as forcing-ground, both the Territory and the State as it became in 1907, again requires emphasis, Indian Country for some thirty-plus removed tribal groupings – Apache to Osage, Kiowa to Medoc.

Nor, in matters of Native history, can the Bureau of Indian Affairs go unmentioned. Until 1849 under, revealingly, the War Department, and thereafter the Department of the Interior, the BIA has played nothing if not a quite decisive hand, whether through each appointed Indian Agent, through relocation, or through policy decisions to do with education, land rights, welfare and legal services. Be the starting point Columbus's first enslavement of his 'gentle' Arowaks in the 1490s, or Cortés's defeat of the Aztecs in 1521 with its subsequent *encomienda* slaveholding by the Spanish, or Anglo-Puritan settlement and warfare in Algonquin-named Massachusetts from the 1630s onwards, the westering impulse has found not only a language but a bureaucracy to sanction, and to perpetuate, colonisation.

Notwithstanding an exception like Roger Williams, Rhode Island's founder, the characteristic inflection is to be heard in Mary Rowlandson's celebrated *Narrative of the Captivity and Restauration of Mrs Mary Rowlandson* (1682), where she speaks of the Wampanaoags (the son of whose King Phillip would be sold into Caribbean slavery) as 'murderous wretches [by whom] I should choose rather to be killed . . . than taken alive'. Cotton Mather's *The Wonders of the Invisible World* (1693) saw appropriation of tribal land, again mainly Algonquin, as nothing if not mandated by Christian providence. 'The New Englanders', he writes with all the assurance of Calvinist mission, 'are a people of God settled in those which were once the devil's territories'.

Selective way-stations serialise the process, but what remains constant is precisely this insistent othering, the one collectivised fiction despite the evident variety of tribal culture. The line can be seen to have run from England's establishment of a Board of Commissioners in 1675 in Albany to handle 'Indian Affairs' to the Indian Removal Act in 1803, from Wounded Knee in 1890 to the Dawes General Allotment Act of 1906, and from the Citizenship Act of 1924 to the Wheeler-Howard/Indian Reorganization Act of 1934 and, of recent legislation, the Indian Freedom of Religion Act in 1978. Interpretation of the politics, the imaging, within this history remains wholly ongoing.

Something of this is to be seen in Korzack Ziolkowski's still-unfinished Black Hills rock sculpture of the Lakota-Sioux holy man, Crazy Horse (his actual Sioux name Tashuncauitco). It may well have been an intended counter to Mount Rushmore's Founding Fathers statuary. Yet to any number of Sioux it signals a double desecration, of the Black Hills or *Paha Sapa* meaning Sacred Land, and of the un-Sioux singling out of self over community. That, too, it is situated near Custer, South Dakota, as named after the US Cavalry's long-supposed martyr defeated by Crazy Horse and Sitting Bull at Little Big Horn in 1876, merely compounds the irony.

Latter-day land-claims, from Maine to Alcatraz, Massachusetts to Taos, again bring into play as much fiction as fact. Is this fair due or greed, a latest Indian generation calling time on history or simply an eye to the main chance? In one view, Native America, conspicuously, is owed restitution for land and resources seized, treaties broken. In another, it is a case of Indians as yet again troublesome, unaccommodating of federal or state statute. Liberal conscience especially turns several ways at once. Reclamation may be right, but are the tribal councils of the Chippewa-Ojibway, Mohawk and Paiutes, with their formidable casino and gambling empires, displaying self-reliance, latest American enterprise, or sell-out, a parody of American consumerism?

Equally a challenge to stereotype has been the 'Indian' response to environment. The pro-environment voice has been one thing, as with the Prairie Island Sioux's campaign against Minnesota's Northern State Power nuclear facility near the Upper Mississippi, or the Laguna Pueblo's attempts at redress against the health effects of the local uranium mine. But another, again especially upsetting to liberal well-wishers, has been the negotiation by a number of tribes, or more specifically their tribal councils, to accept nuclear waste on reservation land, the siting of so-called MRS or Monitored Retrieval Storage facilities (a number of tribespeople have asked – who better?). These latter include the Paiutes of Pyramid Lake, Nevada, and the Mescalero Apache in southern New Mexico, the latter unconsulted witnesses to an earlier era's Los Alamos and Manhattan Project atomic-bomb history. Similarly, there has been controversy about the Tuscarora of New York and the Suquanish of Washington State who have created cigarette factories: yet more enterprise, or a betrayal of eco-health, not to say of the once ceremonial-only uses of tobacco?

Views, fictions, once more run in cross-currents. Is this, whatever the economic advantages, a betrayal of ecological good practice or supposed 'Indian' earth values even if tribal people themselves have been known to cause pollution? On the other hand, does not the objection represent a latest form of liberal patronage, the tribes as incapable of making their own political decisions? Whichever holds, tribal no less than the rest of America has at no time been either unconflicted, or free of contradiction, and not least in the rise and increasing quantity of 'urban Indians'. Any one version, some all-purpose 'Indian', again fails to do even minimal service.[20]

Given these styles of paradox, it can be little wonder that, in customary trickster guise, Gerald Vizenor uses an Andy Warhol silkscreen acrylic image of Russell Means, luminary with Dennis Banks of AIM, in warrior regalia, for his cover to *Manifest Manners*. Braided, in a bone choker, apparently silent-wise in demeanour, a pastel brown-red daubed from his forehead to chest, Means looks to be the perfect brave – impassive and to be 'seen' as silent. In fact he is out of time, posed, painterly, a simulation, and truly a fiction, from a New York studio. The profile, in fact, might have been co-opted from Edward S. Curtis, the very image of an image.

Invoking Magritte's 'Ceci n'est pas une pipe', Vizenor sees the Means profile as symptomatic of each endlessly reiterated fiction of 'The Indian', a shadow, a wonderful, and indeed artful, travesty. He speaks of a 'double other'. In a phrase also repeated throughout *Manifest Manners*, and as though in countering obligation, he says of Warhol's fiction of 'the Indian', and implying all other simulations, 'This portrait is not an Indian'.

III

Mainstream American literature, along with its Canadian counterpart, has equally played a part as ambiguous as any in the making of 'Indian fictions'. If Puritan New England and Virginia can be said to have begun the story, the mythopoeia grows and thickens over time. For the New Republic era, Philip Freneau's reference to 'the ancients of the lands' in 'The Indian Burial Ground' (1786) adds more early nostalgia. Charles Brockden Brown's 'brawny and terrific' Indians in *Edgar Huntly* (1799) rework Gothic caricature. Washington Irving's portraits in *A Tour of the Prairies* (1835), *Astoria* (1835) and *The Adventures of Captain Bonneville* (1837) turn to the alternative typology of the tribes as heroic, figurings of Adamic renewal and health.

Incontestably, however, it is James Fenimore Cooper's five-part Leatherstocking cycle which supplies the best-known *mythus*. From *The Last of the Mohicans* (1826) onwards, Chingachgook enters Euro-American consciousness as the *beau idéal* of tribal typology, Good Indian to Magua as Bad Indian, or on D. H. Lawrence's reckoning 'wife' to Natty Bumppo. Michael Mann's 1993 movie of the novel, with Daniel Day-Lewis and Russell Means in the key roles, may well try for a politically correct update. But, no less than the original, and allowing for the novel's claims as early-American parable of frontier and rights of ownership, it also perpetuates one of the best-known, and enduring, of all fictions of 'Indians'.

The makers of the American Renaissance work most of the variations. In *The Narrative of Arthur Gordon Pym* (1838), Edgar Allan Poe contributes Dirk Peters, the mixedblood and distortedly muscled son of a fur-trader and 'an Indian woman of the tribe of Upsarokas'. In *Nature* (1836), Emerson's Transcendentalist manifesto envisages Columbus, and the Europe which bred him, nearing 'the shore of America; – before it, the beach lined with savages'. For Thoreau, in *Walden* (1852), tribal America embodies Nature's atavistic lodestones ('I have seen Penobscot Indians', he writes evidentially). Hawthorne, in line with his best-known genre, speaks in 'Roger Malvin's Burial' (1832) of Indian warfare as 'naturally susceptible of the moonlight of romance'. Whitman, in 'Song of Myself' (1855), includes in his vistas the 'Indian' as trader in memorabilia, trinketry, the 'squaw wrapt in her yellow-hemmed cloth . . . offering mocassins and beadbags for sale'.

It falls, perversely, to another easterner, the New York-born Herman Melville, sea-goer, whalerman, perhaps best to discern the dazzling elusiveness, the *trompe l'œil*, in American perceptions of 'the Indian'. Who more personifies the very fiction of 'the Indian' than the harpooner Queequeg in *Moby-Dick* (1851), if a South Seas Islander (from 'Kokovoko . . . a place not down on any map') then also the tattooed bearer of a tomahawk pipe of peace? Were further confirmation needed, Melville rarely bettered a chapter like 'The Metaphysics of Indian-Hating' in *The Confidence-Man* (1857), as canny a deflation of savagism as any he wrote.

Two subsequent writers can be said to anticipate the twentieth century. For all his otherwise enlightened racial views, Mark Twain in *The Adventures of Tom Sawyer* (1876) contributes the 'half-breed' Injun Joe, a stereotype as dire as any, and who dies as much encaved in the fearing white psyche as in any specific riverside Missouri. On another tack, one can turn to Helen Hunt Jackson's *A Century of Dishonor . . . A Sketch of the United States Government's Dealings with Some of the Indian Tribes* (1881), an angry, well-taken indictment of the duplicity of government, land speculator and Indian Agent alike.

Modern 'Indian' story looks to Willa Cather's *The Professor's House* (1925), with its contrast of attenuated modern America as against 'Blue Mesa' tribal America; William Faulkner's Yoknapatawpha cycle in its vast genealogical white, black and Chickasaw peopling; and Ernest Hemingway's Michigan 'Indian' sequence featuring Nick Adams in which Natives become the very sentinels for his code of grace under pressure.

In their wake, notably, have come Ken Kesey's *One Flew Over the Cuckoo's Nest* (1962), his Cautionary Tale of America as mental institution and with Chief Bromden as Native 'schizo' narrator; Thomas Berger's *Little Big Man* (1964) as frontier dark comedy of Native and homesteader lives caught up in the history of Custer, the Sioux and Little Big Horn in 1876; Arthur Kopit's send-up play of the Buffalo Bill legend in *Indians* (1968); and Tony Hillerman's ongoing Navajo-Pueblo police mystery series, few more striking than his Anasazi story *A Thief of Time* (1968) with Sergeant Jim Chee and Lieutenant Joe Leaphorn. Memorable as each is, their very attractiveness lies in the quality of fiction over fact.

White written discursive efforts at understanding Indian-Native disjuncture have by no means gone missing. Edmund Wilson was early into the fray with *Apologies to the Iroquois* (1959). Leslie Fiedler, in a typical show of flamboyance, turned to the 'Indians' of mainstream page and screen in *The Return of the Vanishing American* (1968). Dee Brown did seminal groundwork in seeking a Native perspective to American history, and especially the frontier, in *Bury My Heart at Wounded Knee* (1970). Each manages a degree of rejoinder to the mask, and the proliferation of counter-masks, in which Native America has been attired by non-Native America.[21]

IV

Given these often competing crosslights, how best for the Native author indeed to write Native fiction, to unauthor, as need be, each 'Indian fiction'? The arising ambiguities have been equally many and pose their own challenges. *The Life and Adventures of Joaquin Murieta, the Celebrated California Bandit* (1854), by the Cherokee-descended John Rollin Ridge, as the first known Native novel, actually offers Mexican thief adventure. It may well, however, imply an 'Indian', a Native, story, inside its tale of 'Spanish' dispossession and seizure. *Cogewea, the Half-Blood* (1927), by the Okanogan-born Mourning Dove (Christine Quintasket), the first novel by a Native woman, tells a stirring romance of mixedblood life yet in terms of Western ranch property and romance.

Sundown (1934), by John Joseph Mathews (Osage), turns to Oklahoma oil politics, on the one hand wild-scatting white bravura and on the other white-Osage interface and tribal disinheritance as centred in the mixedblood figure of Chal (for Challenge) Windzer. *The Surrounded* (1936), by D'Arcy McNickle (Cree-Metis, enrolled Salish), turns upon Archilde Leon, mixedblood son of a Flathead mother and Spanish father as heir to the spacious western Montana of the Salish, yet, finally, entrapped within the white–Native encounter acted out upon its terrain. Momaday's *House Made of Dawn* ushered in talk of a Native American Renaissance, in many ways a well-meant hurrah. But even that would bring into play more paradox, not to say vexation.

For allowing that less than a dozen Native-authored novels had hitherto been published, or that Momaday acknowledges knowing little at the time of Native writing, was this, again, to confirm some prior literary void? At the same time, if a renaissance, and literary scholarship to match, there has been, has that not led to ever greater excavation, a circling back into hitherto under-recognised ancestries of Native word and story? In fact, and no less than Momaday, the generation of Welch, Silko and Erdrich, not to mention Vizenor, are to be recognised as having emerged from anything but a Native literary vacuum.[22]

V

Midway into James Welch's *Winter in the Blood* (1974), his bemused and unnamed Montana Blackfeet narrator makes a near-classic observation: 'Again I felt that helplessness of being in a world of stalking white men' (p. 120). It carries all the novel's darkly laconic tone, the historic role-reversal of the hunter hunted. The one contemporary life, as may be, but the effect is to imply a larger, more collective dislocation, at once serious and yet often close to some comedy of errors. For all, too, the self-drift, drinking, absurd chance encounters, and each accusing shaft of memory, Welch's story is anything but one of sentimentality. It points, toughly and with acknowledgement of what has been lost, back into the sustenance of tribal legacy. To this end, Welch develops a first-person voice full of quizzicality in which worlds clash yet, often enough, overlap and even collude.

From his return home past the borrow-pit, with its implication of earth lost or evacuated, to his mother, Teresa First Raise, and her new husband Lame Bull, through to the epiphanous recognition of the blind Yellow Calf as his true Blackfeet grandfather as against 'the half-breed Doagie' (p. 159) and the funny-serious burial of his grandmother, the narrator might almost be snared in two landscapes. The one evokes literal Dodson, Montana, its township bars and commerce, along with his mother's Reservation valley holding of hay, alfalfa and fishing country. The other bears 'the presence of ghosts' (p. 159), the line of family which includes the snowdrift drunken death of First Raise, his father, and of Mose, the fourteen-year-old brother mangled and then killed in a cattle round-up whom the narrator might once have saved. Between the two, disjuncture indeed holds sway: 'I was as distant from myself as a hawk from the moon' (p. 2).

These different terrains throw up confusions, charades, which only slowly begin to clear. His Cree woman, whom he thinks to marry, unmanningly steals his gun and razor, then haunts him through the memory of her teeth made green by drinking crème de menthe. Nature itself can seem out of joint, 'cockeyed' as Yellow Calf, calls it, in which meadowlarks sing in mock-chorus, pheasants gabble, magpies as tricksters argue, a hawk shot by the narrator in childhood is remembered only for its unmoving tongue, his long-time horse 'Bird' dies pulled down by mud, and the fish have disappeared from the river.

The story of Amos, the pet duck which survives as its siblings drown, bespeaks another family given over to dysfunction, self-drowned. The episode shadows forward to the early tribal widowhood and abandonment of his grandmother; his mother's marriage to First Raise as drinker and who could make white men laugh, yet also a handyman, and who was found dead-frozen in the borrow-pit with his arm pointing homeward; and the narrator's always accusing culpability in the accident and death of Mose. Throughout an Eliotic note sounds, Montana, if once a Native ecology, then also now dry season, rainlessness, a place for grail and fisher-king.

Each encounter for the narrator adds to the displacement. Who, exactly, is the aeroplane man from Malta, clad in white hunter garb, carrying a teddy bear and five boxes of chocolate-covered cherries, and who hires him to get to Canada before his arrest by 'the two suits' as a possible FBI fugitive? His own mother's letter to the Harlem priest, with whom she drinks but who refuses Native parishioners burial in tribal ground, he finds himself, almost unself-comprehendingly, moved to destroy. His overnight encounter with the bar-fly Malvina, one in a line of several women, edges into fantasy, rough yet maudlin and even comic sex, with its bedroom gallery of the woman's photographs. All of these conflate in his hungover reverie, dream picaresque. The hitchhike back home, in which he gets a lift with a family of Hutterites, exposes him both to a father who asks if 'Indians' eat river turtles, having his picture taken like some curio, and a daughter the very instance of anaemia, a sickly whiteness.

Only in his understanding of the example of Yellow Calf, and the love and succour he once gave to the grandmother and to Teresa as the child he fathers with her, does the narrator begin to glimpse a way to confront the unbalance of his life. His bad leg, dating back to Mose's death, has localised the larger malaise, life lived at a limp. But Yellow Calf's revelation, and the linkage it supplies into a better order of Native being, together with the grandmother's burial, become processes of birth. For even as he wears his father's patched-up suit, Teresa dons red lipstick, coat, high heels and a black cupcake hat, Lame Bull makes a preposterous funeral speech, and the coffin fails to wedge evenly in the ground, rain has at last fallen again. The old lady's pouch, and with it her arrowhead, he himself returns to the earth. Absurdity, comic-absurdly as befits, has begun to dissolve.

As for the first time, and true to his age of thirty-two against the endless taunts of being called a boy, the narrator finds adulthood in a historic Blackfeet and Gros Ventre continuity of name, family, tribe, land, and call to health. He makes a self-promise to have his leg fixed and, a vintage touch of Welch irony, even marriage to his Cree. The signs of disjuncture remain, nowhere more so than in the inspired motley and rhetoric at the grandmother's funeral. But they do so also in relation to the signs of juncture, life over death. *Winter in the Blood* fuses a sense of carnival into seriousness, the narrator's life as Native *comédie humaine*, a jugglery, yet also the promise of order to be won from that same discordance.

VI

'Ts'its'tsi'nako, Thought Woman . . . is sitting in her room thinking of a story now/ I'm telling you the story/she is thinking' (p. 1). Leslie Marmon Silko's opening verse in *Ceremony* (1977) beckoningly, and quite exactly, gives the rationale of her novel. The account of Tayo as damaged Second World War returnee, as mixedblood, and as linked into the Laguna reservation drought and the nearby Los Alamos atomic tests, could not imply a more evident contemporaneity. At every turn, however, and within the sunrise-to-sunrise frame, Silko grounds her novel in, and makes it a parallel with, a Laguna-Keres and allied story of creation-myth, witchery, vision quest and healing. This sustained interaction, a double fiction doubly told, has deservedly won the novel a centre place within Native American fiction.

The intertextual link to *House Made of Dawn* has been much noted. But Silko's novel is, and remains, emphatically her own, a narrative about 'ceremony' yet, reflexively, itself that self-same ceremony. At the opening, Tayo's 'humid dreams of black night' (p. 5), his 'fever voices' (p. 6), and specifically the Pacific jungle killing of his uncle Josiah and cousin Rocky, along with Japanese soldiery, are said to be tangled up 'like colored threads from old Grandma's wicker sewing basket' (p. 6). At the close, and after the war-veteran deaths of Harley and Pinkie, and the banishment of Emo, yet also Tayo's restoration from the 'battle fatigue' (p. 31) which has caused him repeatedly to drink and vomit, Old Grandma observes: ' "It seems like I already heard these stories before . . . only thing is, the names sound different" ' (p. 260). This reiteration Silko tells in terms of Tayo's literal return to Laguna, yet also of his return to a sustaining myth-world, a cosmos which coheres.

In this, his passage takes him through the encounters with key healing medicine figures. Ku'oosh starts the process with his herbs, bundles and 'old dialect'. Josiah's paramour, Night Swan, part-Mexican dancer of flamenco, prophetess, and herself an incarnation of Thought Woman, gives him love and vision of the pathway to recovery. The Navajo healer Betonie, who updates the ceremonies with his telephone books and similar items, recentres him through sandpainting, prayer-stick, ritual cut, and the five hoops, and sends him on to find the missing spotted cattle. The healer-lover Ts'eh Montaño, an incarnation of Yellow Woman and companion to the Mountain Lion Man, gives him power to resist further 'witchery', whether his own (the refusal to kill Emo) or that visited on, and perpetuated by, the white world. He regains, however slowly or at cost, tongue (early described as 'the carcass of a tiny rodent', p. 15), body, and indeed, finally, enters the kiva as himself newborn medicine man, for the moment at least, both the healed and healer.

In situating Tayo's story within each legend of Corn and Reed Woman, Ck'o'yo and other tricksters, Hummingbird, Pollen Boy, and their spirit company, Silko unravels a story both actual and ethnomythic. Her protagonist's war zones, abroad, at home, or in figures of drift like Emo or the Apache-Ute woman Helen Jean from Towac reservation, she tells as wholly specific in time and place. Yet it is a place synchronous with, and to be understood through, a tribal vision of the world. Illness and cure, whether of Tayo, or of postwar Laguna itself, is told throughout *Ceremony* as literal, yet also as though the shadow-act of the 'fifth world' (p. 68).

In the one, the terms in play arise out of Philippine warfare, post-traumatic disorder, 'white' hospital treatment, bars, the barbed-wire fencing of the land (Tayo's quest for the lost cattle comes up against such fencing), the drought, and ultimately the bomb. In the other, they are those of Pa'caya'nyi's bad magic (pp. 46–9) or the mythical witch gathering ('It was Indian witchery that made white people in the first place', p. 132), against which the deities of sun, cloud, corn and water provide good stories and tribal ceremonies of health. In depicting Tayo's course, from death-in-life ('He was tired of fighting off the dreams and the voices', p. 26) to his own sunrise, Silko writes the one and yet the multiple fiction and, at every turn, with a command of style to match.

VII

As typical a moment as any in Louise Erdrich's *The Beet Queen* occurs when Russell Kashpaw, Chippewa from North Dakota and a Korean war veteran, is honoured by his state as its 'most decorated hero'. In fact Russell has been shot to pieces, has become an alcoholic, and needs a wheelchair after suffering a stroke. As the celebrants mill about, he sees himself as if in a Chippewa death vision:

> this was the road that old-time Chippewas talked about, the four-day road, the road of death. He'd just started out.
> I'm dead now, he thought with calm wonder.
> At first he was sorry that it had happened in public, instead of some private place. Then he was glad, and he was also glad to see that he hadn't lost his sense of humor even now. It struck him as so funny that the town he'd lived in and the members of the American Legion were solemnly saluting a dead Indian, that he started to shake with laughter. (p. 300)

A number of Erdrich hallmarks come into play: tribal history as a mix of defeat and victory, the 'four-day road' to indicate Chippewa cosmology, the smack at stereotype as, once again, in 'The only good Indian is a dead Indian', and the irony which can envisage the transformation of Russell as maimed 'dead' Indian into all-American 'live' patriot. Russell's musings, moreover, give off just the right laconi-cism, tough, rueful, yet free of self-pity. In building this, and the rest of her Chippewa world at the US–Canada border, Erdrich barely misses a step, lives, families and histories webbed, or intercircled, one into the other, and yet, at the same time, full of missed connection like the history behind their making.

'Indian', for Erdrich, has never meant cheerfully harmonious tribal community. If, figuratively, there is indeed an 'Indian' pattern to her fiction, one of revolving wheel, then it is a wheel as often broken as not, full of odd spokes, shards, lives caught out by circumstance. Her story-logic so foregoes all easeful circularity in favour of doublings-back, switches, events subject to their own paradoxical rounds of fracture. Characters, mainly from Chippewa dynasties like the Kashpaws, Lamartines and Morrisseys, touch, move on, intermarry and feud, always persuasively human, yet as if the inhabitants of an only dimly perceived circle within America's upper midwest.

Taken in sequence, both *The Beet Queen*, and story-cycles like *Love Medicine* (1984, expanded version 1993) and *Tracks* (1988), would seem to move back and forth through both space and time, in one perspective three decades of Argus, North Dakota, and its surrounding reservations and burial grounds, and in another Chippewa history from the turn of the century down into the 1980s. Yet novel or cycle each functions as complete in itself. Erdrich genuinely startles and compels, her early work quick to win an accolade from Philip Roth as 'the most interesting new novelist to have appeared in years'.

At first sight, *The Beet Queen* indeed suggests something less than Native-centred narrative, which is not to say the Kashpaws and their kin do not make frequent appearances. But the novel's 'Indianness' lies as much in its oblique style of narrative as in any given explicit 'Indian' theme. If wheel or hoop are to be thought 'Indian', then the story, as it doubles back and forth on itself, almost turns inside out that sense of circle.

Told across a thirty-year span and again through linking first-person voices, *The*

Beet Queen opens with Mary and Karl Adare, aged eleven and fourteen respectively in 1932, who arrive illicitly by boxcar in Argus, North Dakota, to claim kin with Fritzie and Pete, their aunt and uncle and the owners of Kozka's Meats. Their mother, Adelaide, recently widowed and nothing if not crazy for romance, has dumped not only them but also a newborn baby brother to fly south from Minnesota to Florida with the Great Omar, a none-too-successful aviator stuntman. It is a first of many separations, lives whose connection is their apparent disconnection.

At Argus, the two Adare children themselves part company. Karl, alarmed by a fierce dog, jumps back on the train only to find himself in the amorous clinch of a hobo who rejoices in the name of Giles Saint Ambrose. Despite believing he has found love, Karl plunges out of the train, only to break both his legs and be nursed back to health by the journeying Fleur Pillager, Chippewa medicine woman. Subsequently raised in a Catholic orphanage, he then takes to the road as a salesman of farm and household gadgetry, still to find connection, love, nexus. Mary, meantime, goes about the wheel of her life in shared disjunctive manner. Her girlhood she spends in fierce tension with her disturbed, glamour-struck cousin Sita, in childhood the human centre of what Argus dubs a religious miracle yet also a spinsterish Old Maid and purveyor of beef and pork who takes over the meat business. Hers, too, has become oddity, a life at the circle's rim.

The lives of the two Adares, however, are but two spokes in the wheel. Celestine James, part-Indian and Mary's lifelong friend, allows Karl to father a child on her, whom Mary virtually adopts and promptly names Dot. But Dot's actual given name is Wallacene. This links us to Wallace Keff, also Dot's self-appointed guardian and the bachelor president of the Argus Chamber of Commerce. Wallace is the man responsible for introducing sugar beet into the region as a sure-fire cash crop. His life, in turn, circles into that of Karl Adare. For he lives with a lonely secret. The only experience which in any way transforms an otherwise stale round of Babbittry is his darkly comic sexual encounter with Mary's driven but seductive brother. Clementine, too, contributes her brother to the ongoing circle, namely Russell Kashpaw, the Korean war veteran more dead than alive. He, if no one else, can see his own breakage inside the Chippewa wheel.

It is to Dot, however, that the novel finally reverts, with further linking turns into the lives of Adelaide, Sita, the lost Adare who surfaces as Father Miller, a Catholic priest, and others in the Kashpaw and related dynasties. As Wallace Keff intends it, Dot will be the Queen in Argus's Sugar Beet Festival. But, again, the wheel turns unexpectedly. She sees that things have been rigged in her favour, gives way to a fury of her own, and, like her grandmother Adelaide before her, takes to the skies. That is, she soars off with the local skywriting pilot, only to wheel back to earth when the main events of the festival are over; a last ironic 'Indian' circling indeed.

One vital clue to the links which bring together all these lives resides in an observation made by Celestine James as she watches with her newborn baby by Karl a small white spider busy about its labours: 'A web was forming, a complicated house, that Celestine could not bring herself to destroy' (p. 176). Louise Erdrich could not have spoken better to her novel in its deftly managed apparent illogic. This is a tale bordering on magic, magic history, perhaps, as much as magic realism. For *The Beet Queen* manages to captures the oddity of lives connected in discontinuity, against appearances their own kind of 'Indian circle'.

VIII

Fictions of Indians. Native fictions. The dialectic is far from lost on Thomas King, of mixed Cherokee and Greek stock, raised in California's Central Valley, and long resident in Canada. Looking back to nineteenth-century portraiture of Native life in *All My Relations: An Anthology of Contemporary Canadian Native Fiction* (1990), he recognises the romance, the beckoning power, of mythic Indianness, and at the same time calls for its end:

> The literary stereotypes and cliches for which the period is famous have been, I think, a deterrent to many of us. Feathered warriors on Pinto ponies, laconic chiefs in full regalia, dusky, raven-haired maidens, demonic shamans with eagle-claw rattles and scalping knives are all picturesque and exciting images, but they are, more properly, servants of a non-Native imagination. Rather than try to unravel the complex relationship between the nineteenth-century Indian and the white mind, or to craft a new set of images that still reflects the time but avoids the flat, static depiction of the Native and the two-dimensional quality of the culture, most of us have consciously set our literature in the present, a period that is reasonably free of literary monoliths and which allows for greater latitude in the creation of characters and situations, and, more important, allows us the opportunity to create for ourselves and our respective cultures both a present and a future.

The observation throws a necessary light upon his *Medicine River* (1990), King's portrait of contemporary tribal life, likely Blackfeet, both on the Reserve as the Canadianism has it, and in the nearby township. For all that the novel turns beautifully on trickster humour, a revolving circuit of tease and understatement, there can be little doubt as to its astute seriousness of aim.

'I was used to conversations with Harlen that didn't make much sense and didn't seem to go anywhere' (p. 169). The speaker is Will Sampson, son of Rose Horse Captive and an absentee, long-dead white father who worked in rodeo, describing his friend and *alter ego* Harlen Bigbear. For Harlen it is, community fixer, benign trickster, tribal good spirit, who has brought Will back from Toronto to the Medicine River of Canadian prairie and the Rockies. There he has shrewdly finagled him into setting up his photography business (wonderfully against stereotype given the view of 'Indians' as spooked at the thought of their spirit being stolen by the camera), made him play basketball for the Medicine River Friendship Center team, and sought to get him married to Louise Heavyman, single mother of South Wing, herself teasingly named not after some Indian Princess but after the hospital ward where she was born.

Harlen, in fact, serves as the very figuration of modern Native life, a fixer and mender of lives (some of them in his basketball team like Floyd and Elwood). Yet King makes him no cartoon Noble Indian, all spirituality and oneness with Nature. Harlen Bigbear falls ill with flu, loves tattle and gossip, and typically misreads maps, even getting lost at, of all places, the Little Bighorn. Unlike, too, some latterday Chingachgook or Hiawatha, and having had Will buy, and help repair, an old canoe in a yard sale, he manages to crash it in the whitewater of the upper Medicine River. He is said, contemporarily, to like 'basketball . . . cars . . . golf' (p. 201). For all his savvy, he can also find himself treading lightly round Bertha Morley's scheme, as he mistakenly believes it, to marry him after she has advertised herself in 'The Calgary Centre for the Development of Human Potential' as 'a Blood Indian woman in good health . . . I like to go fishing and hunting, and I play bingo every Thursday' (p. 178).

Will Sampson becomes the recorder, and quite literal image-maker, of Harlen's Medicine River, a kind of *Winesburg, Ohio* George Willard figure, who also frequently brings into play the memory of his own boyhood as a 'non-status Indian' with his brother James and hard-pressed mother. The family thus has both tribe and city in their make-up, an Indianness of the Rockies and Calgary, the Reserve and tough, economically hard-pressed urban life. Each photographic image Will processes in his studio, and its writing-up as story, helps fill out his own circle as much as the reader's.

This holds for his close encounters with not only Harlen and Louise but also the bingo antagonists Big John Yellow Rabbit and Eddie Weaselhead, the 'marriage doctor' Martha Oldcrow, January Pretty Weasel as abused tribal wife, Harlen's storyteller brother, Joe Bigbear, the tribal elder Lionel James, and the self-divided AIM *aficionado* David Plume. Each builds into a live and overall Medicine River, 'Indians now' as it were. Even Will's sense of place changes and grows, Medicine River if a modern Canada, and within it a modern Alberta, of TV, fast food, pick-up trucks, federal and provincial government and the RCMP (or Mounties), then also, an older tribal world of Chief Mountain and Ninastiko with its ceremonies, trickster myths and play.

King's achievement is to write neither nostalgia nor case-study. *Medicine River*, rather, carries its stories as performative, the oral lightly assumed in the written. Motifs old and new blend. The 'leather rattle made of willow and deer hide', for instance, which Will receives from Martha Oldcrow, serves as a Native form of the 'musical top' he buys for South Wing and which, in parallel, makes 'a sweet, humming sound, the pitch changing as it [spins] in its perfect circle' (pp. 260–1). As Will's insights deepen into Harlen's obliquities, not to say into Medicine River itself, and his own rite-of-passage, the novel overall shows a tribal past making its own kind of way into the present.

At one point, even so, Joe Bigbear looks back on his world trips, pondering how the world prefers its 'Indian stories' to be rooted in the 'olden days' versions:

But those people in Germany and Japan and France and Ottawa want to hear about how Indians used to be. I got some real good stories, funny ones, about how things are now, but those people say, no, tell us about the olden days. So I do. (p. 173)

The point perfectly reflects on *Medicine River*'s own workings, a world of present over past, live substance over dead shadow.

For his part, Will thinks of the air flights in which he has fantasised for fellow passengers the father who indeed was the itinerant, drink-addled 'rodeo cowboy' (p. 80), and whose letters he once read to his mother's anger and upset. He makes him into a 'senior engineer with Petro-Canada' (p. 78), a pilot, a career diplomat, and perhaps most to the point given his own vocation, a photographer (p. 80). It throws a fittingly reflexive cast on the novel at large: *Medicine River*'s imaging of Native legacy as always dynamic, as capable as any other of its own inventions or, if need be, its own counter-inventions.

IX

In her poem 'Neighbors' Linda Hogan has a run of lines which might do good service as a prologue to her novel *Mean Spirit* (1990):

> In this country, men have weapons
> they use against themselves
> and others. It is the dying
> watching death. Light a candle.[23]

The story on offer is one of a turn-of-the-century Osage dynasty caught out, murderously, by Oklahoma oil politics – oil, in one of the novel's recurrent images, as the earth's seeping 'blood'. Densely and adroitly webbed throughout, told at gathering pace, and given a large cast of players from oil-scatters to Hill Indians, and from the sinister fixer John Hale to the legendary coyote ghost John Stink, it secures its own 'Indian' mystery-story out of a true American conspiracy still fully to be given light or, indeed, resolution.

Beginning with the unsolved murder in 1922 of beautiful, oil-rich Grace Blanket, Osage fullblood, then the adoption of her daughter Nola by Belle and Moses Greycloud and their extended family, and moving from the invented Oklahoma town of Watona to Washington DC from where the Lakota-born agent, Stacey Red Hawk, takes up the detection, Hogan recreates a tale whose own turns, corners and entanglements she transposes into a genuinely encompassing narrative.

At one level, this is Warren Harding's America as land-grab, a predatory, anything-goes Gatsbyism, with the Osage, like other tribal people pre-1924, in law a non-citizenry whose lands become fenced in, and out, as much by statue and picket as by each instalment in the 'ring of murders' (p. 242). Not that *Mean Spirit* gives way to victim history; quite the contrary. For another level operates, primarily that of Grace's Osage legacy, as carried forward by the Greyclouds and Nola.

It is first to be met with in the surreal, near-oneiric, 'silent bedchamber' opening scene, indoor beds placed outdoors to deal with the nights of an Oklahoma summer. The linkages to the novel's other Native lore are many: the sacred fire maintained by the water-diviner Michael Horse, and whose almanac, *The Book of Horse*, he shows only to Stacey; Sorrow Cave, the many-chambered sacred Osage refuge with its bats and memorial pictographic wall drawings; the Hill Indian watcher-runners who keep guard over Nola; the stallion, Red Shirt, sought and respected by Horse; and Belle's bees which attack and kill the ill-intending Sheriff Gold ('Bees were like Indians, Belle thought to herself, with a circular dance, working together for the survival of the next generations', p. 312).

None of these, for sure, stops the murders of Grace, or a community which includes Benoit, John Thomas, Walker, the Indian deputy Willis, and others. Nor does it wholly explain the role of Hale, or the lawyer Forrest whose son, Will, marries Nola, or the photographer John Tate who finally kills his own wife Ruth, twin sister of Moses Greycloud, or even the deathly black Buick which delivers the killers. For the conspiracy, from 'Watona' to Osage murders elsewhere in America, and even as far away as England, Hogan tells as an always elusive thread, and whose origins lie as much in the federal government as in local Oklahoma white greed and connivance.

Hogan is equally careful not to make all whites into villainy, as Hale's one-time mistress, China, and the departing physician, Dr Black, give witness. Native life equally has its push-and-pull divides, as in the case of the grandson, Ben Greystone, or Belle's daughter, or the fate of the mixedblood preacher Joe Billy and his wife as they work their way out of Baptist Christianity back towards Native belief. Stacey, modern law agent, increasingly remembers his own meaning as a Sioux. But it is the immersion of the Osage themselves, most of all the Hill Osage, in their own sense of time and place and threatened as may be, which offers a counter-resource to the dire workings of the oil conspiracy to hand.

Like King, Hogan in no way veers towards sentimentality. The novel ends, toughly, with the land indeed lost and scarred by rigs and boreholes and the Greyclouds themselves in flight. Hogan's novel can in this respect be thought a species of palimpsest, a Native version of history written over, or at the interstices of, Oklahoma as 'Indian Country'. *Mean Spirit* gives notice of a mystery whose true meaning, its feints and shadows, even for Hogan still await their solution.

X

Louis Owens's *Wolfsong* (1991) makes its Indian Country the Pacific Northwest, specifically the wooded, part-glacier, North Cascades of Washington State, ancestral home of the Salish people, whether Stehemish, Stillaguamish or Skagit. In Tom Joseph's return from college in California, his taking-up of his uncle's wolf mantle, the different visions which take him back into a recovery of his own Native identity, and his eventual retributive dynamiting of a huge water-tank linked to the Honeycutt Copper local mining operation, he becomes a figure both of tribal return and escape, at once self-found and yet fugitive.

In this, Owens's own Forest Service background evidently helps. The landscape and animal scenes are written not only from an experienced observer's eye but from a sense of their past place in the Salish cosmos. The allusions to old-growth cedar, raven, bear, deer, coyote, sweatlodge, and Dakobed as 'the great mother mountain' (p. 88), known in English as Glacier Peak, underlie, and serve as ironic comment on, the copper-mining, logging, and J. D. Hill's road-building operations.

A nice byplay, too, is kept up not only in Tom's loss of his one-time girl, Karen, to Buddy, JD's son, but in the running taunts and cynicism of his beer-swilling brother, Jimmy. A whole community play of opposite forces, in fact, comes into play: Martin Grider, the Forest Ranger, as against Dan Keller, mouthpiece for the mining interests; the well-meaning white loggerman, Vern Reece, as against Buddy and white bullyboy accomplices like Jake Tobin; Jim Joseph's sympathetic white friend, Sam Gravey, as against Mad John, a kind of Holy Fool preacher; and Tom's mixedblood Flathead college friend, McBride, alongside Karen, herself part-Cherokee, as against the white miners.

The essential equation, however, resides in Tom Joseph with his uncle, Jim Joseph, for whose funeral he has returned in the first place. As the 'crazy Indian' who shoots at the roadmakers' machines, Jim Joseph speaks of having seen the ghosts of ancestors, heard chants, and talked to birds and animals. Finally he bequeaths his own 'wolfsong', and with it each inlaid tribal value, to the returnee. It becomes Tom's own inner voice. *Wolfsong*, thereby, takes up Salish lineage as rite-of-memory and yet, and at the same time, its necessary furthering into the future.

In finding himself called to assume his uncle's mantle, one generation for another, Tom takes on Honeycutt Copper and its corporate ethos of cash return and land abuse. But he equally smacks out at hobbyist Sierra Clubbers. His eventual flight, having counter-mined the company's holdings, and with perhaps an echo of the flight of Chief Joseph and his Nez Percé people to the Canadian border in 1873, gives its own gloss to history as repetition. Owens's debut novel offers its own Cautionary Tale, Salish-Cascades and Northwest in its setting as may be, yet a fiction which shrewdly, and throughout, also implies the wholly larger time and landscape of Native America.

XI

'Thomas Builds-the-Fire's stories climbed into your clothes like sand, and gave you itches that could not be scratched' (p. 15). ' "I'm a recovering Catholic" ' (p. 146). 'Nobody ever notices the sober Indians' (p. 151) Few novels, Native-written or otherwise, can quite have made their bow with a wit as punchily comic, and yet serious, as Sherman Alexie's *Reservation Blues* (1995).

The touch is playful, full of well-targeted satiric tease, yet perfectly alive to defeat, even pathos. The novel's Spokane Reservation world has its share of HUD substandard housing, basketball, alcohol babies, competing churches and tribal infighting. But it can also be one of myth, dream memories, jumps in time, benign fakers like 'the end of the world . . . crazy old Indian man' known as 'the-man-who-was-probably-Lakota' (p. 11) and an overseeing musical shaman like Big Mom of nearby Wellpinit Mountain. As in his subsequent full-length fiction, short stories and poetry, Alexie shows himself always the storyteller marvellously quick on his feet, a master of the revels.

From the magical arrival at the reservation crossroads of Robert Johnson, legendary bluesman with his guitar music born of his compact with the devil, white and known as 'the Gentleman', through to the rise of Coyote Springs as a 'warrior band' (p. 77) albeit a rock band, the novel pursues an odyssey across an America of 'Indians' real and imagined. Thomas, 'the misfit storyteller of the Spokane tribe' (p. 5), serves throughout as part goodfellow, part savant and visionary. With Victor Joseph, drinker and bully yet who inherits the guitar and indeed plays like the devil, Junior Polatkin, his binge partner and uncertain drummer, and the two Flatfoot Tribe sisters, Chess and Checkers Warm Water, who sing back-up, together at first with the blonde 'New Age princesses' in turquoise strings and beads, Betty and Veronica, he seeks to make music, 'reservation blues', as a stay against confusion, his own story of understanding.

The results lead into cavalcade, picaresque, from Spokane Indian Reservation to Arlee, Montana as the first of a slew of tavern and other gigs, and from a disastrous visit to a New York recording studio to an eventual journey in Thomas's iconic blue van to Seattle. Each episode en route does bittersweet, and often bitingly funny, service. Johnson's guitar early speaks in its own voice ('The blues always makes us remember', p. 22). CIA and FBI agents disguise themselves as Indians 'but didn't fool anybody because they danced like shit' (p. 34). Father Arnold hovers deliciously between spirit and flesh, between his mission to the Spokane and his passion for Checkers. Thomas's journal lists entries for Coyote. Envious reviews of the group appear in the tribal press (p. 83), not least at the behest of the Tribal Chairman, David Walks Along, whose muscled convict-nephew, Michael White Hawk, exudes threat. A remembered half-fantasy basketball game between Samuel, Thomas's drunkard father, and the cops, becomes a replay of past 'Indian wars'.

Each fade and dissolve happens at high pace, a fiction of fast-moving fictions. Alexie especially shows his paces when Cavalry Records, under the commercial management of latter-day intertextual 'generalship' like that of Phil Sheridan and George Wright, and they, in turn, under a boss named Mr Armstrong, offers the group a studio try-out ('Indians are big these days', p. 224). History, kind of, replays itself. The group, Victor Joseph at least, becomes 'too violent' and trashes the studio. Betty and Veronica, stage Indians to a fault, become the acceptable purveyors of tribal music.

In turn, Big Mom comes to think 'Indian men have started to believe their own publicity and run around acting like the Indians in the movies' (p. 208). Victor trades in Junior to the Devil even as Robert Johnson receives a cedar flute from Big Mom, a life for a death. As he drives out of the reservation, with Chess and Checkers, Thomas finds songs for all the warrior horse spirits of 'Indians' dead and alive (p. 306). The note is fond, restorative, the perfect visionary follow-on to all the mediating comedy of *Reservation Blues*.

XII

In Betty Louise Bell's *Faces in the Moon* (1994), her narrator Lucy Evers, college teacher in California, a recent divorcee from a Jewish husband, and like Bell herself a Cherokee mixedblood daughter, returns to Oklahoma to witness the dying of her long-put-upon yet wayward mother. Lucy summons the Evers lineage as through 'women's voices' and from across a 'kitchen table' (p. 4), a family in which she has grown up as passed-around 'Indian child' and as the grown woman who 'every year [becomes] more Indian' (p. 33). Her homecoming stirs 'thick memory' (p. 33), a litany of anti-romance:

> Dust, outlaws, pretty black-eyed women raising children alone, chopping their way through cotton, good ol' boys and no-good men. Full-blooded grand-mothers, mixedblood renegades and lost generations, whirling across the red earth in forty-nine Chevys, drunk on homemade beer, and aged by years of craving under the hot Oklahoma sun. (p. 5)

The voices which speak to this memory play one into the other, witness and accusation, comfort and recrimination. They each, in turn, however particular, even idiosyncratic, have their origins in the spiral begun from Cherokee displacement and dispossession.

Gracie Evers, never much above poverty, defiantly yet pathetically goes on repeating her credo as one of 'Don't mess with Indian women', to be emulated, always, by her sister's 'Naw, I sure wouldn't wanna do that'. In her drift from man to man, drinking, newspaper cuttings and second-hand clothing, Gracie becomes the perfect gatherer-up of white America's trifles. From the Depression onwards, and in an Oklahoma whose shacks lies in the shadow of historic Fort Sill, hers has been a world of margins, loss more than gain.

Her sister Rozella, known as Auney, plays Gracie's companion colloquist, also a 'lost generation' daughter of Hellen Evers, the grandmother who at her death 'told my mother, then nine years old, would always be watching her from the moon' (p. 56). Auney, equally, lives a life of make-do, aping white fashion to the point where she peroxides her hair to calamitous effect, a woman always voluble yet as uncentred as her sibling.

From a generation before them stands the redoubtable Great Aunt Lizzie Sixkiller Evers, fullblood keeper of Cherokee wisdom, austere Christian, TB-sufferer, and a farmwoman and purveyor of family chronicle who, for a while, raises Lucy. In her, Lucy finds a more complete voice of the history which has made her the child dreamer who once shouted ' "I am Quanah Parker!" ' in identification with the great Kwahadi Comanche leader of the South Plains, eventual cattle-rancher, and mover in the use of peyote out of which would arise the Native American Church. Lizzie acts as a means for Lucy to go back in memory to the 1835 Trail of Tears, to imagine the first Dawes Act tribal enrolment interview of the Georgia-born Robert H. Evers, to call up the Dust Bowl's impact on tribal life, and to situate the Evers line in the larger history of Cherokee names and places.

Accordingly, Lucie writes not the romance of her own child-notebooks which she finds among her mother's belongings, but the ply of hope and poverty in her long, winding family-tribal ancestry. Asked 'What's it like being an Indian?' (p. 59), her reply carries a perfect impatience with fictions and stereotype: 'I wish I had Indian stories, crazy and romantic vignettes . . . Anything to make myself equal to their romance. Instead I can offer only a picture of Momma's rented house, a tiny flat two-bedroom shack in a run-down part of town' (p. 59). Years later, too, when seeking out the Dawes Commission's Cherokee Rolls, an encounter with a supercilious white male librarian at the Oklahoma Historical Society brings on her writer-memorialist's latest answering act of voice, nothing other than 'I am your worst nightmare: I am an Indian with a pen' (p. 192). The riposte does related kinds of duty. For sure, it summarises the edge, the well-placed remembrance, of Bell's own *Faces in the Moon*. Equally it carries forward, with an abruptness surely justified, the resolve of Native America's writers as to their own terms of literary imagining for Native identity.

The kinds of new fiction in evidence, typically, include novels like *The Jailing of Cecilia Capture* (1985) by Janet Campbell Hale (Coeur d'Alene) with its unsparing California portrait of city mixedblood womanhood; *Firesticks* (1993) by Diane Glancy (Cherokee) as an imagist novella of mixedblood heritage, story threads and travel; *The Light People* (1994) by Gordon Henry (Anishinaabe) as a circle of story-soliloquies linking the Ojibway-Chippewa past to present; and *Eye Killers* (1995) by A. A. Carr (Navajo-Laguna Pueblo) with its updated vampire fable as a way into delineating white–Native culture encounter in New Mexico.

These, in shared spirit with Bell's novel, confirm the legacy of 'Indians with a pen', of Native over Indian fictions, and the promise of a quite different literary order of American territories ahead.

NOTES

1. Vine Deloria (1969), *Custer Died for Your Sins: An Indian Manifesto*, New York: Macmillan, p. 10. Reprinted (1988), Norman, OK: University of Oklahoma Press.
2. Leslie Marmon Silko (1981), *Storyteller*, New York: Arcade Publishing, p. 6.
3. Gerald Vizenor (1994), *Manifest Manners: Postindian Warriors of Survivance*, Hanover, NH and London: Wesleyan University Press, pp. 11, 31.
4. Key historical accounts include Alvin M. Josephy (1968), *The Indian Heritage of America*, New York: Knopf; Dee Brown (1970), *Bury My Heart at Wounded Knee: An Indian History of the American West*, New York: Holt, Rinehart and Winston; Angie Debo (1970), *A History of the Indians of the United States*, Norman, OK: University of Oklahoma Press; William Sturtevant (ed.) (1978), *Handbook of North American Indians*, Washington, DC: Smithsonian; Robert M. Utley (1984), *The Indian Frontier of the American West, 1846–1890*, Albuquerque NM: The University of New Mexico Press; Ward Churchill (1994), *Indians Are Us? Culture and Genocide in Native North America*, Monroe, ME: Common Courage; Alvin M. Josephy (1994), *500 Nations: An Illustrated History of North American Indians*, New York: Knopf; and Roger L. Nichols (1998), *Indians in the United States and Canada: A Comparative History*, and edn, Lincoln, NB: University of Nebraska Press.
5. Leslie Marmon Silko (1977), *Ceremony*, New York: Viking Press; Gerald Vizenor (1998), *Fugitive Poses: Native American Indian Scenes of Absence and Presence*, Lincoln, NB: University of Nebraska Press.

6. Gerald Vizenor (1978), *Darkness in Saint Louis Bearheart*, St Paul, MN: Truck Press, revised and reprinted (1990) as *Bearheart: The Heirship Chronicles*, Minneapolis, MN: University of Minnesota Press; izener (1987), *Griever: An American Monkey King in China*, Normal, IL: Illinois State University and Fiction Collective; and *Chancers* (2000), Norman, OK: University of Oklahoma Press. Among the liveliest, and sometimes contentious, literary accounts of Native fiction are Charles R. Larson (1978), *American Indian Fiction*, Albuquerque, NM: University of New Mexico Press; Alan Velie (1982), *Four American Indian Literary Masters: N. Scott Momaday, James Welch, Leslie Marmon Silko and Gerald Vizenor*, Norman, OK: University of Oklahoma Press; Arnold Krupat (1989), *The Voice in the Margin: Native American Literature and the Canon*, Berkeley, CA: University of California Press; Gerald Vizenor (ed.) (1989), *Narrative Chance: Postmodern Discourse on Native American Indian Literatures*, Albuquerque, NM: University of New Mexico; and, as notable a study as any published to date, Louis Owens (1992), *Other Destinies: Understanding the American Indian Novel*, Norman, OK: University of Oklahoma Press; and James Ruppert (1995), *Mediation in Contemporary Native American Fiction*, Norman, OK: University of Oklahoma Press. Few better accounts of pan-American Native culture exist than Gordon Brotherston (1993), *Book of the Fourth World: Reading the Native Americas through their Literature*, New York: Cambridge University Press.
7. Quite one of the fullest analyses is to be found in Robert F. Berkhover Jr (1978), *The White Man's Indian: Images of the American Indian from Columbus to the Present*, New York: Knopf. This, subsequently, has been supplemented by Fergus M. Bordewich (1996), *Killing the White Man's Indian: Reinventing Native Americans at the End of the Twentieth Century*, New York: Anchor-Doubleday.
8. Elizabeth Cook-Lynn (1991), *From the River's Edge*, New York: Arcade, and (1996) *Why I Can't Read Wallace Stegner and Other Essays: A Tribal Voice*, Madison, WI: University of Wisconsin Press, p. 30.
9. For a wide-ranging analysis of these simulations, see S. Elizabeth Bird (ed.) (1996), *Dressing in Feathers: The Construction of the Indian in American Popular Culture*, Boulder, CO: Westview Press. An earlier study covering the ground is Raymond William Stedman (1982), *Shadows of the Indian: Stereotypes in the Twentieth Century*, Norman, OK: University of Oklahoma Press. The issue takes more abrasive form in Bordewich (op. cit.).
10. See Theodora Kroeber (1961), *Ishi in Two Worlds*, Berkeley, CA: University of California Press, CA: and Gerald Vizenor (1994), *Manifest Manners: Postindian Warriors of Survivance*, Hanover, NH: Wesleyan University/University Press of New England. Vizenor has also written a whole play, *Ishi and the Wood Ducks*, full text to be found in Vizenor (ed.) (1995), *Native American Literature: A Brief Introduction and Anthology*, New York: HarperCollins. For a consideration of both see Louis Owens, 'The Last Man of the Stone Age: Gerald Vizenor's *Ishi and the Wood Ducks*', in A. Robert Lee (ed.) (2000), *Loosening the Seams: Interpretations of Gerald Vizenor*, Bowling Green, OH: Bowling Green State University, Popular Press, pp. 133–45.
11. J. D. Salinger (1951), *The Catcher in the Rye*, Boston, MA: Little, Brown, pp. 155–6. As to the museum controversies, none has been greater than that involving the Smithsonian. At least 200 tribal museums have now come into being, not least the National Museum of the Indian in Washington, DC. Typical would be the Makah Cultural Center and Museum in Neah Bay, Washington, the Iroquois Indian Museum in Upper New York, the Pueblo Cultural Center in Albuquerque, New Mexico, the Sioux Indian Museum, the Navajo Tribal Museum in Window Rock, Arizona, and the Wampanoag National Museum in Plymouth, Massachusetts. For a highly relevant account, see Karen Coody Cooper, 'Museums and American Indians: Ambivalent Partners', in Dane Morrison (ed.) (1977), *American Indian Studies: An Interdisciplinary Approach to Contemporary Issues*, New York: Peter Lang, pp. 403–12. The issue is also helpfully explored in Curtis M. Hinsley (1981), *The Smithsonian and the American Indian: Making Moral Anthropology in Victorian America*, Washington, DC: Smithsonian Institution Press.

12. George Catlin (1841), *North American Indians, Being Letters and Notes on Their Manners, Customs, Written during Eight Years Travel among the Wildest Tribes of Indians in America*, New York: Wiley and Putnam. Recent collections include George Catlin, *North American Indians*, edited with an introduction (1989) by Peter Matthiessen, New York: Vintage Books, and George Catlin, *Drawings of the North American Indians*, with an introduction (1994) by Peter H. Hassrick, Garden City, NY: Doubleday. A well-taken analysis is to be found in Mary Sayre Haverstock (1973), *Indian Gallery: The Story of George Catlin*, New York: Four Winds Press. Charles King's Native portraiture is studied in Viola Herma (1976), *The Indian Legacy of Charles Bird King*, New York: Doubleday, Smithsonian Institution Press, and Andrew Consentino (1977), *The Paintings of Charles Bird King*, Washington, DC: National College of Fine Arts. Moran receives due evaluation in Thurman Wilkins with Caroline L. Hinkley (1998), *Thomas Moran: Artist of the Mountains*, 2nd edn, Norman, OK: University of Oklahoma Press. For Frederic Remington, see Michael Edward Shapiro, Peter H. Hassnick et al. (eds) (1998), *Frederic Remington: The Masterworks*, New York: Harry N. Abrams for the Saint Louis Art Museum and Buffalo Bill Historical Center. The work is helpfully annotated in James K. Ballinger, *Frederic Remington* (1989), New York: Harry N. Abrams. The standard Curtis portfolio is Edward S. Curtis, *The North American Indian*, edited by Frederick W. Hodge, 20 vols, Supplement 4 vols, 1907–30. Best commentary includes Christopher M. Lyman (1982), *Vanishing Race and Other Illusions: Photography of Indians by Edward Curtis*, Washington, DC: Smithsonian Institution Press, and Mick Gidley (1998), *Edward Curtis and the North American Indian*, New York: Cambridge University Press. The tradition overall receives intelligent scrutiny in Brian W. Dippie (1982), *The Vanishing American: White Attitudes and US Indian Policy*, Middletown, CT: Wesleyan University Press.

13. A pertinent account is to be found in Chadwick Allen (1996), 'Hero with Two Faces: The Lone Ranger as Treaty Discourse', *American Literature*, 68: 3, 609–38.

14. A considerable body of scholarship attaches to Natives and cinema. Among the most illuminating are Kevin Brownlow (1979), *The War, the West, and the Wilderness*, New York: Knopf; Gretchen M. Bataille and Charles L. P. Silet (eds) (1980), *The Pretend Indians: Images of Native Americans in the Movies*, Ames, IA: Iowa State University Press; Gretchen M. Bataille and Charles L. P. Silet (eds) (1985), *Images of American Indians on Film: An Annotated Bibliography*, New York: Garland; Ellen L. Arnold, 'Reframing the Hollywood Indian: A Feminist Re-reading of *Powwow Highway* and *Thunderheart*', pp. 347–62, and Mary Alice Money, 'Broken Arrows: Images of Native Americans in the Popular Western', pp. 363–88, in Dane Morrison (ed.) (1977), *American Indian Studies*, New York: Peter Lang; and Jacqueline Fitzpatrick (1999), *Celluloid Indians: Native Americans and Film*, Lincoln, NB: University of Nebraska Press. Specifically early film is analysed in Alison Griffiths (1996). 'Science and Spectacle: Native American Representation in Early Cinema', in S. Elizabeth Bird (ed.), *Dressing in Feathers: The Construction of the Indian in American Popular Culture*, Boulder, CO: Westview Press, pp. 79–85.

15. For a relevant study of the Ghost Dance, and its relationship to Wounded Knee and the revivalist movement, see David Humphreys Miller (1959), *Ghost Dance*, Lincoln, NB: University of Nebraska Press; Paul Bailey (1970), *Ghost Dance Messiah*, New York: Tower Publications; Marion F. Briggs and Sarah D. McAnulty (1977), *The Ghost Dance Tragedy at Wounded Knee*, Washington, DC: Smithsonian Institution; Russell Thornton (1986), *We Shall Live Again: The 1870 and 1890 Ghost Dance Movement as Demographic Revitalization*, New York: Cambridge University Press; and Jack Utter (1991), *Wounded Knee and the Ghost Dance Tragedy*, memorial edition, Lake Ann, MI: National Woodlands Publishing Company.

16. *Pocahontas*, directed by Michael Giaimo, Disney Studio, 1995. A Canadian version, the mythology recognised in its very title, offers a comparison – *Pocahontas: The Legend*, directed by Danièle J. Suissa, Protocol Productions, Ontario, 1995. Pocahontas as myth is

also studied in Jennifer Gray Reddish (1995), 'Pocahontas', *Tribal College*, 6: 4 (Spring), 22–3.

17. For overall guides, see Franz Boas (1940), *Race, Language and Culture*, New York: Macmillan; Lyle Campbell and Marianne Mithun (eds) (1979), *The Languages of Native America: Historical and Comparative Assessment*, Austin, TX: University of Texas Press; William Bright (1994), *American Indian Linguistics and Literature*, Berlin: Mouton; and Ives Goddard (1999), *Native Languages and Language Families of North America*, Lincoln, NB: University of Nebraska Press.

18. A greatly helpful essay-collection dealing with oral naming and tradition is Karl Kroeber (ed.) (1997), *Traditional Literatures of the American Indian: Texts and Interpretations*, Lincoln, NB: University of Nebraska Press.

19. Guillermo Gómez-Peña (1990), 'Documented/Undocumented', *LA Weekly*; reprinted in Rick Simonson and Scott Walker (eds) (1992), *The Graywolf Annual Five: Multi-Cultural Literacy*, St Paul, MN: Graywolf Press.

20. Off-reservation and citied Native America is surveyed in Donald L. Fixico (2000), *The Urban Indian Experience in America*, Albuquerque, MN: University of New Mexico Press.

21. Edmund Wilson (1960), *Apologies to the Iroquois*, New York: Farrar Straus; Leslie Fiedler (1968), *The Return of the Vanishing American*, New York: Stein and Day; and Dee Brown (1970), *Bury My Heart at Wounded Knee: An Indian History of the West*, New York: Holt, Rinehart and Winston.

22. A timely study in this respect is to be found in Colin Calloway (1994), *The World Turned Upside Down: Indian Voices from Early America*, New York: St Martin's Press, Bedford Books. I have invoked only selected fiction in this sense of prior Native lineage. A first-ever Native novel by a woman, the Creek-Muskogee S. Alice Callahan's *Wynema* (1891), obviously enters the lists. Autobiography extends from William Apess (Pequot) and Samson Occom (Mohegan) to George Copway's Chippewa self-portrait (1847), *The Life, History, and Travels of Kah-ge-ga-gah-bowh* [George Copway], and from as-told-to writing like *The Life of Ma-ka-tai-me-she-kia-kiak, or Black Hawk*, or the life of the Sioux medicine man recorded by John G. Neihardt as *Black Elk Speaks* (1932), to the classic of Nevada-Paiute upbringing, Sarah Winnemucca (1883), *Life among the Piutes* [sic]: *Their Wrongs and Claims*. Verse looks to the Creek-raised Alexander Posey's dialect *Poems* (1910); he also wrote the newspaper satires known as the Fus Fixico letters. Native drama has a notable early practitioner in the Cherokee-born Lynn Riggs, whose *Green Grow the Lilacs* (1931) became the basis of Rodgers and Hammerstein's folk musical *Oklahoma!* (1943).

23. Linda Hogan (1988), *Savings*, Minneapolis, MN: Coffee House Press.

CHAPTER FIVE

Chicanismo, La Raza, Aztlán

Fictions of Memory

For those of us who listen to the Earth, and to the old legends and myths of the people, the whispers of the blood draw us to our past. (Rudolfo A. Anaya)[1]

There is really only one outstanding quality of Chicano literature and that is that it is informing the vast majority of Americans that there are Americans who look different, live differently, and who have been lost to the rest of America. (José Antonio Villarreal)[2]

A person who has no place to call home, who has no friends, or relatives can still do many things on earth. Many things. But, he can't be a writer; not for long at any rate. It took me a long time to find this out for myself. (Rolando Hinojosa)[3]

Mexican, the voice in his deep dream kept whispering. Mejicano. Chicano. (Nash Candelaria)[4]

I'm a story that never ends. Pull one string and the whole cloth unravels. (Sandra Cisneros)[5]

I might say that I studied Spanish and Hispanic literature . . . because I had to know more about my past, my historical past. (Ron Arias)[6]

I

The publication of *Bless Me, Ultima* in 1972 did service on a number of fronts. In the unfolding of the one life-memory, set within New Mexico and an America emerging out of the Second World War, Anaya had managed a larger, always more resonant *chicanismo*. Deservedly, the novel was recognised for its intimacy yet as a story also deeply historic, even ancestral, a genuine force of time past brought down into the present. With good reason, credit continues to accrue to Rudolfo Anaya as modern literary founder, a novelist who ushered in a new dispensation of Chicano/a, and by implication, Latino/a US literary fiction.

In fact, and inevitably, Anaya was far from a lone voice. José Antonio Villarreal, Rolando Hinojosa, Nash Candelaria, Sandra Cisneros, Ana Castillo and Ron Arias, to invoke no more than the one selective gallery among many, equally speak as prime movers in the shaping of postwar Chicano/a fiction. A huge gallery of poetry and drama, not to mention music and popular culture, has accompanied. In this self-expression, as much as in Anaya's work, the emphasis upon legacy, inheritance, is both symptomatic and inevitable

How else to write about the United States, *Los Estados Unidos de América*, from a Chicano/a perspective without invoking the human passage involved, whether of family, border, religion and *mestizaje*, the weave of Mexico into America and vice versa, English and Spanish as languages which vie and yet overlap, or sense of region to embrace a southwest and west of Texas, Arizona, Colorado, New Mexico, Nevada and California?[7]

Nomenclature comes early into the reckoning. First has to be Chicano itself, and its feminine Chicana (Spanish tends not to capitalise so frequently – hence *chicanismo* and *chicano* or *chicana*).[8] Both evolve out of *Mejicano/a*, softened in pronunciation into *Mechicano/a*, then abbreviated to *Chicano/a*. A recent usage has been *Xicano/a*, the 'x' a gesture to the original Nahuatl pronunciation. *La raza* weighs equally – 'race', 'people', 'root'.[9] A latter day *corrido*, or poem-ballad, like Rodolfo 'Corky' González's 'I am Joaquín/Yo soy Joaquín' (1972), set out in parallel English and Spanish, and early dubbed the Chicano national anthem, emphasises the memorial implications of the term:

La Raza!	¡La Raza!
Méjicano!	¡Méjicano!
Español!	¡Español!
Hispano!	¡Hispano!
Chicano!	¡Chicano!
Or whatever I call myself	o lo que me llamo yo
I look the same	yo parezco lo mismo
I feel the same	yo siento lo mismo
and	yo lloro
sing the same	y
	canto lo mismo.

Aztlán, also originally a Nahuatl word, has served in kind. In one frame, it acts as a wellspring of Aztec reference, whether Quetzacoatl as serpent god, the cosmology of the fifth sun (*El Quinto Sol*), the Aztec emperor Moctezuma II, La Malinche as a prime, and usually treacherous, figure of mestizaje through her spy-mistress relationship with Cortés, or the female pantheon of legend to include La Llorona (the weeping woman), La Gritona (the shouting woman) and La Virgen de Guadalupe as Mexico's own mother saint. In another, and as seen in, say, El Plan Espiritual de Aztlán of 1969 – the work of Alurista, leading poet-activist and co-founder of

Movimiento Estudiantil Chicano de Aztlán (MECHA), it carried a call to remembrance yet at the same time to rally and consciousness. Its concluding paragraph reads:

> With our hearts and our hands in the soil, we declare the independence of our mestizo nation. We are a bronze people with a bronze culture. Before the world, before all our brothers in the bronze continent, we are a nation, we are a union of free pueblos. We are Aztlán.[10]

In this, Aztlán becomes *chicanismo*'s dream both of a past and yet future homeland, at once mnemonic and banner.

For Carlos Cumpián in 'Cuento', Spanish for story or a fiction, Aztlán serves as a goad, a wry reminder of how *chicanismo* continues to elude much of America:

Today I thought I'd call home
So I got on the
Telephone
and said: 'Operator please give me
AZTLAN person to person'

She replied: 'Sorry sir, still checking'

After two minutes –
She asked me to spell it –
So I did –
A-Z-T-L-A-N
She thought I said ICELAND
At first but after the first spelling, she said
What?!!
AZTLAN!
She said is this some
Kind of joke
I said, 'No, you
know where it is'
She said – 'Sir I cannot
Take this call
But if you wish I'll
Let you talk to
My supervisor –'
I said: 'Fine
Put 'em on
I got time' –
Well her supervisor got on the line –
And I told her what

I had said before
>   All she could say was that
>   was the first time she ever heard
>   about it – I said, 'You'll hear more
about it soon!' – and hung up –[11]

Chicanismo, La Raza, Aztlán. Each bespeaks a Mexican, a Mexican American, an American, heritage of particularity, and yet hybridity, and across a spectrum of pueblo, rancho, barrio, city, suburb and, always, given its 2,500 miles in length, border or, as it has become known, borderland. So potent, and continuous, a legacy for a population, on the 2000 census figures, almost four-fifths of America's overall Latino population of 35.3 million (itself, in turn, 12.5 per cent, or 1 in 8, of all Americans), could not but lie within, or behind, most tiers of Chicano writing. It thus can be said to be implicated in both an American and a Mexican literary continuum and yet to possess its own co-ordinates.[12]

II

If one emphasises yet further the historical sediment, the substrata that have made up Chicano culture, it is to underscore the transitions from past to present and the enduring sense of place that its novelists, poets and dramatists have so remembered when making imagined out of actual worlds.

The Olmecs and Mayans provide a founding repository, passed-down legends, belief systems, alphabets and an architecture. *Los aztecas* and the European intrusion of Hernán Cortés in 1519 and his relationship with La Malinche indeed bequeath the memory of *mestizaje*, a turning gyre of bloodline and class endlessly to be repeated and pondered through time. Mexican independence in 1821, in turn, carried a further ambiguity: decolonisation from Spain yet the pending neo-colonial threat of Mexico's northern neighbour.

The Texas–Mexican War of 1836, culminating in the Siege of the Alamo and, in its wake, the defeat of Santa Anna at the Battle of San Jacinto, continues the two-way focus. Told one way, the Siege signals Anglo-American triumphalism to be echoed in the cry 'Remember the Alamo'. Where more so than in John Wayne's 1960 Hollywood movie version with its Lone Star State hurrahs and featuring James Bowie and William B. Travis as the truest of patriot martyrs? Told another way, did not Santa Anna's attack on the fort represent timely resistance, a strike against Yankee expansionism, a view explored in Jesús Salvador Trevino's 1982 film *Seguín*?

The Mexican–American War of 1846–8, and, always, the Treaty of Guadalupe-Hidalgo (1848), adds yet further to this contested history, the one and yet several pasts each competingly remembered. Did Guadalupe-Hidalgo represent fair compromise or was it, incontestably, ratification of Mexican loss as against American theft? The Mexican Revolution of 1910–17 continues this same division of memory: revolution or betrayal, freedom or repression. Pancho Villa and Emiliano Zapata, for their parts, supply the epic names, substance and yet always shadow.

The Sleepy Lagoon murder case of 1942 and the Zoot Suit riots of 1942–3 in Los Angeles equally yield their twofold kinds of memory. In the case of the former, the body of José Diaz, found at the Sleepy Lagoon swimming pond, led to the trial, sentence to San Quentin for murder, and yet eventual release on appeal in October 1944, of members of an East Los Angeles gang. Police and other authorities spoke of hoodlums, out-of-control Latin youth. Chicanos spoke of the racism of the trial judge, the scant evidence, the stereotyping, all, as it seemed, Anglo bias.

As to the Zoot Suit riots, fiercest in June 1943, what most did they signify? They began in wartime bars and dance-halls, a largely southern and white-rural Navy pitched against *pachucos* or barrio youth (also known as *vatos* or *vatos locos* and speaking *caló* or street Spanish) in their baroque cutaway coats, long watch-chains, pegged trousers and broad-brimmed hats.[13] Was this not a kind of shadow war, a resentful Anglo lower class, white, often Bible-protestant, and from largely rural southern backgrounds, playing out its resentment against a domestic 'foreign' enemy, supposedly Mexican, brown and Spanish-speaking, Catholic and of the city?[14]

How, alongside, to remember the 1940s-50s *bracero* (from *brazo* or arm) programmes whereby non-union, subsistence-paid Mexican labour harvested California lettuces, grapes and other produce? Few Chicanos/as would not honour the memory of 1960s activism like César Chávez's United Farm Workers (UFW) with its boycotts and the 1969 Delano and other protest marches and activity against California agribusiness.[15] Chávez, in turn, became the inspiration for Rodolfo 'Corky' González's Denver Crusade for Justice, José Angel Gutíerrez's La Raza Unida in Texas, and Reies López Tijerina's Alianza de Mercedes in New Mexico, leaders, with Chávez himself, who have long become known by political insiders as the Four Horsemen of the Chicano Movement.

More lately, there has been each ongoing documentation and border drama with *la migra* (the US Immigration Service), and the extension of the *barrios*. A key latter-day skirmish turns upon the issue of bilingual education, and the history which lies behind it. 'English, Yes, Only, No' runs one motto, a counter to the 'English Only' campaigns in California and more than twenty other states, and a call to recognition, if nothing else, that America's largest minority overall is indeed no longer African American but Hispanic. Each has contributed to calls for Brown Power, a politics of radical activism, for Latino Civil Rights, and for an end to exploitation and the dire racist lexicon of wetbacks (*mojados*), greasers, spics and the rest.

It was also a reminder that Spanish, be it Chicano Spanish or its Puertorriqueño, Cubano-Americano and other counterparts, can no longer go on being regarded as simply the language of migrant, exile or barrio poverty. For, under US auspices, Spanish has long been made into a signifier of outsiderness, even illiteracy, with English the code of power and ascendancy. Both languages, ironically, have also long been symbiotic. American English exhibits any number of well-known borrowings, like *lasso*, *adobe*, *bronco*, *cinch* or *sombrero*, not to mention the all-purpose *gringo/a*. In mirror fashion, Chicano Spanish borrows from anglicisms to make *watchear la tele* or *kikear* (the drug habit).

Endless repetition on television and other commercials of food terms like *taco*, *tortilla* and *nacho* has made its own mainstream impact, one language's history remembered or, more aptly, misremembered, inside the other, as in Taco Bell's jingle of 'Run for the Border' with its squat cartoon Zapata-figure which led to a notorious court case. In categories like Hispanic, or even the increasingly more favoured Latino or Hispano, some hear a further accusing politics of memory. Both imply a Eurocentric as against indigenous naming, one, moreover, often hedged in white America's condescension as the presumed standard-at-large from which to dispense patronage, a rubric, for this as for other minority ethnicity and culture.

A *corrido* or folk recitation like the 'The Ballad of Gregorio Cortez', adapted by PBS in 1982 from Américo Paredes's version in *With His Pistol in His Hand* (1958), with a script by Victor Villaseñor, author of the intergenerational epic novel *Rain of Gold* (1991), and with Edward James Olmos in the title role, points up the general discrepancy. The tale of a 'Mexican' smallholder in the Texas of 1891 falsely accused of horse theft, it turns on how the word 'horse' in English translates into Spanish as both masculine and feminine, namely *caballo* and *yegua*. At issue, however, is infinitely more than a quirk of philology. The fable speaks on the one hand to Gregorio's Mexican-Chicano ancestry and, on the other, to the Anglo hegemony of the Texas rangers who pursue him and the court that tries him for murder of the sheriff. What is involved is the remembrance of two value systems, two misreadings against an unnecessary cultural divide. Much as English and Spanish might have been saying the same thing, the gap is typical, and in this case, fatal.[16]

In a similar way, Chicano legacy has traditionally been invoked as *campesino* life of crops and herding and festival. But it increasingly also invokes *barrio* and suburban life. East Los Angeles to Houston, Albuquerque to Denver, bear witness to the estimated 60 per cent of Chicanos who have now moved into the cities. If Harlem for African Americans carries the residues of both Dixie and Manhattan, then East Los Angeles for Chicanos looks back both to *el campo* and the exhilarations and losses of inner-city life. In this respect, California holds a special place, at once the dream of *la abundancia* and heir to fables of wealth like a fabled *Las Siete Ciudades de Cibola* yet also a world of unemployment, high infant mortality, school drop-out and crime, the highs and lows of a barrio like East LA. Even so, as the continuing surge of cross-border migration bears out, and despite each amnesty over residence papers, California remains a magnet, history both made and in the making.

One evident manifestation lies in popular culture, whether Cinco de Mayo celebrations, mariachi bands or Los Lobos, low-rider cars, campesino work songs or Latin rap, and all the memorial art form of its foodways whether *burritos*, *frijoles borrachos*, *enchiladas*, *chimichangas*, *mole de gallina* or *tamales*. An ancestral insignia lies in each *ristra* so often to be found in Chicano homes, strings of usually red-brown and other multicoloured dried peppers and long imbued with indigenous folk meanings of earth and harvest. Most families would know a calendar, besides Cinco de Mayo, of *quinceañeras* and *fiestas patrias*.

Mural art especially counts. With a backward glance to classic Mexican names like Diego Rivera, José Clemente Orozco and David Alfaro Siqueiros, few barrios do not vaunt their own vivid manifestations and, not least, by artists of the stature of Judith Baca or José Montoya. Sites, typically, include the Mission District in San Francisco, Lincoln Heights in East LA and Chicano Park, San Diego. Their colorations often hyper-intense, full of folkloric allusion, heroic yet often satiric ('We are Not a Minority' reads one well-known logo), they have served as urban banners, the interactive visual signature of la raza.[17]

Memory, at times nostalgia it can be admitted, runs right through the cultural rebirth of the 1960s, from the music of an early galvanising rockero like Richie Valens to greatly popular groups like the Texas Tornadoes to a Tex-Mex contemporary like Emilio Navaira, and in the actos of Luis Valdez's enduring and always politically aware and worker-activist Teatro Campesino. In train have been the singing of Texas's Selena, not a little given added meaning by her tragic murder in 1995, and California's Linda Ronstadt whose albums like Canciones de Mi Padre give tribute to her own rediscovered or as it has been called her retro-Chicanismo; the comedy of Cheech Marin; and the screenwork and directing of Edward James Olmos whose rise to fame, ironically, was as the Cuban American Lieutenant Castillo in TV's 'designer cop' Florida series Miami Vice.

Few performance texts have more, or better, carried the memories within chicanismo than Guillermo Gómez-Peña's video-text, Border Brujo (1991), or his dazzling, quick-change panel of history vignettes, Warrior for Gringostroika (1993). Both dramatise the complexities of 'border': US-Mexico, Spanish-English (with chilango in between), Aztec as against Euro-American visions of history, Tijuana alongside LA, mestizaje as normative, hybridities of music, food and dress, in all America as indeed one extended border and unceasingly engaged in a rich, necessary process of cultural renewal and transformation. The skills of presentation Gómez-Peña brings to bear appropriately are those of multimedia, memory caught, and projected, as its own kind of fast-moving, synoptic kaleidoscope.

In this latter respect, likewise, a whole body of film has emerged as shared memory. Luis Valdez's Zoot Suit (1981), originally a Teatro Campesino performance script of pachuquismo, Sleepy Lagoon and the riots, was adapted as a screen operetta. La Bamba (1987) offers a film biography of Richie Valens as Latin rock star featuring Los Lobos as the best-known of all Chicano pop groups. Stand and Deliver (1987), the career of Jaime Escalante as pioneer mathematics teacher in the East LA barrio, tackled not only an exemplary teacher but also stereotype. How could barrio teenagers have done so well in Scholastic Aptitude Tests (SATs) without cheating? American Me (1992) yields an unyielding portrait of Mexican Mafia gang and prison life.

For a considerable time, not least on account of Hispanic viewerships, TV had mooted El Pueblo/LA as a programme which would deliver a Chicano version of Roots. That failed to happen, the upshot of studio-management politics and calculations about the likely viewing market. But in 2000 Resurrection Boulevard, centred on the East LA Santiago family, a story of barrio, boxing dynasty, and the fierce competition yet love between generations, made its bow as the first-ever prime-time Chicano serial.

Yet, however collective the memory, *chicanismo* does not yield some unconflicted view of itself. The class hierarchy, for instance, created by the conquistadores, has its modern footfalls, still based on blood, skin colour, landedness, and, often, family name. Old *chicanismo* plays against new, especially between certain New Mexico dynasties and those of supposedly inferior birthright. This calls up the disdain of Spanish-born *gachupines* (its original meaning 'spurs') for colonial-born *criollos* or Creoles, and theirs, in turn for *los indios* (especially *genízaros* as a term for Natives forced to lose their tribal language and to speak only Spanish), for lower-order *mestizos*, and for *negros* (a distinct but Spanish-speaking population).[18]

Splits and divergences of memory run in many directions. How best to regard the process whereby much of *Méjico/México* became the American southwest and west? Was this, indeed, colonial theft or Yankee imperialism masquerading as Manifest Destiny, or even some ambiguous mix of both? How far, in truth, do most present-day Chicanos engage with Mexico? If the Mexican Revolution signals heroic insurrection, not least when at the time if not ignored then daemonised into bolshevik Red Plot by the Hearst Press, what to say of the nearly century-long monopoly of the Partido Revolucionario Institucional (PRI) until the Vicente Fox government was elected in 2001?

Can César Chávez, campesino hero of the 1960s *huelgas* (strikes), friend of Robert Kennedy, heroic icon, continue always to serve as political leadership model in a community risingly suburban and middle-class? How to regard a modern pantheon if not as a culture of no one overriding consensus which includes a fallen New Mexico Democrat politician like Henry Cisneros, a conservative ideologue like Linda Chavez (Bush's nominee as Secretary of Labor in 2000), or an anti-affirmative action writer-journalist and PBS editorialist like Richard Rodriguez? In no way least, how are Chicanas to remember Catholicism – as the home of faith and spiritual sanctuary or, and often enough at the same time, yet another patriarchy able to oppress in matters of marriage, child-raising, contraception, divorce or outside-the-house employment through its own highly gendered rules?

Imagining, and re-imagining, the past may well be, in L. P. Hartley's apt and celebrated phrase in *The Go-Between* (1953), to take up imaginative residence in a 'foreign country' where 'they do things differently'.[19] That, not altogether para-doxically, can be said to hold all the more for America as a culture so often given to the ethos of future possibility. Chicanos, no doubt having known the flavours of defeat as well as those of triumph, have had good reason to dwell upon their past. Whether it was the conquistador regime, a border as redolent of human flight as *El Río Grande*, the history by which Tejas was reconstituted as Texas, or the duality of California as promise and yet denial, the prompt to memory has been ongoing.

For it is this collective memory which has served as solvent for each generation's telling of *la raza*, and nowhere more so than in the literary fictions associated with what rightly, and unignorably, has come to be recognised as a renaissance of Chicano word and narrative.[20]

III

Certainly that has been the case, along with the Anaya of *Bless Me, Ultima* and his subsequent fiction, for Villarreal, Hinojosa, Candelaria, Cisneros and Arias, however differently they have styled their uses of memory. Theirs has been a fiction which can be said to have thrived on the shaping energies of remembrance, a present told and reinvented in the mirrors of the past. They also have been anything but alone.

In a story cycle as delicately imagistic as Tomás Rivera's '. . . *y no se lo tragó la tierra' And the Earth did not Part* (1971), another kind of memory holds sway, that of a single migrant-labour year of Chicano dynasty headed for Iuta (Utah) in which all other similar years and journeys are to be discerned. Raymond Barrio's *The Plum Plum Pickers* (1971) makes for a linking memorialisation, this time set in California's Santa Clara Valley during the Reagan governorship. Its indictments of labour exploitation and racism take the form of memory as again accusation, indictment.

Spanish-language fictions, with versions in English to follow, extend the ranks. In *Peregrinos de Aztlán* (1974), Miguel Méndez takes a more vernacular direction through the memories of Loreto Maldonado, car-washer in Tijuana, an anatomy of border life, poverty, Yaqui identity, *mestizaje*, and remembered dreams of Mexican revolution and freedom. For his part, Alejandro Morales in *Caras viejas y vino nuevo* (1975), to appear in English-language versions as *Old Faces and New Wine* in 1981 and *Barrio on the Edge* in 1998, transposes a version of 1960s *barrio* Los Angeles into a kind of working archetype, as brutal as it is incarcerative.

English-language authorings offer a complement. Daniel Cano's *Pepe Rios* (1991) attempts historical fiction of an older kind, the Mexican Revolution as an Epilogue of sorts to *Nueva España* and Prologue to a new order of *chicanismo*. Arturo Islas looks to memory as myth in *The Rain God* (1984), the portrait of a Tex-Mex dynasty descended in the aftermath of the Mexican Revolution through the imperturbable matriarch Mama Chona. The first-person novels of John Rechy, from *City of Night* (1963) onwards, and taken up with midnight cowboy and citied Gay America hustle, have either been shunned or de-ethnicised as part of an 'alternative' sexual tradition. In their different modes of using *chicanismo* as memory, and in one or two languages, all of these fictions in fact can lay claim to a shared lever or fulcrum, a heritage of time and voice given its own dialogic measure.

Memory has equally shaped an increasingly emergent Chicana fiction, in whose ranks Sandra Cisneros has been little short of a luminary.[21] Isabella Ríos's *Victuum* (1976), through the psychism of its narrator, Valentina Ballesternos, renders woman-centred history as a kind of ongoing dream script. Ana Castillo's *The Mixquiahuala Letters* (1986), epistolary in design, casts its remembrance of women's intimacy not only as story of north–south but as a past metafictionally reconstructing itself as a present-continuous. The Americas as remembered historic *mestizaje* she further takes-up in her fantasia, *Sapogonia* (1990), and in her almanac-memoir, *So Far from God* (1993). To this end, the formulation offered in *Massacre of the Dreamers:*

Essays on Xicanisma (1994) succinctly draws together the powerful memorial implications of a border inheritance for her fiction:

> Dreamers and Magicians, Brujas y Curanderas: As descendants of Mexic Amerindians, ours *is* a formidable and undeniable legacy . . . Our collective memories . . . hold the antidote to that profound sense of alienation many experience in white dominant society. (pp. 15–16)

Roberta Fernández's *Intaglio: A Novel in Six Stories* (1990) offers the portraiture of six turn-of-the-century women on the Río Grande border, a gifted work of oppressed lives, femininities. Cherrié Moraga's storytelling (and essay-work), of which the anthology she co-edited with Gloria Anzaldúa, *This Bridge Called My Back: Writings by Radical Women of Color* (1981), and her *Loving in the War Years* (1983) and her *The Last Generation* (1993) can be thought symptomatic, yields yet another kind of remembrance, that of the silence which, by historic writ, has surrounded lesbian life in a culture of patriarchy.

Demetria Martínez remembers the Latin America of *los desaparecidos* in *Mother Tongue* (1994), a 'story's medicine', as she calls it, of El Salvador politics and the US as both accomplice and yet sanctuary. For Denise Chávez in *Face of an Angel* (1994), memory centres on Soveida Dosamantes, and the women in her Mexican American dynasty of the southwest, whose lives have been spent 'in service' whether as in Sovieda's case in El Farol Mexican Restaurant or as domestics and cleaners in other workplaces. The upshot is a female-worker epic, antic, even roistering at times, but full of the remembered toughness of everyday Chicana life.

In narrative poetry, Corky González, however frequently invoked his 'I am Joaquín/Yo soy Joaquín', has been one of any number of memorial voices. Subsequent poetry to remember *chicanismo* as ancient and cross-cultural in its making as a historic way of being (or *manera de ser*) would include José Montoya's street-vernacular or *caló* verse narrative 'El Louie', Carmen Tafolla's adeptly syncretic iteration of Chicano/a identity in 'La Isabela de Guadalupe y el Apache Mío Cid', and Jimmy Santiago Baca's itinerary landscape poems in *Martín and Meditations on the South Valley* (1987) which develop a memory both of southwest landscape and *mestizaje* – to reflect the Chicano and Native components in his own make-up.

Literatura chicanesca, non-Chicano writing about Chicano life and culture, affords another styling of memory in John Nichols's *The Milagro Beanfield War* (1974), the first in a trilogy to include *The Magic Journey* (1978) and *The Nirvana Blues* (1981). However specific to the 1970s, or a New Mexico valley, its drama of contested water rights again calls up the inlaid older history of Indian, Mexican and Anglo conflict that, across four centuries, took New Mexico from a Spanish colony to a territory to America's forty-seventh state. Joe Mondragón finds himself fighting Ladd Devine and his Miracle Valley Recreation Area Development for the right to irrigate his land. In fact, what Nichols portrays tacitly is the fight for the Chicano heritage in which the bean field acts as a trope for the very soil, the nurturing medium, of a whole people's history.

Nichols's novel and the Redford–Esparza movie of 1988 (with its appropriately multiethnic cast of Ruben Blades, Carlos Riquelme, Sonia Braga and Christopher Walken) can so play fact against *el mundo de los espíritus*, the genuine historicity of the past as open to the figural reconstruction first of the written and then of screen. It has had a controversial companion piece in Danny Santiago's *Famous All Over Town* (1983), an East LA adolescent life in the person of Chato Medina which turned out to be faux-authorship, a deliberate imposture. Ethnic transvestism had again shown its literary hand.

Yet as all these texts remember *chicanismo*, so they inevitably contest and dissolve mainstream evasion of, not to say deformation and decreation of, its different legacies. Perhaps, overall, and based upon quite another literary domain, that of England's Elizabethan and Jacobean drama, Frances A. Yates's notion of memory theatre applies best – the forms of the past, in this case of conjoined Americas, always to be remembered, and re-remembered, and however obliquely, in the forms of the present.[22]

IV

If modern Chicano fiction looks to an inaugurating work, mixed literary achievement as may be, it would have to be José Villarreal's *Pocho* (1959). Set between two wars, those of the Mexican Revolution and the Second World War, the novel situates the life of its writer-protagonist, Richard Rubio, within his family's passage from Mexico to California. *El norte* carries a double loading, that of hope and loss, a dream and an awakening. 'Pocho', as Villarreal's text makes clear, suggests a self caught between opposed worlds, neither 'wholly Mexican' nor 'wholly American' (p. 62); often enough, historically, it has carried a smack of denigration, as blandness or colourlessness.

On the one hand, Richard looks to his father, Juan Rubio, a one-time *Villista* and soldier peasant of the Mexican Revolution who brings the force of memory of battles for campesino freedom, his past, even his own *mestizaje*, into the Santa Clara Valley where he settles with his family. On the other, Richard looks to the accumulating memory of his own. His is a world as much English-speaking as Spanish, a modern America if a would-be haven of opportunity which also implicates him in racial slur – 'ya souvabitchen black Messican' (p. 68). He will break with the family Catholicism, witness the ravages of migrant labour, find himself of an age with zoot-suited *pachucos* and, no small ethnic confusion of loyalties as another colour-marked American, sign on with the Navy in the wake of Pearl Harbor.

'A strange metamorphosis' (p. 132) is how the novel has Richard designate this history, one which memorially subjects past to present and at the same time that same present to its own future. Each stopping-off place adds definition. Consuelo, Richard's mother, invokes for him their shared Aztec-Castillian legacy of *indio*, *mejicano* and *español* as idiom, yet she also sees the implications of border and generational language-gap – 'we cannot even speak to you in your own language' (p. 61). A Portuguese settler from the Azores encourages his book-reading, the voice of another culture to add to his neighbourhood's Chicano, Native and Japanese American mix. In the process of his own Americanisation, he will witness the break-up of his parents, sexual stereotypes (notably Anglo fascination with the supposedly unfettered Latin libido), and the everyday harassment by the police and the growers and their agents of migrant Mexicans.

Pocho has met with criticism for veering towards documentary, but it nevertheless gives drama to all these plotlines, an abiding early modern fiction of the process, in all its ambiguity, of Mexican-into-Chicano presence. Villarreal evidently writes from a period before the 1960s and the emergence of militant Brown Power politics, a transition borne out in how Richard finds himself bound to 'America and the American way of life' yet 'saddened to see the Mexican tradition begin to disappear' (p. 132).

But Richard's own reading interests, his early story and related autobiographical compositions, and even the way he thinks back upon his sexual initiations, give pointers to the writer-in-the-making. His, in time, is to become the 'consciousness of his race' who, from a family upbringing of contingency and the temporary, will indeed translate this phase of *la raza* into the permanence of the written word. In this, and to advantage, he might be said to find a parallel in his better-known namesake, the 'Richard' of Richard Wright's *Black Boy* (1945). *Pocho* has its limitations, but it remains a marker, both memorable and memorial, in making literary narrative of *chicanismo*.

V

In *Klail City y sus alrededores* (1976), reissued in English as *Klail City* (1987), and in the rest of the dozen volumes which make up his Klail City Death Trip Series, Rolando Hinojosa subjects the lower Río Grande Valley of south Texas to Faulknerian rules. The locus is Belken County, a kind of Tex-Mex border kingdom, from the Depression-era through the postwar years and the Korean War, and down to the present. Not the least of Hinojosa's feats is to invoke this world, in his own Spanish phrase, as *estampas*, in the sense of imprints, with each novel a collage of story, sketch, poem and colloquy, and in English and Spanish, and with his own cross-translations of both. In *The Valley* (1983), Hinojosa further echoes Faulkner in supplying a prefatory map of the terrain.

Klail City looks to three narrators, Rafe Buenrostro, Jehu Malacara and P. Galindo and to generational flashbacks to both 'Anglo Klail' and 'Mexican Klail' (p. 119). The upshot is lively, collagist narrative, Belken County Chronicles, to quote the Prologue, as though indeed underwritten by 'that old, tired meanderer, the Río Grande' (p. 118). Each tributary episode, thereby, the emphasis mainly on 'Texas Mexicans' (p. 9), serves as an immediacy of event, family, character ('one shouldn't expect to find legendary heroes here', p. 9), religion, even murder, yet at the same time always the memorial flow of its border past into the present.

The opening vignette offers a symptomatic tale. Don Servando as Tamez clan patriarch has to deal with the eldest son Joaquín's having got Jovita de Anda pregnant. The summary marriage, birth of a daughter Gertrudis, and the return to Klail neighbourhood life as one of everyday normality, gives an old and familiar mistake new impetus, not least in Hinojosa's command of the ways of discretion and the push and pull of family politics.

In train follow episodes at once highly specific yet again imbued in ritual: the 'cantina monologue' (p. 16) about Choche Markham as local sell-out and coward; Rafe, as bartender in the *Aquí Me Quedo* bar, listening to a Klail regular like Echevarría and his story of the Widow Sóstenes and her Mexican Revolution pension; the 'clear memory' (p. 25) of Echevarría about the violent Buenrostro-Leguizamón feud over land; Rafe Buenrosto's portrait of elders like Don Marcial de Anda ('a religious, pious soul [who] used to sell homemade candy under the palm grove at the corner of Klail and Cooke boulevard', p. 30) and Don Aureliano Mora ('the father to Ambrosio Mora, a World War II vet shot and killed by Belken County Deputy Sheriff right in front of Klail's J. C. Penney Store on a Palm Sunday', p. 36); and, in sequences called 'The Searchers', the yearly rite of 'the migrant trail' (p. 67) north to Indiana, Michigan and Minnesota and in which the Múzquiz husband and wife of Bascom, Klail County, are killed when their pick-up overturns on Route 365.

Time past plays into the present throughout. In the story of Ambrosio Mora's murder, Don Manuel Guzman ('Klail's lone mexicano cop', p. 112) likens Klail Mexicans to 'Greeks whose homes have been taken over by Romans' (p. 38). Tom Purdy, a Michigan English teacher and an Anglo, is remembered for how he helped Texas migrant workers in his native state. Klail High School is re-seen through Rafe's memory of its alumni and romances at a class reunion ('The Homecoming', pp. 137–43). The town's past population is invoked through the war memorial and the memories of the undertaker Damián Lucero who 'makes his living burying the dead and their secret sins' (p. 122). The story of Tomás Imas (a play of words in Spanish meaning Tomás and more), a Catholic who converts to pentecostalist and missionary, gives the measure of a changing Tex-Mex regime. Earlier Klail City is recalled variously through its founder, General Rufus T. Klail, the Spanish flu epidemic of 1920, and in how the re-election of Big Foot Parkinson as Anglo Sheriff of Belken County becomes a reprise of the politics of power relationship between Anglo and Chicano Klail since the 1840s.

Barbershop or street, memories of Klail High or Korea, swimming in the Río Grande or listening to politics in the park near the railroad depot: each story carries its sense of place as history. Hinojosa's achievement is to give Klail City, 'Belken' and its *alrededores* (in the sense of whereabouts or environs), as at once, and equally, a remembered present in kind with its remembered past.

VI

'But his thoughts carried him farther. Across the ocean to the source, the begin-nings' (p. 13). Jose Rafa's pondering of his New Mexico dynasty, and of the past to which it belongs, in the first volume of Nash Candelaria's trilogy, *Memories of the Alhambra* (1977), *Not by the Sword* (1982) and *Inheritance of Strangers* (1985), can serve as a gloss for the whole sequence. Each invokes a distinct phase in the evolution of Chicano history while at the same time building into the larger, more encompassing memory. One reverberation is made to play against another. Pre-European Mexico, then 1492, *Nueva España* and all the enravelled heritage of *los aztecas* and *los conquistadores*, inaugurates the story. The always controversial Treaty of Guadalupe-Hidalgo in 1848 which made the Río Grande the boundary between the USA and Mexico, and then the admission of California to the Union in 1850 as the thirty-first state, supplies a modern counterpart, annexations which lead to the emergence of a contemporary southwest and west.

If, at times, Candelaria has been felt to go too slowly, to risk a certain inertness, he cannot be faulted for ambition. His fiction seeks nothing less than to remember a whole multicultural ebb and flow in the making of *chicanismo*, a history, but also in William Styron's celebrated phrase, 'a meditation on history'.[23] *Memories of the Alhambra*, too, as a title consciously taken over from the composer Albéniz, gives added resonance, the hispanicity of Spain as both a European past and yet American present.

For José himself, the memories within *Memories of the Alhambra* begin with the family move from Albuquerque to California in the 1920s, a move into the barrio even as he dreams his dynast's dream of pure Castillianism. When, years later, after his father's funeral and at the behest of the fake genealogist Señor de Sintierra ('Without Land'), he takes off for Mexico in the hope of discovering high-born roots, no paradox can disabuse him of the fantasy. The Virgen de Guadalupe may be a Catholic saint, but her indigenous originals are to be seen in everyday streets and byways. If Mexico for him calls up conquistador heroism, what price the cantina murder he witnesses or his flashback to the time when he himself was detained at the border as a suspected illegal? His, in other words, is selective memory, the wished-for over the actual.

Pushing on in hopes of an ideal past by which to judge the present, he crosses to Spain, his hope of conquistador patrimony secreted as he believes in yet another genealogy, *The Archives of the Indies*. But the Spain he finds is anything but imperium, more village poverty than a world of court and hidalgo. In his encounter with Señor Benator, *Morisco* businessman, moreover, a memory of still deeper paradox is brought to bear. Spanish racial purity, quite as much as its Hispano-American offshoots, has been an illusion from the start, its genealogies variously Visigoth, Andalusian, Catalan, Galician, Basque, Gypsy, Jewish and Moorish. Thus the 'Recuerdos de la Alhambra' Jose hears in Sevilla with Benator (harking back to an Islamic emirate of no less than eight centuries) again points to the blurs and overlap of even the original *Hispanidad*. Rafa's heart attack could not be more emblematic, the deadly price of memory as idealisation.

His son Joe, decried by his cousins as 'an anglicized Chicano – which was almost nothing at all', and yet a multiculturalist in the making, is left to understand his family's competing skeins of memory. 'Words. Feelings. Wheels inside of wheels inside of wheels', he ponders, 'With the need for different words. Accurate words' (p. 183). The best memory for him, and by implication for the Rafa inheritance and all *chicanismo*, points to a sense of history, a language, able to recognise and then accept cross-culture, and within it 'winners and losers both' (p. 184).

Not by the Sword takes as its present the Mexican-American War of 1846–8, unravelling through its principal figure, Father Jose Antonio Rafa III (Tercero, as he is known to the family), a fierce, mid-nineteenth-century historical bid for ascendancy between the Spanish and the Anglos, with the Indian population a muted third presence. Yet another novel itself a memory, it draws on a sequence of incremental other memories: the original Spanish land grants; the intrigue centred on Santa Fe's *palacio de los gobernadores*; the Albuquerque militias formed to combat the Yankees; the saga of Tercero's adventurist twin brother which involves the Comanches, Utes and Navajos; and the eventual Treaty of Guadalupe-Hidalgo signed in February 1848. Even the interpolated story of Michael Dalton, the Irishman known as *El Gaélico*, involves a memory within a memory of the Mexican-American War. In telling, too, of his own abandonment of priesthood in favour of marriage and his accession to the Rafa patrimony, Tercero blends the personal into a wider history, two kinds of memory interwoven into one.

By *Inheritance of Strangers*, 'a work of fiction based on history' (Author's Note), Tercero has become the *abuelo*, an elder and oral archivist, the time and place now 'Los Rafas, U.S. Territory of New Mexico, 1890'. The story he tells, of dark, internecine land wars with Yankee buccaneers on one side and the vigilante *Hijos de Libertad* on the other, has a listener in fourteen-year-old Leonardo Rafa, the grandson most bewitched by (as Candelaria has Tercero call these memories) his 'recitations'. The arc of memory once more is wide – the Taos Rebellion and the death of his brother Carlos, the saga of Don Pedro Bacas unhinged by the Yankee murder of his family. But if memory exhilarates Leonardo, it also leads directly to his death as the boy embroils himself in a misconceived honour code. Yet by the novel's end, Tercero is to be heard telling another grandson, another Carlos Rafa, 'Once upon a time . . . there was a land called New Mexico' (p. 268).

Memory, as throughout the Rafa trilogy, embarks upon a latest version of the past, one, as Candelaria leaves little doubt, still not finally told, still in process of being released from within the circles of memory of all its successive tellers.

VII

'Estos cuentitos.' Sandra Cisneros's inviting, homespun diminutive could not better underwrite the Tex-Mex *chicanismo* of *Woman Hollering Creek and Other Stories* (1991). The note is one of the cultural memory as intimacy, a *Dubliners*-like *latina* cycle of childhood, family, religion and love affairs told through the two overlapping vernaculars of English and Spanish. 'You must remember to keep writing', says a dying aunt to Esperanza Cordero, child fabulist of *The House on Mango Street* (1983), 'It will keep you free' (p. 61). The twenty-odd stories that comprise *Woman Hollering Creek* might be thought of as a further making good, a bouquet, yet another *ristra* of Chicano/a remembrance.

The characteristic accent is set in opening stories like 'My Lucy Friend Who

Smells like Corn', with its childlike word-inversion and remembered fidgets of little-girlhood; or 'Eleven', which beautifully calls back from memory a girl's mortification at being thought by her teacher, Mrs. Price, to be the owner of a tatty, left-behind sweater 'that smells like cottage cheese' (p. 8); or 'Mericans', set in the context of Mexican-Chicano churchgoing ('Why do churches smell like the inside of an ear?' (p. 19), asks the girl narrator), a shrewdly pitched vignette about Anglo patronage in which a picture-taking tourist woman observes, '"But you speak English"' and the girl's brother replies as if in memory of all such condescension, '"Yeah . . . we're Mericans"' (p. 20).

Another memory lies behind the reflexivity of 'Tepeyac', in which the storyteller thinks back, in sequence, to Abuelito or grandfather, to the family store, and to a particular *cinco de mayo* on the Mexican side of the border. She confides: 'It is me who will remember when everything else is forgotten' (p. 23). The observation implies a whole larger freight of remembrance of time as place, family as self.

Such is to be heard in 'One Holy Night', the story of a sexual first encounter, pregnancy and birth, but told also as the echo of a Mayan fertility legend. In 'My Tocaya', a black comedy of mistaken identity, the doubling assumes an unexpected form – that of a schoolgirl fantasy, the missing child as the storyteller's own martyr figure of Other. 'Never Marry a Mexican' tells of remembered love, in particular one she has shared with a father and son, to be looked back to in the 'amphibious' teacher-artist-narrator's mind as evidence of some parallel universe of gender. 'Little Miracles, Kept Promises' offers a fond harking back to the often imploring *milagritos* safety-pinned to effigies of the Virgin and name saints. As each message builds into a mosaic, an even further-back memory takes shape, that of a first, dark, Aztec cosmos, the generative source of all *chicanismo*.

'Woman Hollering Creek' as the title story depends on yet other forms of intertwined memory: one of a failed, abusive and cross-border marriage, another of the legend of *la llorona*, actuality and myth as joint testimony to the rage against patriarchy. '*Bien* Pretty', on a lighter note, acts as the narrator's self-watchful recollection of her affair with Flavio Michoacán ('I'd never made love in Spanish before', p. 153): love itself as its own kind of *mestizaje* which can cause the world to seem a field of chattering *urracas* or magpies. The story, however, affords another dimension. Thinking of the time Flavio hit his thumb with a hammer, she observes, 'He never yelled "Ouch!" he said "¡Ay!" The true test of a native Spanish speaker' (p. 153). In that '¡Ay!' lies also the larger memory, the intimacy indeed, of a *chicanismo* called back by Cisneros with quite winning idiosyncrasy.

VIII

In Ron Arias's *The Road to Tamazunchale* (1975), Chicano fiction reaches, una-shamedly, the shores of magic realism. Although a novella, it nevertheless suggests Cervantean expansiveness, with an increment of Latin *fantasía* in its echo of Carlos Fuentes's *Cambio de Piel/Change of Skin* (1967).[24] Memory thus becomes a source of metamorphosis in which Fausto Tejada, ex-salesman of encyclopaedias and an East

Los Angeles *anciano* and widower, can face the imminence of his own death with his remembrances of life.

'Suddenly the monstrous dread of dying seized his mind . . . No! he shouted . . . As long as I breathe, it won't happen' (p. 29). His memories can be literal enough, especially of his put-upon and accusing dead wife, Evangelina, and their chorus-like parakeet, Tico-Tico. But they are just as likely to take on Ovidian invention, an imagined flight into the Peruvian jungles, or a sailor-smuggling scam across the border at Tijuana. He can leave one time-period for another, that of the Nahua-Aztecs and Incas, the Lima of the sixteenth century, the early twentieth-century Tamazunchale (a literal Moctezuma River Valley town but again fantasy, an implied wordplay on 'Thomas and Charlie'), and, finally, barrio Los Angeles networked by the modernity of its street life and everyday *caló*.

Don Fausto, who finds his Sancho Panza in the *pachuco* Mario, true to his magus-like name revels in these magical powers of memory, acts of imaginative life whereby death is held in abeyance. The anachronistic shepherd Marcelino Huanca, thus, can direct his sheep through rush-hour traffic as if to silhouette an earlier timezone of herdsmanship within the era of the freeway. Equally he can advise Tejada on how to ensure his own futurity by an ancestral act of stone-upon-stone ritual. Tejada can both literally disrobe and, in imagination, peel off his own dying skin in a replay of the Aztec immortality rite of Xipe Topec.

Other memories add further transformative meaning: the body of a *mojado*, a wetback, brought back to life in a tribal revival ceremony; a community theatre group reflexively performing a play called 'The Road to Tamazunchale', which then disappears into the night sky; a *puta* who guides the old man into a jungle clearing where, sexually exhilarated, he joins in a tribal mourning. If these, too, are memories, they speak to the myths and arcana of *chicanismo*, remembrance as its own form of wizardry.

Tejada travels through an actual continuum of bookshops, a restaurant echoingly called the Cuatro Milpas (Four Cornfields), a picnic in the equally well-named Elysian Fields, and a film set in which he and Mario are taken for Hollywood extras. Yet always there is the other continuum, that of surrealised recall, which supplies the life-giving memory of a larger Azteca-Chicano history. On the one hand, beset with Kleenex, meals prepared by his niece, his old man's clothes and knick-knacks, he lies dying of heart failure in his room. But in imagination he is clad not in a dressing-gown but in a conquistador cloak, grasps not a hoe but a regal crook, and, a latter-day Orpheus, feels himself called not to a void but to Elysium.

It is this cumulative memory that allows him to defeat death even as death defeats him. Tamazunchale, in turn, acts as the sign, the index of all such metamorphosis, at once endemically familiar (at least as reflected through Los Angeles) and endemically other. *The Road to Tamazunchale*, in other words, brings Chicano memory full circle. It offers a memory fiction not only of the past, not even only of the present, but in Arias's novel as magic-realist playfield, of nothing other than the future.

NOTES

1. Rudolfo A. Anaya (1986), *A Chicano in China*, Albuquerque, NM: University of New Mexico Press.
2. José Antonio Villarreal (1980), Juan Bruce-Novoa (ed.), *Chicano Authors: Inquiry by Interview*, Austin, TX: University of Texas Press.
3. Rolando Hinojosa (1987), *Klail City*, Houston, TX: Arte Público Press.
4. Nash Candelaria (1977), *Memories of the Alhambra*, Palo Alto, CA: Cibola Press.
5. Sandra Cisneros (1991), *Woman Hollering Creek and Other Stories*, New York: Random House.
6. Ron Arias (1980), Juan Bruce-Novoa (ed.), *Chicano Authors: Inquiry by Interview*, Austin, TX: University of Texas Press.
7. The following are among the best accounts of Chicano history and politics: George I. Sánchez (1940), *Forgotten People: A Study of New Mexicans*, Albuquerque, NM: Horn; Carey MacWilliams (1948), *North from Mexico: The Spanish-Speaking People of the United States*, New York: Greenwood Press; Matt S. Meier and Feliciano Rivera (1972), *The Chicanos: A History of Mexican-Americans*, New York: Hill and Wang; Rodolfo Acuña (1972), *Occupied America: The Chicano's Struggle towards Liberation*, San Francisco, CA: Canfield Press – still a highly controversial text; Richard Griswold de Castillo (1979), *The Los Angeles Barrio, 1850–1890: A Social History*, Berkeley, CA: University of California Press; Marcia T. Garcia et al. (eds) (1984), *History, Culture and Society: Chicano Studies in the 1980s*, Ypsilanti, MI: Bilingual Press/Editorial Bilingüe, National Association of Chicano Studies; Alfredo Mirandé (1985), *The Chicano Experience: An Alternative Perspective*, Notre Dame, IN: University of Notre Dame Press; Rodolfo O. de la Garza et al. (eds) (1985), *The Mexican American Experience*, Austin, TX: University of Texas Press; and Renate von Bardeleben, Dietrich Briesemeister and Juan Bruce-Novoa (eds) (1986), *Missions in Conflict: Essays on US–Mexican Relations and Chicano Culture*, Tübingen: Gunter Verlag. For an alert and challenging account of the literary implications of *mestizaje*, see Rafael Pérez-Torres (1998), 'Chicano Ethnicity, Cultural Hybridity, and the Mestizo Voice', *American Literature*, 70:1 (March): 153–76.
8. An informed account is to be found in Andrew D. Cohen and Anthony F. Beltramo (eds) (1975), *El Lenguaje de los Chicanos: Regional and Social Characteristics Used by Mexican-Americans*, Arlington, VA: Center for Applied Linguistics.
9. See, especially, Matt S. Meier and Feliciano Rivera (1974), *Readings on La Raza: The Twentieth Century*, New York: Hill and Wang.
10. 'El Plan Espiritual de Aztlán' is reprinted in Rudolfo Anaya and Francisco Lomelí (eds) (1989), *Aztlán: Essays on the Chicano Homeland*, Albuquerque, NM: University of New Mexico Press. Its four paragraphs are also available in broadsheet form.
11. Carlos Cumpián (1990), *Coyote Sun*, Chicago, IL: MARCH/Abrazo Press.
12. The source for these figures is Betsy Guzman, *The Hispanic Population, Census 2000 Brief*, US Census Bureau, US Department of Commerce, Economics and Statistics Administration, C2 KBRO 1–3 May 2001, p. 2.
13. *Caló* has been increasingly recognised as a Spanish in its own right, as borne out in Dogoberto Fuentes and José A. López (eds) (1974), *Barrio Language Dictionary: First Dictionary of Caló*, Los Angeles, CA: Southland Press.
14. A persuasive interpretation of these events is given in Mauricio Mazón (1979), *The Zoot-Suit Riots: The Psychology of Symbolic Annihilation*, Austin, TX: University of Texas Press.
15. An important contemporary record, and by an essayist and novelist of note, is John Gregory Dunne (1967), *Delano: The Story of the California Grape Strike*, New York: Farrar, Straus and Giroux.
16. Américo Paredes (1979), *'With His Pistol in His Hand': A Border Ballad and Its Hero*, Austin, TX: University of Texas Press.

17. A volume which reproduces many of these murals and provides a helpful gloss is Eve Sperling Cockcroft and Holly Barnet-Sánchez (eds) (1990), *Signs from the Heart: California Chicano Murals*, Venice, CA: Social and Public Art Resource Center; reprinted (1993), Albuquerque, NM: University of New Mexico Press.

18. For the implications of this nomenclature, see Alfred Yankaur, 'Hispanic/Latino – What's in a Name?', and David E. Hayes-Bautista and Jorge Chapa, 'Latino Terminology: Conceptual Bases for Standardized Terminology', both in *American Journal of Public Health*, 77:1 (1987), 61–8. I am grateful to Dr Arthur Campo, formerly of the School of Education, University of Colorado at Boulder, for directing me to these references. For an account of *genízaro* culture, see Brenda M. Romero (2002), 'The Indita Genre of New Mexico: Gender and Cultural Identification', in Norma E. Cantú and Olga Nájera-Ramírez (eds), *Chicana Traditions: Continuity and Change*, Champaign, IL: University of Illinois Press pp. 56–80.

19. L. P. Hartley (1953), Prologue, *The Go-Between*, London: Hamilton.

20. The literary-critical confirmation of this renaissance has been given active continuance in a number of studies since the 1980s. These are listed in the Secondary Bibliography, but their range of concerns can be noted as follows. Juan Bruce-Novoa (1982), *Chicano Authors: A Response to Chaos*, Austin, TX: University of Texas Press, argues for a distinctive kind of imaginative space, hybrid, border, a compelling mix of actual and mythic. Edited collections like María Herrera-Sobek (1985), *Beyond Stereotypes: The Critical Analysis of Chicana Literature*, Binghamton, NY: Bilingual Press/Editorial Bilingüe, and Asunción Horno-Delgado (1989), *Breaking Boundaries: Latina Writing and Critical Readings*, Amherst, MA: University of Massachusetts Press, hypothesise a distinctive *chicana* feminism with readings to match, a body of self-expression able to challenge and transcend customary gender and role boundaries. For Ramón Saldívar (1990), *Chicano Narrative: The Dialectics of Difference*, Madison, WI: University of Wisconsin Press, Héctor Calderón and José David Saldívar (eds) (1991), *Criticism in the Borderlands: Studies in Chicano Literature, Culture, and Ideology*, Durham, NC: Duke University Press, José David Saldívar (1997), *Border Matters: Remapping American Cultural Studies*, Berkeley, CA: University of California Press, and Alfred Arteaga (1997), *Chicano Poetics: Heterotexts and Hybridities*, Cambridge: Cambridge University Press, the challenge is to bring to bear a critical aesthetic sufficiently particularist to meet *chicanismo* as both high and popular culture in terms of location, border, bilingualism, code-switch and the interacting co-presence of Spanish- and English-language literary forms.

21. For a helpful overall reprise, see Bridget Kevane (2001), 'The Hispanic Absence in the North American Canon', *Journal of American Studies*, 35:1 (April), 95–109.

22. The phrase recurs in Frances A. Yates (1966), *The Art of Memory*, London: Routledge Kegan Paul and Chicago, IL: University of Chicago Press.

23. William Styron (1968), *The Confessions of Nat Turner: A Meditation on History*, New York: Random House.

24. Carlos Fuentes (1967), *Cambio de Piel*, México: Joaquín Mortiz.

CHAPTER SIX

Eat a Bowl of Tea

Fictions of America's Asia, Fictions of Asia's America

Down from the gardens of Asia descending radiating . . .
  (Walt Whitman)[1]

lately I've been asked, as a writer, why there are not more Asian Americans represented in American literature. (Amy Tan)[2]

I wandered ghostlike amidst the mainstream of America, treading unaware on a culture that lay buried like a lost civilization. (R. A. Sasaki)[3]

The further west we go, we'll hit east;
the deeper down we dig, we'll find China.
  (Marilyn Chin)[4]

I

Whitman's 'Passage to India' affords an early port of entry. His 'gardens of Asia', or, in another enduring phrase from the poem, 'myths asiatic', might well provide headings for the fictions of Asia within virtually all of Euro-America's literary and popular culture. But when Frank Chin, and his co-editors Jeffery Paul Chan, Lawson Fusao Inada and Shawn Wong, published *AIIIEEEEE! An Anthology of Asian-American Writers* in 1974, and its successor, *The Big Aiiieeeee! An Anthology of Chinese American and Japanese American Literature* in 1991, their two compendia of fiction, memoir, poetry, essay and drama, 300 and 600 pages respectively, bore witness to a new order of things. This was to be a literary regime possessed, repossessed, of its own peopling, timeline, diversity of idiom and origins, Asia's America rather than America's Asia, or yet more accurately, that of Asian America.[5]

The 'Aiiieeeee' of both titles, the editors explained, was meant as a rebuff to the assumption of a missing literature, along with the one-dimensionality of voice routinely attributed to Asians in fiction, screen, radio and comic book. The Introduction carried all the tone of embattlement, the call to rally:

The Asian Americans here are elegant or repulsive, angry and bitter, militantly anti-white or not, not out of any sense of perversity or revenge but of honesty. America's dishonesty – and its racist white supremacy passed off as love and acceptance – has kept seven generations of Asian Americans off the air, off the streets, and praised us for being Asiatically no-show. A lot is lost forever. But from the few decades of writing we have recovered from seven generations, it is clear that we have a lot of elegant, angry and bitter life to show. We are showing off. If the reader is shocked, it is due to his own ignorance of Asian America. We're not new here. Aiiieeeee!![6]

Chinese American playwright, storywriter and controversialist, Chin especially would give graphic expression to this exclusion from the American literary map both in his essay-contribution to *The Big Aiiieeeee!*, 'Come All Ye Asian American Writers of the Real and the Fake', and in a 1976 reissue of John Okada's pioneer Japanese American novel, *No-No Boy* (1957):

What if there were no whites in American literary history. There is no Melville, no Mark Twain, no Kay Boyle, no Gertrude Stein . . . a white American writer would feel edgy if all the books written in America were by blacks, browns, reds, yellows, and all whites had ever published were cook-books full of recipes for apple pie and fried chicken. That's what I grew up with . . . in our 150 years, nine Chinamen generations, four Japanese generations, three Filipino, two Korean, not one of us had an urge to say what and who's who about ourselves.[7]

In this light, and in frequent other venues, he has long taken aim at white-mainstream travesties both of Asia and Asian America. The list includes Shangri La and Yellow Peril, Heathen Chinee and buck-toothed Japanese, China Doll, Tokyo Rose, the Picture Bride, Filipino/a labourer and house servant and Vietnamese bar-girl. Model-minority or gatekeeper stereotypes likewise have long provoked his disdain, whether Asian American communities as models of good, meaning un-troublesome civic behaviour, the computer whizz-kid as norm, or an attributed 'American' success-by-hardwork of Korean or Bengali storekeeper. Literature, he has become identified as arguing, has an obligation to offer fictions, precisely, of the real as against the fake, a restorative human complexity in the imagining of Asian America.[8]

For Chin, this also means contending against two further kinds of obstacle. On the one hand, Asiaphobia still holds, not least as both an actual and ideological memory of war – Pearl Harbor, the Pacific campaigns of the Second World War, Red China, Korea, the quagmire of Vietnam. On the other, Asia-exoticism comes into play, notably in film and TV. The panorama has been of varying kinds, designer orientalism from slit-thigh skirts to Mao suits, chopstick fast foods from stir-fry chow mein to sushi or kimchee, 1960s flirtations with yoga, Transcen-dental Meditation and tai-chi, martial arts made over into suburban fads like kung fu, tae-kwondo and karate, pop music to include David Bowie's 'Little China Girl' and the disco hit 'Kung Fu Fighting', or the icon of Yoko Ono as John Lennon's Asian and loved-hated widow queen. Within all of it persists Asian America itself, worlds of time and word far from any fortune cookie or commercial version, fact amid fiction.

No fictions, for Chin as for fellow authors, could more have done the work of stereotype than Charlie Chan and Fu Manchu. The one, created by Earl Derr Biggers and who makes his entrance in *The House Without a Key* (1925), was all Hawaiian-Chinese singsong, etiquette, hobbled walk and mandarin ratiocination. The other, from the pen of an avid aryanist like Sax Rohmer (Arthur Sarsfield Ward), his choice of pen-name a giveaway, and first introduced in novels like *The Insidious Dr. Fu Manchu* (1913), embodies the Tong fiend criminal, full of designs to conquer America and the white western order and a fount of sexual miasma. That both would be played by white actors, Sidney Toler, Warner Oland and Peter Ustinov in the case of Chan, Boris Karloff and Christopher Lee in the case of Fu Manchu, makes for its own ironic commentary.[9]

They would bequeath the considerable progeny of a 1930s pulp comic-book figure like Shiwan Khan in *The Shadow*, Ming the Merciless in the Flash Gordon films with interplanetary death ray to match, the triad gangsters of Dashiell Hammett's *The Continental Op* (1945), John P. Marquand's Mr Moto, and the scientist title figure, replete with prosthetic metal hands, of the 1962 James Bond film *Dr No*, in which 007, suave, sexually all-conquering, serves once again as the embodiment of white governance.[10]

There also has arisen the issue of supposed in-house literary collusion. Not only was Maxine Hong Kingston, as an 'icon of our pride', to be indicted for 'cultural fraud' but so, too, fellow writers like Amy Tan and the playwright David Henry Hwang. 'Engineers of stereotype' would be just one of Chin's charges. Kingston's *The Woman Warrior* had misused, or rather mis-gendered, the Fa Mu Lan legend or chant, an English-language version of which Chin reprints in 'Come All Ye Asian American Writers of the Real and the Fake'. She skews the original to falsely indict China as patriarchal trap or abyss, a version he derides as that of 'despicable Chinamen propelling a sadistically misogynist culture'.[11] Kingston, to be sure, would in time have her own fond-satiric comeback, Chin transformed into Wittman Ah Sing as 1960s San Francisco Chinaman, beatnik and writer, in her pointedly titled *Tripmaster Monkey: His Fake Book* (1989).[12]

Amy Tan's duck-swan vignette at the beginning of *The Joy Luck Club* similarly contravenes authentic Chinese animal fable. No Chinese fairytale, says Chin, ever taught 'male dominance and the inferiority of women'. Hwang, for his part in M. *Butterfly* (1988), and for all his update of Puccini and use of transvestism as a disguise metaphor both of sexuality and colonialism, is said to perpetuate rather than subvert western fantasy. Asians, men especially, so emerge as inveterate, envious, and passive-feminine worshippers of the white body. The play, furthermore, amounts to a perpetuation of 'Christian Americanised Chinese' autobiographies like Pardee Lowe's *Father and Glorious Descendant* (1943) and Jade Snow Wong's *Fifth Chinese*

Daughter (1945), assimilationist in its view of America, evasive of all mention of exclusion legislation and bias, and denigratory of China.[13]

The *Aiiieeeee!* anthologies, even as they begin to seem part of a past era, are not to be denied. Quarrelsome, no punches pulled, they may have been; but, at the time, where was acclaim to be found, say, of Carlos Bulosan as the worker-radical voice of *America is in the Heart* (1946), or of Toshio Mori as the founding Japanese American storywriter of *Yokohama, California* (1949) – especially a story like 'The Woman Who Makes Swell Doughnuts' in which foodway becomes a metaphor of life-appetite, or of Hisaye Yamamoto as the author of 'Yoneko's Earthwake', the fine-edged story of a *sansei* child's half-comic close encounter with Baptist America during a California earthquake, and which would appear in her *Seventeen Syllables and Other Stories* (1988)? With *The Big Aiiieeeee!* the original sixteen selections expanded to over thirty, from *An English-Chinese Phrase Book* of Wong Sam and his assistants (first published in 1875) through to a chapter from Joy Kogawa's *Obasan* (1982), her Japanese Canadian novel of Second World War internment in wasteland Alberta and told with rare command in the invented autobiographical persona of Naomi Nakane. The fare was heady, at the very least bracing.

The editors themselves were to be seen as not just collecting the evidence for, but through their own writings helping make happen, this change of Asian American literary status. Chin's arguments for better understanding of China's Three Kingdoms heritage, or of the Tongs, or of Confucian writ, was one thing. In *The Chickencoop Chinaman* (1972), with its exorcism of the John Chinaman stereotype and the first-ever Asian American play to be performed on Broadway, or a story collection like *The Chinaman Pacific & Frisco R. R. Co.* (1988) with its humanising memory of sojourner life as coolie, railworker and launderer, or a novel like *Donald Duk* (1991) whose young title hero works past his cartoon name into a tough yet affectionate coming of age in the fifteen-day lantern festival and foodways of San Francisco's Chinatown, he had also put down his own creative marker.

The anthologies also served to showcase Jeffery Paul Chan's stories, whether the circling dream reverie of 'Auntie Tsia Lies Dying' (1971), a tough, accusing tale of Nevada back-country sinophobia like 'Jackrabbit' (1974) or a cleverly against-stereotype episode of suburban adultery between neighbours, a Jewish husband and a Chinese wife, in 'The Chinese in Hiafa' (1974).[14] Lawson Fusao Inada could draw from the poems in his *Before the War: Poems as They Happened* (1971), the traumas of the 1940s Japanese American internment camps, the opprobrium of a Japanese name or face in postwar America, caught with first-person vividness. Shawn Wong contributed a sequence from *Homebase* (1979), his lyric first novel told as an interaction of memories across four Chinese generations from 1840s Gold Rush to the California student radicalism of the 1960s.

Chin, along with his co-editors, and both fondly and unfondly, have come to be called the 'four horsemen' of this new Asian American literary order. This is doubtless to overstate, not to say imply an Asian American male hierarchy and to step round their insufficient recognition of Asian American woman-authored writing. The exclusion of Kingston and Tan, to the unpersuaded, had as much a look of chauvinist meanness as critique. Other anthology terrains, furthermore, notably of Indo-America and other South Asia, or a Pacific Rim to include Hawai'i and the Philippines, or indeed of Asian American women's writing, have built up, together with a raft of Asian American Studies journals and university departments.[15]

This augmenting sense of depth and width to Asian American scriptural lineage, for many, confirms not just a past but prospective literary-cultural efflorescence. The *Aiiieeeee!* anthologies, polemic included, may well begin to assume the look of past era. But their intervention deserves every recognition for having been as timely as they were passionate. They continue to supply a departure point, whether as frame or anti-frame, for those recent literary fictions generated by, and given over to, Asian America and which have most made the running.[16]

II

The sheer volume of Asia-lore within perceived US culture, high and popular, could hardly not have had considerable pre-emptive effect. Whitman, throughout the nine versions of *Leaves of Grass* (1855–92), makes no secret of his affinities with 'worship ancient and modern', the 'Shastras and Vedas'. Emerson's Transcendentalism, especially as reflected in *Nature* (1836), 'The Divinity School Address' (1838) and 'The Oversoul' (1841), shows a striking inwardness with notions of karma, nirvana and Confucian analect. Thoreau's *Walden* (1854) draws interactingly upon Yankee self-reliance and Asian zen, the Pond as mirror and koan. For Melville in *Moby-Dick* (1851), western plays against eastern myth, the fierce, capitalist quest of Ahab and the *Pequod* for oil transformed into a quest for cosmic light and in whose pursuit the text aligns Judaeo-Christianity with Hindu, Farsee and Buddhist belief systems. Even at America's literary High Renaissance, Asia can be seen to have become entrenched as a marker of alien otherness.

Subsequent literary tradition has worked by now familiar changes: Jack London's Yellow Peril vampirism in stories like 'The Unparalleled Invasion'; Lafcadio Hearn's turn-of-the-century *japonerie*; Pound's modernist interest in Confucianism in the Pisan *Cantos*; the supposed China values of a bestseller like Pearl Buck's *The Good Earth* (1931); the tantrism of Beats such as Ginsberg, Kerouac, Snyder or Kaufman; or Alaska as figurative Mekong or other Asian killing-field in Mailer's *Why Are We In Vietnam?* (1967). Atlantic as may have been its best-known origins, America has thereby long known itself to be a place of Pacific interests, not to say fictions, born of an East well beyond its own West.[17]

America's film, TV and stage Asia likewise possesses its own genealogy. War cinema runs from *The Sands of Iwo Jima* (1946), with its Marine Corps heroism as against Japanese soldiery as line or swarm, to *The Manchurian Candidate* (1962), with Communism as a Chinese-Korean and Cold War fifth column of brainwash and would-be assassination, to *The Green Berets* (1968), John Wayne's patriot salute to US Special Forces in Vietnam. In each, Asia serves as foe or conspiracy. Vietnam undoubtedly changes things, a litany of best-known movies as battlefields of mind and guilt as much as village and jungle warfare. *The Deer Hunter* (1978) carries the war's psychic wound into rural Pennsylvania. *Apocalypse Now* (1979) delivers an Asian upriver Heart of Darkness. *Platoon* (1986) depicts the US soldier column as secret sharer with the Viet Cong. *Full Metal Jacket* (1987) implies a Vietnam as much existential as military-political labyrinth. 'Vietnam' becomes warning-beacon, Asia as impossible land war, a realm of symbolic as well as actual labyrinth.[18]

Other US film versions of Asia could be said to begin from early two-reeler silents with Chinamen as manikins, given to pigtails and bowings. Josef von Sternberg's *Shanghai Express* (1932), using Marlene Dietrich as personified decadence, offers a China all gambling den, opium and vice. By the time of Roman Polanski's *Chinatown* (1974), classic *film noir* to do with California water politics, and with a powerful sub-theme of incest, the metaphor again becomes Asianness as silence, unfathomability.

This is not to deny a shift, counter-film, as it were. Wayne Wang's *Chan is Missing* (1981) offers a Chinatown at once life-filled, and for all its vernacular, quite fathomable. Alan Parker's *Come See the Paradise* (1991) looks to 1940s Japanese American internment albeit through a *nisei*–white marriage. *The Fall of the I-Hotel* (1976) documents the demise, in San Francisco, of a celebrated Filipino old people's hotel, and the Pacific-West Coast migrant story of its residents. *The New Puritans: The Sikhs of Yuba City* (1987) gives an account of a Punjabi wedding, its ritual, language and family custom transposed to California. The image changes, the fictions grow subtler, more diverse.[19]

TV's Asia-imaging has had few more popular expressions than *Kung Fu* (1972–5), China converted into a Tale of the West, with David Carradine as Kwai Chang Caine, the votary Shaolin priest and Martial Arts master. M*A*S*H (1972–83), with its overlap of the Korean and Vietnam wars, managed to ease the memory of grievous Asian conflict through its Medical Unit vignettes. *The A-Team*, launched in 1983, converts a frontline unit of the kind led by Lieutenant Calley in My Lai into a self-applauding California law-and-order posse, Vietnam as the site of America's least winnable war destigmatised.[20] Subsequent 1980s–1990s TV commodification runs from series like *Karate Kid*, with its white boy given Asian training, to *The Mystery Files of Shelby Woo*, with its teenage Florida sleuth in virtually no respect Chinese American other than appearance.[21]

Stage Asia has its own American history, whether the Rodgers and Hammerstein musical *The King and I* (1951) as Asian court harem suitably brought under western moral etiquette, or *Flower Drum Song* (1958), starring Nancy Kwan, as San Francisco's Chinatown turned into an exotica of costume, girl chorus and romance. An actress like Anna May Wong (1907–61), born Liu Tsong in Los Angeles's Chinatown, could look to a long career, but her roles were invariably stereotypes of the plotter or siren. Latterly, *Miss Saigon* (1989) has brought issues of cultural representation again to the fore. Was not its triangle of white male love, sacrificial Asian bar-girl and child, not more stereotype, a latest turn in Eurasia as a version of tragedy? Broadway found itself involved in a yet further, and greatly bitter controversy, when Jonathan Pryce, a white Briton, was chosen for the lead over an

Asian or Asian American actor. America's Asia's or Asia's America – whose version was to prevail?[22]

III

Given these, and other 'outside' cultural representation, historicity becomes a prerequisite, whether of Chinatown, Japantown, Little Seoul, Little Manila or Little Bombay, or the cultures of Confucianism and Shinto, Buddhism and Hinduism, not to mention hybrid America-Asia cults from the Hare Krishna Movement to the Rev. Sun Myung Moon's Unification Church, or language systems using kanji and ideograph. Such, despite quotas and embargoes, underscores a continuing migrancy to add to the estimated one million Asians who entered the US between the Gold Rush in 1849 and the Immigration Act of 1924.

They, and their Fresh Off the Boat (FOB) descendants, whether the massive number of Overseas Filipino Workers (OFWs), trans-Asians like the Hmong, or Chinese in the 1990s in the wake of Hong Kong's reverting to the People's Republic of China (PRC) – a frequent contrast is made with American-Born Chinese (ABCs) – or immigrant groupings from Thailand to India, make for a nothing if not multivocal Asian America. Demographics underline the point. Currently, Chinese Americans are estimated at 2.4 million, Filipino Americans at 1.9 million, Indo-Pakistani and other South Asians at 1.3 million, Vietnamese Americans at 1.1 million, Korean Americans at 1 million, and Japanese Americans at 800,000.[23]

Chinese America, as the largest Asian American population, looks to a symptomatically complex history: possible pre-Columbian exploration of the Pacific islands; the first indentured sugar workers in Hawai'i in the 1830s; the 20,000 Chinese who arrived in San Francisco in 1852 in search of Gum Sahn or Gold Mountain (more accurately Gamsaan in Cantonese, Jinshan in Mandarin); the founding by Chinese Americans of the Six Companies in 1854; the role of workforce for the Central Pacific and other railroads in the 1860s; and the bitter, historic Exclusion Act of 1882, with its renewal in the Geary Act of 1882, which led to successive 'bachelor' generations denied their wives and families by the legislation.[24] The renewed ban on Asian immigration in 1924, its hard-won repeal, and the ever greater diversity of Overseas Chinese, from Taiwan, Singapore and Hong Kong as well as key emigrant locales like the mainland's southerly Guangdong province as sources of American connection, adds yet further tiering.

Few memories rankle more, however, than that of Angel Island, just off the San Francisco coastline, which from 1910 onwards detained mainly Cantonese Chinese in meanly crowded barracks whose abuse would be caught in the 125 etched-in wall poems. This trove of remembrance of a one-time detention and interrogation bureau, now a museum, is caught in an accusing line reference to 'all kinds of abuse from these barbarians'. Tribute has been both literary and filmic as in a tough, but scrupulous, screen documentary like Felicia Lowe's *Carved in Silence* (1988).[25]

Japanese America, from the westernisation begun with Commodore Perry's landing in Japan in 1853 to the dropping of the atomic bomb on Hiroshima and

Nagasaki in 1945 and the rise of Japan as a postwar world economic power, equally looks to complexity: the *issei* as first generation, with the mainly west-coast *nisei* and *sansei* generations in their wake. Little, however, has been of greater enduring pain than Roosevelt's signing of Executive Order 9066 in 1942 which, in the aftermath of Pearl Harbor, put 120,000 Japanese Americans into camps like Manzanar, Lake Tule, Topaz, Poston and Amache. The camps linger and haunt, whatever the Second World War loyalty and bravery of the all-*nisei* 442 Regimental Combat team, the absence of a single proven betrayal, or the slow legal processes for redress.[26] Garrett Hongo's poem, 'Stepchild', speaks to the ongoing power of internment to shame and silence:

> It's not talked about.
> Not shared.
> Someone pulled out the tongues
> of every Nisei
> raped by the felons
> of Relocation.[27]

Other Asian America has been no less dense or knotted. Korean Americans, for all their dramatic increase in numbers in the 1960s, look back to a migrancy begun (largely, again, to Hawai'i) as early as 1902, Japanese annexation from 1910–45 and within it the 1919 uprising, the Korean War (1950–3), the division of the peninsula at the 38th Parallel, and the counter-regimes of Syngman Rhee and Kim Il Sung. The history of Korea-in-America has had a recent unfolding in the Korean–Black divisions over storekeeper wealth and black community resentment in Los Angeles's 1992 South Central riots following the Rodney King affair.[28]

The Philippines, the US's only literal colony in the wake of the Spanish American War of 1898, has from the outset served as a source of US migrant labour, a history to include each Rizal Day Festival, the false promise of Independence in the Tydings-McDuffie Act of 1934, the America-supported Marcos dictatorship (1972–86), and an evolving American community from the *manongs*, or elder brothers, and *pensionados*, or scholarship generation to include leading *pinoy* literary names like Bienvenido N. Santos, through to FLIPS, the current acronym for younger Filipino Americans. Ongoing migrancy to add to those families and communities long established, and a rising birthrate, suggests that Filipino America will eventually become the largest population of Asian and Pacific Island origins in the US.[29]

Vietnamese Americans find themselves heirs to a cryptic roll-call of Vietnam as patria, a once-Communist north and 'free' south, and always, mainstream America's most ambiguous war memory – a lost conflict, a defeated US soldiery, guilt, bravura. Even so, and from the first boat-people onwards, Saigon becomes Little Saigon, Hanoi becomes Little Hanoi. South Asians, from Indo-Pakistan, Bangla Desh, Sri Lanka or Myanmar, and to include Nepal or the Maldives, and in languages from Hindi to Urdu, Bengali to Sinhalese, and in consequence of British imperialism and the Raj as often as not in English, yet further complicate the notion of any totalised

Asian America. Each, in this respect, has increasingly looked to a new order of Asian American voice, its own body of American literary fiction.[30]

One key symbolism lies in the commissioning of Maya Lin, a Chinese American architect then a mere twenty-two years old, to design the Vietnam Veterans Memorial in Washington, DC. The controversies were several. On its unveiling in 1982, some thought its sunken, V-shaped black granite wall, engraved only with the names of the American dead, too stark. Should it not have been more like Arlington Cemetery's Iwo Jima sculpture, forty feet high, flag held valiantly, true patriotism? Did not prejudice, however muted, feature, the choice of a designer of Asian American background, a woman, and especially one educated at a WASP bastion like Yale? These implications once more point to the Asia folded into America's history, whether in the form of demography, art or, quite inescapably, its literary fictions.

IV

To designate John Okada's *No-No Boy* (1957) and Louis Chu's *Eat a Bowl of Tea* (1961) a founding tier of the Asian American novel is, once again, anything but to imply a prior literary void. The former, with its portrait of *nisei* alienation set in postwar Seattle and Portland, and the latter a novel of 'bachelor' China dynasty in New York City and full of dark comedy and verbal play and bite, in fact can look to turn-of-the-century-written fictions such, notably, as the Chinese-Eurasian sisters Edith Eaton (who assumed the name Sui Sin Far) and Winnifred Eaton (who, complicatingly, opted for the Japanese pseudonym Onoto Watanna), the former born in England and the latter in Montreal. Ethnic chameleon is still to be heard as a term for both. Edith Eaton's story-sequence, *Mrs Spring Fragance* (1912), with its Pacific Coast Chinese lives, and Winnifred Eaton's novels begun with *Miss Numè of Japan: A Japanese-American Romance* (1899), with its east–west pairs of Japanese and American lovers, have increasingly come to be thought Asian American literary coming-of-age landmarks.

'Everything Japanese and everyone Japanese became despicable' (p. vii). So Okada's Preface, using Pearl Harbor as touchstone, sets the tone for *No-No Boy*. 'Sneaky Japs', 'the camps', 'relocation', 'Go back to Tokyo, boy', 'saboteurs', 'Shinto freaks', in the novel's further opening phrases, act as mnemonics, a sour historic context, for the return of Ichiro Yamada to Seattle after his four years of camp and prison. His No to the America of 9066, and in consequence his No to wartime military service (technically No to the draft and to the pledge of allegiance), leaves him in search of what he recurrently calls 'pattern', a moral logic, to citizenship his by birth yet abused by latest Yellow Peril phobia. The achievement of Okada's fiction is to explore the arising fissures, Ichiro caught within, and between, each competing call of identity.

His two grocer-store parents give a first instance. His mother edges into the madness of denial. Japan, for her, is truly the Chrysanthemum Kingdom, a descended-from-the-gods imperium which, according to letters from Japanese family in Brazil, is about to ferry her home by ship. All else, Japanese starvation or military defeat, she takes for American conspiracy, a war ruse. Impaired, anorexic, she drowns, to be found in the family bath by her returnee son. His kindly, if ineffectual, father decays into alcoholism, an *issei* for whom neither Japan nor America can be safe domicile. Taro, his younger brother, repudiates him, citizen-warrior who signs on for the army in compensation for Ichiro's refusal. It is a family caught out by Pacific war, by generational gap, and for sure, by 'relocation' ('It wasn't all right to be American and Japanese. You had to be one or the other', p. 91).

Seattle, and Portland, for Ichiro, equally become landscapes of divided claim and loyalty. Eto, a one-time school friend, whom he meets on return, swears at him as treacherous, even though he has finagled his own exemption from army service. Kenji, whose leg has been severed and turned cancerous in war service, gives him friendship, love, even as the two of them drive to a Portland Vets hospital where Kenji will die in a last operation. His invaded leg shadows the diseased national body politic. Kenji's friend, Eri, sees in Ichiro the figure of her husband Ralph, on war service in Germany, but who refuses to return for shame at an elder brother who has decamped to Japan. Drawn to her as she is to him, Ichiro cannot play shadow-husband any more than he can any other faux self in the novel's unfolding series.

This screen of doubleness, Japanese America as overwhelmingly masked, or suspect, gives *No-No Boy* its inclusive impetus. Ichiro revisits his one-time engineering dean but cannot bring himself, marred as he is by camp and prison, to resume 'normal' studies at the university. A Mr Carrick, in Portland, who speaks of the camps as 'a big mistake' (p. 150), offers him a good job which he turns down as if unable to accept even a well-meaning white world. A Mr Morrison, in Seattle, likewise, offers him a position in the ironically named Rehabilitation Center, again which he refuses. American normality, whether study or employment, for him has been undermined by American un-normality. Ichiro's price is that of inner distance, the self alienated as much from itself as America in general.

In the Club Oriental, a kind of drinking-place microcosm of different Seattle ethnicities, its Japanese, Chinese, Black and other regulars divide warningly among themselves. Ichiro sees in them, as in himself, further expressions of displacement. He gets caught up in name-calling, fights, a stabbing, outward yet also inward scar. 'It was a prison for ever' (p. 40), he surmises of the America which has embroiled him in the paradox of having actually to choose his own unfreedom in despite of the nation's 'elusive insinuation of promise' (p. 251). Okada's fiction gives every ground to be thought pioneer, a portrait of American and Japanese war fought far from any overseas battlefield.

In Louis Chu's *Eat a Bowl of Tea*, another enclave of American history finds its own aptest fiction, a novel of 1940s New York 'bachelor' Chinatown with its inside laws of Tong, dynasty, face and foodway, yet also, and at the same time, a novel of second-generation Chinese America told as a drama of sexual impotence, cuckoldry (the novel's phrase is 'love thievery', p. 198) and eventual restoration of family dynasty. Chu's liveliness works throughout to capture the daily pace of mah jong, race bets and mealtimes, the circling intrigues and gossip, and the Cantonese slang in English of 'Wow your mother', 'Go sell your ass, you stinky dead snake' and 'you dead person'. It is a Chinatown evolved of two matching worlds elsewhere, the one that of village and family South China of Kwantung and the other that of Manhattan's Lower East Side, and yet, whether one-room dormitory, restaurant or barbershop, also and at the same time in Chu's fashioning a live, enactive Chinese American world in its own existential right.

The arranged marriage of Ben Loy, waiter, and Mei Oi, his sent-for bride from Sun Lung Lay village in China, and the family lines of their respective fathers Wah Gay and Lee Gong, speaks not only to 'bachelor' Chinatown and their own earlier arrival at Ellis Island in the 1920s, but to the making of successor Chinatowns and regimes beyond. That Ben, no sexual innocent, suffers impotence, that Mei Oi, beauteous, educated, a prize, enters a dalliance with, and becomes pregnant by Ah Song, 'the club-house hanger-on' (p. 69) and 'lone wolf' (p. 216), and that the fathers enter into a pact of truce and connivance to make things right just as they have in the original marriage, generates a near-comedy of charade and revenge. Chu shows himself, at every fast-paced turn, the adept at Restoration-style sexual revels, Chinatown as 'gossipy community' (p. 151), abrim in local custom, talk, scandal.

Yet, vernacular as may be, there can be no doubt in *Eat a Bowl of Tea* of an enclosing larger history. This is a Chinatown world at once the upshot of US Exclusion laws with its ritual anti-Asianism and of a China of self-sustaining community practice, whether clan solidarity like that of the Wang Association, ginseng cures, a baby's 'first haircut', Tong benevolent-society aid, or calendar ceremonies of dress and gift. The one story, thereby, engagingly harbours the other, the west as east, the east as west, and neither of them a utopia.

Wah Gay's slicing-off of Ah Song's ear as virtual *film noir*, the latter's banishment, Ben's own return to herb-induced potency as he consumes each 'bowl of tea', and the birth of the child whatever its fathering, become the gathering and simultaneous signs of an end to enforced bachelordom and of a new era of family. As the two fathers move on from their cronyish Manhattan under the rules of 'face', and Ben and Mei Oi transfer from New York to San Francisco's Chinatown, the novel points to an end to impotence, be it sexual or social and cultural. Both family dynasties, and the China-inheritances out of which they arise, look to a Chinese American life well beyond any and all 'exclusion'.

Louis Chu's achievement lies in giving place and generational process lively, full recognition, *Eat a Bowl of Tea* as a fiction which, with quite brilliant and expressive contrariety, shows against whatever historic odds a China being born of America, an America of China.

V

Chinese American fiction, in the aftermath of Louis Chu, has been greatly well served, whether by Maxine Hong Kingston or Frank Chin themselves, or a line to include Shawn Wong and Gish Jen, and as notably as any, by Amy Tan. Not only did *The Joy Luck Club* deservedly become a *succès d'estime*, but successor novels to include *The Kitchen God's Wife* (1991), with its 'hidden' China pasts of Jiang Weili from Shanghai to America, and *The Hundred Secret Senses* (1995), with its contrasting Chinese and American half-sisterhood of Olivia Bishop and Kwan. Tan, for good reason, enters any reckoning of Asia America's literary stock.

Yet other directions could look variously to Diana Chang's *The Frontiers of Love* (1956) with its portrait of the travails of Eurasianism and set in Shanghai under Japanese occupation, to Ruthanne Lum McCunn's *Thousand Pieces of Gold* (1981), the self-billed 'biographical novel' of Lalu Nathoy, stolen Chinagirl, concubine, Gold Rush participant and eventual Idaho homesteader, or to Gus Lee's *China Boy* (1991), middlebrow, documentary, the early life of Kai Ting as one of Chinese boy-warriordom in San Francisco's mainly black Panhandle area. Fae Myenne Ng's *Bone* (1993) gives another intimate, crafted version of generational leave-takings and stayings-on in San Francisco's Chinatown. If a Chinese America plural in its fictions, that, duly, has been no more than of a kind with a Chinese America plural in its history.

Tan's *The Joy Luck Club*, bestseller as it became, always drew a certain amount of critical fire. Frank Chin was indeed early to lay down the charge of 'fake Chinese fairy tale', a China refashioned to western taste, west-coast sino-exotica. But there was also widespread agreement as to the novel's virtuosity. Tan's triumph was to be found in her command of the cross-storyings, through sixteen episodes, of the novel's four mothers and daughters and which hinge China with Chinese America, Chinawomen mothers in inspired, and often wonderfully just off-cue, colloquy with a Chinese American daughter generation.

The title story sets up a pointer with its remembrance of Suyuan Woo's 'black sesame-seed soup' as against Aunt Lin's 'red bean soup'. Either the two soups are *cahbudwo*, 'the same', or a case of *butong*, the latter glossed as 'would like to be the same' and so 'the better half of mixed intentions' (pp. 5–6). This almost sameness again arises when Jing-Mei Woo, first of the daughters, succeeds her mother Suyuan Woo, dead of 'cerebral aneurysm' (p. 5), at the Joy Luck Club, but where she faces a father who believes his wife 'was killed by her own thoughts' (p. 5).

The pattern is repeated. Rose Hsu Jordan's mother, An-mei Hsu, having attended the First Chinese Baptist Church, has a leatherette Bible which Confucianly winds up 'wedged under a too-short table leg, a way for her to correct the imbalances of life' (p. 122). Waverly Jong, in liberal outrage, asks her mother, Lindo Jong, about Chinese torture. She elicits the reply:

> 'Chinese people do business, do medicine, do painting. Not lazy like American people. We do torture. Best torture.' (p. 92)

Lena St Clair hears a similarly double-version story from her mother, Ying-ying St Clair. A great-grandfather once sentenced a beggar to a cruel death. But 'the dead man came back and killed my great-grandfather. Either that, or he died of influenza one week later' (p. 104). Waverly Jong contends that 'I'm my own person', only to have her mother rejoin 'How can she be her own person? When did I give her up?'

(p. 290). In other words, these views and exchanges displace even as they serve to connect, mother and daughter, China and America. They find themselves crossed by a semantics prone always to make the one continuum into two and yet which oddly, or at least under different cultural auspices, retells each mother's story in that of the daughter.

Jing-Mei 'June' Woo has to supply her own mother's missing discourse. She makes the trip to China, encouraged by the others, as an act of completion ('I realize I've never really known what it means to be Chinese', p. 307). She has earlier thought only of gaps, the human fissure between herself and Suyuan Woo and of the other mothers and their daughters:

> And then it occurs to me. They are frightened. In me, they see their own daughters, just as ignorant, just as unmindful of the truths and hopes they have brought to America. They see daughters who grow impatient when their mothers talk Chinese, who think they are stupid when they explain things in fractured English. They see that joy and luck do not mean the same to their daughters, that to these closed American-born minds 'joy luck' is not a word, it does not exist. (p. 31)

But in China she does find more: her mother's, and so her own, lost family of twin half-sisters. Against time, distance, separation, connection takes hold. As a Chinese American woman looking upon her Chinese kin, and despite language or migration, she is able to see, finally, and in the most pertinent of talk metaphors, 'the same mouth' (p. 332).

Each of the Joy Luck Club's other mothers, likewise, match linkage with fracture. An-Mei Hsu, in 'Magpies', places the breakdown of her daughter's marriage in the context of her own mother's wrenching, sacrificial Second Wife history with the merchant Wu Tsing. Ying-ying St Clair, in 'Waiting between the Trees', interprets the marriage of her daughter, Lena, in terms of her own utterly contrasting eastern and western marriages. Lindo Jong, in 'Queen Mother of the Western Skies', ponders, and compares, the transpositions of how 'face' operates as an etiquette, a mode of relationship, first in China and then in America.

Whether the focus turns on Shanghai or San Francisco, China under Mao or America under Eisenhower, the foodway of wok or microwave, this joined but discrepant crossply of talk, memory, story, governs throughout the text. Jing-mei Woo offers a working key or lever in her response to her mother's account of Chinese and Jewish ways of playing mah jong with its comic, non-explicatory leaps of logic: 'These kinds of explanations made me feel my mother and I spoke two different languages, which we did. I talked to her in English, she answered back in Chinese' (p. 23).

China history, America history. Eastern family, western family. The one language silhouetted against the other. Each shadows, even as it competes with, its counterpart, a shared but at the same time unshared matrilineage. Tan's achievement in *The*

Joy Luck Club is to bring each competing half into dynamic balance, specific family stories yet always part of a larger story, with the club's mah jong table a sounding board as much for truth as wager. Dialogics can rarely have found more fertile ground, China, America, Chinese America, all, under Tan's direction, bound into their several but one telling.

China-in-America as both legacy and prospect has quite another styling in Shawn Wong's *Homebase* (1979). Novella-length, spare, lyric, it first looks back through its California-raised narrator's own orphaning at fifteen to the older, dynastic 'orphaning' of the three generations of Chan-Chinamen who precede him, in all over a century of living in America and of becoming American. It takes the form of self-query, a meditation, by the narrator Rainsford Chan:

> I never kept a diary. Those words were useless. I chose the land around me, my grandfather's America, to give me some meaning and place here, to build something around me, to establish my tradition. I wanted to know exactly what I had left . . . (pp. 47–8)

The tradition he finds left refers him to his great-grandfather's struggle working on the Central Pacific Railroad in the Sierra Nevada; to the grandfather who became nothing less than a 'Chinese *vaquero*' working ranches in Wyoming and elsewhere; and to a father who serves time as an airman in Guam. In this light, the will to self-inscription, the making of identity, makes every sense – 'I am the son of my fathers, my grandfathers, and I have a story to tell about my history' (p. 9).

He ponders the lost years of all the Chans (a surname, he explains, which can also mean California). These bring into play the Asiaphobic nineteenth-century Exclusion Acts which caused his great-grandfather to send his grandfather back to China; the searing loneliness of the first Chinamen without their womenfolk; the bitter detentions of Angel Island (Wong offers an inspired recreation of interrogation procedure); and the loss in himself of a language and his sense of self-travesty as a memorialist from the 1950s and early 1960s, clad in his Fraternity House jacket and sneakers. In this he speaks of himself as the American Chinaboy, a Chinese American who once learned to sing 'Home on the Range' with his father as though a true anthem to American nationality.

The will to re-affiliation with his Chan dynasty becomes also a re-appropriation of prior voice, his own narration as colloquium or archive: 'And I knew that I was . . . my father's son, that he was Grandfather's son and Grandfather was Great Grandfather's son . . . and that . . . we were all the same man' (p. 86). In linking vein, he thinks back to the death of his mother in her flower shop, to the uncle and aunt who then continued his upbringing, and to the passed-down stories, letters, diaries, mementos and placenames across the West as each imbued with Chan presence. In each he recognises story, pattern. 'I pick up the pieces like I'm collecting bones' (p. 94), he witnesses, an image itself deeply imbued in Chinese memory of the remains of sojourners sent back to the homeland for reburial.

But Rainsford Chan is also American progeny. Off hiking with a fifteen-year-old blonde California girl, he defiantly, and ruefully, vaunts their pairing as the expression of his claim to an America which so infrequently has claimed him:

And now in America I say to her that I have no place in America, after four generations there is nothing except what America tells me about the pride of being foreign, a visitor from a China I've never seen, never been to, and never care about. Or, at best, here in my country I am still living at the fringe, the edge of China. So now I take this fifteen-year-old blond-haired body with me on the road . . . she is the true dream of my capture of America . . . My patronizing blond-haired, whining, pouting bride . . . is America. She tells me things about me that I am not. America patronizes me and loves me and tells me that I am the product of the richest and oldest culture in the history of the world. She credits me with all the inventions of modern life, when in fact I have nothing of my own in America . . . (p. 66)

'In fact' Chan has something most potently his own, namely his own reconstitutive act of telling. He has acquired, remembered, outrightly imagined when necessary, enough Chan history to repudiate all past orphanage and, at the same time, to envisage this Chinese past as a way into his own Chinese American future. He also thinks of a tariff, a new order of inspiration. 'After 125 years of our life here', he asserts, 'I do not want just a home that time allowed me to have. America must give me legends with spirit' (p. 95). An admiring reader would argue *Homebase* to be exactly Shawn Wong's own legend with spirit, the telling of a past, a present, as a route into history still in process and fully yet to arrive.

'Bu yao fa feng . . . stop acting crazy' (p. 217). A better working gloss would be hard to come by for the world of Gish Jen's *Typical American* (1991). For Helen Chang's reprimand to her children, Callie (Kailan or Open Orchid in Chinese) and Mona (Mengna or Dream Graceful), applies in equal part to all the Changs and their immigrant circle, the quest for Chinese equilibrium amid American disequilibrium.

Ralph Chang, the jug-eared Yifeng as was, who leaves 1940s China to take up a Ph.D. fellowship in engineering in New York and who progresses from one kind of self-bewildering American close encounter to the next, is seized by a fantasy to make millionaire bucks from a fast-food chicken restaurant. Theresa Chang MD, the sister he once called Bai Xiao or Know-It-All, and whose affair with Ralph's married Head of Department amounts to a parody of the American hospital romance, herself suffers near-fatal injury in a Gatsbyesque car accident brought on by Ralph's own bad driving and the dog the Changs have bought to certify their credentials as *bona fide* American suburbanites. Grover Ding, raised Chinese American, and as practised, and mysterious, an adept in Yankee double-dealing as Bellow's Dr Tamkin in *Seize the Day* (1956), plays sexual courtier to Helen at the same time as seducing Ralph with prospects of instantaneous, and to be sure shady, all-American wealth.

Each, throughout Jen's novel, suggests Americanisation as a comedy of errors, a process startlingly funny the one moment, yet wry, even bitter, the next. For *Typical American* offers ethnic fantasia in which otherness is itself othered, displacement given its own deftest ironic scrutiny. Which gap is the greater, asks Jen's text, China as 'enormous circumspection', a 'terraced society', or America as 'spread-out' (p. 178), 'a wilderness of freedoms' (p. 142)? How to reconcile, at another reach, the Chinese-Confucian goal of 'reunification' with the American-Franklinesque goal of 'the self-made man'?

This sense of cultural divide, and of the spaces between, the novel especially locates in the Changs' acquisition of English and, not least, the family's relish in thinking themselves Chang-kees as against Yankees. Helen contrasts her Chinese-language and American-language worlds as follows:

> In China . . . the world . . . was like a skating rink, a finite space, walled. Words inevitably rebounded. Here the world was enormous, all endless horizon; her words arced and disappeared as though into a wind-chopped ocean. (p. 85)

Theresa, for her part, struggles

> to put her Chinese thoughts into English. But now she had English thoughts too – that was true also. They all did. There were things they did not know how to say in Chinese. The language of *outside the house* had seeped well inside – Cadillac, Pyrex, subway, Coney Island, Ringling Brothers and Barnum and Bailey Circus. Transistor radio. Theresa and Helen and Ralph slipped from tongue to tongue like turtles taking to land, taking to sea; though one remained their more natural element, both had become essential. (pp. 123–4)

Ralph's reaction to workaday Manhattan summarises the contrast yet more succinctly. 'The very air smelled of oil', he observes, 'Nothing was made of bamboo' (p. 8).

'It's an American story' (p. 3), assures the opening sentence. But however so, it is also one whose comic dividends lie in Jen's exploration of Chinese and American discrepancy. Confucius vies with Franklin. More terrestrially, the small (and so unprivate) dynastic home in Jiangsu province, near Shanghai, contrasts with the Changs' eventual tract (and so spacious) home in Tarrytown, New York, complete with its accoutrements of lawn, fitted kitchen, garage, central heating, and family and other separate rooms ('All bespoke bounty, and peace, a world never ending', p. 271).

Prophetically, and in preparing for America, Ralph learns the gap between Chinese and English verbs to be infinitely more than one of grammar. A whole world-view is entailed:

> What's taken for granted in English . . . is spelled out in Chinese . . .; there's even a verb construction for this purpose. *Ting de jian* in Mandarin means, one listens and hears. *Ting bu jian* means, one listens but fails to hear. (p. 4)

If, too, his father cites Confucian lore ('*Opposites begin in one another*', p. 5), Yifeng-Ralph's way to America sets himself a Franklin-cum-Gatsby schedule ('I will do five minutes of calisthenics daily', p. 6).

Further disjunctures crowd in on him. To get to New York, he travels cross-country from the Golden Gate Bridge, at once east to west and west to east. If he can grandly ponder world-historical movements in the light of the Fall of Manchuria ('Kingdoms rise up, kingdoms collapse', p. 22), he can also, mundanely, fall for the large-breasted Cammy, the university's Foreign Student Office secretary with whom he fantasises American love and a honeymoon in Paris. Instead of Yifeng, in English 'Intent on the Peak', she selects the homespun Ralph as a name for him. Where once he has learned grammar-book English, he now learns a slew of Americanisms in a bar – 'dames' and 'dough' (p. 17) prime among them. Heir, as may be, to fables of the Three Kingdoms, he also hears another kind of fable from a would-be landlady: 'I don't rent to no Chinks. So far's I'm concerned they bring bugs' (p. 31).

'This is America you're in' (p. 40), Dr Pinkus, his antagonistic doctoral supervisor, tells him, a warning to lose his wary, indirect Chinese ways. But which America? On marrying the very Chinese, and supposedly very docile, Helen, formerly Hailan or Sea-Blue, he in fact finds her the readiest American housewife (to his patriarchal amazement she fixes the boiler in their apartment). 'Typical American' becomes his, and the family's, mantra for each acquired new reality or phrase, whether they have the matter right or not.

New York, '*the* American city', as Ralph thinks it, compels yet distorts him as though beyond the reach of all Chinese criteria – 'So clangorous – such screeching, rumbling, blaring, banging! Such hiss! Everything buzzed . . . No equation could begin to describe it all' (p. 182). If engineering palls for him, 'imagineering' (p. 82), as he calls it, does not ('Anything could happen, this was America', p. 42). Even his 'non-life' (p. 34) in the blood-splattered abattoir which supplies a Chinese restaurant where he is forced to work in order to pay for his studies, smell and offal, fails to give him a working hold on American reality.

For Ralph imagines himself at one with the dream so Faustianly dangled before him by Grover Ding as Chinese American fixer, charmer and villain, and by his own exhilarated reading of self-promotional manuals such as Norman Vincent Peale's *The Power of Positive Thinking*, or *Making Money, Be Your Own Boss!* and *Ninety Days to Power and Success*. He even lines his office with Babbitry, uplift-speak or 'inspirational quotes' of the kind 'ALL RICHES BEGIN IN AN IDEA' or 'WHAT YOU CAN CONCEIVE, YOU CAN ACHIEVE' (p. 198). For in Yifeng-Ralph the two regimes, China and America, can literally be seen to be about a new genesis, ever ambiguous, that of Chinese American.

The upshot of his urge to American well-being, satiety, is Ralph's Chicken Palace, the deflationary implications of whose name escapes him – and in preparation for which he practises endlessly on a cash-register even as Helen betrays him in the room above with Grover ('Ralph . . . all blind focus, saw nothing but the register', p. 218). That the whole restaurant scheme is based on Grover's wheeler-dealing, and will literally collapse (the diners, absurdly, moved to ever more low-level tables), matches an America of dream with scam, hope with betrayal.

Each of Ralph's reeling, comic pratfalls, however, together with Helen's dalliance, Grover's dubiously supposed imprisonment for tax-evasion (has he or has he not been doing time for his finagling?) and, above all, Theresa's accident, bring him to a hard-won acknowledgement of illusion, the snares built into desire. He sees, accordingly, that if China has become a 'thing recalled' then America, as he has believed it, is also 'no America' (p. 296). A new, and chastening, synthesis is required: 'A man was the sum of his limits; freedom only made him see how much so' (p. 296).

But against this winter-time 'bleak understanding', he also calls to mind a 'heartening' summer's day in which Theresa has been frolicking with Old Chao, her lover (p. 296). It points him to the world he still has, intimate, imperfect yet whole of itself, none other than his and the family's 'house' of Chinese America. In showing how the Changs of China become the Changs of America, or as *Typical American* again expresses it Chang-kees become Yankees, Jen tells another Asian American Cautionary Tale, and one wholly as contemplative as it is witty.

VI

In Cynthia Kadohata's *The Floating World* (1989), Japan-in-America is given both as the everyday remembrance of family transition from east to west and contemporary picaresque. Set in the 1950s, and told through the precocious, Holden Caulfield voice of Olivia Ann, *sansei* teenager, it works as a kind of seriocomic road drama. The family's search for seasonal work across the small-town Pacific west and Dixie south, in the wake of internment, calls up every kind of quirk and niche, not least travelling as in itself a home. Life, for Olivia, falls under its own governing Japanese Americanness with in play due governing laws of gravity, being, motion, and even language.

Kadohata, like Gish Jen, begins with names, etymology as, again, a kind of dynastic journey through time. She first has Olivia invoke Japan's granting of patronymics to her *issei* grandparents and other commoners in the 1870s. After emigration to Hawai'i, and the Second World War, enrolment in school requires the next generation to cede their *nisei* names of Satoru, Yukiko, Mariko, Haruko and Sadamu to Roger, Lily, Laura, Ann and Roy. Finally, on the mainland, and in due turn, their *sansei* offspring shift from Japanese to American ('My brothers and I all have American names: Benjamin Todd, Peter Edward, and me, Olivia Ann', p. 2). This evolving nomenclature as marker is not lost on Olivia herself. Of even her own family, she observes: 'Today their Japanese names are just shadows following them' (p. 3).

This, however, as she and her family travel through America's 'unstable world' (p. 3), is not to reckon without her tough, acerbic, thrice-married *obasan*. 'My father wanted us to call her Grandma – more American' (p. 5), but *obasan* it is who unyieldingly carries Japan into America, full of ceremony, elisions of time, tea, memories of her husbands, sayings and story. ' "My memories are a string of pearls and rocks" ' (p. 24), she witnesses. Olivia, whom she harries and pinches as her own contrary way of loving her, even hears her speaking American dreams in Japanese.

When, albeit in her eighties, she surprises the family by dying (where more appositely than in a California motel?), she has already taught the family to perceive the world of the *hakujin*, the white people of America, through her imported screens of Japaneseness:

> My grandmother liked to tell us about herself during evenings when we all sat talking in front of motels or houses we stayed at. We were traveling in what she called ukiyo, the floating world. The floating world was the gas station attendants, restaurants, and jobs we depended on, the motel towns floating in the middle of fields and mountains . . . *We* were stable, traveling through an unstable world while my father looked for jobs. (pp. 2–3)

The gloss is perfect for Olivia's own on-the-road close encounters, each western substance and yet also eastern shadow.

Her opening brush with a quietly crazed ex-professor points the way. Only her grandmother's Japanese guile, her smile, saves Olivia from likely murder ('Hakujin don't know when a smile is an insult', she tells the girl, p. 8). Fostered out to Isamu, a lonely Japanese farmer in Nebraska whose daughter has spurned him, Olivia helps him write out his entire world in a phonebook containing only seven names. En route to Gibson, Arkansas, she summons up her childhood as always transition ('Pictures of one world fading as another took its place', p. 55). In Gibson, she translates her grandmother's diaries, each a 'revelation' ('And I liked the two languages, Japanese and English, how each contained thoughts you couldn't express exactly in the other', p. 91). She also finds love with the southern-accented *nisei*, David Tanizaki, a relationship whose passion has its own oblique correlation in her job as factory chicken-sexer.

In stepping west, to Los Angeles, she enters the 'secret world' of Andy Chin, Chinese American corrupt car-fixer. There, too, she fantasises a conversation with her long-dead father ('I'd never met a ghost before', p. 158), takes over his vending-machine route as owner-repairwoman across California, Arizona and Nevada, and heads out, finally, for one more Huck-like, night-time foray ('It was high time I left', p. 161). Unbraiding these, along with the earlier recesses of her history, and each improbable turn in the lives of her *obasan* and parents, gives *The Floating World* its presiding mix of truth and irreality.

Native-born, even aspirant all-American 'baton-twirler' and 'shortstop', Olivia confronts her America as real yet floating, West yet always East. She glosses this doubling as follows: 'Someone was always seeing a ghost or having a hunch or hearing a rumor. No idea had a definite form; every fact could dissolve into fiction' (p. 32). This, on her part, and behind her on Kadohata's, is truly to put America under Japanese auspices, Japanese America as not only tale but telling.

VII

Ronyoung Kim's *Clay Walls* (1986) has long served as a pioneer Korean American fiction of generational transition, its time-span Los Angeles in the 1920s through to the 1940s. The family in view looks to Haesu, the mother, as *yangban* or high-born Korean woman, Chun as her peasant-stock husband, and Faye as their American daughter. It falls to Faye, rather than to either of her two brothers, Harold and John, reflexively to observe 'I haven't found a book yet written about the people I know' (p. 297). Kim's novel bids precisely to meet this desideratum.

'I feel like I'm living with blindfolds over my eyes' (p. 25), Haesu tells her friend Clara Yim. Though the observation bears on her struggle to acquire English, she might be speaking of her life in general. Korea has meant Japanese rule, uncertain escape to America, loss of extended family, and the break-up of her marriage to the lower-class Chun. Role and counter-role mix. American has meant working as maidservant-cleaner in a California mansion whose luxuries both attract and taunt her. To purchase her own home, she must use the ruse of having Chun's white partner, Charlie Bancroft, pretend to be the buyer. Would-be American loyalist, she has, nevertheless, to witness her son Harold suffer anti-Asian rejection from a WASP academy. Neither Korea nor America serves as true domicile for a Korean generation whose losses must seek redemption in its Korean American offspring.

Haesu's work as a seamstress becomes her only means of keeping the family afloat, the more so with the news that North Korea has appropriated land she once bought in Quaksan. Literally, she cannot go home again. In fact, unwittingly, she resembles an Asian Penelope, stitching, embroidering, her family, and the Korea they perpetuate, into America. Kim uses this trope to shrewd, unintrusive effect, an American family web reluctantly woven of Korean strands.

Chun, for his part, shows a more Taoist, and so accepting, disposition. The children, he allows, can be simultaneously the history within both their Korean names (Culyong, Keeyong and Inyong) and their American counterparts (Harold, John and Faye). If Haesu favours politics as secretary to *Koreans for Progressive Reforms*, he works to create an American grocery business. But, as the odds pursue him with the loss of a government contract, his gambling, and the life he ekes out as a farmworker and bellhop before his lonesome death in Reno, he comes to recognise that the Korean 'clay walls' (Kim herself has termed them 'earthen walls') he once thought to build into, and around, his American life have not served. For him, as for Haesu, this has been unwalled history, Korea-to-America migrancy as loss in equal part with gain.

There remains, principally, Faye, who takes over the first-person narration of the novel. The paradoxes of her upbringing press from the outset. She is raised in porous, eclectic America – Jewish, Chinese, Black, but, by her mother's ruling, 'No Japanese friends' (p. 211). She learns quickly enough the cost, and ambiguity, of America's shifting preferences for one Asia over another. On the one hand, 'Being at war with Japan meant mainstream Americans and I were on the same side . . . I'm glad it wasn't the Koreans who bombed Pearl Harbor' (p. 262). On the other, when

Harold, her brother, enters the ranks, as an 'oriental' he is turned down for marine officer training. CK, her friend, also Korean American, finds himself in a further twist when he is given command of an all-*nisei* regiment. Faye can be told by her mother that 'the Americans are a better people than our enemy' (p. 271), but she, and the other children, after Pearl Harbor, are made to wear self-protective badges saying 'Korean' (p. 261).

Nor does the spiral stop there. Daniel Lee, the Korean American medical student from Connecticut with whom Faye's American future appears to lie, confides, however woodenly, 'WASP assumptions require that I be one thing and my ancestry demands another' (p. 297). In this light, and as if to acquire her own bearings, she says to him: 'So you've been to Korea . . . tell me about it' (pp. 291–2). Ronyoung Kim's *Clay Walls* pitches her couple to suggest a Korean American future, but only as they will, or can, negotiate the balance of both the Korea and the America within.

VIII

Bienvenido N. Santos belongs in the Filipino American literary generation halfway between those of Carlos Bulosan, 1940s luminary fiction-writer and the autobiographer of *America is in the Heart* (1946), and Jessica Hagedom, feisty performance-artist, musician and poet and the novelist of *Dogeaters* (1980). His *What the Hell For You Left Your Heart in San Francisco* (1987) explores the life, the times, of David Dante Tolosa, 'new Filipino immigrant' (p. 20) yet with permanent residence status in the America of the 1970s.

An opponent of Marcos's 'New Society' Philippines, with its army-born and America-supported authoritarianism, Tolosa also finds himself bound upon negotiation of an America itself of race-line and easy sexual morality. Not a little disingenuously, Santos has him term his account 'random notes' (p. 1). Tolosa's diary, in fact, could not be a more structured fiction, the sequencing of the plotline, the parallels, even the shows of improvisation, those of a first-person novel.

Various kinds of eventfulness work across, and contrast with, each other. Tolosa's own life and employment by a rich middle-class Filipino medical community to begin a magazine of Filipino life plays against his memory of village Filipino hardship. The luxury of the life he lives at the Diamond Heights home of his principal sponsors, Doctors Pacifico and Imelda Sotto, gives the point yet sharper emphasis. In a linked paradox, the Sottos, respectively, are a vasectomy specialist and she a paediatrician, while their own daughter Estela is deformed, brain- and nerve-damaged. Within this frame, Santos has Tolosa serve as the voice, the archivist, of the evolving curve of Filipino into Filipino American identity.

In one respect, his becomes a close encounter of generations: the *pinoy* elders of whom Cesar Pilapil, or Tingting, the seventy-year old I-Hotel resident with whom he plays tennis, acts as a representative; the Sottos as expatriate monied and professional Filipino clique; the FLIP students who initially question his relevance and authority when he teaches a course in Philippine culture at the local college; and the indulged American offspring of Professor Jaime, his one-time teacher. In another,

Diamond Heights becomes his platform for his reflections on the nexus of Filipino and American, not least in his night-time talks with Sotto. Yet another trajectory lies in his memories of New York to Salt Lake City travel, his various romances in the city – with Judy and Karen, both drop-outs – and his growing recognition that the magazine will not happen as it looks to give an image of Filipino life far from the bourgeois money and socialising of the Sottos and their friends.

Within these lies a series of inward soliloquy, David, or Deedee, as reflexive consciousness. He dreams, hauntedly, of his lost migrant-worker father in San Francisco and, equally, of his once endlessly-in-waiting village mother in the Philippines. His 'Notes to Myself' for the would-be magazine become the life-markers of actual bottom-of-the-order Filipino American life, whether Little Manila, the always-present *chismis* or gossip, or the issue of old age for a Filipino generation brought over as cheap labour. Even his class syllabus becomes a fiction ingredient, academic Philippine-study with its due reading lists and class assignment as a route back into quite unacademic Philippine-life.

In Estela, dream and frailty combine, the physically and brain-damaged Sotto daughter who delights only in the dazzle of light of San Francisco at night ('a sheet of sparkling jewels', p. 182). For just as the Sottos give Estela a telescope to gaze upon the city, so, with an eye as often saddened as uplifted, Tolosa also sees, and re-envisions, the city as uncertain Filipino-American landscape. Santos's *What the Hell For You Left Your Heart in San Francisco*, to be sure, gives but the one version. But, in the process of delineating yet another Asian America, it wins its place as the fiction of an American home still to become wholly, and unambiguously, a Filipino home.

IX

In *Blue Dragon, White Tiger: A Tet Story* (1983), Tran Van Dinh supplies opening co-ordinates, a calendar, for his novel of America-in-Vietnam and Vietnam-in-America:

> The Blue Dragon represents spring and tenderness, the White Tiger, winter and force. All beings on earth are affected by the constant struggle between the Blue Dragon and the White Tiger.
>
> A Traditional Vietnamese Belief

This dragon–tiger dialectic takes form by beginning with a love story in Amherst, Massachusetts, moving back into Vietnam as war zone, and closing with its diplomat protagonist, Tran Van Minh, applying in Thailand for an American visa. More precisely, it frames Minh's enlistment in the Communist cause during the Vietnam War, his stint as an NFL representative in Paris, his return to unified Vietnam after the fall of Saigon, and his final defection to America. If at times more than a touch essayistic, the novel does best as a book of mirrors, two warring nations each the accusing reflection of the other and each, themselves, internally at war.

'It is obvious that the root of the war is in Washington, not Saigon' (p. 38). The words are those of Long Van, Minh's ideological fellow traveller in Vietnam. But they also indicate the novel's own ideological thrust, the fine line which argues that Ho Chi Minh's Marxism should have been allowed to compete for allegiance without French or American intrusion. Tran Van Minh, thereby, becomes a witness to each contending party: old-time Vietnamese nationalism like that of his father, Hue, as against the opportunism of a Marshall Ky or General Thieu; Buddhist-led reform as against the state terror of each successive ruling clique in the south; ARVN as against the Viet Cong; and, ultimately, America as the source of Minh's personal happiness yet of devastation to his own country. Tet in Vietnam, or Tet in America, Dinh leaves little doubt of the paradox of 'constant struggle.'

Minh carries most of these divisions within himself. He has half-brothers who fight both for the south and the north (the former killed by renegades among his own men). His lover, Jennifer Sloane, having gone to Vietnam with a Quaker group, falls victim to an American B52 raid. The scholarly father who tells him that 'It's an American wood that sets the Vietnamese house on fire' (p. 66) is himself murdered by Vietnamese soldiers. A black US officer, Bradley, with whom he strikes up a friendship, he translates to a friend as saying 'while . . . fighting for freedom in Vietnam, his people at home haven't any' (p. 89). If once a subscriber to the collective will in the Party, he relishes, equally, the liberation of his own will as a writer in New York.

Nor does this play of contradiction end with Minh's leaving for Vietnam for the final time. When, in his mind's eye, he sees himself kneeling 'at the foot of the Statue of Liberty' (p. 334), he also sees himself as the bearer of 'the historic Vietnam he held in his heart' (p. 334). Given marring occasional editorial intrusions by its author, *Blue Dragon, White Tiger* makes its best asset the parallel imagining of Vietnam and America, each ensnared in a politics of contradiction, in its own kind of fiction.

X

Migration, ethnic passage, especially if European, often enough has been told as the forward step, the arduous but essentially affirming rise into accepted American identity. But another version also enters the telling, America as new world to be met with· at near-defeating expense. Two fictions, South Asian in their referencing and both woman-narrated, offer precisely this kind of portraiture, lives written as from Burma/Myanmar and from India and bound into a US destiny which involves self-transformation as violence, barely contained division.

Wendy Law-Yone's *The Coffin Tree* (1983) can be thought a tale of two pathologies, those of the narrator in her mid-twenties and of her half-brother Shan, sibling refugees from the Burmese military coup which causes them to flee, initially, to New York, and then into an America of further collapse and attempted suicide. Initially there persists the Burma of memory, the father a legendary founder of the People's Army, the narrator's mother a lost beauty dead on giving birth, and Shan's mother a half-mythic village madwoman. Rangoon as capital, monsoons, a mean, ghostly grandmother ('her body was a shrunken vegetable', p. 3), fussed aunts, banyan and tamarind tree, gunny sack and elephant grass, give the circumstantial litany, along with the eventual tanks, and the 'the tattoo of gunfire' (p. 29) and 'unexplained arrests' (p. 31).

Subsequently there is the world of '"You'll be free in America"' (p. 43) as supposed by the father, yet for the sister-narrator and her brother one of selves as bound as unbound. If, on the one hand, 'escapees from an imprisoned land' (p. 149), theirs in a world of freedom becomes 'continued imprisonment' (p. 171). This is America as 'colossal obstacle course' (p. 45), the drift into indigency and always a disabling hunger at once as figural as physical.

Uncertain parasitic stays with the father's Manhattan contacts confirm 'the extent of our defeat' (p. 59). Of Mr Morrison, one-time safari-shirted visitor to Burma, the unnamed sister observes: 'We were faces out of past he didn't appear eager to recall' (p. 47). At a subsequent stage, they are taken in by the Lanes in the East Seventies, 'serving in effect as fulltime caretakers' (p. 59) to a large, messy family yet themselves uncared-for and 'full of inadmissible fears' (p. 61). In an economy of dollar abundance, she takes jobs as a low-paid bank-teller, even as her brother deludedly tries to become a sailor and adventurer headed for the Bahamas and based in Pensacola.

The narrator's eventual collapse, and confinement to 'Ward 3 East' in a psychiatric hospital after gouging her arm in an attempted suicide and with its virtual relearning of language and meaning, gives one curve. Shan's decline into psychosis, worsened by malaria, cheap-motel life in South Carolina and Florida, and his traumatising rape at a Vermont hotel which leaves him 'stripped of his dreams, his beliefs, his supports – blank' (p. 76), gives another. In this, the novel's organising metaphor of the coffin tree, however likely, it is explained, a species of juniper tree, serves perfectly: the tree as growth and yet one which supplies coffin wood, life as ever close to, and yet paradoxically energised by, the presence of death.

As the sister begins to win back a 'narrow sanity' (p. 103), her mind turns back to the 'balance' (p. 148) of being held acrobatically as a child in her father's hands. Her Burmese life, however, has become an American life, and only precariously at one with itself. Law-Yone offers a fiction of anything but ready Franklinism. In a style full of memorial nuance, she depicts, discomfortingly, and at no compromise, a New World suffused in old pain.

Bharati Mukherjee's *Jasmine* (1989) equally offers no roseate version of migrancy. But, across settings from Hasnapur in the Punjab to the Florida Keys, New York to Iowa, and if also a fiction of setback and different kinds of self-fissure, it also affirms appetite, exuberance, an America, and vestigially an India, of different kinds of 'becoming' (p. 5). 'The zig-zag route is straightest' (p. 101) confides the title heroine, the perfect legend for a woman who can as readily invoke 'the scale of Brahma' (p. 60) as a US farm-country's 'self-absorption' (p. 171). For hers is indeed a tale of evolving incarnations, her serial life-identity as a woman, from Asia to America.

In no respect is this to be met with more emphatically than in the heroine's tracing of her name, 'Jane, Jasmine, Jyoti' (p. 21), to which must be added her self-naming as Kali, tongue-sliced avatar in killing the rapist in whose boat she lands illegally in

America, and Jase as Manhattan mistress-lover. Each of these names carries a history, a life 'greedy with wants and reckless from hope' (p. 241). Mukherjee's strength, if for some of her readership in fact a weakness, is to tell a story actual and yet self-monitoring, that of an 'I' at once first-person self and yet aware of its own fictions as that self. Each stage of the novel, as it interlaces event and timeline, gives witness.

In Hasnapur, a village astrologer predicts 'widowhood and exile' (p. 3), prophecy she ponders as 'lifetimes ago' (p. 3) from Baden, Elsa County, Iowa. Between the two, her identities accrete, and multiply, a self ever more composite. As Jyoti, she is the fourteen-year-old Hindu bride of the 'modern' Prakash Vijh, his Jasmine, yet the unwitting cause of his bombing murder by a Sikh nationalist and heir to her husband's dream of becoming an American business virtuoso. As Kali, and en route from the Punjab city of Jullundhar to her own intended widow-burning or *sati* in Florida, she kills Half-Face, the Vietnam-scarred shipper of herself and other human contraband, who has raped her, and whose name as Bubba she mishears and conflates into the Hindu name Baba. In the aftermath of the killing, she burns both her own and her husband's clothes, which she speaks of as her own rebirthing. As Jase, she enters into love with Taylor Hayes, Columbia university professor, and surrogate motherhood to Duff, his daughter by Wylie, the wife about to abscond with the economist Stuart Eschelman. Transformation could not be more sudden, the discard of old clothes and assumption of new as the expression of old into new identity, a continuum of self-construction.

Stepping westwards to Iowa, she becomes Jane, that is Jane Ripplemeyer, wife to the spine-fractured agricultural banker, Bud Ripplemeyer, having been unable to prevent his shooting by the crazed debtor, Harlan Kroener, and foster mother to Du, their adopted Vietnamese whizz-kid son known to his contemporaries as Yogi and with an Asian history, if anything, more traumatic than her own. These all she invokes from present-day Iowa prairie and its world of township, farm, Mennonites, Bud's still-in-love former wife Karin who runs a suicide helpline, and Mother Ripplemeyer. If now the adept American, as inward with TV commercials as driving, she remains equally Indian. Yankee self-help co-exists with her sense of a cosmos of infinite transformation under Vishnu and Lord Rama. Her haunting by Sukhwinder as the killer of Prakash, amid Partition politics, is added to by his reappearance in New York and has caused her to flee to Iowa for fear of what he might do to Taylor and Duff. More mundanely, these worlds of west and east also join in each interplay of western and eastern food ('pot roast and gobi aloo', p. 213).

This 'geometry . . . twisted, tangled, and intertwined', to give a line from her prefatory citation of James Gleick's *Chaos*, holds right through to the novel's close. Prakesh's widow yet newly pregnant with Bud's child, sane witness to the insanity and hanging of the young hog-farmer Darrel Lutz, she steps, finally, from the midwest towards a still further west, a still further America, with California-bound Taylor and Duff. Motion, whirl, more transformation, karma, in no way diminishes.

Asia, one more time, infiltrates, and shapes, America. But it does so also uniquely, its passage embodied in the alternating and extravagant currents of Jasmine's life as both gentle and murderous, everyday and magical ('I shuttled between identities', p. 77). Whatever the murmurings by a number of postcolonial critics as to the India of the novel, Mukherjee's novel offers a bold, and boldly stylish, fiction of self and nation, the one as much as the other caught up in the literal life-and-death, but wholly irresistible, making of multicultural American identity.

XI

No less than each other fiction, *Jasmine* helps fill out, and at the same time particularise, this overall topography of literary Asian America. In offering the narratives of an America drawn from, and always augmented by, China, Japan, Korea, the Philippines, Vietnam or India as one of many South Asian points of origin, what finds expression is always dialectic. Asian 'othering' seeks, and achieves, its own riposte. Memory can summon one-time migrancy, odds of language, a historic unwelcome. But, in calling up push and change, even setback, it can equally often look to the successful generational emergence of America as a new homeland, efficacy for some, hard times still for others. If, in all these respects, Asian American fiction makes for any one generic kind, it does so in ways as multivocal and contrary, and as likely to favour the exception as not, as any other in American fiction.

NOTES

1. Walt Whitman (1868), 'Passage to India', published in the 'Annex' to *Leaves of Grass* (1871).
2. Amy Tan (1990), 'Mother Tongue', The Threepenny Review, republished in Joyce Carol Oates and Robert Atwan (eds) (1991), *The Best American Essays 1991*, New York: Tickner & Fields, pp. 196–202.
3. R. A. Sasaki (1991), *The Loom and Other Stories*, St Paul, MN: Graywolf Press.
4. Marilyn Chin (1994), *The Phoenix Gone, the Terrace Empty*, Minneapolis: Milkweed Editions.
5. Frank Chin, Jeffery Paul Chan, Lawson Fusao Inada and Shawn Wong (eds) (1974), *AIIIEEEEE! An Anthology of Asian-American Writers*, Washington, DC: Howard University Press; Frank Chin, Jeffery Paul Chan, Lawson Fusao Inada and Shawn Wong (eds) (1991), *The Big Aiiieeeee! An Anthology of Chinese American and Japanese American Literature*, New York: Meridian/Penguin.
6. Preface, *AIIIEEEE!: An Anthology of Asian-American Writers*, p. xxxi.
7. Frank Chin, Afterword to John Okada (1970, 1976), *No-No Boy*, Seattle, WA: University of Washington Press, pp. 253–4. Okada's novel was originally published as (1957) *No-No Boy*, Rutherford, VT: Charles Tuttle. 'Come All Ye Asian American Writers of the Real and the Fake', *The Big Aiiieeeee!*, pp. 1–92.
8. A most useful pamphlet which deals with these and other comic-strip stereotypes is Charles Hardy and Gail F. Stern (eds) (1986), *Ethnic Images in the Comics* Philadelphia, PA: Balch Institute of Ethnic Studies.
9. Earl Derr Biggers (1925), *The House Without a Key*, New York: Collier. There followed (1925) *The Chinese Parrot: A Novel*, New York: Grosset and (1928) *Behind That Curtain*, Indianapolis, IN: Bobbs. Sax Rohmer (1913), *The Insidious Dr Fu Manchu*, New York: McBrode, also published as (1920) *The Insidious Dr Fu Manchu: Being a Somewhat Detailed*

Account of Nayland Smith and His Trailing of the Sinister Chinaman, New York: A. L. Burt. In its wake followed novels like (1936) *President Fu Manchu*, Garden City, NY. Doubleday, for the Crime Club, and (1948) *Shadow of Fu Manchu*, Garden City, NY: Doubleday, for the Crime Club.

10. Dashiell Hammett (1945), *The Continental Op*, New York: Spivak, and John P. Marquand (1938), *Mr Moto's Three Aces*, Boston, MA: Little, Brown.

11. 'Come All Ye Asian American Writers of the Real and the Fake', p. 26.

12. For a well-argued response to Chin's critique, see Sau Ling-Wong (1999), 'Kingston's Handling of Traditional Chinese Sources', in Shirley Geok-Lin (ed.), *Approaches to Teaching Kingston's 'The Woman Warrior'*, New York: Modern Language Association.

13. David Hwang (1988), *M. Butterfly*, New York: Penguin. His other best-known play (1983), *F.O.B.*, in *Broken Promises: Four Plays*, New York: Avon, uses F.O.B., 'Fresh off the Boat, as a kind of joke mantra. Analysis of the M. *Butterfly* controversy is to be found in Robert Skloot (1990), 'Breaking the Butterfly: The Politics of David Henry Hwang', *Modern Drama*, 33: 1 (March), 59–66; Dorrine K. Kondo (1990), 'M. *Butterfly*: Orientalism, Gender and Critique of Essentialist Identity', *Cultural Critique* (Fall), 5–29; and Angela Pao (1992), 'The Critic and the Butterfly: Sociocultural Contexts and the Reception of David Henry Hwang's M. *Butterfly*', *Amerasia Journal*, 18:3, (1989) 1–16. See also David Henry Hwang (1989), 'Evolving a Multicultural Tradition', *MELUS*, 16:3 (Fall), 16–19.

14. These appeared as follows: 'Auntie Tsia Lies Dying' in *Aion*, 1:2 (1971), 'Jackrabbit' in *Yardbird*, 3 (1974), and 'The Chinese in Haifa' in *AIIIEEEEE!* (1974).

15. The relevant anthologies are listed in the bibliography.

16. The best-known journals include *Aion* (1970–1), *Amerasia Journal* (1971–), *Asian American Review* (1972–6), *The Journal of Ethnic Studies* (1972–), *Bamboo Ridge: The Hawaii Writers' Quarterly* (1971–), *MELUS* (1975–), *Yardbird* (1971–6), *Quilt* (1980–), *Hitting Critical Mass* (1993–) and *Journal of Asian American Studies* (1998–).

17. Jack London's 'The Unparalleled Invasion' is included in his (1929) *'Moon Face' and Other Stories*, New York: Macmillan. Subsequent texts are as follows: Lafcadio Hearn (1894), *Glimpses of Unfamiliar Japan*, Boston, MA and New York: Houghton Mifflin; Ezra Pound (1915), *Cathay*, London: Mathews, and (1955) *Cantos*, complete and revised edition, New York: New Directions; Pearl Buck (1931), *The Good Earth*, New York: John Day; Allen Ginsberg (1956), *Howl and Other Poems*, San Francisco, CA: City Lights Books; Jack Kerouac (1957), *On the Road*, New York: Viking; and Norman Mailer (1967) *Why Are We in Vietnam?*, New York: Putnam.

18. A careful sense of context for these films is supplied in Philip West, Steven I. Levine and Jackie Hiltz (eds) (1998), *America's Wars in Asia: A Cultural Approach to History and Memory*, Armonk, NY: M. E. Sharpe.

19. Relevant studies include Eugene Franklin Wong (1978), *Visual Media Racism: Asians in the American Motion Pictures*, New York: Arno Press; Gina Marchetti (1993), *Romance and the 'Yellow Peril': Race, Sex, and Discursive Strategies in Hollywood Fiction*, Berkeley, CA: University of California Press; Ella Shohat and Robert Stam (1994), *Unthinking Eurocentrism: Multiculturalism and the Media*, New York: Routledge; and Matthew Bernstein and Gaylin Studler (eds) (1997), *Visions of the East: Orientalism in Film*, New Brunswick, NJ: Rutgers University Press.

20. An overview is offered in J. Fred McDonald (1985), *Televising the Red Menace: The Video Road to Vietnam*, New York: Praeger.

21. See Bernice Chu (ed), *Asian American Media Reference Guide*, New York: Asian Cinevison.

22. A considerable performance scholarship has emerged, notably Trinh Minh-ha (1991), *When the Moon Waxes Red: Representation, Gender and Cultural Politics*, New York and London: Routledge; James Moy (1993), *Marginal Sights: Staging the Chinese in America*,

Iowa City, IA: University of Iowa Press; Marilyn Ivy, *Discourses of the Vanishing: Modernity, Phantoms, Japan*, Chicago, IL: University of Chicago Press; Josephine Lee (1997), *Performing Asian America: Race and Ethnicity on the Contemporary Stage*, Philadelphia, PA: Temple University Press; and, an especially sharp reading of the M. *Butterfly* and *Miss Saigon* controversies, Dorrine Kondo (1997), *About Face: Performing Race in Fashion and Theater*, New York and London: Routledge.

23. For general context, see Hyung-Chan Kim (ed.) (1986), *Dictionary of Asian American History*, Westport, CT: Greenwood Press; Roger Daniels (1988), *Asian American: Chinese and Japanese in America since 1850*, Seattle, WA: University of Washington Press; Susheng Chang (1991), *Asian Americans: An Interpretive History*, Boston, MA: Twayne; Shirley Hune Kim, Hyung-Chan Kim, Stephen S. Fujita and Amy Ling (eds) (1991), *Asian Americans: Comparative and Global Perspectives*, Pullman, WA: Washington State University Press; Yen le Espiritu, *Asian American Panethnicity: Bridging Institutions and Identities*, Philadelphia, PA: Temple University Press; Karin Aquilar-San Juan (ed.) (1994), *The State of Asian America: Activism and Resistance in the 1990s*, Boston, MA: South End Press; and David Palumbo-Liu (1999), *The State of Asian America: Historical Crossings of a Racial Frontier*, Stanford, CA: Stanford University Press.

24. A greatly important anthology which reflects early Chinese immigration to west-coast America is Marlon K. Hom (ed.) (1987), *Songs of Gold Mountain: Cantonese Rhymes from San Francisco Chinatown*, Berkeley, CA: University of California Press.

25. Histories include Loren W. Fessler (1983), *Chinese in America: Stereotyped Past, Changing Present*, New York: Vantage; Shih-Shan Tsai (1986), *The Chinese Experience in America*, Bloomington, IN: Indiana University Press; Lynn Penn (1990), *Sons of the Yellow Emperor: A History of the Chinese Diaspora*, Boston, MA: Little, Brown; Susheng Chan (ed.) (1991), *Entry Denied: Exclusion and the Chinese Community in America*, Philadelphia, PA: Temple University Press; and Jonathan Spence (1999), *The Chan's Great Continent: China in Western Minds*, New York and Harmondsworth: Penguin. Angel Island is documented in Him Mark Lan, Genny Lim and Judy Yung (eds) (1980), *Poetry and History of Chinese Immigration: Angel Island 1910–1940*, Seattle, WA and London: University of Washington Press, along with *Carved in Silence*, directed by Felicia Lowe, NAATA 1988.

26. Among the best accounts of Japanese American history are Harry H. L. Kitano (1969), *Japanese Americans: The Evolution of a Subculture*, Englewood Cliffs, NJ: Prentice Hall; Robert A. Wilson and Bill Hosoka (1980), *East to America: A History of the Japanese in the United States*, New York: William Morrow; Yuki Ichioka (1988), *The Issei: The World of the First-Generation Japanese Immigrants 1885–1924*, New York: The Free Press; and David O'Brien and Stephen F. Fujita (1991), *The Japanese American Experience*, Bloomington, IN: Indiana University Press. The classic account of 9066 is Michi Weglyn (1976), *Years of Infamy: The Untold Story of America's Concentration Camps*, New York: William Morrow. See also Yasuko I. Takeza (1995), *Breaking the Silence: Redress and Japanese Ethnicity*, Ithaca, NY: Cornell University Press.

27. Garrett Hongo (1982), *Yellow Light*, Middletown, CT: Wesleyan University Press.

28. An overall history is to be found in Bon-Young Choy (1975), *Koreans in America*, Chicago, IL: Nelson-Hall.

29. See Jesse Quinsaat et al. (eds) (1976), *Letters in Exile: An Introductory Reader of the History of the Filipinos in America*, University of California at Los Angeles, CA: Resource Development and Publications, Asian American Studies Center; Fred Cordova (1983), *Filipinos: Forgotten Asian Americans*, Dubuque, IA: Kendall/Hunt Publishing; Antonio J. A. Pido (1986), *The Filipinos in America*, Staten Island, NY: Center for Migration Studies; and E. San Juan Jr (1998), *From Exile to Diaspora: Versions of the Filipino Experience in the United States*, Boulder, CO: Westview Press.

30. These histories receive attention in James A. Freeman (1989), *Hearts of Sorrow: Vietnamese-*

American Lives, Stanford, CA: Stanford University Press; Roger Daniels (1989), *History of Indian Immigration to the United States: An Interpretive Essay*, New York: The Asia Society; S. Parmatra Saran (1985), *The Asian Indian Experience in the United States*, Cambridge, MA: Schnekman; and Keith H. Quincy (1988), *Hmong: History of a People*, Cheney, WA: University of Washington Press.

CHAPTER SEVEN

Sites

Indian Country, Asiatown, Black City, Barrio, Borderland, Migrancy

All events and experiences are local, somewhere. And all human enhancements of events and experiences – all the arts – are regional in the sense that they derive from immediate relation to felt life.

It is this immediacy that distinguishes art. And paradoxically the more local the feeling in art, the more all people can share in it; for that vivid encounter with the stuff of the world is our common ground. (William Stafford)[1]

I

Location, location, location. Real-estate professionals in the USA have become famed, if not notorious, for the use of this mantra with its promise of ever-enhancing market value or congeniality of vista. But the built-in repetition might as readily be applied to the focus of a whole round of literary-ethnic fiction. For location, especially in how, etymologically, it calls up *locus*, and in William Stafford's sense 'being local', gives a ready pointer to ethnicity as cultural site.

Whether as tribal homeland, Asiatown, black inner city, barrio, or a historic borderland like that of the USA and Mexico, or even, paradoxically, migrancy as its own kind of location, ethnicity has always been more than a one-note category. The novels and stories which give confirmation, quite evidently, turn on anything but site as dollar investment. Quite the contrary: they speak from, and to, place, and with it time, as a veritable multidimensional ecology of being, and always with its own porous borders and shifts of contour.

This, in turn, is also to acknowledge that as much as the affiliation can be one of necessary intimacy, it can also be the source of any amount of mixed or volatile emotion and open to ongoing revision of status. Whichever the case, and in their discrete yet interlinking and comparative ways, these fictions supply an index to America as a series of ethnic-cultural loci both as geography and as what any Latino community would recognise to be *una manera de ser*, a way of being, each inside America at large yet with its own human dynamic and texture of memory.

II

'Indian country' has long been a phrase likely to arouse an immediate caveat. Whose naming is it – that of the conquering white frontier, and so loaded up in savagist mystique, or that of the tribes, to whom, historically, landownership as against use was an alien construct?

Nonetheless, it has long had play, whether under Euro-settlement and from the Puritans onwards as beckoning but feared *terra incognita* or, under Native-centred understanding, an inhabitation of woodland, hill country, prairie, pueblo or coast in which a massive variety of cultures have had, and still have, their being. In the fictions of James Welch and Louise Erdrich, two among literary fiction's plurality of Native worlds, Blackfeet and Chippewa, find major articulation.

With *Fools Crow* (1986), James Welch develops a rare, almost unique picture of tribal Montana in the late 1860s. Welch himself has been insistent, however, upon how, from the start, his interest was in more than spectatorship or topography. His aim, throughout, is a tribally centred dimension, belief system, clan and kinship, language and naming, in all the filled human space of Blackfeet culture:

> My main point in writing this book is to present the Blackfeet way of life – daily life, hunting, raiding, ceremonies, mores, belief, preparing hides and food – before the whites made real inroads into their culture. The Indian had a different reality and I try to present that.[2]

Centred in the life of Fools Crow, originally White Man's Dog, and whose change of name marks his coming-of-age as warrior and medicine man, the novel from the outset takes great care to set up a meticulous Native-animist geography. The Montana Rockies become 'the Backbone of the World', the moon 'Night Red Light', the sun 'Sun Chief', winter 'the Cold-Maker', death 'Shadow Land', and the ancestral Blackfeet deities 'the Above Ones'. Shadow nomenclature as may be when given in English transliteration, each, even so, points to a Blackfeet sense of cosmos and nature-cycle born of its own ordering semantics.

For this is Blackfeet life alive in circumstantiality, the three bands of the Pikuni, Kainah and Siksika, and their subdivision into warrior societies, as well as Fools Crow's family of Rides at the Door, his father, mother, and his wife Red Paint and child. Welch carefully delineates a working round of hunt, raid, sweatlodge, courtship, migrations between summer and winter camps, intimacy with Nature and its animals, birds and sounds, diplomacy with other Blackfeet and, unsentimentally, tribal rivalries and different acts of human pettiness and crime. Time joins seamlessly to place, belief to practice, Blackfeet cosmology to Blackfeet everyday existence. Louis Owens has persuasive grounds for terming the novel 'an act of cultural recovery'.[3]

Napikwans, white men, operate at a distance, as though situated at the spatial-temporal periphery. This is not to underestimate the trauma for the tribe of the Baker Massacre of 1870, in which 173 Pikunis, mostly women and children, were destroyed by the military mainly at the behest of local cattlemen. Nor is it to downplay the devastating impact of different waves of white-imported smallpox. Both are given place in Welch's novel, but as incidents, however important, within yet others. The effect is to replace the usual emphasis of frontier, farm settlement and the cavalry with a tribal perspective, so inverting the usual formula of the 'winning' of the west.

Tribal memory presides. Fools Crow, for instance, remembers 'the stories told by his grandfather of the origins of the constellations. He had been young then and it all seemed simple. There were only the people, the stars, and the blackhorns' (p. 93). Whatever the self-estimate of white explorers, the settlers and their covered wagons, or even the military, as white people they are initially thought of in trickster vein and tribal humour: 'At first we thought these Napikwans were animals and incapable of reproducing with human beings' (p. 66).

Blackfeet history, in general, becomes one of uncertain equipoise, a tough, savvy tribal order, yet also vulnerable to a changing America. Welch, to his credit, once more eschews any hint of sentimentality. If the Pikunis hold to a warrior etiquette, they also have renegades capable of destructive, indeed murderous, action, as in the case of Owl's Child and his followers. Their situation becomes one of Pikuni continuity yet possible rupture, history as know-how, survival, a way of being, and yet history as also the threat of diminution and erasure. It is a dynamic shrewdly perceived in the observation of the mixedblood scout Joe Kipp: 'These people have not changed, thought Kipp, but the world they live in has. You could look at it one of two ways: either their world was shrinking or that other world, the one the white man brought with him, is expanding' (p. 252).

Fools Crow's closing pilgrimage to Feather Woman as shaman, and as led in imagination by the spirit Nitsokou, becomes in effect a search for Blackfeet destiny. He is shown a scroll, a parchment of signs and predictions, which serves as prophecy: 'Fools Crow thought of the final design on the yellow skin in Feather Woman's Lodge. He saw the Napikwan children playing and laughing in a world that they possessed. And he saw the Pikuni children, quiet and huddled together, alone and foreign in their own country' (p. 386). In this 'final design', past and future join to set inheritance against dispossession. Welch's closing note as to Blackfeet siting is historic, chastening.

With both *Love Medicine* (1984, 1993) and *Tracks* (1988), Louise Erdrich shows another unique hand in the creation of Native site, two story-cycles of Chippewa life within a border USA of North Dakota and Montana and a turning wheel of human overlap and counterpoint. Each story, a number of them told in monologue, stands complete in itself but always as augmented by the overall linkage of mixedblood-Chippewa dynasty, a homeland, however, and from pre-contact to modernity, evoked as one of the living not dead.

Love Medicine, fourteen pieces to which four more were added in the 1993 edition, inaugurates the Kashpaw-Lamartine cycle. In 'The World's Greatest Fishermen', the four-part first story, a Chippewa woman, June Kashpaw, wills her own death after much drinking and a casual sex encounter with a 'mud engineer' (p. 3) by walking into the night-time snows and Chinook wind outside of Williston, North Dakota ('oil boomtown', p. 1). Her death, that of a woman lost to her own best promise, and its aftermath for her divorced husband Gordie, her niece Albertine Johnson and mother Zelda, her Grandmother Kashaw and Great-uncle Eli, her cousin Nector and the family adoptee Lipsha Morrissey, supplies a kind of warning shadow for the lives still to be unfolded.

This is reservation culture toughly told as damage, missed chance, love which can turn bitter. Yet behind the rivalries and splits, as behind the intrusion of the white-owned oil business and other exploitation, Erdrich points always to older, and larger, Chippewa history. As the cycle expands, other Kashpaws and Lamartines enter, together with the Lazarres, Pillagers, Morrisseys, Nanapushes and Adares, each severally bound into a linked but broken hoop. White against red values clash. Odd couplings and liaisons and births take place. Families vie for ever-reducing land. Slithers of Anishinaabe speech entwine themselves in dialogue and each narrative's English. Yet for each crack or fissure there is connection, life-histories whose very divergences themselves make a revolving circle.

The stories, in turn, deal with the tensions between a French-exported Catholicism and Chippewa belief ('Saint Marie' and 'Flesh and Blood'); the unexpected, comic turns of tribal conjure as against Catholic observance in affairs of the heart ('Love Medicine'); the role of drink and alcoholism in Chippewa history ('Crown of Thorns'); sexual permutations within an extended family regime ('Lulu's Boys'); Vietnam and the return of the damaged Henry Lamartine ('The Red Convertible'); and actual tribal reality in an era of mythified or cartoon Indians ('The Plunge of the Brave'). As serious in implication as these themes evidently are, Erdrich keeps them free of solemnity or sentimentalism. Narrators, accordingly, can settle old scores, adjust the record as fits, complain or justify, only to have correctives supplied by others in the wheel.

Lulu Lamartine in 'The Good Tears' offers a key instance. 'I'm going to tell you about the men' (p. 277), she announces, in short order to catalogue Nector Kashpaw, the 'rifraff Morrissey' and the brothers Henry and Bev Lamartine, in all a black comedy of revolving marriages and relationships. But if she recognises her own wayward path, the quick sexual fix over anything long-term, she also keeps her eye on the more encompassing displacement:

> All through my life I never did believe in human measurement. Numbers, time, inches, feet. All are just ploys for cutting nature down to size. I know the grand scheme of the world is beyond our brains to fathom, so I don't try, just let it in. I don't believe in numbering God's creatures. I never let the United States census in my door, even though they say it's good for Indians. Well, quote me. I say that every time they counted us they knew the precise number to get rid of. (pp. 281–2)

Not only does this project a richly singular characterisation, but a history, a tribal sense of America, which cycles into Native lives well beyond her own. Erdrich's feat, throughout, is to make one idiom of story precisely imply others.

Tracks steps back an increment in time to the years running from winter 1912 to spring 1924, and narrates across its nine stories the double jeopardy suffered by the Chippewa from pneumonia and the loss of tribal lands to outside speculators. Two voices preside, those of old Nanapush, Chippewa tribal chairman, and of Pauline Lamartine, would-be Catholic martyr, who despite her every effort to break free of her Chippewa allegiances finds herself hexed and drawn back into her Indian heritage.

A third, and crucial, human point of reference is given in the person of Fleur Pillager. Varyingly she is thought a witch, a lover and a loved one, and at one point Erdrich calls her in Anishinaabe a *mide* or visionary. To her daughter, Lulu Pillager, she offers special testimony, the wisdom of self-acceptance against odds and the hostility of her detractors. In their three voices, Chippewa culture, as site past and present, once more takes on live continuity, a resistance, however humanly vexed, to closure.

Nanapush, for his part, speaks out of the past ('I guided the last buffalo hunt. I saw the last bear shot', p. 2). His is the witness to government treaty, allotment, the creation of tribal police, and above all to the disease in which 'Our tribe unraveled like a coarse rope' (p. 2). He knows, too, that 'Nanapush is a name that loses power every time that it is written and stored in a government file' (p. 32). Yet he is also 'oldtime Anishinaabe warrior' (p. 116), guardian of tribal memory, good medicine, a repository of hunting and preservation skills.

Pauline's furious attempts to divest herself of her Indian identity ('Pauline schemed to gain attention by telling odd tales that created damage', p. 39) thus make a necessary ironic point of contrast. She engages in the most baroque Catholicism, would-be martyr and saint, tries a bevy of men, and hovers between sanity and unhingement. Between Nanapush and Pauline, and in each alternating act of story, they tell the larger and even more important story of how, against history, the Chippewas in all their breakage have managed by near-miracle to endure.

Like its predecessors, *Tracks* does not always afford too easy or immediate access, but it continues to exhibit Erdrich's mastery of cyclical narrative. The history which gives rise to each voice may well deal in bitterest loss but not at the expense of self-pity. Nowhere does this show more affectingly than in the account given by Pauline Lamartine of a prophetic early moment in the life of Nanapush. The memory is tragic yet salutary, a warning and yet a celebration:

> As a young man, he had guided a buffalo expedition for whites. He said the animals understood what was happening, how they were dwindling. He said that when the smoke cleared and hulks lay scattered everywhere, a day's worth of shooting for only the tongues and hides, the beasts that survived grew strange and unusual. They lost their minds. They bucked, screamed and stamped, tossed the carcasses and grazed on flesh. They tried their best to cripple one another, to fall or die. They tried suicide. They tried to do away with their young. They knew they were going, saw their end. He said while the whites all slept through the terrible night he kept watch, that the groaning

never stopped, that the plain below him was alive, a sea turned against itself, and when the thunder came, then and only then, did the madness cease. He saw their spirits slip between the lightning sheets. (pp. 139–40)

The stories in *Tracks*, as the title implies, function as pathways into a composite but always unique legacy, the Chippewa as shadowed by colonial death and yet kept in being by sheer human vitality and the will to survive. Tragedies of displacement, each outbreak of disease, remain undeniable, but not so as to crowd out each redeeming liaison and continuity, not to mention the comic pratfalls of desire, marriage or religious practice. Both in its fissures and its joinings, Erdrich's world of Native dynasty becomes as vertical as horizontal, the Chippewa life within her fiction made over into the site of a history and culture longer, and richer, than any one moment of reservation or township.

III

The sites of Asian America, given every contrast the one with the other, equally proliferate: Angel Island to Chinatown, Japantown to Manzanar, each Korea-town, Little Manila or Little Bombay, the Sikhs of California's Yuba City to the Vietnamese of Louisiana's Lake Charles, and always the islands of Hawai'i as pan-Asian, indeed pan-American, metropolis. Each of these communities, of necessity, assumes its own present tense, and yet always in relation to massive layers of prior cultural memory. As much, thereby, as Asian America has been given to contemporary telling, in this shaping residual sense, it looks to telling already told.

Whether, more precisely, Japanese America as 1930s–1940s township and flower-nursery West Oakland in the stories of Toshio Mori, or the Chinatown Vancouver and Chinatown San Francisco of novels by Sky Lee and Fae Myenne Ng, or Korean American borough politics in New York as conceived by Chang-rae Lee, or the Vietnam of the Mekong Delta and then the Mekong Grocery in Falls Church, Virginia, of Lan Cao, these fictions all give expression to an Asian America or Canada always the two sites in one. Each offers a mutuality of substance and silhouette, Asian American ethnicity, if told as the lived-in present, then anything but forgetful of the lived-in past.

In no sense is this truer than in the 1930s San Leandro community world of Toshio Mori's *Yokohama, California* (1949, 1985), twenty-two stories whose nuancing of Japan-in-America has rarely been bettered. Mori, as has become well known, amounts to a true literary-recovery story. His California birth in 1910, work in the family nursery business, internment in the Topaz Camp in Utah despite a brother wounded on overseas army service and where he became camp historian, meant delayed publication of his stories in book form. Yet on appearance that, too, came hedged in ambiguity, whether the well-meant but custodial Introduction by William Saroyan, bestselling Armenian American author of California blue-collar life ('He is a natural born writer . . . [yet] . . . it will be better for him when [he] learns to be more lucid') or, for all of Mori's own mention of it, the too easily misleading comparison with the 'grotesque' of Sherwood Anderson's *Winesburg, Ohio* (1919).

The two stories Mori was to add later act as their own kind of framing. 'Tomorrow is Coming, Children', told in the voice of an interned grandmother without explicit mention of any camp, implies its own act of affiliation, un-self-pitying and also unrecriminatory ('Ah San Francisco, my dream city . . . I belong here', p. 20). 'Slant Eyed Americans', the title phrasing its own ironic rebuke, again points to a choice of loyalties, and in which a Japanese American son, like any other American son, leaves patriotically for war ('Our people's honor depends on you Nisei soldiers', his mother tells him, p. 135). Both, with all of Mori's characteristic understatement, point to Japanese American life as also, and endemically, American life, despite that same America's act of seeking to make those of Japanese descent surrogate prisoners of war for the Japan which attacked Pearl Harbor.

'Lil' Yokohama' bears home the point in yet another way. An imagistic mosaic, it builds a portrait of 'our community' (p. 71) as live, full, everyday America ('we have twenty-four hours every day', p. 71). A taxonomy accumulates. Baseball loyalties take the form of the Alameda Taiiku vs San Jose Asahis with due family fans and popcorn. The school day parallels the work day. The death of the long-time gardener, Mr Komai, occurs as the same time as the sansei birth of Franklin Susumu Amano. Yukio Takaki, painter living on Seventh Street, throws an observing eye on the scene. Sam Suda expands his fruit market. Satoru Ugaki gets married. The sight of a new Oldsmobile Eight causes a stir. Ray Tatemoto leaves to study journalism in New York. The daily *Mainichi News* makes its appearance. Housewives read, radios blast out Benny Goodman's jazz, school ends. 'The day is here and is Lil' Yokohama's day' (p. 76), runs Mori's gloss, apt, deliberately low-key, the confirmation of a community wholly ordinary in its activity and rhythm.

Yet this poetry of the everyday, so discreetly rendered, contains its own threat of counterface: that in which Japanese America is to be seen as alien, a fifth column, latest Yellow Peril. The ordinary turns extraordinary, and the prospect of camp as against house, desert as against township. Mori rightly spells out nothing, a narrative of the unsaid as much as the said. It makes the point exactly, and movingly, the one America shadowed in the other.

It also, and unmistakably, underlines how the art of each of the other stories in *Yokohama, California* delivers the interiority of Japanese America. In 'The Woman Who Makes Swell Doughnuts', a child gives witness to the alimentary craft, the sheer life art, of the old woman known as Mama whose doughnuts carry the flavours of time, history, the very tissue of human creativity. In 'The Seventh Street Philosopher', Motoji Tsunoda, seeming oddball monologist, embodies a force of brave passion as he speaks, absurdly and yet not, to a lecture hall of seven people. In 'Three Japanese Mothers', the women, Kiku, Tane and Tomi, all sixty-ish, link their family greenhouse and flower cultivation to the destinies of their respective sons, a subtle hinging of the past which brought them from Hiroshima, Japan, the present which is Washington township, California, and the Japanese America which will be the future generation. Toshio Mori's subtleties endow these, and all the other lives he tells, with a quite superb miniaturist touch, the local as the always larger site.

Kae Ying Woo, present-day narrator of Sky Lee's dense, threaded novel of Chinese Vancouver, *Disappearing Moon Cafe* (1991), sets herself to transgress what she terms 'chinese-in-Canada' silence and invisibility, a 'secret code' (p. 180). The history she unravels, circling into the twentieth century from Wong Gwei Chang's arrival in 1892 with a mission to return to China the bones of dead coolies who once worked on the Canadian Pacific Railway, through to the birth of her own son, Robert Man Jook Lee, in 1986, amounts to panorama, each time-panel dated and given its own standing. Each, however, across warring love-hates, patrilinear and matrilinear lines, looks to the Disappearing Moon Cafe of the 1920s, 'the busiest, largest restaurant in Chinatown' (p. 24) as reference point. For the Wong dynasty, as others in the making of the Chinese-in-Canada, it becomes hearthstone, meal-table, an ongoing archive.

The three generations in question not only shape and hex each other, at one point as near-incest, but do so within the paired geographies of east and west, China and Canada, an Asiatown at once Vancouver's city of China and China's own city of Vancouver. For Kae Ying Woo, 'the well-kept secret I actually unearthed years ago' (p. 23), circuitous, knotted, always resistant, becomes also yet another double thread: a history busy in the facts of timeline and dynasty, and yet, in her very reclamation of it, a fiction of her own imagining.

The first tier of Wong Gwei Chang, and his abandoned first wife Kelora Chen (a crossblood of mixed Chinese and Native-Canadian parentage), and his redoubtable second wife, Lee Mui Lan, centres indeed on 'Disappearing Moon Cafe, 50 East Pender Street, Vancouver, British Columbia' (p. 23). Beginning from Canada's Exclusion Act of 1923 and the sinophobic and sexually fraught 'Janet Smith case' of 1924 ('A white woman is murdered! The prime suspect is a Chinese houseboy named Wong Foon Sing! Chopsticks drop and clatter in surprise! Clumps of rice stick in throats . . .', p. 66), Lee offers a Chinatown evolved from the 'old ways' of the Chinese-only Tang People's Street into modern Chinese Vancouver, at once Chinese *and* English-speaking.

The near-comedy of genealogical miscalculation which descends on the second generation of Wong Choy Fuk, son of Gwei Chang, and Lee Mui, his designated wife, Chan Fong Mei, and his concubine, Song Ang, among other doings wonderfully undercuts male primogeniture as assumed Chinese writ. Lee offers family as a *tableau vivant* of deals struck, guerilla campaigns, needs denied or seized, inside coverups, and each located within the competing different orbits of family, gender and age. Lee Mui turns slowly from Empress of all she surveys to Empress denied. Fong Mei moves from silence to speech and woman-slave to woman-warrior. Choy Fuk evolves from doted-upon legitimate son to doting father. Wong Ting An, offspring of Gwei Chang and Kelora, rises from abandoned illegitimate son to reinstituted heir. Under Moon Cafe rules, and, as Sky Lee manages the story, each reversal or aboutface becomes the norm, its own kind of working order.

The saga manages an even greater about-turn with the third generation and Kae's almost blood-related parents, Beatrice and Keeman. However unwittingly, they reintegrate the line through their marriage, but not without the price of the suicide of Beatrice's sister, Suzie. Between Beatrice and her mother, Fong Mei, lies both tension and transition: 'while Fong Mei hated this country, which had done nothing except disqualify her, Beatrice had grown up a thoroughly small-town canadian' (p. 164). In the prohibited love of Beatrice and Keeman lies a contract made against received order, the overturn of an old China by a new. Suzie can achieve no such about-turn: she hates 'Granny's dumb China rules' (p. 176), wants out, and takes her own life as a prisoner destroyed rather than saved or enhanced by the mix of regimes. Appropriately enough, she loses in a miscarriage the last son, the last male Wong heir, freeing the way for a regime of daughters. If, however, Beatrice and Keeman give the sign of new Chinese survival, Suzie gives the sign of an old Chinese cost.

This cumulative account, given in story-episode and first-person memory, letter and dialogue, and not least played out against the PRC and 'Overseas Chinese' perspective of Hermia Chow, Swiss-raised, international, eventually filters and weaves into the one connected sequence. The unfolding of the story, as it falls to her to recreate, she quite appropriately thinks 'the heavy chant of the storyteller' (p. 237). For she it is, freed dynastically to be both Chinese westerner and western Chinawoman, who now authors the very dynasty which once authored her.

China-history, as she recreates it, thus becomes Canada-history, or rather Chinese Canadian history, each, however, and across all the human interstices, bound up quite dazzlingly in her word, her imagining. *Disappearing Moon Cafe* depicts the Asiatown of East Pender Street as a peopling always actual and historic, and yet, and at the same time, called back into being as though players in a consummate fiction. Kae's account, as Sky Lee creates it, offers a voice to suit for a China site, if true to history, also true to story.

'#2–4–6 UPDAIRE' (p. 183). So Faye Myenne Ng's *Bone* (1993) designates the Fu-Leong apartment in Salmon Alley, Chinatown, San Francisco. The family comprises Mah, matriarch and baby-store proprietor, her second husband Leon, merchant sailor and odd-job tinkerer, and the sisters – Leila, in whose voice the novel is narrated, Ona, whose suicide leap provides the novel's emotional lodestone, and Nina, who literally has decamped from the Chinatown she thinks of as stasis to New York and avian life as a flight attendant. The 'old blue sign' (p. 193), later to become 'backdaire' (p. 194), perfectly enciphers in its midway Chinglish another Asiatown made up in equal part of an ongoing Chinese past and an ongoing Chinese American present. As Leila leaves no doubt: 'There was a time when Salmon Alley was our whole world' (p. 176).

Thinking back, however, to when with her then lover and eventual husband, Mason Louie, she drove to Salmon Alley to tell Mah about Ona's fatal jump from the Nam Ping Yuen building, Leila imagines this 'whole world' seen only from outside: 'Looking out, I thought, So this is what Chinatown looks like from inside those dark Greyhound buses; this slow view, these strange color combinations, these narrow streets, this is what tourists come to see' (p. 145). In fact, for her, a quite less narrow human order would be hard to imagine. Intrigue, griefs, competing languages, gossip, a diasporic China of rift and reconciliation, all play into the Chinatown family dynasty to be understood, in another of Ng's best metaphors, as time-zones situated the one inside the other.

Ng tells *Bone* as a series of story-folds, Mah and her daughters caught up in a serial began in an originary China, continued over in Chinese San Francisco, and if in one sense history as repetition then history as also renewal in form and sequence. Mah's first marriage to Lyman Fu, who abandons her and Leila for the new Gum Sahn of Australia, gives a point of departure. Leon Leong, Lyman's successor, looks backs to his Angel island and paper-son history yet also looks forward to a mainland history quite the opposite of paper marriage and family. Mah's adultery with Tommy Hom while working as a seamstress, and Leon's bitter return to the bachelor hotel, the *San Fran* ('our family's oldest place, our beginning place, our new China' (p. 4), as Leila cryptically describes it on account of Grandfather Leong's early residence there), looks to two faces of generational love and marriage. Even Leon's ill-fated laundry venture with Dai Gor, or Big Brother, the Peruvian-Chinese Luciano Ong, gives another contrast, life on land as against his frequent absences at sea. Finally, Leon's haunting, confused search for the cemetery bones of dead Chinese ancestors, during the Ghost Festival, links inextricably in his own mind to the death of his beloved daughter Ona.

This sense of life throughout *Bone* as always human interplay and dialectic Ng accomplishes with genuine finesse. Mah's bitter ginseng tea contrasts with Leila's restaurant-going, her Chinatown baby store with Leila's Bay Area job as a high-school counsellor. Leon's euphoric Dream of Gold Mountain alternates with his disillusioned outbursts against America as 'this lie of a country' (p. 103). Ona as one of a new generation finds only oldest self-abandon, and eventually death, in drugs, while Nina escapes to New York, but returns with the announcement of having had an abortion.

Leila herself, 'I'm the stepdaughter of a paper son' (p. 61), yet also American-born modern daughter, finds herself narrator-participant for these back-and-forths of heritage and dynasty. If Leon can say 'You're inside Chinatown; it's safe . . . Outside it's different' (p. 181), she herself seeks 'something that would unlock me from Mah, this alley, Chinatown' (p. 184). She cites Nina as saying of both Leon and Mah 'their parenting [was] chop suey, a little of everything' (p. 110). She grows up snared between Salmon Alley as past Asiatown even as she does a job counselling the Chinese American children who will become the future generation. In this respect, she thinks with envy of how Nina has become a China guide and so has 'a whole map of China in her head; I had Chinatown, the Mission, Tenderloin' (p. 28).

Time, dynasty, however, do change for her. When, for the last time, she leaves Salmon Alley with Mason, past and new life join. He, their marriage, point forward. Yet the 'old blue sign, #2-4-6 UPDAIRE' (p. 193) reminds her always 'to look back, to remember' (p. 194). The one 'backdaire' (p. 194) site of Chinese American life Leila carries 'in my heart' (p. 194) as her 'reassurance' (p. 194), the trove of family and memory with which to enter not only other Chinese, but all next and further, America.

Chang-rae Lee's *Native Speaker* (1995) looks to quite another Asian American site, a Korean American turf of politics and power-brokerage set in the 1980s New York borough of multi-ethnic Queens. Its story of Henry Park, son of a brutally hard-working immigrant and grocerman father, employee in a murky American surveillance outfit, and a spy on the rise and fall of John Kwang as Korean American councilman from Flushing and possible New York mayor, however, points to always intriguingly deeper fare: the way identity, personal, ethnic, American, is constructed. One clue lies early in Park's assertion, as he builds up his report, that 'My necessary invention was John Kwang' (p. 130).

For this is Asian America as one ethnicity in a spectrum of American ethnicity itself then told as 'spy' territory. The designated public identity is pursued for the individual identity within: the Park family, the silent Korean housekeeper sent for on the mother's death (a Korean-speaker only) who arrives bearing bottled *kimchee* and Korean dried vegetables, Kwang himself and his warring Asian, Black and Hispanic constituencies, and Henry Park as narrator-detective. His own stilled cross-marriage to the Scots American Lelia, and the loss of their beloved child, Mitt, who has once mimickingly called his father '*chink*, a *jap*, and a *gook*' and sung the lines 'Charlie Chan, face as flat as pan' (p. 96) and has died in a fortuitous choking incident, gives its own haunting centre, and mystery, to the story.

In this, Lee's very spirals of style, each ellipsis and phrase (Lelia's pen-marked itineraries as she plans out her European escape from Henry a 'messy bruise of ink', p. 3), are somehow to be seen as implicated in the guises involved in investigating New York, metropolis and suburb, for the lives sited as Asian American. If Henry Park's father will struggle in his adopted language, his son, reflecting Lee's own authorship, will take his own domain over the very language of immigrancy and the play of racial markers just as Lelia uses her own speech-therapy skills to release into word children with 'physiological defects like cleft palates and tied tongues' (p. 2).

As Henry Park plunges ever deeper into Kwang's life as a first-ever public Korean American politician, the novel opens into anything but mere thriller or caper. Its subject indeed can be thought that of language itself, or at least the politics of language. What *are* the languages of foreignness, of ethnicity, of Asianness and Americanness, and how do their powers impinge upon the individual life? These issues slowly emerge through each circling of plot, whether the intrigues of Hoagland as the domestic spy-agency head, Eduardo as his agent-in-place, Lelia's own early list of her husband's traits to include '*False speaker of language*' (p. 5) or, centrally, John Kwang's councilman politicking, be it financial or sexual.

The latter, which culminates in a disaster of scandal and arrest, and which began as the Korean system of *ggeh* but became finagled into an American financial scam, supplies an enclosing irony. What is it to be perceived as Korean American or any other Asian hyphenation? What language of politics, and conversely politics of language, best applies? Lee has not always won plaudits. There has been talk of too involuted a plot and idiom, a taste for the garish or inflated phrase. Such, by far, is to miss the point: *Native Speaker* brings not only a daring of style to bear, but an often simply luminous intelligence.

With good reason, the text speaks of New York, indeed America, as 'a city of words' (p. 319), and offers a last scene in which Henry aids Lelia with more speech-impaired children. 'Taking care of every last pitch and accent . . . I hear her speaking a dozen lovely and native languages, calling out all the difficult names of who we are' (p. 324), he witnesses. Korean America, we are invited to consider both on the basis of the spiralled Kwang story, and Henry Park's own within it, belongs among those 'difficult names', another of America's ethnic sites full of language and yet, at the same time still, and always, to find its own fullest language.

Lan Cao's *Monkey Bridge* (1997), told as the memoir-novel of Mai Nguyen, Vietnamese American daughter to her stroke-ridden mother, Nguyen Van Binh, who fled Saigon in 1975 and who is dying in an Arlington, Virginia hospital, also ponders Asia and America as contrasting languages. Thinking of her mother, and her friend, Mrs Bay, the two refugee Vietnamese women from Ba Xuyen province, with whom she plans an expansion of their Mekong Grocery, Mai observes: 'In many ways, they continued to live in a geography of thoughts defined by a map of a country that no longer existed in terms I could understand' (p. 66)

Cao handles this ongoing endoublement of Vietnam with meticulous flair, the one the mother's world of Buddhist-karmic Vietnam history with its endlessly warring ghosts to be appeased or hexed ('a starved sea-horse waiting for happier days', p. 150), the other which has become a part of her daughter's adoptive westernness as a TV warground of napalm, A-teams and strategic hamlet (Saigon 'a combustion of burning chemicals and fuel', p. 74). In the mystery story at its centre, that of Baba Quan, at once mythic grandfather, cuckold, Viet Cong agent and Mekong killer-revenger, there is also to be read the inadequacy of all cultural binaries, any one simple opposing otherness.

Vietnam as these two joined, yet divided, kinds of site plays throughout. The former lies inside Tet, rice ceremony, the betel tree, the Chinese solar calendar, the mother's Buddhist endowment of big ears and the way she bequeaths their meaning to her daughter as a bastion against harm, and the monkey bridge as an image of an always precarious life-balance. The other is to be perceived as Little Saigon, the Virginia enclave of exiles, food and custom where Vietnam can somehow be miniaturised and made safe. But if even ex-GIs shop there, that is not to say that each Vietnamese face other than reminds, in both ways, of a war lost and a peace not yet won.

For Mai, the challenge, as she says of herself, is to find her own monkey bridge between a 'subverted interior' (p. 2) and the exterior worlds of the Vietnam ghosted by America and the America by Vietnam. 'The Vietnam delivered to America had passed beyond reclamation. It was no longer mine to explain' (p. 128), she observes. Both, even so, live deep, and abidingly, within her. Cao, on the one hand, has Mai overlap with Maxine Hong Kingston's woman warrior in her self-identification with one of the mythic Trung sisters (fighters, ironically, against invading Chinese), a Vietnamese figure of survival. With the intervention, on the other hand, of her adoptive Connecticut parents, the ex-US colonel, Michael, his wife Mary, together with the promise of a 'new' education at Mount Holyoke as America's oldest women's college, hers will also be Americanisation. She is right to think the transition that of 'an outsider with inside information' (p. 212).

In settings which, appropriately enough, turn upon images of fissure and surgical repair, whether the hospital treatment of a mother's stroke or the divides of grammar between English and Vietnamese ('There is no fixed "I" or "you" in Vietnamese', p. 144), she finds herself called upon to make wholes of parts. One kind of pathway is indicated in her mother's belief in Asian astrology, fortune-telling, Vietnamese destinies of chance to be foreseen and countered. Another lies in her mother's obsession with TV's Jaime Sommers, the Bionic Woman as an American self remade. Mai inherits both, two sites of time and place each, also, with its own 'languages' of life and death. As given in *Monkey Bridge*, their resolution, in all its multicultural challenge, will lie in her own powers of Vietnamese American bridging.

IV

No black city, or black inner city, has more seized the world's imagination than Harlem, at once striking, indissoluble fact, and at the same time, from the Jazz Era 1920s to the Black Power 1960s, and then well beyond, the very stuff of legend. If in one vista the ghetto, a world of tenement, crime and mean streets, there have always been other Harlems. They include those of church and domestic respectability, politics, domestic employment downtown whether as maid or porter, and an effervescence of jazz and blues, ragtime and rap, eateries and after-midnight venues. That the stories of its citizenry, its brownstones and storefront churches, its 125th Street, and each memorial reference back to Dixie, not to mention Harlem argot and style, have fed into almost every kind of literary genre has been as inevitable as it has been compelling.[4]

Claude McKay's *Home to Harlem* (1928), as well known as any fiction from the New Negro era, and for all the author's Jamaican origins, gives an insider's exuberant, street-level portrait. Langston Hughes's bar-room Jesse Simple stories, begun in the *Chicago Defender* in 1943, tell another fond, anecdotal Harlem, but not without its own keen-eyed irony. James Baldwin's *Go Tell It on the Mountain* (1952), by contrast, offers Harlem in the wake of the Depression, edging into ghetto, a clash of flesh and spirit told against a backdrop of fervid southern memory and pentecostalism. Louise Meriwether's *Daddy was a Number Runner* (1970) also looks back to the 1930s as a girl's-eye view of Harlem, the uncertain route into black womanhood amid street and poverty.

Chester Himes's Coffin Ed Jones/Grave Digger Johnson *romans policiers*, inaugurated with *For Love of Imabelle* (1957), turn Harlem into comic-surreal crime labyrinth, a milling world of citied hustle, masquerade, a humanity at once preyed upon and predatory. William Melvin Kelly's *dem* (1967) again opens Harlem to the fantastical, black city and white suburb as mutual distortion, a hall of mirrors. For Robert Deane Pharr in *SRO* (1971), Harlem centres in 119th Street's Hotel Logan as the ground zero of human spirit, the reduction of existence through the supply-and-demand of heroin, drink and prostitution, to exactly, and searingly, single-room occupancy. A line of women's authorship would invoke Nella Larsen's *Passing* (1929), with its subtle interaction of gender and racial identity, Ann Petry's *The Street* (1946), whose life of Lutie Johnson points to Harlem's clubland glitter and yet tenement threat, or Rosa Guy's *A Measure of Time* (1983), in which the life of Dorine Davis as a 'booster' or thief is set within a twentieth-century Dixie-to-Manhattan panorama. Each of these, however different, speaks to Harlem's great wellsprings of life, its seeming near-inexhaustibility.

In Toni Morrison's *Jazz* (1992), Harlem as live axis, the lodestone of Afro-America's past inside present, takes on further unique form. Morrison has long been recognised to have attempted her own unfolding of American history, from *The Bluest Eye* (1970), and its portrait of Pecola Breedlove's descent into self-hate in her quest for blue-eyed beauty and a redemptive family love, through to *Paradise* (1998), with its parable of black women's community refuge. Each of her other best-known novels, to include *Song of Solomon* (1977), with its inspired use of the 'flying African' mythos, and *Tar Baby* (1981), with its black-diasporic linkage of Africa, the Caribbean and Afro-America, similarly works within a specific panel of time and place. These chronological staging grounds, together, make for an encompassing whole, Morrison's version of the historical route from slavery to the modern city.

Jazz adds yet another link and with its own virtuosity. Set in a 1920s time-present, yet with dips into earlier tiers of black life, and given over to the stirring love triangle of Joe Trace, his wife Violet, and Dorcas, history elides into a kind of ballad, as it were talked, and then written, as a Harlem blues. 'He fell for an eighteen-year-old girl with one of those deepdown, spooky loves' (p. 3). The novel opens in the voice of a narrator always privy to all the gathering detail of this 'bewilderment' (p. 6), at once familiar, chorusy, not a little censorious, yet, and by clear authorial design, less and less certain of her ground by the end of the story. The novel as much turns on Morrison's feats of style as it does on the actual love affair, its command of viewpoint and pace.

The immediate landscape is the Harlem of Lenox Avenue and 140th Street, with 3 January 1926 as its immediate season, winter cold at its bitterest. 'I'm crazy about this City' (p. 7) confides the narrator, 'Do what you please in the City, it is there to back and frame you no matter what you do' (pp. 8–9). In one incarnation, this is Harlem at its crest of style as black metropolis, hub, full of the Jazz Age energy of round-midnight clubs like the *Mexico*, of speakeasies, eateries, 'clarinets and love-making' (p. 7). The city colour draws yet further from Garveyist parades, Harlem Hospital, and even the gaudy commercial logos for drink and good times pasted on to Harlem's walls.

But in a matching incarnation Joe and Violet, figures like Dorcas's keenly etched seamstress aunt with her own fund of respectability and who has had the raising of the girl (and who will eventually, no doubt contrarily, befriend Violet), and always the narrator behind them, serve also to remind of domestic and street-intimate Harlem. This vista looks to tenanted brownstones, the stoop, grocery shopping, everyday jobs and meals and apartment life. As, too, a one-time 'young country couple' (p. 30) from Vesper County, Virginia, they also show Harlem to have drawn black-southern remembrance, cotton, the jukes, food or idiom, into its own citied way of being.

Joe Trace's lonely passion for a teenage girl, that of a fifty-odd-year-old 'sample case man' (p. 73) selling Cleopatra toiletries, his eventual shooting of Dorcas Manfred as she moves on from him to Acton, her chosen and insouciant younger blade, and Dorcas's dying refusal to name Joe as her killer, might indeed be ballad. Morrison found the source of her story in a James Van Der Zee photograph of a Harlem corpse and Camille Billops's *The Harlem Book of the Dead* (1978). The unhinged attack of Violet, neighbourhood hair-stylist, on Dorcas's corpse with a knife in order to mutilate her face, becomes a latest episode in eccentricity – she has earlier tried to steal a baby and once simply has sat down in a crowded street ('Joe never learned of Violet's public crazinesses', p. 22). She, like him, will eventually give herself to a secret-sharer vigil before Dorcas's photograph as the 'bold, unsmiling girl staring from the mantelpiece' (p. 12). The text's description of these events as 'the mystery of love' (p. 5) could not be better vindicated.

Out of Dorcas's life, and image, moreover, the novel is able to disinter a whole ambient history, that of the Great Migration, 'a wave of black people running from want and violence' (p. 33). It is as part of this migration that Joe and Violet have stepped north in 1906 carrying their respective family spirals of back-country history (he abandoned by his parents and raised by kindly foster-parents, she the daughter of a suicide) aboard the near-mythic train travelling through Baltimore and on to New York. The story looks back to their first encounter 'under a walnut tree' (p. 30), cotton-picking, and the singular lineages of kin which will travel with them as they board the 'colored section of the Southern Sky' (p. 30). If indeed blues narrative, *Jazz* loses no touch with a sense of the quotidian, Joe's ascent from fish-cleaner to doorside salesman, Violet's leg-tiredness from her hair work.

The effect is mosaic, circles of organising and contrapuntal image. Violet's empty birdcages, especially that of the parrot which could say 'I love you' (p. 24) and where she secretes the knife used on Dorcas, calls up Flaubert's 'Un cœur simple' in its imaging of desire and loss. Joe's morose love for Dorcas, sudden, yet then acted on as though a campaign, has him saying 'I didn't fall in love. I rose in it' (p. 135). Dorcas, never wholly a beauty as her friend Felice bears witness, but spirited, needy, primed to seize upon adventure and an identity of her own, is to be seen on the day of her death dancing with Acton amid 'dazzle and mischief' (p. 188), 'a heartbreaking vocal' (p. 188). 'Dorcas let herself die' (p. 209) confirms Felice, as if the dying girl would rather seal her best times forever than live on in recrimination.

The novel's two parallel flashbacks, Joe's abandonment as a child, the origins of his name as Trace, and his one-time tree-top sleeping, and Violet's family history through her Baltimore grandmother, True Belle, with its story of the mulatto Golden Gray and Joe's likely wild-woman mother, might be Dixie genealogy in microcosm. They both give witness to survival from out of the distortion of slavery, each historic southern code of black and whiteness and the race-politics, domestic and social, to which they have given rise. Even more, they point to the need to find, and make and sustain, 'family' as conditions best allow.

'Joe is wondering about all this on an icy day in January' (p. 180), runs Morrison's narrative as the fatal dénouement of his passion grows near. It supplies just the right run-up. The reader is again returned to the behest of a narrator at once guardian of the tale, yet also speculative, querulous, as to the understandability of the emotions which will move Joe to kill Dorcas as one love, and then, in resignation, return him to 'old-time love' (p. 228) with Violet. If she, as a stylist of Afro-hair, like Joe has been a purveyor of 'beauty', gossip, ironically, has conflated her name into Violent. The two of them, at the end of *Jazz*, normal and yet odd, the rising talk of the neighbourhood, remain as sentinels to what the narrator terms 'rogue' happenings.

For them, and for Dorcas, love has been both the intoxication of desire and yet the stillness of routine, dream and yet reality, nothing if not indeed a reckoning, a blues. The novel's circling story, and its circling narrator in kind, does every kind of justice. For this is a Harlem whose literal music, along with the music of its everyday life and word, Morrison makes into the very seam of her novel. It also gives a reminder that, however humanly particular, this remains but the one Harlem archive, and site, among an abundance of others.

V

East Los Angeles ('East Los'), Barelas in Albuquerque, San Antonio or Denver, 'Spanish' Harlem, Dade County's Little Havana, Salvadoran or Dominican Chicago, all, and severally, give currency to 'barrio' as Spanish-into-English term, its own world-within-a-world. The hum of vernacular Spanish, Catholicism often fused with *santería*, trademark Latino music and foodways, and each style of extended family, have made for easy recognition. If, too, 'barrio' has been taken to signify a culture marked by much poverty, and with it 'the street' of gang crime and drugs, that has not held across the board; it has always harboured other kinds of life. Nor has the barrio been but one kind of community as borne out in the middle-class émigré Cuban world of Florida as against that which has evolved in Los Angeles or Manhattan.

In Alejandro Morales's *Caras viejas y vino nuevo/Barrio on the Edge* (1975, 1998) and Nicholasa Mohr's *Nilda* (1973), two comparative fictions are indeed to be met with, Chicano East Los Angeles told as a Notes from Underground and Puerto Rican *Nueva York* told as through the tough, but affectionate, prism of a girl's coming of age. For Morales the idiom becomes near-hallucinatory, the speed and violence of *pachuco* lives drawn into the novel's realist-scatological grain. Mohr sets her pitch at a warmer, more affectionate angle, a poetry of remembrance.

'El barrio no cambia; parece que jamás cambiará'/'The barrio does not change; it seems it will never change' (p. 65; p. 64).[5] The narrator's comment in *Caras viejas y vino nuevo* gives working measure: a vision, more than not, of endgame. In the dual lives, and deaths, of the friends Julián and Mateo, Morales locates young life caught out by old despair, poverty, family feuding, addiction, alcohol. A drug-high fatal car-crash will kill the long-fated Julián. Mateo, more contemplative, a thinker, will die of leukaemia ('Death began talking to him', p. 108). If more for Julián than for Mateo, willfulness presides, the barrio as the adrenalin of violent turf and gang war, low-rider drag races, and always a sexuality full of compensating immediacy.

The temptation might have been to write only unrelieved Lower Depth or what the text designates 'el filo de la estirpe'/'La Raza's bottled up rage' (p. 165; p. 164). But, not unlike Hubert Selby's *Last Exit to Brooklyn*, the novel's voices give mediating depth and counterpoint. A back-and-forth timeline holds. It would be hard to miss the conscious insistence upon this one time and place as the figuration of each other like barrio, a world locked into itself as against 'el otro lado', the other side, of Anglo LA. Morales thereby can portray the barrio as stasis, yet also, in every kind of manifestation, suffused in human passion, if enclosure then also, and however perverse its forms of expression, a wellspring of energy.

This dialectic holds throughout. An opening wedding degenerates into 'barrio war' (p. 42). Julián laments the death through heart disease of his beloved mother, Margo, only to blame and feud with his authoritarian father Don Edmundo along with Doña Matilde as Margo's successor. The funeral degenerates into near-farce, Margo's demise a prompt not to reconciliation but to renewed father–son imbroglio. With Julián's own *compañera*, Virgy, love is bartered for sex, intimacy for more drugs. Little wonder the myth-figure of La Llorona, the weeping woman, is invoked at different moments: her spirit that of chorus to chaos and deformation.

If Mateo's family points up a better order, especially in his dying reflections as to past Christmas Eves and the memory of Father Carlos's long-ago 'socials', both he and Julián have their sorties with the *vatos locos*, the Buenasuerte brothers, their names belying their anything-for-kicks malevolence, and meaning, ironically, Good Luck. These gang outings act as their own counter-ritual: the different orgies and drug sessions, Mateo's brute back-of-the-car sex with the druggie-hooker Barbara, and for Mateo his final car disaster and for Julián his final hospitalisation. Morales keeps his novel tight, its very idiom as uneaseful as the world it depicts. If this is death-in-life, then Morales provides a last reminder in his allusion to the nearby 'hornos', or brick kilns, the barrio sited as enwalling hell.

For Nicholasa Mohr in *Nilda*, the barrio has its odds, but to nothing of this extent. 'Nilda loved telling stories about New York to her two best friends because they had never been there' (p. 163). In so locating her title figure, rather, Mohr shows her typically about storytelling business. For the novel, in an immediate way, is *Bildungsroman*, a portrait of the artist as Nuyorican pre-adolescent girl coming alive to her own creative powers against citied and Second World War *pobreza*.

But it also offers the dramatised remembrance of Puerto Rican New York as cultural site, a round of tenement housing, schooling, Nilda's Spanish-born sick stepfather, her valiant but always struggling mother, the siblings and older-generation relatives (especially the slightly crazed Aunt Delia who vows she speaks only Spanish but reads the paper in English), the welfare visits, summer camp, and her own dual-language heritage; in sum, barrio life as childhood's theatre, and all of it inscribed within Nilda's first-generation American consciousness. The novel may well have been published as a juvenile fiction, the contrast in every way with Piri Thomas's *Down These Mean Streets* (1967) as the chronicle of Nuyorican street life and crime-and-drugs. But it would be a mistake to think Mohr's directing hand less than adult.

For Nilda Ramírez, ten years old in July 1941, the terms of the barrio are set early. She grows up on the block, a 'familiar world of noise, heat and crowds' (p. 16). Summers become a shimmer of the city's 'intense heat' (p. 3). She remembers hearing *la policía* refer to 'the whole damned bunch of you spicks' (p. 6). As she contemplates the mainly Irish-run Catholic church, she wonders 'if Puerto Ricans were ever allowed to be nuns, fathers, or brothers' (p. 16). When she visits the mother of Sophie, the girl her brother Jimmy has taken up with, she hears: 'My Sophie, my daughter, is dead. She run off with a nigger and now she's dead' (p. 88). Welfare becomes routine and, often, a charade. Her stepfather dies. Life for the family is struggle, clothes, food, endless improvisation to make the rent, and always the circuit of white prejudice.

Yet, against these odds, Nilda finds necessary and redemptive value, sanctuary even, in her world. She calls up a childhood which, amid duress, is also fondness, the intimacy of remembered first things. That can be street camaraderie, the reading of the barrio newspaper *La Prensa*, the comic-grotesque episode in *La Iglesia Pentecostal* in which Don Justicio urinates in full view of the congregation to show his contempt for clericalism, her mother's half-zany seances with the neighbourhood *espiritista* Doña Tiofila, the memory of youth gangs like the Lightnings and the Barons, or her sense of caring for her baby sister and her love of often absentee brothers. It can even be the summer heat.

She allies this world, in turn, to her own emerging creativity. Mohr directs the reader early to Nilda's 'box of things' (p. 50), a storage not unlike that belonging to Mick Kelley in Carson McCuller's *The Heart is a Lonely Hunter*. On her way home, she stops at a tunnel in 104th Street – 'Sometimes when she was alone she would sing, enjoying the resonance of her own voice as it filled the dark chamber' (p. 58). Above all, she looks back to the self-discovery bound into a Fourth of July trip into the country which she links to her mother's memory of Puerto Rico: 'Nilda remembered her mother's description of Puerto Rico's beautiful mountainous countryside covered with bright flowers and red flamboyant trees' (p. 153). At these summer camps, she recalls her 'secret garden' (p. 158), a resource she will need on her mother's death which coincides, ironically, with the end of the Second World War.

As the novel closes, she is to be seen showing her friend Claudia drawings of the 'trail' into that garden, itself the figure of all that has been the meaning of her life and which act to join Puerto Rico both as Caribbean island and as Manhattan. It gives coordinates, place and time, to her own emerging self-definition. In this, *Nilda* joins other fictions by Mohr, *El Bronx Remembered* (1975), *Felita* (1979), *In Nueva York* (1979), *Going Home* (1986) and *Rituals of Survival: A Woman's Portfolio* (1985), in making her Nuyorican past imaginatively present, remembrance as the portal into the sites, the ethnicity, which has brought her womanhood from out of girlhood.

The barrio, in mainstream US parlance, has long been associated with stigma, that of citied ethnic pit, danger zone, a humanity of colour somehow irredeemably cornered. Few, for sure, would deny blight, the dangers and risk. But in Mohr, as in Morales, and however different their fictions, that has always been to tell part for whole. No panglossian version applies for either. But in their different stylings they both render the barrio as American sites of life whatever the forces of anti-life.

VI

If it has fallen to anyone to bid for contemporary laureateship of the US–Mexico border, southwest and west, the name, once again, has to be that of Guillermo Gómez-Peña.[6] His performance scripts, videos, the Aztec, campesino and mariachi costuming, the ingenious language-switches and amalgams (one being *Naftazteca*) all invite re-emphasis, as again does a piece like *Border Brujo* which had its premier at the Centro de la Raza, San Diego, in 1988. They all give live inflection to the borderland of Tijuana's estimated 40 million crossings per year as a hatch of migrancies, whether Native, Mexican, Mestizo/a, other South American and, the other way round, even Anglo. The vocabulary in play, likewise, bears both past and present: the whole concept of *el norte* as the promise of work and economic sufficiency, together with *la migra* (immigration authorities), *coyote* (smuggler), *mula* (carrier), *maquiladora* (border cheap-labour factory) and the human drama built into documented/undocumented. Nor has the interface of sexual and ethnic identity been lost on him, the transgender universe of feminist, hetero, gay and bisexual people as its own kind of borderland to be linked in kind, and variety, with US ethnicity as *mestizaje*.

A recent cinematic fiction like John Sayles's *Lone Star* (1996) offers a comparative bearing. A revisionist western, as it has been called, and set in the emblematically named Frontera, Texas, its mystery story of a murder cover-up involving the revered lawman, Buddy Deeds, and the corrupt sheriff, Charley Wade, opens into a nexus of cross-border lives and relationship. In Sam Deeds's vexed relationship with the memory of his own father, and with the schoolteacher Pilar Cruz, Sayles throws a lens literally, and figuratively, upon Tex-Mex history at large to embrace both Mexican and Anglo legacy, the multicultural clash and yet (especially in the case of Sam and Pilar) the intimate overlap of family, language, time and land.

Pilar's struggles to teach multicultural history in her classroom offer one refraction. Sam, among others, turns in memory to earlier border history, whether the Spanish land grants, *mestizaje* and the rise of *chicanismo*, white farming, oil and other settlement, US military force, or labour employment and migrancy. Sayles resorts also to an inspired use of desert and township landscape, a play of habitat to which the interaction of Mexican and Texas-country soundtracks gives its own confirming colour. Taken with the multiethnic ensemble, *Lone Star* makes for a cinema to challenge historical cliché, a USA–Mexico of no single but always hybrid ethnic destinies, border film in every sense.

In Miguel Méndez, to whose novel *Peregrinos de Aztlán/Pilgrims in Aztlán* (1974) Gómez-Peña has paid frequent homage, the border has a yet earlier, and equally formidable, literary incarnation.[7] Méndez's own birth in Bisbee, Arizona, five miles from the Sonora of much of his upbringing, could not have given him more symptomatic education, at once bilingual and bicultural. Not inappropriately, his novel has been said to have had a kind of border life of its own in terms of reception, three times issued in Spanish and, in 1992, for the first time, in English. Located in Tijuana, and in the person of the old car-washer Loreto Maldonado, it plays a spatially narrow border-town USA–Mexico with its river and traffic of all kinds into a highly diverse human width to embrace Yaqui, Mexican, Chicano and American histories.

The Mexican Revolution intersects with a 1960s time-present of Vietnam and the counter-culture, populations south and north of the border each its own plurality yet also long spliced into each other. Tijuana itself emerges as the very image of interzone, a confluence of idioms, class, street poverty and landed affluence, and the memory of wars fought nationally and abroad, in all a joined, but often fractured and unequal, hemispheric America. Méndez embodies this multinarrative in the person of Loreto as Yaqui veteran of the Zapata–Villa era, both its heroism and sell-outs. His dying years amid Tijuana's contemporary hustle, the drugs, the sex and other tourism, and always the cars as fetishes of speed and glamour, act as ironic epilogue to a history of far older borders of time and site.

At the novel's opening, Loreto is said to have almost given up on 'ordenar recuerdos en fila cronológica/'[arranging] his memories in chronological order' (p. 10; p. 8). In fact, Méndez takes on the task for him, flashbacks and past vignettes played against ongoing street life and in which Loreto's 'cerebro lleno de redes'/ 'headful of cobwebs' (p. 25; p. 21), and to whose costs his lost knee bears witness, is un-cobwebbed into the novel's overall story-mosaic.

In one trajectory, he remembers his role alongside the Yaqui soldier-hero, Chayo Cuamea, the guerilla campaigns, the blood and suffering of the fight for populist freedom, and then the PRI's betrayals, together with figures like Lorenzo the Yaqui as Native *curandero* and sage. In another, he lives in a present of the prostitute La Malquerida (badly loved), a girl betrayed into the sale of her own womanhood, the Mexican millionaire Mario Dávalos de Cocuch and his wife whose money in part comes from brothel-ownership, and a street community which includes the herb-vendor, Doña Candelita, the son of an impoverished Chicano family, Frankie Pérez, who is drafted into death in Vietnam as against 'life' in America, and the obese, addled street figure of Kite. Anglos enter in the form of Judge Rudolph Smith, whose double standard in dealing with white as against Mexican-Chicano plaintiffs is palpable, and whose hippie son's rejection of him and his wife carries its own judicial irony.

Méndez's feat is to render Tijuana as a complex of sites. A border city, it reaches into Mexican migrant deserts and campesino work farms. Space and time join as US cars, chariots of modern affluence and commodity, cross and recross terrain full of indigeneity and memory and whose Aztec markings lie in the closing use of the tiger-and-eagle allusion. Loreto acts as the human bridge, rich in his very pauperisation. If, to be sure, a Yaqui, he also, incrementally, bears his own transformation into Mexican, Chicano and American. The novel's sympathies palpably veer towards him, and his kind, but they nevertheless keep to a balance. For *Peregrinos de Aztlán/*

Pilgrims in Aztlán depicts Tijuana as cultural meeting-place, and yet fissure, neither the one Mexico, nor the one America, and if indeed vintage borderland then possessed of its own borders within.

VII

To invoke, from within a Chicano perspective, migrancy as yet another kind of site, even homeland, evidently, bespeaks a paradox. Is not seasonal farm labour, by definition, transience, motion, not the one locale but many? Yet few texts have better expressed the sense of the abiding permanence of family, worker life and community, than Tomás Rivera's '. . . *y no se lo tragó la tierra'* / . . . *And the Earth did not Part* (1971). Written as a two-language text, each with its own code-switching, and reissued in 1987 in two new translations from the Spanish by the poet Evangelina Vigil-Piñon, and by Rivera's friend Rolando Hinojosa as, infinitely to the point, *This Migrant Earth* (1975), it offers storytelling to recall Sherwood Anderson's *Winesburg, Ohio* and, at its best, Joyce's *Dubliners*.[8]

The memory of tough field labour, low pay, temporary shack housing, campesino Catholicism, each truck-ride to a next Anglo farm or town, and always the balladry of *la raza*, has long become historic myth. Leading Chicano/a poets, to include Tino Villanueva, Gary Soto and Lorna Dee Cervantes, have all made migrancy and its customs a major theme. The distinction of Rivera's text, however, lies in transforming a seeming actual 1940s–50s year, and journey, into story continuum, full of live grain and detail. Each of the fourteen vignettes, however discrete, at the same time makes for diorama, a gathering whole.

'That year was lost to him/*Aquel año se lo perdió'* (p. 5). The opening sentence, English or Spanish, almost Proustianly blurs the one time-past into time as continuous present (in Hinojosa's version 'Lost, that was what that year was to him'). 'And that was just one year', the narrator later insists; 'I'll have to come here to recall all the other years' (p. 159). A first story, which calls up a child shot and killed by the farm boss for drinking water instead of working, alternates with a successive one centred in a mother's desperate prayer for her absent GI son in Korea. The narrator's recollection of anti-Mexican taunts in the schoolyard leads on to a further recollection of being sequestered with an unhinged, murderous old couple. His further sense of displacement is given its most forceful expression when, in boyhood, having gone out at midnight to taunt the devil, then to demand explanation of God for the death of his father and brother, he finds his apostasy has not led to his own destruction (hence the alternative translated title in English of *And The Earth did not Devour Him*).

All the cycle, in fact, operates from this schema of time past as time continuous, the one event shadowed or counter-figured in the other. The boy's Catholic communion-going becomes entangled in an irreverent counting of possible sins and also the sight of a naked couple having sex in a nearby dry-cleaning store. Five neighbour children, the Garcías, are grotesquely burned to death after the father has rubbed alcohol on their bodies for a well-meant and home-based boxing match. A love-struck young migrant worker kills himself, after being rejected at a San Antonio dance, by touching a power cable and causing the town to plunge into darkness. A Tex-Mex mother suffers a nervous breakdown in the city store as, confusedly, she seeks to steal Christmas presents for her children. A number of neighbourhood families allow themselves to be duped by salesmen who promise super-enlarged photographs of relatives or missing sons. Each gives idiom to human hope over reality, a wished-for community of presence over the snares, the gaps, entailed by migrancy as absence.

Above all, in 'When We Arrive'/'*Cuando Ileguemos*', the human cattle-truck whose engine burns out en route to the midwest becomes the very image of migrancy with the dawn sky as comfort. The effect is lyric, poignant, a ballad of sorts, a reminder that whatever the shifting venue or locale in the search for work, each family carries its own meaning of home. To that end, Rivera himself might be said to put in a fleeting appearance in the figure of Bartolo, poet-historian of the workers and their *comunidad*:

> Bartolo passed through the town every December when he figured that most of the people had returned from work up north. He always came by selling his poems. By the end of the first day, they were almost sold out because the names of the people of the town appeared in the poems. And when he read them aloud it was something emotional and serious. I recall that one time he told the people to read the poems out loud because the spoken word was the seed of love in the darkness. (p. 154)

Rivera finds his surrogate in Bartolo who, in turn, links to the alternating voices of adult and child of 'I recall'. '. . . *y no se lo tragó la tierra*'/. . . *And the Earth did not Part* thereby acknowledges its own kind of telling and, relatedly, its own kind of tale. That, in turn, serves to underline a further and shared end. Paradox as may be, it lies in how migrancy is to be thought a permanent cultural site in which the Chicano cycle of the shifts and transitions of seasonal work meets, fuses, and is given its own memorial, in one of the deservedly best-admired story-cycles in ethnic modern fiction.

VIII

Terms like location, locale, or the local, offer no fixed schematic, some rulebook paradigm. But they do point up how, within ethnic fiction, 'site' becomes always as much time as place, an accumulation of memory.

That is also to say that particularity of site, as it expresses itself in literary narrative, cannot but harbour the larger human resonance, a single imagined American world the mirror of worlds still larger, interconnected and beyond. Whether Indian Country or Asiatown, black city or barrio, borderland or migrancy, and in fiction or life, the notion of ethnic site can only be thought margin from a vantage point which imagines itself to be somehow unsited and always quite beyond location.

NOTES

1. William Stafford (1980), 'On Being Local', *Bamboo Ridge*, 9 (December).
2. Cited in Ron McFarland (ed.) (1986), *James Welch*, Lewiston, ID: Confluence Press, p. 161.
3. Louis Owens (1982), *Other Destinies: Understanding the American Indian Novel*, Norman, OK: University of Oklahoma Press, p. 128.
4. Literary-cultural scholarship about Harlem has been extensive. Two notable recent contributions are David Levering Lewis (1981), *When Harlem Was in Vogue*, New York: Knopf, and Jervis Anderson (1982), *This Was Harlem: A Cultural Portrait, 1900–1950*, New York: Farrar, Straus and Giroux. I have attempted an overall account in 'Harlem on My Mind: Fictions of a Black Metropolis', originally published in Graham Clarke (ed.) (1988), *The American City: Literary and Cultural Perspectives*, London: Vision Press, and expanded in A. Robert Lee (1998), *Designs of Blackness: Mappings in the Literature and Culture of Afro-America*, London: Pluto Press, pp. 50–71.
5. The publication of a dual-language text is invaluable. The quotations are taken from Alejandro Morales (1998), *Caras viejas y vino nuevo/Barrio on the Edge*, translated by Francisco Lomelí, Tempe, AZ: Bilingual Press/Editorial *Bilingüe*. The quotations in English are from this version.
6. A liveliest attempt to explore the cultural plurality of the southwest and west as borderland is to be found in José David Saldívar (1997), *Border Matters: Remapping American Cultural Studies*, Berkeley, CA: University of California Press.
7. The Spanish-language text cited here is Miguel Méndez-M. (1974, 1979), *Peregrinos de Aztlán*, Berkeley, CA: Editorial Justa Publications. The English-language version is Miguel Méndez (1992), *Pilgrims in Aztlán*, translated by David William Foster, Tempe, AZ: Bilingual Press/Editorial Bilingüe.
8. Tomás Rivera (1985), *This Migrant Earth*, translated by Rolando Hinojosa, Houston, TX: Arte Público Press.

CHAPTER EIGHT

Island America

Hawai'i, Puerto Rico, the Philippines, Cuba, the Dominican Republic, Haiti

Island.
Look to a map to prove the concept mute.
All waters have a source and this connection renders earth
island.
  (James Thomas Stevens (Akwesasne Mohawk))[1]

Indentured to dreams
we imagine America,
the soft green breast of a green island
almost a mirage before our eyes.
  (Russell Leong)[2]

The place where I was born,
that mote in a cartographer's eye,
interests you? . . .
In truth, I confess to spending my youth
guarding the fire by the beach, waiting
to be rescued from the futile round of
paradisial life.
How do I like the big city?
City lights are just as bright
as the stars that enticed me then;
the traffic ebbs and rises like the tides
in a crowd,
everyone is an island.
  (Judith Ortiz Cofer)[3]

I

To advance America as an island, indeed a multicultural island, might seem to invite a certain suspension of disbelief. Is not its defining topography that of continental land mass, the sum of forested New England, Appalachia, the Mississippi River, prairie Wyoming, the cotton South, Texas, the Rockies and the Grand Canyon, Alaska's tundra and the California sierras? Is not its Grand Narrative, for the most part, that of a chosen people, Anglo-America, and that of an extending frontier to join east to west, Atlantic to Pacific?

Yet, as re-underlined in James Thomas Stevens's poem, Native America has long seen the earth in its entirety as an island, and America, in particular, as Turtle Island. In Russell Leong one hears, for all the echo of Gatsbyism, an Asian imagining of America as 'green island', at once 'soft green breast' and 'mirage'. Judith Ortiz Cofer muses upon a lineage which links the Spanish-speaking Caribbean, New Jersey, and the island which can be self. America, throughout, is to be met with as indeed islands, or rather inter-islands, a serial of multi-peopled ethnicities and life.

Literal island geography can hardly be doubted, from the Atlantic's Puerto Rico to the Pacific's Hawai'i, from Ellis Island to Angel Island. The prospect includes the New York of Long Island and Manhattan, the offshore islands of the Carolinas and Georgia, and the small-island Minnesota of the lakes. Empire inevitably enters the reckoning, America as successor power to Europe out of which Hawai'i becomes a US state, Puerto Rico a commonwealth. Others, like the Philippines, Cuba, the Dominican Republic and Haiti, however eventually and after struggle independent of European imperium, have also long known US hemispheric politics. All, in the process, look to migrancy, past and continuing, into the US mainland.

At the same time, and not a little in consequence, the figurative sense of the USA as islanded comes into play, whether begun in Native creation-myth or in the form of the Ancient World's Atlantis and Shakespeare's Brave New World. These islands, the original ones of Atlantic and Pacific, and those 'imported' into continental America, so take on more oblique significance, a remembering, and for sure a reinvention, as the one or another kind of fiction. The sense of 'double' island, Cuba and Cuban America, say, as actual and yet always mythic, not only a literal force of place or time-line but also of competing forms of memory and talk, holds across the board. Each, in this double, and often multiple, play of meaning gives a composite dynamic to the notion of 'island' America overall.[4]

In the literary fictions which best apply, these kinds of interacting islandedness invite their own scrutiny, the one American geography, actuality or myth, bound up with the other. For the stories they tell, inescapably, and memorably, speak out of, and to, the very making of multicultural identity in America.

II

Hawaii, in indigenous spelling Hawai'i, for good reason offers a first vantage point. Its archipelago of Oahu, with Honolulu as capital and Pearl City and Waikiki Beach among its best-known locations, Hawai'i itself as the Big Island, and Maui, Kauai and the lesser islands, is ever more pointed to as America's multicultural paradigm. East intersects with west, even as its million-plus population, and status since 1959 as America's fiftieth state, redefines both.

The population mix could not be more indicative, at once indigenous (*kanaka*),

Caucasian-American (*haole*, with a modification as local *haole*), European (Portuguese, to a lesser extent French, German), and Asian (Japanese, Chinese, Filipino, Korean). Each respective language reflects this mix of ethnicity, Hawaiian as official co-language with English, standard to pidgin, a Portuguese less of vocabulary than lilt and intonation, and the primary Asian tongues. Those of Hawaiian nationalist persuasion see the islands as still colonial, a suppression of indigenous claims and rights. Others speak of how Hawai'i has become simply more present-day America, allowing for its own uniqueness of locale in any number of ways quite as much mainland as Pacific. For yet others, by east–west and island demography, it gives evidence of postcoloniality, nothing if not transnational America.

Certainly its history has given rise to a pattern of differing perceptions. The Polynesia of volcanic genesis, from likely first settlement in the fifth century, also has its indigenous myths of deity and origin. Cook's landing in 1778 begins the incursion of a despoiling imperialist west even as it throws up the image of paradise. Brute European- and US-owned nineteenth-century sugar and other plantations, whose labour force would be augmented from Japan, China and the Philippines, further perpetuates, even as it contradicts, the notion of South Seas pastoral. The American-engineered installation of Queen Lili'ukalani in 1887, and then her deposition in 1894, alternates monarchy with formal annexation in 1898. Pearl Harbor, under the 'day of infamy' Japanese attack of 7 December 1941, becomes an icon of treachery and yet Second World War rally. Recent US statehood throws an ironic light on islands which have been variously kingdom and republic. As much as Hawai'i has become US and Asian tourist playground, that, in no way, is to say it has ceased to be working Pacific.

Literary and popular culture bearings, equally, give their own contrary skeins of portraiture. Melville's *Omoo* (1847), Yankee sailor picaresque yet also critique of Western depredation, and Mark Twain's *Following the Equator* (1897), Hawai'i as idyll yet spoiled garden, suggest something of the bequeathed ambiguity. If James Michener's *Hawaii* (1959) offers South Seas middlebrow epic, a confection both of research and invented dynasty as easy on the eye as it has been prolific in sales, Kazuo Miyamoto's quasi-autobiographical *Hawaii: End of the Rainbow* (1964, 1968) also gives history a fictional guise as the story of Japanese settlement from Hawaiian indenture to Second World War internment. Ethnicity within fictions has been as rich as it has been contrastive. In Carolyn Lei-lanilau's *Ono Ono Girl's Hula* (1997), its author Hawaiian of Hakka Chinese stock, being 'more or less Chinese' (p. 28) as an island identity is explored in the persona of its woman narrator. The upshot is novel-collage, a postmodern riff, in which the languages of ethnicity, sexuality and the will to writerliness form a lively, and often comic, intertext. Gary Pak's *A Ricepaper Airplane* (1998) looks to a Hawai'i of Korean family shaping, labour migrancy, settlement and memory all caught within a delicate command of voice.[5]

Hawaii Five-0, the longest-running crime drama in American TV history (1968–80), for all its famous opening shot of a Honolulu breaking ocean wave, turns Hawai'i into a kind of white police fiefdom. Jack Lord's Steve McGarrett, Elvis-quiffed, clipped of speech, battles an array of mainly 'oriental' gangsters, above all Wo Fat as played by Khigh Dhiegh. Subliminally or not, the series was always race-loaded, 'Asian' Hawai'i under white mainland law-and-order guardianship as the footfall of ancestral resistance to Yellow Peril. By contrast, and for literary purposes, one turns, admiringly, to *Bamboo Ridge: The Hawaii Writers' Quarterly*, both the semi-annual journal established by Eric Chock and Darrell H. Y. Lum in 1978, and whose luminaries range from poets like Wing Tek Lum and Cathy Song to a fiction-writer like Gary Pak, and the publishing house associated with its activities.[6]

The title stories of three short-story collections help supply a still fuller frame. Jessica Kawasuna Saiki's 'From the Lanai' offers a beautifully judged ironic picture of *haole* disconnection.[7] Hattie Crumb, financially well-placed Cleveland wife, indeed sees only from the lanai or veranda, a kind of borrowed, or there but not there, Hawaiian existence. Her vista needs the housekeeper Shiz as cultural interpreter of the Japanese Hamada family who work for her, of their wish to harvest the garden mangoes, and who have a new baby. In her rocker, she has a 'reverie' of snow and chill, the weatherly index of her distance from the unmonied but richer humanity about her and whose emblems are to be found in the surrounding papaya and jacaranda. Sylvia Watanabe's 'Talking to the Dead' likewise points to Hawai'i as harbouring a ceremony-world of life and death beneath any apparent surface.[8] In the figure of Aunty Talking to the Dead, the 'half-Hawaiian kahuna lady', Yuri, the wayward and gangly heroine, learns truths of life, her own included, and of death, well beyond those of the family mortician business. Aunty, from beyond her own death and with eyes still open, serves as necessary linkage into island time and remembrance.

In 'Hawaiian Cowboys', John Yau, Boston-raised poet and art critic of Anglo-Chinese parentage, turns the image of Hawai'i another way.[9] In its role as holiday island, a Big Island Hawai'i of cowboy-clad locals and tourist chic, it becomes the image of a failing marriage, the one island for another. For the narrator, and his wife Janet, he of Chinese-Dutch and she of English stock, and renting a friend's house in the hills ('made of black lava', p. 96), their growing mutual distance plays against other couples 'made up of different races and cultures' (p. 97), not to say the cowboys who are 'Asian or Hawaiian, Chinese, Japanese, Filipino, Polynesian, and Samoan' (p. 100). The island as fact yet metaphor operates throughout, whether Hawai'i itself as 'an island with an appetite . . . the ocean, volcanoes, and jungles are like hungry, angry infants' (p. 99), or the marriage as one of many 'islands within islands' (p. 102). Yau gives a perfect pointer and gloss in the following exchange between the couple:

'Haraki . . . the old woman who owns the general store, just asked me what island I'm from . . .
'So,' my wife asks, 'what did you say?'
I wasn't quite expecting this response, but I go on.
'I told her I was from Manhattan.' (p. 88)

Of Hawaiian longer fiction, Milton Murayama's *All I Asking for is My Body* (1975) and Lois-Ann Yamanaka's *Blu's Hanging* (1997) amount to a line of continuity, the

1930s past and 1990s present as two eras within the one overall locale. In the former, a novella in three parts, plantation Hawai'i and first-into-second-generation family as both continuity and conflict finds its best-known memorialist. Although centred in Japanese American life on Maui, that of the Oyama family honour bound to redeem ancestral debt and the one ethnicity of the story's several, Murayama leaves little doubt of its linkage into more general island labour. No South Seas pastoral again holds, whether in the class ladder with the owner-overseer Mr Nelson at its top or in the different ethnic rankings. In fact the reverse holds, life and image cast by the text in unsparing excremental terms:

> The camp, I realized, was planned and built around its sewage system. The half dozen rows of underground concrete ditches, two feet wide and three feet deep, ran from the higher to the lower slope of the camp into the concrete irrigation ditch on the lower perimeter of the camp. An outhouse built over the sewage ditch had two pairs of back-to-back toilets and serviced four houses. Shit too was organized according to the plantation pyramid. Mr. Nelson was top shit on the highest slope, then there were the Portuguese, the Spanish, and *nisei lunas* with their indoor toilets which flushed into those same ditches, then Japanese Camp, and Filipino Camp. (p. 96)

In the Oyamas, however, lives at once full of human edge and vitality, and told in both standard and pidgin dialogue often with dark humour and ingenious code-switches from English to Japanese, the story finds its sustaining mark. Two islands clash, the originating Japan of the parents, patriarchal, Buddhist, full of inlaid etiquette and requirements of filial duty, and the Hawai'i of demeaning labour. Japanese family is set against American individualism, group against self.

Generations, in kind, also collide, whether the narrator Kiyoshi or his elder brother, Toshio, 'first son' yet unwilling heir to old custom, ever and quite unfilially battling his fisherman father and seamstress mother, and who will find vicarious escape from them and plantation servitude in his boxing. The advent of Pearl Harbor and the Second World War, and the enlistment of Kyoshi into the US army, blends the one kind of division into the other.

Each of the three sections adroitly explores this islanded play of tensions. In 'I'll Crack Your Head *Kotsun*', the boy Kyoshi comes to learn that his friendship with Makot Suzuki, son of the only Japanese family in the Filipino camp, is somehow blighted, the object of his parents' prohibition. In fact, Makot's mother is the Filipino camp prostitute, kimonoed and powdered for trade, her red cheek spots the very badge of harlotry. Her laughter at Kyoshi's politeness to her conceals bitter irony, her demeaning sale of all dignity. Makot's father, likewise, in his Ford Model T, has become a kind of gaudy pimp-castratus. Kyoshi's break from Makot, a boy generous in his share of meals, adventure and movie tickets, shadows the plantation's larger divide-and-rule protocols, whether the interethnic demarcation of the camps or the intra-ethnic rules which, for the Oyama parents, render Mrs Suzuki a pariah.

'The Substitute' nicely conflates Japanese belief into Hawaiian reality, the mother's sickness and likely death assuaged by the death of *Obadan*, the grand-father's older sister, long a kind of family matriarch. In the 'American' aspect of telling, the mother is simply a woman whose illness cannot be paid for, whose life is circled by debt, and whose loss of teeth, faints and general debility bespeak a life lived little above subsistence. In the 'Japanese' aspect, the mother is a creature of *bachi*, retribution or punishment, a Shinto-Buddhist play of cosmic forces in which she sees her unworthiness mirrored in illness, hospitalisation, the twice-over near-death of her husband, and the damage caused by a *tsunami*. When *Obadan* dies, herself once the black sheep of the family on account of having run away and divorced and remarried, the mother feels she has acted as a death substitute, her surrogate. In a laconic touch, Kyoshi reminds her, for all that she sees spiritual pattern, that she will now need to get new teeth. Japan and Hawai'i as island worlds, if they play the one against the other, also, and however contrarily, once again play into each other.

The third and most substantial section, 'All I Asking for is My Body', centres on the two brothers, sibling boxers, Toshio initially the cane field lackey as worn down by day labour as by the grit and toilet conditions of the camp house he shares with his parents at 173 Pig Pen Avenue, Kyoshi the schoolboy who listens to the *haole* schoolteacher, Mr Snook, in his call for worker solidarity with striking Filipinos. In Toshio's rebellion against the family debt (he dares call his grandfather a *dorobo* or thief), as in the call to loyalty when America declares war on Japan (and Toshio insists his Japanese citizenry be rescinded), the division augments and deepens. Each of the boxing fights, in Kahana and other Maui venues, or in Honolulu, fugitively re-enacts and eases the *kotsun* or slaps of the father, the Oyamas rifted by family law just as their community has been rifted by Hawai'i's martial law.

Sexual needs and awakenings, under camp conditions, become furtive, mastur-batory, for Kyoshi a voyeur's uncertain pleasure as he watches women in a bath-house. His mother's latest pregnancy, a seventh child, parallels Toshio's intending marriage, one more overlap and yet conflict of generations. It makes for another right touch of irony that Kyoshi, having become a flyweight, wins $6,130 at dice as he is enlisting, and in the cheque he sends to repay the family debt offers a younger brother's redemption of an older brother's destiny. His accompanying scribbled note, 'See you after the War' (p. 103), makes the necessary point. American fortune plays against Japanese fortune, an apt ending to Murayama's landmark portrait of unfinished island negotiations of past into future.

If Lois-Ann Yamanaka has long argued for de-exoticising Hawai'i, then her *Blu's Hanging* (1997), even more than *Saturday Night at the Pahala Theatre* (1993) and *Wild Meat and the Bully Burgers* (1996) with their celebratory mix of vernacular life, often in off-colour pidgin, and unflinching portraits of island racism, could not better have delivered on the resolve. Nothing in the way of some media version of a surf-and-pleasure Pacific holds. Rather, and in the voice of Ivah Ogata, its thirteen-year-old narrator, the novel turns upon contemporary class poverty for a Japanese American family, adolescent sexuality to include Ivah's own body-changes and the molestation of nieces and then male rape of Ivah's brother Blu by a Filipino 'uncle' neighbour, and the drift of a hardworking but vulnerable father into drug-taking. That Yamanaka won an Asian American literary prize for *Blu's Hanging*, which was then rescinded on the grounds that it stigmatised the Filipino community, added further to its controversy.

In Ivah, the novel not only has a prepossessing Hawaiian girl thrust into adulthood before her time but a perfect vantage point to locate Hawai'i as the clash as much as the complement of gender, class and ethnicity. At her mother's death from medicine originally intended to clear the leprosy which also haunts her father, she takes on sibling den duties: helpmate to her young sister Maisie, who has been rendered if not mute then speech-impaired by the loss of the mother and who is helped by the teacher Miss Ito, and companion to Blu, compulsive in his eating and near-androgynously overweight, sexual, the eventual object of abuse and yet a musician and singer.

Violation, in fact, carries a charge throughout, whether the memory of plantation Hawai'i, leprosy, compensating American fast food for the family hunger ('We eat mayonnaise bread for a long time after Mama's funeral' (p. 3), the book begins), the mocking 'pastoral' intrusion of *Gilligan's Island* and similar TV escape drama, Poppy's love of easy-listening music like 'Moon River' even as his life of two jobs and three children brings on decay, Maisie's silence and eventual fractured words, or the manoeuvres of twenty-year-old Uncle Paulo who both seduces the winsome schoolgirl Paulette and trusses and rapes Blu. The hanging of the Ogatas' kittens by the Reyes sisters, family nieces acting unfamilially, gives its own not-so-oblique parallel.

That Ivah finally is awarded a high-school scholarship to Honolulu makes for the point of arrival for her own hard-won subduing, in life and word, of chaos, a family haunted by its lost mother. Hawaiian islandedness for the Oyamas, as Yamanaka portrays it, gives off fondness, sibling warmth and care, and yet also, and unsparingly, a grasp of the Pacific as hard-won migrant legacy, generational gains and losses. It is a resonance, and nuance, which invites all due recognition.

III

> In my books I follow memories, *cuentos*, events, and characters that I see as my guides to what Virginia Woolf calls 'moments of being' in my life and in the United States. It is a process of discovery. My books are neither Puerto Rican emigrant history not sociological case studies; at least, I didn't write them as such. . . . I re-envision the scenes of my youth and transform them through my imagination . . . into a collage that means Puerto Rico to me, that gives shape to my individual vision.[10]

Judith Ortiz Cofer's declaration gives an illuminating gloss to her writing career, whether *The Line of the Sun* (1989) situated in the parallel Puerto Rican worlds of Caribbean island and American mainland, or *Silent Dancing: A Partial Remembrance of a Puerto Rican Childhood* (1990), with its invocation of island visits from her New

Jersey 'vertical barrio' to her grandmother's 'casa de Mamá' (and about which she muses 'why not call it a fiction?', p. 13), or *The Latin Deli* (1993), poems and prose vignettes derived from El Building in Paterson, New Jersey, where she spent her girlhood. Puerto Rico, it has not been lost on Ortiz Cofer or writers who share her origins, has rarely meant fewer than two kinds of reference.

In one, it is the island of Columbus's landing, said to have been named by Juan Ponce de León with the words '¡Ay que puerto rico!' (what a perfect port!), and whose Arawak-Taino origins, together with the Spanish-African mix, cause it to be known indigenously as Borinquen and its people Borinqueños. This is the island currently designated Estado Libre Asociado de Puerto Rico, or Autonomous Commonwealth, and whose citizens hold US citizenship, after a history which evolves from the Spanish-American War of 1898 and continues in the tensions between *independentistas* and those favouring the present political status.

In the other, it has meant, notably, Spanish Harlem, more precisely East Harlem as situated between 116th and 145th Streets in Upper Manhattan, the upshot of a migration which has continued down the century from 1898 through Operation Bootstrap of the 1950s. Nuyoricans themselves would also recognise a wider outreach into New Jersey, Chicago, Los Angeles or Hawai'i, sufficient to make Puertorri-queños the second largest Hispanic community in America, 3.5 million in all or 11 per cent of the whole.

Nuyorriqueñismo has looked to its own variety of cultural expression. In Piri Thomas's *Down These Mean Streets* (1967), it signified ghetto tenancy, drugs, crime, a world descending into vortex. In *West Side Story*, Broadway musical and film (1961), with a score by Leonard Bernstein and Stephen Sondheim, and Rita Moreno and Natalie Wood in dubbed roles, it became musical baroque, a Latin street-gang version of *Romeo and Juliet*. In Geraldo Rivera, lawyer and journalist, it has a well-known TV personality whose talk-show which launched in 1987 has long become a viewing staple. Nicholasa Mohr, in *Nilda* (1973) as in her other fiction, acts as Nuyorican literary benchmark, which is not to overlook inventively flighted ethnic parody like Ed Vega's *The Comeback* (1985).

No literary-cultural institution, however, has more held sway than the Nuyorican Poets' Cafe, begun in the 1960s, at once gathering place and performance arena, and whose 'nationalist' luminaries have included the poets Tato Laviera, Miguel Algarín, Sandra María Esteves, Papo Meléndez and Pedro Pietri. Other fellow Riqueños, literary or otherwise, have sought a different kind of base, whether under the multicultural banner like Victor Hernández Cruz or Aurora Levins Morales, or working-class Boston like Martín Espada or, in Ortiz Cofer's own case, Atlanta, Georgia. Together, even so, and in every difference of idiom, they bear witness to Puerto Rico as islandedness at once pastoral and city.

This lies at the very heart of *The Line of the Sun*, Ortiz Cofer's Truman-era migration novel of the Vivente dynasty as told by her narrator, Marisol, heir both to the island and to El Building. If greatly eventful, especially the life of the uncle Guzmán, it serves also as a portrait of competing Puerto Rican intimacies, those of the fictive Salud as island community ('*The town of Salud was the result of a miracle*

. . .', p. 45) and of El Building ('which the residents seemed intent upon turning into a bizarre facsimile of an island barrio', p. 220) as the route into a larger America.

Both represent mixed regimes. Salud, true to its name meaning 'health', can be at once Taino kingdom, an Eden of guavas, tamarinds or yucca (pp. 133–4), yet also the provincial meanness which will cause Guzmán to be turned into the *niño del diablo*, not least by his mother Mamá Cielo, as he engages in a forbidden love with Rosa, the older spiritist and *puta*. If a world of clan respectability and priests, Salud is also one of cockfights, jealous gossip (to include the likely gay relationship of Mamá Cielo's other son, Carmelo, who will die in Korea, with the young priest Padrecito César), the casino run by Doña Amparo, and Mr Clement as American owner of the canefields. Family hardship, be it birthing or employment, can draw comfort in the island's abundance, and at the very same time, be mocked by it.

El Building becomes the base from within which Marisol's father Rafael, frequent absentee sailor, and her mother Ramona, find the means to a livelihood, and yet also a source of threat through the crowdedness, drugs and violence which will leave Guzmán nearly dead of a knife attack. On the one hand, any given Christmas fills the hallways with 'the smells of coconut candy and pasteles' (p. 186), the memory of island festival and well-being. Yet its basement can mean sexual danger to Marisol, and its streets, not just access to her Catholic school, but to a larger underworld of forbidden knowledge, gang activity, and the ever-present possibility of rape.

The novel brings these two layered domains into relationship in yet other ways. The fire, at a time of lay-offs, strikes and police surveillance, which breaks out in consequence of a session conducted by Elba, the exotic black *santera*, points exactly to how yet more of the island has been carried into the city. Marisol and Guzmán, uncle and niece, in like manner become allies of deed and word, he the benign 'underground' fugitive in life who has once survived by hustling on the New York subway, she the secret biographer. *Riqueños* they both remain, he in his eventual recuperative return to Puerto Rico and she in America, yet with a difference not just of generation, or gender, but in how each must find the best meaning of island legacy.

The Latin Deli serves almost as a companion-piece, a gloss, for Ortiz Cofer's novel, a round of self-bearings told as anecdote, letter and poem. El Building supplies one lodestone, variously 'gray prison' ('American history', p. 14), dream-palace for unchaperoned teenage love ('Twist and Shout', p. 22) and a place 'filled with the life energies of generations of other Island people' (p. 93). The island itself supplies another, one of loved but ailing grandparents ('The Witch's Husband'), an old man's magical death clinging to dolphins which take him out to sea ('Letter from a Caribbean Island'), and of 'warm, vegetative air' ('Juana: An Old Story', p. 81). Out of both, she maps her own evolution as child, woman, mother and writer, the Puerto Rico of the Caribbean and of New Jersey, in all their joined complexity, as but two islands in the successive creation of identity.

IV

Jessica Hagedorn's *Dogeaters* (1990), understandably, was thought on appearance to have made the Philippines into a species of *film noir*. For the world it seeks to dramatise, 'our tropical archipelago of 7100 known islands' (p. 100), replete with its 'eighty languages and dialects', 'loyal believers', 'blood feuds', 'torrid green world', and 'legacy of colonialism' (p. 100), reads as one upon which has been grafted a metropolis wholly in kind, Manila as edge city, power labyrinth and feeding ground.

On the one hand, this is the Philippines as counter-Eden, its reptile and insect life almost a rebuke to the nirvana implied by Jean Mallat in his celebrated *The Philippines* (1846). Citing, in her Preface, his insouciant observation that Filipinos 'have the greatest respect for sleeping persons', Hagedorn counters with her own hallucinatory version:

> We are serenaded by mournful gecko lizards, preyed on by vampire bats and other *asuwangs*, protected by *kapre* giants crouching in acacia trees, enchanted by malevolent spirits living in caves and sacred termite-dwellings. The humid landscape swarms with prehistoric, horned warrior beetles with armored shells, flies with gleaming emerald eyes, and speckled brown *mariposa* butterflies the size of sparrows. Eagles nest in mountain peaks; in certain regions and seasons the sky blackens with humming locusts and flocks of divebomber cockroaches. Invisible mosquitoes lurk in the foliage, said to infect children with a mysterious fever that literally cooks the brain, causing hallucinations, insanity, or death. (p. 100)

Under Marcos-style authority it has, in turn, become also urban tropic. However resilient its everyday vernacular diversity, it exists under a politics of military rule, huge private wealth, detention, prison, drugs and brothels. The sex industry vies with fervent Catholicism. Poverty breeds dreams of glamour. No more baroque a measure of the gaudiness amid the dispossession is to be met with than the Imelda Marcos figure. Hagedorn leaves little doubt as to the implication of her different soubriquets as the 'Madame' or 'iron butterfly' (p. 221).

Orchestrated, ostensibly, by Rio Gonzaga, Filipina author-exile from New York and an America which has saturated Manila in its politics, film, music and fashion, *Dogeaters* offers a series of story-panels, thirty-plus vignettes. Each story episode, letter and memoir, together with the all-pervasive *tsismis* or gossip as conducted in a hybrid of English, Tagalog and residual Spanish, thereby in design as much as substance re-enacts the 'plot' of class and power within Philippines society itself. In this the novel can be said to subject an Asian-Philippine terrain to both the Latin American magicalism of García Márquez or Vargas Llosa and the New Journalism reportage techniques of Hunter Thompson, Tom Wolfe and the Norman Mailer of *Miami and the Siege of Chicago* (1968).

The upshot, full of its own compositional speed and transformation, even to the point of extravagance, is narrative in no way to be thought out of keeping with the world it seeks to transcribe. Yet in her insistence upon locality of voice, be it girl-talk, family conversation, grocery, flirtation and bar-speak or vernacular English–Tagalog switches, Hagedorn acts throughout to challenge, if not subvert, any one supposed national voice. Filipino history, thereby, is shown always to spar against, yet oddly to replicate, that of the United States (Umberto Eco's notion of seeing one culture through its 'absolute fake' applies, Manila as US city in both silhouette and substance).

Dogeaters highlights, with due irony, President William McKinley's rationale for colonising the country in 1898. The lavishly nomenclatured Beauty Competitions, of which 'Miss Universal Universe' (p. 218) is typical, outbid even their American originals. Each costume-romance film put out by the Mahubay Studios might be Filipino Hollywood. TV like *Love Letters* and *Maid of the Philippines* uses formulae derived from American daytime soaps. Hispanic or Afro-US pop fills the airwaves, as youth music, the modernity of American sound. *The Monte Vista Golf & Country Club* acts as the icon of First World wealth amid Third World poverty (its claims to genteel exclusivity, MEMBERS & GUESTS ONLY, mocked, alongside, by the revealing PLEASE DEPOSIT ALL FIREARMS HERE, p. 184). The SPORTEX supermarket mall, out of reach for most Filipinos, embodies American consumer plenitude. The 'news' as told in the Marcos-fearing *The Metro Manila Daily* replaces journalism with pseudo-journalism. Tabloid glossies like *Celebrity Pinoy* echo US gossip columns. Citied Filipino society, on this reckoning, conducts much of its cultural life inside the wrap, or skin, of its American counterpart.

The rent-boy and disc jockey, Joey Sands, his father a black GI and his mother a Manila streetwalker, might be yet another figuration of the interplay. A groupie for US glitz, long-time drug addict, love-object to the German cinematographer, Rainer, his unwitting witness to the murder of Senator Domingo Avila puts him in a New People's Army opposition group, part of the 'for hire' militia politics. Tito Alvarez and Nestor Noralez as TV producers-stars, and Cora Camacho as glamorous but ageing TV interviewer, give their own Tinsel Town media gloss to actual reality. Romeo Rosales and Trinidad Gamboa, he an actor working as a waiter and she a Sportex factory employee, aspire to American screen romance amid Filipino un-romance.

Hagedorn leaves no doubt of an island world at once host and virus. Avila is gunned down by government apparatchiks, Filipino yet also American assassination. General Nicasio Ledesma parodies Marcos and other US-sponsored military authority figures as would-be guardian to the nation even as he reveals himself the sadist, torturing, exquisitely, with *Love Letters* playing on television. His dalliance with the drug-addled, beauteous mistress, Lolita Luna, is engaged in even as his wife acts the role of model Catholic penitent. The ten or so First Families, each with their own power interests, feature alongside the Church under the righteous, but unfortunately true-named, Cardinal Sin. The liberal-Jewish Goldenbergs, well-meaning to a fault, are rewarded with the irony of a next American Embassy posting in Saudi Arabia.

The lavish hispanism of each Filipino name further mimics the political theatre:

Boomboom Alacran (alacrán the Spanish for scorpion) as the transvestite bar-owner who works as Perlita and belongs to a fantastical business empire, Cherry Pie Lozano, and, inevitably, the President's wife, Madame Galactica as she is known from her beauty-pageant days. This, in Hagedorn's version, is Imelda as Americanised holograph, 'Queen of Beauty Queens', 'coiffed and complacent' in her 'custom-made peau-de-soie pumps', and given to the ritual warning 'God save us from the day my husband steps down from this glorious country!' (p. 221). She laments, explicitly, not having become a movie actor ('I was going to call myself Rose Tacloban', p. 224). Instead, coyness itself, she sees herself called to a higher mission. 'I am simply here', she avers, 'to carry out our Lord's wishes' (p. 224). Self-invented in life, she becomes Hagedorn's perfect satiric invention, whether the celebrated shoe cellars, coiffure, singing or, above all, soap-opera role as Manila's own Eva Perón. If, indeed, a 'mysterious fever' (p. 100) holds, American as much as Filipino, dust amid dream, she gives it face, body, its very language.

The whole, throughout, is held in Rio as the Filipina who has become the Filipina American. Pucha, her cousin, offers a kind of prophetic word when, in 1956, sipping TruCola and under the eyes of their *yaya* or chaperone, she and Rio gossiped about *All That Heaven Allows* and the roles played by Rock Hudson, Jane Wyman and Agnes Moorhead. The film, seen in the 'air-conditioned darkness' (p. 3) of Manila's Avenue Theater, could not better situate the screen fantasy of America within the life fantasy of the Philippines. An age later, both cousins will far better understand how their island homeland has indeed been caught up in its own form of dark cinema.

Its dangers and betrayals, even a homebody like Pucha recognises, hover every-where, and not least, or unreflexively, in Rio's resolve to chronicle this dual Philippines of home and abroad. Pucha's letter warns 'Nothing is impossible, I suppose, with that crazy imagination of yours. I'm not surprised by anything you do or say, but if I were you, *prima*, I'd leave well enough alone' (p. 249). This, within the plotline of the novel itself, speaks to one kind of risk. But it also points to the imaginatively larger and anything but 'left well alone' risk within Hagedorn's bold, inventive fiction, a spilling of family secrets, Philippines reality as its own kind of American irreality.

V

Cuba, pre-Fidel or post-Fidel, has long compelled America's interest. As Spanish slave, sugar and tobacco colonial fiefdom, it made for one kind of early lure. The liberationist figure of José Martí, and then the Spanish-American War of 1898, brought the island into still closer ambit. The US corporation and casino playground it became under Fulgencio Batista (1929–59) led to Fidel Castro's 1959 revolution with Che Guevara as Marxist co-helmsman. The litany of hostility, thereafter, meant Cold War boycott, the abortive Bay of Pigs invasion of 1961, the Missile Crisis of 1962, and the Mariel Boatlift of 1980 which deposited some 135,000 refugees in Florida. It has been from this history that Cuban America, in any modern sense, has been born. Little Havana, Miami, inside Florida's metropolitan Dade County, acts as its heartland.

The ongoing spectacle of the *balseros*, or boat people, from among the estimated 10 per cent of all Cubans to have fled their homeland, would win latter-day CNN and other global media attention in the figure of six-year-old Elián González in December 1999. He had nearly drowned, as in fact his mother did, crossing the Florida Straits. If, at one level, a child custody battle within the González-Brotón family, this became the very expression of the Cuba–America divide. Whose boy was Elián, Cuba's or Cuban America's? The affair may well have involved Fidel himself, Janet Reno as US Attorney General, Larry King interviews, the Immigration and Naturalization Service (INS), unofficial adoption by the cousin Marileysis González, night-time troopers seizing the child, and pundits on child and domicile rights. Elián, finally, may well have been returned to his father, Juan Miguel. But the heart of the matter lay in Cuba's America and America's Cuba, with Cuban America the upshot, two islands of ideology, two mutual political fictions.

For Havana, that has meant *gusanos*, or worms, in the sense of betrayers and ingrates. For most of America, it summons an image of true patriots, victim refugees from Communist dictatorship, however, in fact, un-monolithic the community. The tension remains fuelled by each fierce anti-*fidelista* 'exile' political group, well financed, active in their lobbying, and whose influence led to legislation like Congress's Helms-Burton Act (1996) which established the American right to sue the Castro regime for restoration of confiscated US property.

Popular culture, in turn, adds its own co-ordinates, whether Miami's Calle Ocho as hub, everyday foodways and community murals and newspapers, or the reach into other Cuban communities from New York to Los Angeles. Music, a fusion of African and Latin, and whether salsa, mambo, cha-cha or son, supplies an ever-present backdrop, be it Tito Puente and his Latin Jazz Ensemble in the 1960s, Gloria Estefan and the Miami Sound Machine in the 1990s, or the re-emergence of Cuba's own Buena Vista Social Club. Inevitably, Cuban American literary fictions have greatly augmented this process of self-definition.

Oscar Hijuelos's *The Mambo Kings Play Songs of Love* (1989) won immediate headlines, novel and film. Its exhilarating story as conjured into being by the nephew Eugenio of the brothers César and Néstor Castillo, their journey from Havana to New York to perform with their cousin Desi Arnaz on the *I Love Lucy Show*, and their decline from show-business stardom into isolation and drink, seemed to offer the very thing at its core, a triumphant-sad mambo in narrative form. For as much as the novel turns upon liberating Latin heat, music and sexuality, it also implies requiem, loves competed over, won and lost, a Cuba itself caught up in, and yet frequently betrayed by, its own politics of promise. Roberto Fernández's *La vida es un especial/Life is a Bargain* (1982) takes the story on to contemporary Miami, his spiky, teasingly irreverent and even grotesque foray into the community foibles, with all due *chisme* or gossip, of evolving Florida-Cuban exile life.

Two generational fictions, Cristina Garcia's *Dreaming in Cuban* (1992) and Virgil Suarez's *Latin Jazz* (1989), the one centred in the Revolution and the other in the

Mariel Boatlift, confirm the ongoing delineation. For Pilar Puente, in whom *Dreaming in Cuban* has its eventual Cuban American voice as daughter to the fiercely anti-Fidel Lourdes Puente and granddaughter to the Fidel-adoring Celia del Pino, née Almeida, Cuba could not more be there and yet not be there: 'Cuba is a peculiar exile, I think, an island-colony. We can reach it by a thirty-minute charter flight from Miami, yet never reach it at all' (p. 219).

How, for her, as she rises from a vexed Brooklyn art-punk girlhood into becoming a full-time painter, to negotiate an island palpably actual and yet impossibly steeped in myths both of heroic revolution and despotism? How to find balance from a heritage which means a warring family of both New York and Havana, Miami and the Sierra Maestra, capitalism and communism, English and Spanish, American freedom and the Committee for the Defence of the Revolution, the music of Cuba's Beny Moré and Greenwich Village's Lou Reed, and the women of three family generations with the patriarch, Jorge del Pino, at once alive and yet a ghost?

Garcia's novel achieves an intricate *table ronde* of dynasty across three generations, the lattice for island lives which carry the division, as well as the bridge (el puente), of facing American worlds. In Celia, 'new socialist woman' (p. 107), devotee of the revolution, coastal spotter for the regime of post-Bay of Pigs invaders, and judge in the People's Court, the island finds both its romance and sickness. Her love for Jorge and their three offspring, for the long-ago Spanish lover, Gustavo, to whom she writes letters of desire never posted, and for Castro as *el líder*, gives one emphasis. Her breakdowns giving birth, hospitalisations, and breast cancer, and her struggle to encompass the different fates of her children, gives another. She embodies Cuba's dream of perfection, and yet its ailing body, utopian island hope, and yet setback.

Each offspring carries this division further. Lourdes Puente, raped by soldiers of the revolution, sets up and prospers as expatriate owner of her baroque Yankee Doodle Bakery in Brooklyn. Alternatingly fat, and slim, she becomes a part-time auxiliary cop even as, in imagination, she talks with the ex-merchant marine father whose own cancer has brought him in his last years to New York for treatment. Hers becomes fervid US patriotism, an America to redeem Cuba as island of the ideologically damned ('What America needs, Lourdes and her father agree, is another Joe McCarthy to set things right again', p. 171). Only half in fantasy will she see herself as Castro's assassin.

Felicia, her sister, flighty, excitable, impossibly three times married, and anything but in keeping with her name, spirals into madness, after a fraught and ever more eccentric relationship with her twins Luz and Milagro and son Ivanito. In being drawn towards a *santería* cult ('she had a true vocation for the supernatural', p. 186), and whose ministrations fail to cure her illness, she embodies yet another Cuba, rooted in Africa and Native lore. The Pino son, Javier, one-time chemistry winner, and who returns from Czech exile, becomes a drunk, Marxism's burnt-out case.

In them, and their families, not to mention her Tía Alicia who names her children after 1940s Hollywood movie stars, Pilar Puente has her Cuban, and Cuban American *herencia*. 'I'm still waiting for my life to begin' (p. 179), she has reason to say as she strives to find her own terms of womanhood. Each principal act she takes will be a mix of affiliation and liberation: the early runaway to Miami; the brat-art satiric Statue of Liberty she makes for her mother's business; and her eventual visit to Cuba where she will paint watercolours of her Abuela Celia and, in turn, be given a copy of Lorca and Celia's folder of letters to Gustavo. This is the island whose Havana, in an apt phrase, she will describe as full of 'noise and decay and painted ladyness' (p. 235). Garcia's invitingly styled novel, a triumph of image throughout, acts true to the title, Cuba, whether Caribbean or carried to America, as real in dream as wakefulness.

Virgil Suarez's *Latin Jazz* opens with the long-time Havana saying 'If we lose each other, honey, meet me in Miami' (Preface). It sits well with the novel at large. For around the figure of Hugo Carranza, fugitive from Cuba's political prison-camp of Cochiquero ('this charred territory', p. 3), Suarez develops a canvas also of three generations, and to span Havana, California and eventually Key West, Florida. If it concedes little to the Cuba of Fidel, 'the dead buried by the living' (p. 269), or favours a more realist-documentary pattern than *Dreaming in Cuban*, this is not to deny a novel full of event.

The Cuban America of Hugo's family, that of his father Esteban, his sister Lilián and her husband Angel Falcón, who run a Los Angeles ice-cream business, and of his nephew Diego, a musician at Los Angeles's Toucan Club with his own marital problems and amours, all point to a post-Cuba and for which the Mariel episode is but the latest escape. This, throughout, makes for a Cuba un-islanded, or more accurately re-islanded, even though Esteban, early dispossessed by Fidel's regime of his pharmacy, and his friend Domingo likewise debarred from practising law, in a nice touch of black comedy plot a return to the literal island to bury the ashes they have dug up in Los Angeles of Esteban's dead wife, Concha. Her voice, too, is to be heard from beyond death – warm, choric, that of a lost and yet returned Cuba.

Hugo's hard-won return, the flash-backs to revolutionary action, disenchantment with *fidelismo*, risks, bribes, near-drowning, re-encounter with his lover Lucinda, and final entry back into his family in Miami, comes over at pace. It also plays against the story of Diego as next-generation Cuban American, musician, pending divorcee and lover of the beautiful Maruchi, but also a man close to the edge of hustle and drugs. Suarez clearly, but unsentimentally, is about Cuba as one kind of island reborn as another.

VI

I hadn't fit into any of the stories – that was the problem – like Cinderella's ugly sister with a shoe store worth of discards – not the love story, the sob story, the homegirl-made-good story. That's why I came back to the island . . .

A happy immigrant home might have offset the unwelcome; the six of us marching abreast, arms hooked into each other's, singing the USA anthem to the tune of a good merengue. But as the plane lifted off from our motherland island, the ground of *familia* gave and the craziness started.

I began writing in earnest . . .[11]

Julia Alvarez's summary of childhood flight from La República Dominicana, American young womanhood, and revisitation to the island, gives a perfect context to *How the García Girls Lost Their Accents* (1991) as the novel by which she established her reputation. In ¡Yo! (1997), published six years later, she even, and with a flourish of irony, intertextualises its very making and impact. 'Yo', the Spanish for 'I', and abbreviation for Yolanda as the García Girl who has become a celebrated author, is cannily answered by those of her family whose lives, and secrets, she has flaunted. The tease gains further for how it arises out of Alvarez's own fictionalisation of her history as a member of the island's well-born élite caught up in the larger interplay of US–Dominican Republic relationship.

That relationship itself offers an ambiguous mix of fact and fiction: Hispaniola, or Little Spain, as 'discovered' by Columbus (its Taino name Quisqueya), the various US interventions (1916–24, 1965), co-island with Haiti not just in Caribbean lushness but military politics (above all the Trujillo dictatorship of 1930–71), and an island poverty which can somehow comport with the American glamour of a Dominican-born *haut couturier* like Oscar de la Renta. The Dominica exported into America carries with it these, and the yet further irony of the search for haven within a mainland, however beckoning, or even redemptive, also, and as often as not, inimical to its interests.

'"I am given up, Mami! It is no hope for the island. I will become *un dominican-york*"' (p. 107). The words belong to Carlos García, MD and Green Card refugee in the aftermath of a failed, and CIA-involved, plot against Trujillo and, three years on, who has just sworn the Pledge of Allegiance. His fractured language exactly locates the sense of history behind *How the García Girls Lost Their Accents*. For whatever its backdrop of flight and escape, the novel turns upon the gains and setbacks of Americanisation as played out in the Dominican parentage of Carlos and Laura García (Papi and Mami), and the Dominican American daughterhood of Carla, Sandra (Sandi), Yolanda (Yoyo, Joe, Joey) and Sofia (Fifi). At issue, and middle-class as may be the focus, is an America of yet more island transitions.

Alvarez's distinctive crafting of the story crosses not only three periods, 1989–1972, 1970–1960 and 1960–1956, and the interaction of New York and Santo Domingo, but deploys the sisters' voices as though consortium, a dialogical round. Yolanda's voice, that of schoolteacher, one-time poet and storyteller, and a divorcee who has had a breakdown ('she spoke in riddles', p. 79), supplies prologue and epilogue.

In the time-present opening chapter, she makes a wistful return journey into the island's interior in search of guava as a form of recovered identity. ' "Here she comes, Miss America" ' (p. 4), says a cousin. She finds beauty, language, a lived-in landscape, but also threat, and the undeniability of having become American. In the last chapter, she is the Yolanda of her childhood inside the protective family compound, the story of her grandmother's gift of a drum, and her encounter with a kitten, a one-eyed black Haitian maid whom she associates with Voodoo, a stranger and his dog, and a darkened shed. Shadowed in memory, each fuses for her, and for her art, into 'story ghosts and story devils' (p. 290). Both sequences point to a Dominica there, but at the same time also fugitive, intervened in, and sheened for her, by America. The family's story, and the growing-up of each sister whose clothes and belongings, de-individuatingly, were once all colour-coded by their mother, takes place as a menu of gain and defeat within these points in time.

In 'Floor Show', one of Alvarez's best vignettes, Dr García and the family endure a humiliating 'Spanish' hotel evening at the invitation of the Fannings, he a patronising colleague who has found work for García, and his wife an increasingly flamboyant drunk. The paining need to show gratitude, the girls' skewed and uncertain etiquette, the gift to Fifi of a 'Spanish señorita' barbie doll, the kitsch flamenco, and even the bad food, all make for a portrait of immigrant America at cost. For Laura García, in 'Daughter of Invention', America becomes comic Ben Franklin territory where she takes to making 'inventions' deludedly thinking them aids to a better household life. In one sense, she has moved on from her prescribed Catholic wife-mother role in Dominica, in another she verges on a parody of the American can-do ethos.

To the daughters, initially, America represents an escape act, a lurch into the call and sparkle of modernity:

> We began to develop a taste for the American teenage good life, and soon, Island was old hat, man. Island was the hair-and-nails crowd, chaperones, and icky boys with their macho strutting and hairy chests with gold chains and teensy gold crucifixes. By the end of a couple of years away from home, we had *more* than adjusted. (pp. 108–9)

For each, however, the adjustment will be again mixed fare, Dominican strictness of womanhood suddenly exposed to American 1960s laxity of dope, contraception, lovers, and always the beguilement of the immediate over the long term. Yolanda's self-fissure speaks to the one kind of consequence, the would-be custodial writer of her own divided life and marriage as well as literary syntax.

Carla, the eldest and the most still-Dominican on arrival in America, and viciously taunted in childhood by Irish boy schoolmates and surprised by her own body in adolescence, becomes a psychologist. Her advocacy of assimilationist behaviour, or 'fading into walls' ('Trespass', p. 164), becomes a mask to cover Dominican and all other difference. Sandi, in contrast, becomes a compulsive, the self-consuming lister of books and a woman quite unassimilable, indeed broken, by an America so abundant in choice. Fifi takes yet another turn, American errant teenager sent back to Dominica, 'rescued' by her sisters, and finally the maverick lover of a German and mother of two. Having been repudiated by her father, she, ironically, becomes the good Dominican daughter in supplying him with the grandson heir he craves.

In each of these different García family lives, 'so many husbands, homes, jobs, wrong turns among them' (p. 11) as Yolanda observes, the island serves as continuing reality and shadow, a middle-class Dominica of two countries.

If, for her part, Alvarez leaves no doubt of her family's privilege, Junot Díaz, author of the meticulously worked eleven-part story-cycle, *Drown* (1996), looks to a terrain of lower-class barrio, whether island Santo Domingo or immigrant New Jersey. Held together through the vernacular of idiom of Yunior, with its ready barrio *caló* and throwaway obscenity, each instalment casts a cool, almost clinical, eye upon the migrant Dominican family history of Ramón and Virta de las Casas, and their offspring Rafa and Ramón (Yunior's baptismal name). Theirs, whether on the island or on America's urban east coast, emerges as the tough wearing human cost of getting beyond subsistence, the will to make America their own.

'Life smacks everybody around' (p. 134), observes one of the father's friends after he has fled the family and begun his northward passage to New Jersey. Ramón himself, casual worker, bigamous father to a second family, receives his own share, in common with Virta, the literally diminished wife, and Nilda, the second spouse. He, like his sons, also doles it out, a cruelty somehow almost intrinsic to survival. This is both Dominica, and America, shorn of heroics, a diet of casual labour, betrayal, pinched and furtive sex, drugs. Díaz favours no upward-mobility mythic virtue. His stories, rather, and persuasively, abound in dispossession, a brilliantly pitched Dominica-to-America migrancy of the manoeuvres, often wayward and full of lies and dispute, to do whatever might be required to keep just ahead of defeat.

'Ysrael', as the opening story and set in Ocoa, Dominica, has the brothers stalking, and then victimising, a boy so marred by a facial birth defect that he needs a mask; one cruelty joined in another. 'Fiesta 1980' turns the other way, a visit to the Bronx apartment of Tía Yrma ('furnished in Contemporary Dominican Tacky', p. 24) for a cheap booze-and-dance. En route, and back, Rafa suffers his usual car sickness to be threatened physically, and as always, by the father who owns a shiny green new van, about whom Yunior has written a school essay 'MY FATHER THE TORTURER', and to whose infidelity with a Puerto Rican woman both brothers have become conspiratorial boy witnesses. The two stories draw from lives of shared and hard-edged contingency throughout.

'Aurora', as named after a drug-thin girl, and set against a background in which Yunior has become a partner in street dealing, portrays romance tenement-style, a coupling amid heroin, theft and broken-in apartments. 'Aguantando', a key vignette, relays Yunior's dawning recognition in the Dominica of his childhood of his father as permanent absentee ('this waiting for him was all a sham', p. 54) even as he fantasises his return ('gold on his fingers, cologne on his neck, a silk shirt', p. 69). 'Edison, New Jersey' depicts Yunior, and his co-worker Wayne, as installers of pool tables for the suburban rich, a perfect cameo of Dominican labour amid American class privilege. In the title story, 'Drown', Díaz speaks to the ambivalence of Yunior's sexual encounter and friendship with the gay, college-bound Beto, a glimpse of the vulnerability behind the masks of toughness required to survive in the kind of Dominican America dramatised with so evident an insider's touch throughout *Drown*.

VII

Haiti, its origins also Arawak-Taino-Carib and slave African, yet French-Creole rather than Spanish, equally has looked to its mainland American counter-face. For Little Haiti, whether situated in Brooklyn or Miami and other Florida, has increasingly emerged as alternate realm, another island derived of migrancy and with an evolving American identity in its own right. Both incarnations of Haiti, even so, could not but look to shared repositories of memory.

One kind turns upon heroism, that of Toussaint de l'Ouverture as insurrectionist and slave liberator in the 1790s and the Independent Republic of 1804, even if the legacy would become 'President for Life' Papa Doc Duvalier (1957–71), Baby Doc Duvalier (1971–86), and the uncertain succession of Jean-Bertrand Aristide (elected in 1990, deposed in 1991, and reinstated in 1994). Another looks to poverty and sugar-cane servitude largely under neo-colonial US plantation ownership, one of banks and 'dollar diplomacy' with, in support, the invasions of 1916, 1924 and Marines presence until 1934. Haiti's own violence most notably summons the regime of the Tontons Macoutes as fearsome, often arbitrary, militia rule and diktat. On its own terms, it remains the poorest country in the hemisphere, a one-in-four population of abject poverty. Haiti-in-America affords the 1997 case of Abner Louima, arrested after a nightclub scuffle, sexually brutalised by officers from Brooklyn's 70th Precinct, and widely recognised as symptomatic of police racism against Haitians as immigrant underclass.

Within both kinds of setback, Caribbean and American, persists, of necessity, the saving continuity of Creole culture as extended family, work, language, food, music, and, always, the religious hybridity of Catholicism and santería. Whether island Haiti or America's Haiti, and with no underplaying of their bittersweet transitions and interactions, such has found a deservedly acclaimed literary custodian in Edwidge Danticat. In both her novel, *Breath, Eyes, Memory* (1994), moreover, and the stories of *Krik? Krak!* (1995), hers is a version overwhelmingly to be understood through its women, an intimate, and bridging, island to mainland gynocracy. The opening and closing pieces bear home the point. The Haiti-based 'Children of the Sea', with its poignancy of a dead child thrown into the ocean by boat-people, becomes also the remembrance of island story itself. The New York-based 'Caroline's Wedding', a handicapped sister's nuptials, subtly refigures the transition from Haiti to America.

For Sophie Caco, in *Breath, Eyes, Memory*, the journey from Croix-des-Rosets to Brooklyn becomes also one from childhood under the tutelage of Grandmè Ifé, Tante Atie, and then her expatriate mother, Martine, into eventual marriage to the Louisiana musician Joseph, and on to her mothering of their child Brigitte in Providence, Rhode Island. If, for Sophie, America can be 'a place where you can lose yourself easily' (p. 103), so Haiti, for Tante Atie, can be where 'I am losing myself . . . too' (p. 104). Yet in the passage between the two lies also passage from loss to self-retrieval, a journey through, and into yet different, strengths of womanhood.

Love and damage, indeed, contend across the four generations. The grandmother refuses to wear black for the loss of a fond husband dead of sunstroke in the canefields yet who she believes lives always. Tante Atie, the spinster who even so gives unstinting and adoptive mother-love to Sophie, can be both saint and tippler. Martine, would-be good mother, suffers lifelong nightmares as consequence of the canefield Tonton rape which has produced Sophie, a double mastectomy, and will eventually kill herself and the unborn child she has conceived in late age with the lavishly named Brooklyn-Haitian, Marc Jolibois Francis Legrand Moravien Chevalier, the one man who in fact has loved her. Each history, Haitian and American, offers a linking thread.

Sophie herself will suffer her own trauma and liberation. She deflowers herself with a pestle in protest at patriarchal island custom which insists upon being tested for virginity. She suffers bulimia, a not-so-hidden compulsion to gorge on America yet disgorge its abundance. A loss of sexual feeling, and yet instant pregnancy, her will to love and yet need for an abuse support group, shadow her marriage to Joseph. Only, finally, as she buries the mother who has told her 'You have become very American' (p. 179), will she speak, and begin to dissolve, both her own unfatherly fathering, and at the same time the violations inherent in the mutual history of Haiti and America. 'I ran through the field, attacking the cane' (p. 233), she recalls, as though to free herself of both.

At issue, on the one hand, is the Haiti of her mother's 'twenty-five years of being raped' (p. 217) and the Macoutes's latest killing, and, on the other, the America which has 'called us "boat people" and "stinking Haitians"' (p. 66). It is a liberation to embrace what Sophie's grandmother calls in creole 'Paròl gin pié zèl. The words can give wings to your feet' (p. 234). The accusing bitter-sweetness of the canefields, their lavish, colourful promise betrayed in the vast, cruel history they actually signify, might finally be transcended.

That, in turn, is to seize upon Haiti's own alternative legacy, its counter-narrative, one for Edwidge of shared womanhood, health of body and spirit, santería and the figuration of a goddess like Erzulie, ring shouts brought from Africa, the 'Krik, Krak' by which African-Creole storytelling is enacted and, in each, the redemption of self-possession. Therein, as the finely conceived *Breath, Eyes, Memory* portrays it, lies passage out of the ensnaring historic losses of Haiti, and Haiti-America, and into an identity of true 'island' freedom.

VIII

The 'islands' of American fiction have long, and readily, made their bid for attention. Turtle island, and its myriad constituent and interconnecting sub-islands, serves as a perfect trope for America as multicultural order, its endlessly transforming human chain of ethnicities. Atlantic and Pacific, inshore and offshore, migrancy as a bridge in time as much as space, one language for another, it has been an America whose calls to literary telling have clearly been irresistible. The upshot has been a dynamic conjugation: island fictions, fictions of island, each wholly indispensable in the composite imagining of both American selves and the American self.

NOTES

1. James Thomas Stevens (1994), *Tokinish*, Staten Island, NY: First Intensity Press; reprinted in (2002), *Combing the Snakes from His Hair*, East Lansing, MI: Michigan State University Press.

2. Russell Leong (1993), 'The Country of Dreams and Dust', in *The Country of Dreams and Dust*, Albuquerque, NM: West End Press, p. 24.

3. Judith Ortiz Cofer (1987), 'The Idea of Islands', in *Terms of Survival*, Houston, TX: Arte Público Press.

4. Judith Ortiz Cofer (1993) reinforces the point in 'American History', in *The Latin Deli*, Athens, GA: University of Georgia: 'I had learned to listen to my parents' dreams, which were spoken in Spanish, as fairy tales, like the stories about life in the island paradise of Puerto Rico before I was born' (p. 10).

5. James Michener (1959), *Hawaii*, New York: Random House, and Kazuo Miyamoto (1964, 1968), *Hawaii: End of the Rainbow*, Rutland, VT: Charles E. Tuttle. Much as Michener's novel took all before it, a kind of easy-read panorama, it had the effect of obscuring writing done by Hawaiian authorship itself. Ironically, it was in 1959 that a pioneer anthology, with an introduction by Michener, appeared, but to little success – namely A. Grove Day and Carl Stroven (eds) (1959), *A Hawaiian Reader*, New York: Appleton-Century-Crofts.

6. Quite the best overall account of Hawai'i in literature remains Stephen H. Sumida (1991), *And the View from Shore: Literary Traditions of Hawai'i*, Seattle, WA: University of Washington Press. For a cultural area-studies account, spanning Cook to *Hawaii Five-0*, Melville to *Baywatch*, together with Los Angeles, Honolulu and Taipei as ocean-arena 'hub cities', few more infectious works of analysis have appeared than Rob Wilson (2000), *Reimagining the American Pacific: From 'South Pacific' to Bamboo Ridge and Beyond*, Durham, NC: Duke University Press.

7. Jessica Kawasuna Saiki (1991), 'From the Lanai', in *From the Lanai and Other Hawaii Stories*, Minneapolis, MN: New Rivers Press, pp. 39–43.

8. Sylvia Watanabe (1992), 'Talking to the Dead', in *Talking to the Dead and Other Stories*, New York: Doubleday, pp. 104–18.

9. John Yau (1995), 'Hawaiian Cowboys', in *Hawaiian Cowboys*, Santa Rosa, CA: Black Arrow Press, pp. 87–102.

10. Judith Ortiz Cofer (2000), *Woman in Front of the Sun: On Becoming a Writer*, Athens, GA: The University of Georgia Press, p. 114.

11. Julia Alvarez (1995), *The Other Side/El Otro Lado*, New York: Dutton, pp. 116–17.

CHAPTER NINE

The Postmodern Turn

Metafiction, Playfield, Ventriloquy

I define *postmodern* as incredulity towards metanarratives . . . The grand narrative has lost its credibility. (Jean-François Lyotard)[1]

The novel is an imaginary paradise of individuals. It is the territory where no one possesses the truth, neither Anna nor Karenin, but where everyone has the right to be understood, both Anna and Karenin. (Milan Kundera)[2]

Criticisms of directions in postmodern thinking should not obscure insights it may offer that open up our understanding of African-American experience. The critique of essentialism encouraged by postmodernist thought is useful for African-Americans concerned with reformulating outmoded notions of identity. We have too long had imposed upon us, both from the outside and the inside, a narrow constricting notion of blackness. Postmodern critiques of essentialism which challenge notions of universality and static over-determined identity within mass culture and mass consciousness can open up new possibilities for the construction of the self and the assertion of agency. (bell hooks)[3]

I

Postmodern US multicultural fiction? The term could readily look suspect, a tease, some categorical sleight of hand, even a contradiction. Modernism there may be, the New Negro writings of the 1920s and of African American luminaries from Zora Neale Hurston to Ralph Ellison, or the Native fictions of Scott Momaday and Leslie Marmon Silko, or Chicano and Asian American self-referencing autobiography of the kind to be met with in Oscar Zeta Acosta and Maxine Hong Kingston. But that, surely, amounts to sufficient muster, a show of experimentalism here, a certain reflexivity there. Postmodernism, however, with its relish of bricolage, contingency, travesty or pastiche, its mosaics of fragmentation and discontinuity, and always its sense of irony at the notion of any one overarching truth, makes for a bridge too far.[4]

US multicultural literature, it goes on being said, and certainly under Black, Native, Latino/a and Asian auspices, has been called upon to deal in lives usually too hard-fought, too 'real', to opt for a self-avowedly textual repertoire of metafiction, playfield or ventriloquy. Does not that explain why, for long, American ethnic fiction was thought most properly housed within naturalism-realism?[5] Given chattel and plantation slavery, or Native and Mexican-Chicano dispossession, or the travails of Asian migrancy, and for all the refusal of stasis and victimry, would not the severity of these remembered histories be at risk of being parlayed into fabulation for its own sake, some obscurantist literary gamesmanship?

Yet, across a considerable body of authorings, the upshot invites being thought quite otherwise. In each of the relevant postmodern texts, the damaging construct-edness of race, pre-emptive binaries of otherness, and the cultural power-politics of naming, have been held up to new orders of scrutiny, as has the saving creativity and resilience of the lives being told. Their fashioning subverts not only the presiding ideologies of American master narratives but their very techniques, be they naturalist-realist, modernist, or any supposed register between. An extraordinary compositional vitality, in fact, has emerged, full of self-circling pivot and irony, and rarely conceived as anything but against the grain.

In this respect, the highlight falls on Ishmael Reed's Afro-signifying and syncret-isms in *Flight to Canada* (1976) and *Mumbo Jumbo* (1972), Gerald Vizenor's post-indian mixedblood-trickster aesthetic in *Bearheart* (1978, 1990) and *The Heirs of Columbus* (1991), Ana Castillo's reflexive update of magic realism and epistolarity in *The Mixquiahuala Letters* (1986) and, respectively, Maxine Hong Kingston's *Trip-master Monkey* (1989) as both given over to, and at the same time itself an enactment of, Chinese American talk-story, and Teresa Hak Kyung Cha's *DICTEE* (1982) as the polyphonic 'voicing' of Korean lineage and womanhood silenced, and divided, within a connecting frame of Japanese colonialism, two-nation status, US migration and the politics of gender.

Counter-hegemonic voice, to use a current phrase, takes on fresh impetus, one which links into, even if it does not exactly reproduce, the postcoloniality theorised by Homi Bhabha or Gayatri Spivak with its necessary hybridity both of migrant life-history and arising styles of narrative. Prior equations of protest, usually nation- or class-based, are simply, though actually not so simply, superseded. Alleged 'realist' fictions, once thought normative in their linear or cause-and-effect patterning, can be held up, if not teased, for their coercive artificiality. The emphasis, rather, becomes one of reverse imagining, the taking back of possession. For, in entering the ranks of the postmodern, these texts not only reappropriate lives from routine, and usually condescending, labelling as 'US ethnic', or even multicultural, but subject these self-same discourses to, exactly, their own metafictive, playfield and ventri-loquial regimes of invention and signification.

Postcolonial, or transnational, English-language fiction has become familiar enough in names as diverse as those of Salman Rushdie and Maryse Condé, Keri Hulme and Abdulrazak Gurnah, Timothy Mo and Buchi Emecheta. But recognition of the extent to which US ethnic-designated narrative borders on, if it does not exactly share, the terrain, is also due. In the case of Black, Native, Latino/a and Asian American writing, colonialism, especially internal, subalternism, and even empire, can be said to figure, but with necessary adjustments. For America yields its own kind of postmodern national space, a uniquely self-aware and competitive arena of identity, and evolved through histories linked to, but either subsequent to or situated at a remove from, those of the European imperium visited on Africa, Asia and most of Latin America.[6]

Literary modernism, it is usually said, betrays a nostalgia for some supposed universal unity of belief or culture within its shored fragments, its myth-worlds, as in Pound's *Cantos*, Eliot's *The Wasteland* or Joyce's *Ulysses*. With postmodernism, however, the game and its narrative levers change, a scepticism that any such unity does, or indeed can, exist. Is not Roland Barthes's example of the peeling of the onion only to reveal skin-layers, no evident core, best suited? One says yes but with reservations. The US ethnic fictions in play certainly offer their own revolving circuits of sign and semiotics. But they do so from a history of lives contemplating themselves as having already been made subject to a kind of pre-existing American virtual reality, a lived-out, or lived-through, multi-screen, literal and figurative, and from early print or cartoon to DVD, of attributed identities, masks, simulations and stereotype.

Why not, then, virtual counter-texts, or surtexts, of their own multicultural kind, and quite as much given to postmodernist manoeuvre as names like Nabokov, or an American roll-call to include John Barth, Thomas Pynchon, William Gaddis, Ron Sukenick, Donald Barthelme and Raymond Federman? To imagine that multi-cultural writers somehow would, or indeed should, have eschewed the opportunities afforded by this imaginative option, and not have taken their fiction to the reflexive edge, has always been to do a disservice. To admirers, at least, the eventuality of this resort to a simultaneity of timelines, floating narrators along with floating signifiers, and renderings of the world as anything but linear, has been exhilarating. It suggests the word as much to have taken possession of American ethnic history as to have been possessed by it, and, in so doing, to have made for a quite wholly new and freeing historical efficacy.

US ethnic literary voice, on this reckoning, moves yet more through, or beyond, or simply around, some minority niche. It both refuses the cultural governance of whiteness, and its pre-emptive boundaries, as usually assumed universal marker of value, and at the same time challenges any too-narrow cultural-nationalist ideology. The loss of the real, again to invoke Baudrillard, exerts its own kind of relevance. How best to free any given ethnicity from static definition? How best to recognise disjuncture as much as continuity in the lives so designated? Nor can the histories involved comfortably be thought the one thing, the one place, be it reservation, ghetto, Asiatown or barrio. Access to a 'glocal' world-order courtesy of satellite, or web, or cheap travel, and even for those generally thought disempowered, is not to be denied. Ethnicity, in this sense, and without denying any given intimacy or discretion of lineage, can be said to have become as international as national. In the same spirit, and in an echo of Randolph Bourne, there has been a move to replace 'US ethnic literature' as a term with 'US transnational literature'.[7]

Related new questioning, alongside, also enters. Who, actually, invented American ethnicity? How real, in its own turn, is it? Who, both, is it, and yet performs it? What not only of crossed or mixed ethnicity but different kinds of ethnic gendering? What plies of ethnicity arise in the face of serial migrancy? Is there such a thing, in America, as non-ethnicity? For some, the postmodern text will always reflect cultural exhaustion, a sense of endgame, narratives of depthlessness. But, for others, it carries edge, appetite, literature's way of undermining and complicating all easy 'reality' culture. In consequence, it can little surprise that literary-ideological contretemps continue to stir, and in the multicultural literary arena no less than elsewhere. The contending forces of debate have especially been drawn to what is, or might be, or should be, any given due line or mode of ethnic writing.

Within African American tradition, the attritional Black Aesthetic agenda of the 1960s never wholly disappeared with its call for Afrocentricity, a militant direction to all acts of black literary voice. Signifying, with its own reflexive tactics of wordplay and imagery and whose unique origins lie in African, oral-slave and musical heritage, to be sure, has won fuller recognition. But an old worry is still to be heard and which bell hooks is not alone in voicing. How, convincingly, to reconcile demands that African American writing engage the historically actual terms of life out of which it arises with black texts as playfields, and which, in multiple ways and to multiple effect, circle around their own textual self-knowing?[8]

A well-known Native American spat broke out in the 1980s in consequence of Leslie Marmon Silko's review of Louise Erdrich's *The Beet Queen* and which turned upon oral-community as against too scriptural, or elusively postmodern, a mode of text. It has taken new and equally fierce polemical shape in Elizabeth Cook-Lynn's strictures against 'American Indian intellectualism'. This she ascribes to a supposed overly professorial, largely mixedblood and off-reservation cadre to include, among others, Gerald Vizenor, Wendy Rose, Louis Owens and Diane Glancy. Yet, as Vizenor especially has argued, have not 'Indians' since American discovery, if not prospectively long before, been imaged in most western culture as precisely cartoon, Noble or Devil, and with always the mongrel half-breed to add to the fray? For him, Native people were metafictions *avant la lettre*, 'double others', 'a bankable simulation', as he calls them in *Manifest Manners*. Owens, in his turn, hypothesises 'this phantom artifact called "Indian"'. How for them, as for like-minded other Native writers, to resist subjecting this kind of pre-emptive Indianness to postmodern interrogation?[9]

Latino/a polemic has been equally contrary. The talk of a US–Mexico border aesthetic by Gómez-Peña and others has raised the stakes as to not only an American national cultural text but even a cultural-nationalist ethnic text. How does post-modernism change the terms of reference, the border as also virtuality, a site not just of literal migrancy but of mind and the reflective oscillations of myth? In the discursive practice of figures like Gloria Anzaldúa and Cherríe Moraga, sympto-matically in their *This Bridge Called My Back: Writings By Radical Women of Color* (1981), the grounds are offered for a renegotiation of gender identity free of patriarchy both in, and beyond, the Hispanic community. But for them, as for most of their contributors, the issue runs far beyond. Gender, quite postmodernly, and whether straight, bi- or gay, is to be understood as much for its cultural and social construction as for biology, in effect yet another species of self-aware and performative human text.[10]

Frank Chin, in his intervention on fake and authentic China myths, can look to latest kinds of Asian American counterpart, as can Epifanio San Juan, in his association of postmodern style with a kind of consumer-goods aesthetic and to which he believes a fellow-Filipino/a author like Jessica Hagedorn gives hostage. David Mura, for instance, author of *The Colors of Desire* (1995) and *A Male Grief: Notes on Pornography and Addiction* (1996), as well as the autobiography, *Turning Japanese: Memoirs of a Sansei* (1991), has won praise but also severe ideological critique both from those who accuse him of fake confession and from a number of Asian American feminists. Yet his, too, has been a postmodern stand, the articulation of a self-aware 'Asian' sexual identity out to repudiate long-time and exotic passive-aggressive fictionalisation by the mainstream even as it acts to watch, and explore, its own plural sense of eros.[11]

The emphasis, throughout, must indeed fall on the postmodern *turn*. No absoluteness applies, ideological or generic, some instant litmus-paper test as to credential. Rather there becomes evident a style of consciousness, and narrative, which steps from inside to outside in terms of focalisation. But, however the eddies of argument are best to be resolved, they underline, an irony no doubt in its own right, the degree to which ethnic fiction has become implicated in the intellectual dramas of postmodernism.

Diehards continue to speak of the mere will to virtuosity. Those more welcoming of postmodern narration, however, look to the challenge of its dislocations, the bold, even heady, unfixing of history's received versions and, with it, the unfixing of genre or any prescribed rhetoric of fiction. For them, othering itself becomes othered. The imagined margin turns the tables and seizes not only upon its own rights, but its own reflexive-playful possibilities, of imagining. Allowing for each greater or lesser success, this is to acknowledge, in vision as in genre, how America's ethnic fiction has also put into contention its own, often enough startling, textual lien on the postmodern.[12]

II

Sometimes I feel that the condition of the Afro-American writer in this country is so strange that one has to go to the supernatural for an analogy. Manipulation of the word has always been related in the mind to the manipulation of nature. One utters a few words and stones roll aside, the dead are raised and the river beds emptied of their contents.[13]

Ishmael Reed, writing in 1970, offers typically figurative, and engaging, notice if not exactly of a wholesale change of imaginative regime then of redirected bearings, a different tone. Given the flourish of early narrative fantasias like *The Free-Lance Pallbearers* (1967), with its irreverent tilts at Nixonian America, or *Yellow Back Radio*

Broke-Down (1969), with its send-up of frontier lore, here not only would be, but already was, the African American novel's own zestful, and not a little magical, empire of signs. Texts which deconstruct themselves, history as synchronicity, riffs on ethnic cliché, swerves of wit and parody, have become hallmarks.

Flight to Canada and *Mumbo Jumbo* add especially to Reed's postmodern litany, two takes on key American epochs as much for their passed-down 'authoring' as historical actuality. The former steps into the nineteenth century, a daring, at times witheringly funny, meta-narrative of Lincoln-era southern slaveholding under rules of mask, double-speak and charade. The latter conjures a neo-Hoodoo 1920s mystery story which contrasts black creativity, Jes Grew, and whether jazz or literary word, with a puritan white-masonic America, if not, indeed, the western world in general. Subsequent fictions, to include *The Last Days of Louisiana Red* (1974), his pillorying of corporate America, *Reckless Eyeballing* (1986), his controversial swipe at strong-arm feminism, and *Japanese by Spring* (1993), his campus novel of US Asiaphobia, show no lessening of a taste for postmodern carnival.

Reed, assuredly, has been anything but a sole flag-bearer. William Demby contributes his McLuhan-influenced and, as he calls it, 'cubist' novel of the world as media reality, a Rome-centred fiction of the real in *The Catacombs* (1965). John Edgar Wideman transposes an American back-to-Africa journey into oneiric monologue in *Hurry Home* (1970). Clarence Major, in *NO* (1973), fuses a murder mystery into the trope for the authorly detection of reality. Carlene Hatcher Polite writes, in her own term, a free-form 'jazz text' of the black female body caught between possession and autonomy, the competitive power-plays within gender as much as colour, in *Sister X and the Victims of Foul Play* (1975). All need to be entered into the reckoning. But Reed's own fictions have been uniquely sharp-eyed, full of liberating challenge even as they give off the most genuine congeniality.

As to *Flight to Canada*, the notion of the America of slaveholding and its aftermath, not to mention of civil war, as pastiche shadowland, to be sure, involves risks of tact. How best to lower the ironic postmodern boom on history much of which has become sacrosanct, whether 'the peculiar institution' and escape, the Old South, Lincoln, *Uncle Tom's Cabin*, the postbellum rise of America as capitalist triumph, or even Canada as supposed Freedom Trail haven? For as Reed tells his story of Raven Quickskill, plantation fugitive and pen-man of the valedictory poem which shares its title with the novel ('*I have done my Liza Leap/& am safe in the arms of/Canada*', p. 11), and of his battle, respectively, against Arthur Swille as gargoyle Virginian-Southern planter, and Yankee Jack as pirate, wine connoisseur and Northern entrepreneur, he is about giving metafictive guise to America's weightiest national drama.

In the novel's framing of matters, who is to be entrusted with Afro-America's story or, with an eye to the larger frame, that of the nation-at-large? Aided by each purposive jibe and squib (the radio's 'Beecher Hour show' p. 122, the announcement, 'there will be a garden party reading of Edgar Poe', p. 128, or Lincoln's 'having visions of himself as a statue' p. 142), Reed's ends are perfectly served by making Quickskill into black meta-author. Ventriloquist at large and post-slave speechgiver, and writer possessed by his guede or Haitian god-spirit, he it is who will return from Canada once more to take up his pen.

For all of Reed's shows of scholarly know-how, his complexities of voice and styling, he has not always had an easy critical passage. Charges speak of a stand-up comedy of the page, showtime or cartoon. But these too easily allow the companionability of his playfield text, and its narrator, to overtake an infinitely savvier achievement, that of *Flight to Canada* as palimpsest. The one kind of earlier slave narrative is written over by the other, slavery-time freedom-seekers and 'patrollers' reconceived under latter-day terms of contemporary freedom-seekers and repossession men.

The outcome is a fiction which can overlap time ('Slave/Catchers waitin on me/ At Trailways', p. 11), which can have Princess Quaw Quaw Tralalarala, herself a 'love terrorist' update of Pocahontas (p. 118) and eventual Blondin-like tightrope walker, observe (of all times) during a sexual tryst with Quickskill '"You're . . . you're too . . . too ethnic. You should be more universal! More universal"' (p. 107), and wherein Lincoln ('Gary Cooper-awkward', p. 31), just as reflexively, can find himself noting that 'myths fly' (p. 43). Trickster writ holds throughout, the one historical currency inside the other, the one voice inhabited by the other.

In Reed's Dixie, the Swille plantation features as surreal Camelot, an Arthurian outpost, yet also the headquarters of a contemporary multinational corporation. Swille himself doubles as slaveholder and latter-day CEO, American-born yet wholly admiring of the self-flagellating white-royal England of Queen Victoria, Prince Albert and Gladstone. Ms Swille plays plantation mistress to a fault yet also TV- and diet-obsessed modern housewife ('"She looks real Emancipated"' says the malapropising Mama Barracuda, p. 122). Swille's albino son, Moe, acts as a parody of white slave-offspring, lookalike son yet kept at a distance. The legitimate heir, Mitchell, would-be African anthropologist yet killed by a 'heart of darkness' Congolese crocodile, becomes a ghost whose skull his father places in the National Archives. If that mimics usual anthropological practice, it also wins Swille tax exemption. The Usher-like appearance of Vivian, Swille's 'chaste Southern belle' sister ('We were married in Death', p. 148) yet his partner in incest and necrophilia, further theatricalises the pageant, more life Gothic acted out as stage Gothic.

Alongside runs the Afro-south of Quickskill's fellow escapees, the slave figure of 40s who, on his houseboat in Canada, speaks of 'Virginia everywhere' (p. 87), Stray Leechfield who will sell out to white sexual interest in black flesh as a porn star, Mama Barracuda as grotesque dominatrix-mammy, and Uncle Robin and Aunt Judy, two 'puttin on ole massa' house servants to a fault yet heirs to the estate after Swille is burned to death by his wife. Under their regime, and having visited the Ashanti lands, the estate, known as the Castle, become a centre for black craftsmen, artists, writers – in whose fashioning, Quickskill's among them, America's 'other' history will not just be recognised but further told and built. All are heirs to what Reed has Swille designate *Dysaesthetica Aethipica*, 'the disease causing Negroes to run away' (p. 27).

Were not this dark comedy enough, Abraham Lincoln, 'The Player', visits the slave quarters with 'Hello Dolly' playing in the background and delivers the Emancipation Proclamation less as the moral high ground than as expedient campaign politics. Helicopters overfly the grounds. Cameo appearances are made by TV's Harry Reasoner and Barbara Walters, the actor Yul Brynner, the black Augustan poet Phillis Wheatley and a bardic Walt Whitman ('He stood in the corner . . . sniffing a lilac', p. 94). Mrs Stowe as 'Old Harriet. Naughty Harriet' (p. 15), abolitionist and yet vintage Victorian prude, is invoked for accusing Byron of pornography, for her physical dislike of Lincoln and, above all, for stealing the gri-gri or life story of Father Josiah Henson, purported model for her title character, in Uncle Tom's Cabin. On-the-spot and unsparing 'reality TV' interviews are broadcast of the Lincoln assassination from the Ford Theatre out of which John Wilkes Booth, one-time Dixie thespian, emerges as 'America's first Romantic Assassin' (p. 115). The south could not be more costume drama for real:

> Raised by mammies, the South is dandyish, foppish, pimpish; its writers are Scott, Poe, Wilde, Tennyson; its assassin left behind a trunk in which was found 'clothes in fine silk velvets; silks, ermine and crimson; and also hats, caps, plumes, boots, shoes, etc.' (p. 153)

The north, likewise, edges into mythic kingdom, Boston as 'Emancipation City', Buffalo and Niagara Falls as 'leap to freedom' staging posts, and Canada as metaphoric site of Quickskill's interwoven freedom of body and word ('He was so much against slavery that he had begun to include prose and poetry in the same book, so that there would be no arbitrary boundaries between them . . . Each man to his own Canada', p. 99). Aeroplane bookings are needed to give anti-slavery lectures, and William Wells Brown enters to gives conference and platform-delivery commercial advice. Yankee Jack, speculator and anything-for-sale entrepreneur, ascends the capitalist ladder and, not least, in the commodification of his own wife, Quaw-Quaw, as ethnic chic ('She was popular on the college circuit, performing Indian dances', p. 103). If the south affects Arcadia, this is the north as parody Franklin, a Yankeedom of all-out market commercialism.

In both, the novel points to Reed's use of Quickskill as master of each quick-change and dissolve within, as much as of, his own text. But he also shares something of his custodial spirit with the south's most haunted, if not haunting, author, Edgar Allan, Poe, or Eddie Poe as, faux-intimately, Quickskill dubs him. Custodian of the darker reaches of the psyche, whether mansion, pit or maelstrom, symboliste by French adoption, who better contends as precursor of America's literary postmodernism? In this light, there can be little doubt of a writerly affinity to connect the black-phobic visions of the South's whitest author with the black-affirming visions of Ishmael Reed as delivered through Quickskill:

> Why isn't Edgar Allan Poe recognized as the principal biographer of that strange war? Fiction you say? Where does fact begin and fiction leave off? Why does the perfectly rational, in its own time, often sound like mumbo-jumbo? Where did it leave off for

Poe, prophet of a civilization buried alive, where, according to witnesses, people were often whipped for no reason. No reason? Will we ever know, since there are so few traces left of the civilization the planters called 'the fairest civilization the sun ever shone upon', and the slaves called 'Satan's Kingdom.' Poe got it all down. Poe says more in a few stories than all of the volumes by historians. Volumes about that war. The Civil War. The Spirit War. Douglass, Tubman and Bibb all believing in omens, consulting conjure and carrying unseen amulets on their persons. Lincoln, the American Christ, who dies on Good Friday. Harriet saying that God wrote Uncle Tom's Cabin. *Which God? Some gods will mount any horse.* (pp. 18–19)

Raven as ornithological-symbolic bird underlines the link in how it calls up both Poe's best-known poem and Quickskill's name, the south's prophet of a 'civilization buried alive' and Reed's invented slave-fugitive. As to Quickskill, he takes up the implications of his naming in his use of black and Native flight imagery to utter the continuity of an America of slaveholding and escape as indeed a 'strange' haunting. A century and a half on from 'The Raven' (1845), *Flight to Canada* in all its overlapping textual self-disguise as both novel and poem-prologue, invites being thought quite one of the canniest, not to say canniest postmodern, literary requiems.

Early into *Mumbo Jumbo*, Reed supplies an etymology for his novel's title, its use in English as a casual synonym for gibberish nicely rebuked by its Mandingo lexical root as a term of exorcism, and which, with teasing scholarly touch, he cites from the American Heritage Dictionary. For throughout a text he dubs Neo-Hoodoo in kind, and in which Vodoun serves as bas-relief to Warren Harding's 1920s, and Pharaonic and Graeco-Roman allusion to Jazz Age politics, Reed indeed sets himself to play the exorcist of a west which, even as it has exploited, has largely inferiorised and infantilised the massive, and eclectically various, cultural legacy both of Africa and Afro-America.

The result becomes nothing short of a deconstructive raid on the edifice known as western civilisation. The text fuses detective story with religio-cultural mythology, recondite dips into Egyptian, Greek, Haitian and Harlem lore with medieval Templar-masonic conspiracy. Yet further loopings use page layouts of strip cartoon, photography, newspaper extracts, telegrams, and even a diagram of bomb tonnage dropped in the Second World War. Reed himself, signing himself 'I.R.', has no hesitation in intruding as commentator, or authorial player, in his own narrative. But, whatever the sleight-of-hand, he can rarely be said to have conceived more serious comedy.

The plotline, or rather plot-circling, turns back on itself as though anti-plot. The mysterious outbreak of a black-originated cultural fever called Jes Grew ('Ask Louis Armstrong, Bessie Smith, your poets, your painters . . .', p. 52) plays against a white unicultural America under the would-be sway of Atonists. These serve as heirs to the Templars, and their medieval New World Order, whose masonic agents Reed calls the Wallflower Order, 'a society of enforcers established when the Atonists triumphed over the West' (p. 189). Theirs has been the installing of 'an anti-Jes

Grew' President Warren Harding (p. 17), with 'Calvinist editorial writers' (p. 17) who inveigh against the dangers to the civilised world of a 'negritude' of Vodoun, Jazz, talk, round-midnight style, and specifically as part of the age, the dancing of the Funky Butt or Black Bottom rather than the waltz.

Mumbo Jumbo, collage, narrative-within-a-narrative, bears down exactly upon how the massive plurality of black custom has been reduced to atavism or, as Reed cites accusingly, Freud's 'black tide of mud' (p. 211). Another gloss, equally accusing, is added in the observation 'If [Jes Grew] could not find its text then it would be mistaken for entertainment' (p. 211). The implied issue lies in asking how to find, to speak, or to write, blackness not only in the face of so much would-be anaesthetising cultural whiteness but as itself not one but many texts.

Harding, and the guardians of 'sacred' whiteness, epitomise one pole of how western culture has come to express itself. In PaPa LaBas, 'astrodetective' (p. 64) and 'detective of the metaphysical' (p. 212), 'obeah-man' (p. 45) and 'fugitive-hermit' (p. 45), however, Reed imagines another, the conjure figure as nemesis to unravel the true plot whereby blackness, in all its multicultural energy of history, speech, religion, art and music, has indeed been made into mumbo-jumbo. It is this blackness that Reed summons as a 'liturgy without a text' (p. 6), a feast or plenitude of loas. For the single 'text' that LaBas is employed to find, the 'synthetic master-text' as it has been called, in fact cannot be found. There cannot be, is not, any *one* Book of Blackness.[14]

This, on Reed's part, amounts to anything but fashionable indeterminacy, mere postmodern chic. Quite the contrary: it holds to the wholly serious need to grasp cultural blackness as indeed without closure. As the listed manifestations of Jes Grew bear out, Scott Joplin to Charlie Parker and John Coltrane, the Blues, dances like the Eagle Rock or Buzzard Stoop, all the black language arts, and each literary fiction (pp. 211–12), blackness operates, as Reed cites from Arna Bontemps's slave-insurrection novel, *Black Thunder* (p. 218), like a pendulum, at once dialectical, mobile, fluid.

In other words, the tactics of postmodern voice, its fragmentation and use of visual as much as spoken or scriptural trace, could not be better placed to unpack not some essentialist blackness but a necessary diversity of black cultural imagination. That spans the Egypt of Osiris-Isis resurrection myth, the Africa of Ogoun and Damballah, the Haiti of Vodoun practice and Independence-era generalship, and the 'conjure' New Orleans of Marie Laveau and Place Congo. 1920s Harlem, street as much as New Negro salon, becomes but one of its many epicentres. It can justly be asked that, if LaBas and his company are enjoined to seek one text of blackness, is not *Mumbo Jumbo* conceived, and angled, as a rejoinder, a script about there being no such script, only multitextuality?

Few could doubt Reed's deflationary talents, each keen-eyed jibe. Freud, faced with Afro-America, faints ('What he saw must have been unsettling to this man accustomed to the gay Waltzing circles of Austria', p. 208). An invented caricature like Bill Musclewhite moves from Police Commissioner to 'Curator of the Center of Art Detention' (p. 42). The *Mu'tafikah*, a 'Black, Yellow and Red' multicultural gang led by LaBas's associate, Berbelang, in a reversal of western custodianship, are seen to be 'looting the museums and shipping the plunder back to where it came from' (p. 15). A 'Talking Android' is introduced by the Wall Flower clique to mouth black platitudes, and in speech and writing to utter a species of one-note blackness, mock-ebonics. Others, in shared manner, become the butt of the text's irony, by-the-book Marxists, narrow black nationalists, third-rate literary critics who speak only of 'protest' and the like, and Mormons as symptomatic of unimaginative and unifocal religious mythmakers.

The action swerves and accelerates. Linkages track intertextually one into the other. The cast enters and exits in quick-moving fades, to include a white New Orleans mayor and floozy and for whom Jes Grew signifies 'the end of Civilization As We Know It' (p. 4); Abdul Hamid as savvy, long-time student of black culture as multiplicity and yet, finally, a species of Elijah Muhammad – puritan and nationalist; Black Herman as LaBas's 'Jes Grew' fellow-gumshoe; and Hinckle Von Vampton, his name an echo of Carl Van Vechten, whose would-be cultural magistracy over Renaissance Harlem is borne out in his newspaper sign 'NEGRO VIEWPOINT WANTED' (p. 76).

Little wonder that Reed has LaBas speak of his understanding of 'the certain Native American Indian tribe reputed to have punished a man for lacking a sense of humor' (p. 97). It may well be in that same spirit that as a coda to his novel he includes a 104-item bibliography. If that points to *Mumbo Jumbo* as supplying one of postmodernism's fictional textbooks, it could, quite as readily, take on reverse status as one of postmodernism's textbook fictions.

III

'I believe we're all invented as Indians', observes Gerald Vizenor in a celebrated 1981 interview.[15] 'Indian is a nominal simulation of racialism and colonialism, an invented name, unheard in native oral languages', he further amplifies in a 1995 autobiographical essay.[16] Both give points of departure. How to de-invent 'the Indian', and to re-invent, in his signature phrase, *postindian* identity? The goal holds throughout his fiction of Native-trickster feints and transgression, the fantastical realism, the Rabelaisian carnival. If Vizenor is best to be described as postmodern, it would be to emphasise no mere passing feat of style, considerable though that can be, but how inventively fierce, even brutal-comic, yet always subtle, has been his counter-imagining to Indians as harlequin, hologram, chimera, the one or another kind of pre-emptive cultural shadow. *Bearheart: The Heirship Chronicles* (1978, 1990), tribal-visionary and baroque pilgrimage, and *The Heirs of Columbus* (1991), pastiche of 1492 in which Columbus features as not Genoese but a Mayan-descended mixedblood tribal homecomer, make for symptomatic offerings from within his truly ample body of authorship.

Griever: An American Monkey King in China (1987), in aligning Griever de Hocus as Native trickster with Sun Wu-k'ung as the trickster of Chinese operas, and replete in the simian lore of both traditions, uses its Gulliverism to take shies at capitalist and Marxist shibboleth. *The Trickster of Liberty: Tribal Heirs to a Wild Baronage at Petronia*

(1988) turns its antic, Berkeley-set story of anthropology, computers and Native Studies academic politics into a detection-plot as much of American history as purloined relics. In *Dead Voices: Natural Agonies in the New World* (1992), Vizenor enters Beckett terrain, yet also downtown Oakland, a shaman vision with due invocation of the Anishinaabe earthdiver creation-figure of Naanabozho, and of the wisewoman Bagese transformed into bear voice, as figurative mirrors by which to take on Native meaning.

Hotline Healers: An Almost Browne Novel (1997) puts 'Indians' under White Earth trickster rules, not least its cross-genre of story-cycle as novel and its spectacle of the Blank Book business created by Almost. *Chancers* (2000) looks again to the spectacle of museumised Natives. Skulls are reborn as dancers in a California ritual of exorcism. Trickster eroticism includes resurrection through sex with mummified Native remains as a restoring of life to exhibits. Names from Ishi to Phoebe Hearst and Alfred Kroeber as stellar anthropologist are variously invoked in the novel's guying of any attributed social-science fixity to Native identity.

It takes little acquaintanceship to recognise that both *Bearheart* and *The Heirs of Columbus* give off shared challenge, apocalypse in one, subverted Columbian discovery myth in the other. That is not to suggest that Vizenor has laid exclusive claim to the trickster's magic box. James Welch's *Winter in the Blood* negotiates displacement into its own narrative form, Native *cauchemar* but also dark, often absurdist comedy. Leslie Marmon Silko's *Almanac of the Dead*, with its compendious eco-genealogy of western damage to Native, and specifically Pueblo, time and culture, is rightly thought as much an epic of postmodern voice as cartography. Sherman Alexie's *Reservation Blues* gives every grounds for being considered the shrewdly targeted replay of one Indian War era in another, a Native-centred Comedy of Errors. But it does emphasize Vizenor's own singular tackling of the massive historical ruptures and deformations which, as he sees it, Native America has found itself obliged not only to survive but outwit.

Bearheart, at first view, might readily call up Chaucer, Dante or Cervantes in its use of the *peregrinus* motif. But the travels in play, from the start, clearly belong to quite another order of irreality. They involve entering, and traversing, an America as much bereft of spiritual balance as of oil and petroleum energy, at once toxic, cannibal and literally unlit. Yet for all the dystopian impulse, and as in not only Swift but the artwork of Hieronymus Bosch or George Grosz, Vizenor's own Book of the Grotesque at the same time offers therapy towards better historical grace. If 'war words and terminal creeds' (p. 11) serve as his codings for Native life conventionally told as though in savagist monochrome, or having been put under malign siege from sources that collaborationistically can also be Native along with non-Native, then the novel acts as trickster countermand.

The manuscript given by Saint Louis Bearheart to Songidee migwam, AIM radical whose sacred Anishinaabe name she too readily discloses on breaking into the BIA offices, might indeed be a story brought out of hiding. The passage it tells of Proude Cedarfair, fourth of his name, and of his wife, Rosina Parent, from the 'sovereign circle' (p. 3) of sacred cedar trees at '*migis* sandridge' (p. 13) in the Upper Mississippi (or as cited from Anishinaabe the *misibi*) to Chaco Canyon as 'vision window' (p. 238) and into the Fourth World, Vizenor pitches as a kind of puppet drama. His 'circus pilgrims' (p. 96), each a fantastical mixedblood whose number includes the seven clown crows and the mongrels Pure Gumption and Private Jones, travel the abandoned interstate highways of America as though across a wasteland of darkest dream. The frequency of violence and death, the extravagant sexuality, have sometimes aroused shock-horror puritanical complaint. Yet, at the very outset, Vizenor would seem to have issued a kind of Native-cum-postmodern authorial health warning ('The bear is me now' reads the opening line, p. vii).

The very names of the pilgrims, and their tics or manners, do reflexive service, starting with Bearheart as woodland tribester yet also ursine spirit-healer, and whose repeated *ha ha ha haah* gives its own ironic acoustic to the novel. Of Rosina, Native woman, the text observes: 'She did not see herself in the abstract as a series of changing ideologies' (p. 35). Others, usually mixedblood, assume a shared magical or mongrel physiology, whether Benito Saint Plumero, lover of a green woman statue, and in an old Native piece of bawdy possessed of the endlessly in-service giant penis known as President Jackson, or Pio Wissakode-winni, 'parawoman mixedblood mammoth clown', alleged male rapist given female hormones and caught sexually midway, or Belladonna Darwin-Winter Catcher, born at Wounded Knee of Lakota father and white mother, and who will die of a poisoned cookie for her narcissistic blather about Mother Earth and related feathers-and-warpaint tribal cliché.

The company extends to Bishop Omax Parasimo, wearer of three metamasks in aiding tribal people to shelter, and who will die of lightning strike; Dr Wilde Coxwain, dispenser of fake tribal history, and his male lover, Justice Pardone Cozener, lawyer illiterate; Sir Cecil Staples, 'monarch of unleaded gasoline' (p. 99), bald, toothless, skin-poisoned custodian of What Cheer Trailer Ruins, the Evil Gambler of Anishinaabe and other tribal myth (a life for five gallons of petrol), and the gargoyle mixedblood who will die by one of his own killing-devices only when defeated in the game of chance by Proude; Lilith Mae Farrier, abused daughter and mocked one-time teacher, yet loving sexual partner to her twin boxer dogs, who destroys herself by fire having lost to Sir Cecil; and Inawa Biwide, orphan, victim of torture at New Mexico's Palace of Governors, pure spirit in a world of excremental history who will step into the Fourth World with Bearheart.

In their Brobdingnagian encounters, Vizenor seeks to skewer the legacy of America as Manifest Destiny, Native man-trap, and gasoline and foodway culture. 'Interstate' perfectly applies, asphalt routeway yet also the index of a half-human condition. *Bearheart*, appropriately, works as a narrative theatre of episode and mask, one violent metamorphosis set against another. Often Vizenor accoutres them in a rhetoric long identified as his own but which, as ever, works to unfix fixity, the sediments of co-optive past usage: survivance, transmotion, paramask, terminal creed, vision bear, shaman crow or panic hole. The opening collusion with the federals by Jordan Coward, gin-soaked and blustering chairman of the nearby reservation, to have the Bearheart cedars felled by federal agents serves as perfect image of sell-out, tree-killing petty power as anti-life. It provides a curtain-raiser to the darker, at times near-hallucinatory, sequences to follow.

Any number stand out. At the Scapehouse on Callus Road, the novel envisages a thirteen-woman poet commune of Weirds and Sensitives, literally poisoned womanhood given to animal-eating, cancer, and group orgy with Bigfoot. At Big Walker, the pilgrims barely avoid death as oil-scavenging whites try to seize the silver cabriolet they have been given only to burn to death in the flames. What Cheer yields Sir Cecil, parody aristocrat and bad spirit, to be followed by the novel's most graphic horror, that of the 'Hlastic Haces', the Dunfries colony of cripples whose body parts, and faces especially, have been so eaten by cancers as to leave them unable to pronounce 'Plastic Faces'. When Little Big Mouse, white-woman companion to the giant pilgrim, Sun Bear Sun, seeks to console them with a strip-tease, they lust and masturbate, eventually to cause her death by dismemberment, ruined and parasite ghouls.

At the Bioavaricious Regional Word Hospital, language itself comes under imagining as equally cancered, more terminal creed in the form of government or canonical history and never less so than in regard to Native America. At the Witch Hunt Restaurant, the target is what Vizenor terms Fast Food Fascism, hanging 'witch' women served as edible take-outs. At the city of Orion, by contrast, hospitality is to be exchanged for live spoken story, a suspicion of how, yet again, the fixed written word exerts its own imprisoning. Sun Bear Sun, for example, captured along with the other pilgrims by white authority at the Palace of Governors, is left 'answering unanswerable questions' (p. 230). These different close encounters, and as one after another pilgrim dies or abandons the journey, will lead into Bearheart's own final and transcending bear-entry into the Fourth World.

'Postmodern' likely only begins to cover the turnings of Bearheart, its command of satiric reversal or grotesquery. Native fiction is often construed as different orders of emergence, vision or homing story.[17] Each indeed plays its part in Vizenor's novel. It is the trickster ethos, however, Native-oral or postmodern-reflexive, if not an interplay of both, which above all gives it narrative energy. A Mrs Grundyism, distractingly, may on occasion have surfaced about maverick violence or offending sex. But the wholly more consequential challenge should not be doubted, tribal history imagined as tribal meta-history, Native America imagined as an awakening from nightmare.

The Heirs of Columbus exhibits similar daring, more trickster unplotting of the plots of history, not one, but a whole series of interwoven, and resolutely postmodern, detective stories. To be sure, Vizenor was far from alone in alighting upon Columbus as entrenched US foundational myth-figure in time for 1992. But few authors, Native or not, circle as deftly, or provocatively, around the usual either–or historiography aroused by Columbus. Under the novel's construing, better, altogether richer, speculative 'crime-detection' is invited as to the binary of Atlantic braveheart or zealot coloniser, not to mention all the ensuing New Found Land hagiography and its implications for America's Native peoples. The Heirs of Columbus aspires to nothing less than a re-envisioning of US history, a trickster telling of the Columbian legacy to capture its millennial contradiction, rift and zaniness.

What, then, if the Columbus of 1492, not least as seen from America's vaunted quincentenary year, were to be thought a returning crossblood Mayan, Sephardic Jew, maybe converso, and exile as much as indigenous Italian? What if, by union with a Native lover, Samana (her name from Samana Cay), he were imagined as the part-begetter of a whole crossblood hemisphere? What, under trickster irony, if he were to be counter-discovered and civilised by those actually anything but Godless and uncivilised indigenes to whom, often with mad intoxicated religiosity, he imagined himself the bringer of God and civilisation?

Vizenor's stroke is to have his own novel sleuth these versions, and the arising myths which have enclosed Native peoples, through the storyteller Columbus 'heirs' gathered at the Stone Tavern by the headwaters of the Mississippi. Shadowing Columbus, and five centuries on, they themselves will move to 'found' a new mixedblood nation at Point Assinaka in America's northwest. The original Columbus connects to Stone Columbus as descendant, owner and talk-show host of the Minnesota bingo-barge, *Santa María Casino*, 'anchored on the international border near Big Island in the Lake of the Woods' (p. 6). For *The Heirs of Columbus* is about a portrait of Columbus, and Columbianism, as a serial of historical masks each to be 'overturned' (p. 185) through postmodern fabling, or perhaps more aptly, anti-fabling. The outcome is both a subversion of the 'New World' landfall, with its legacy of cultural genetics, savagism, and the supremacist persistence of a white–Native divide, and a postmodern 'authorial' reclamation of America's founding story.

The mixedblood cadre of detective figures who do the actual groundwork are typical Vizenor hyper-reality figures: Felipa Flowers as ex-model who 'steals back' Native artefacts but goes to her death having failed to listen to shamanistic warnings; Chaine Riel Doumet, ex-military intelligence veteran who believes in story over factual truth; and Lappet Tulip Browne who, among other things, aims to 'detect' the language as much as the politics and economics of Manifest Destiny dominance. A recent critic like Elizabeth Blair helpfully lists the kinds of mystery they are set to fathom, a charge-sheet quite as figurative as literal:

> the theft of the stones from the tavern on the mount; the conquistadors' burning of the triple bear codex; the theft of New World gold; Spain's banishment of the Sephardic Jews; Columbus's enslavement of the Indians; his theft of New World names; Henry Rowe Schoolcraft's theft of medicine pouches; their repatriation or theft by the mixedblood shaman, Transom; Felipa Flowers's repatriation of tribal medicine pouches, ceremonial feathers and bones; the theft of the remains of Columbus and Pocahontas.[18]

The overlapping turns, false trails, clues and reversals in this overall detection makes for a busy weave. Nor does Vizenor rest content in contriving a Feydeau-like maze of sleuth and sleuthed. Explicit Columbus scholarship plays into the plotline, along with a scholarly but always wry bibliographic Epilogue ('Columbus arises in tribal stories that heal with humor the world he wounded', p. 185). Leading names in Indian Studies, Louis Owens or Arnold Krupat notably, enter as though fictional characters. A New York courtroom hearing segues into a fantastical indictment of crimes against Native America whose evidence includes cyber-moccasins, holographic bear sex, and sock magic. The story's real-unreal cartography folds, and unfolds, from the Upper Mississippi, to London's Used Book markets, to Pocahontas's burial site in St George's Church in Gravesend, Kent. Reburial ceremonies are described both for the fictive Felipa Flowers and for the only slightly less non-fictive Pocahontas and Columbus. If, truly, a detective novel, *The Heirs of Columbus* doubles as meta-detective story, the one story tactically set up to situate, and monitor, the other.

A final laser show from Stone's casino projects into the night sky images, among others, of Naanabozho as compassionate trickster, Louis Riel as executed *métis* leader, Crazy Horse and Black Elk as shaman-guides, Jesus, and Columbus himself. It serves as metafictive tableau, a text-inside-a-text of healers and villains altogether more elusive, and virtual, than canonical American history has allowed itself to believe. The result not only keeps in view the competition of pasts secreted inside America's present as connectedly European, Native, crossblood and multicultural, but again confirms each to be ever as mythic as actual. In this, *The Heirs of Columbus*, whether best thought postindian, postmodern, or an interaction of both, delivers a timely instalment of Gerald Vizenor's never less than dazzlingly fertile trickster signwriting.

IV

Ana Castillo's *The Mixquiahuala Letters*, at first sight, would seem to join a long-established lineage, Ovid, Choderlos de Laclos, or Samuel Richardson, and on to a body of contemporary fiction to range from Amos Oz's *Kusfah shekhorah/Black Box* (1986) to Alice Walker's *The Color Purple* (1992). But the forty letters which make up her novel take nothing if not their own postmodern turn. In this, she keeps company with a body of Latino/a authorship accorded 'magic' or reflexive status and whose names have long included the likes of Rudolfo Anaya, Ron Arias and Isabella Ríos.

Teresa's aware, and always writerly, mix of diary, verse, travelogue and colloquium, as she recreates the ongoing rite of intimacy with Alicia as designer-artist *comadre*, first of all amounts not to two-way, but one-way, correspondence. If, too, the letters explore two ethnic styles of womanhood, west-coast Chicana ('i, with dark hair and Asian eyes', p. 21) and east-coast white-New York ('you, some WASP chick or JAP from Manhattan's West Side', p. 44 – JAP, here, meaning Jewish American Princess, and as revealed in the recollection of relationships and journeys which cross Americas south and north of the border), it is the writing itself as a drama of inscription which, finally, and quite as equally, takes imaginative command.

That is, as much as any representational account, the different love affairs, the close encounters with place, the ten-year time-span, the mutual and self-enquiry, even Teresa's abortion and then the birth of her son Vittorio or Alicia's feelings on confronting the suicide of her lover Abdel, Castillo uses epistolarity as also a drama of literary composition, or rather, re-composition. From Letter One's 'Here's the plan: On the 15th you arrive in L.A. i'll pick you up at the airport and head for San Fernando . . .' (p. 11) through to Letter Forty's account of the Abdel shooting ('Your eyes are pinned to the rumpled figure on the kitchen floor . . .' (p. 132), the letters flatter to deceive. Teresa, in fact, takes editorial custodianship of the two lives under one voice, reworks the past as though a continuous present, and shows every awareness of the management of memory, locale, and sequence. The different theatres of identity to ensue, thereby, become a *mise-en-scène* of life into word, but at the same time, and equally, of word into life.

The fond dedication written to 'the master of the game' makes no secret of a prime debt to Julio Cortázar's *Rayuela* (1963), or in English, *Hopscotch*. His novel's dismantling of linear narration, offer of alternative sequences, citied inter-mirrorings of Paris and Buenos Aires, and protagonist doubles of Horacio Oliviera and Traveller, made it one of the founding texts of Latin American magic realism. The echo throughout *The Mixquiahuala Letters* is unmistakable. Castillo's own offer as to possible order, 'For the Conformist', 'For the Cynic' and 'For the Quixotic', to be 'read as separate entities' if so wished, give but an opening indication, the quite explicit bid to bind writer and reader into the necessary co-making of her text.

This same dynamic continues throughout. Each letter not so much reports as re-enacts the two women's 'uterine comprehension', 'sisterhood' and 'solidarity' (p. 18), epistolarity as 'life' text in its own right. Mixquiahuala itself, 'pre-Columbian village of obscurity' with its 'Toltec ruins' and 'benevolent god in exile' (p. 19), not unlike Ron Arias's Tamazunchale, becomes both a point of arrival and of departure, a marker of first Americas and yet of subsequent north–south lives such as those of the Teresas and Alicias lived in them.

An affair like Alicia's with Adán, 'Indian' philanderer in Acapulco, or her long-standing relationship with her Harlem boyfriend, Rodney, are put forth as much for their challenge to telling as for their vexatious personal history. 'Our Aztlán period' (p. 38), centred in 1970s San Francisco and with its wall posters of Geronimo ('remember?' asks Teresa), reads as though itself political chic, mock drama-script. The Vera Cruz episode (Letter Twenty-Two), with its haunted house and *brujo* detail, becomes a would-be act of haunting in its own right, telling once again as tale.

The 'Miss Amerika-in-Drag' scene (Letter Twenty-Three) wonderfully recalls a Gay Beauty Competition ('we were two schoolgirls/in comparison to/sizzling dynamite/silicone/hormone city/Swiss-made caricatures of the female genus' p. 76). But, once more, it does so as narration pitched in kind. In aligning 'shemale' identity, its third-sex queens and sashaying, with straight male behaviour as the two women have known it, Castillo makes her own style also an acting-out. The letter moves through camp, butch-bitch parlance, alongside the remembered love-talk, and threats, within heterosexual close encounter, sexuality, or sexualities, as always performative spectacle.

Teresa's description of her own relationship with the drug-shadowed poet Alexis (Letter Twenty-Nine) speaks of rapture, an all-excluding passion, but also of 'our obsession for the written word' (p. 103). It points utterly to the telling of the lives of Alicia and Teresa. Their correspondence offers the one text posing as two, the one textual process made actively to play inside the other. Put still more succinctly, it can be said to confirm Castillo's postmodern scripting in *The Mixquiahuala Letters*.

V

This fiction is set in the 1960s, a time when some events appeared to occur months or even years anachronistically.

Maxine Hong Kingston's 'Author's Note' leaves little doubt of the likely narrative fare to follow in *Tripmaster Monkey: His Fake Book*. For her reeling, mythy, immensely energetic China-America novel, unique as it is, works in shared vein with the fictions of Reed, Vizenor and Castillo. Certainly Wittman Ah Sing, fifth-generation American Chinaman and self-nominated 'Chinese beatnik', plays the perfect split-screen role, an author himself full of voice yet also the turning point for the novel's own directorial voice.

Reflexively to a fault, Kingston sets him to answer the question 'Do we have a culture that's not the knick-knacks we sell to the bok gwai?' (p. 184) – bok gwai being ghosts, a synonym for collective white America. His mind dwells on an art-drama to embrace China as mainland culture in its three-kingdom, Fa-Mulan, monkey and 'kingdoms rise and fall' myths and, in the same sweep, the allure of America as Gum Sahn in all its history of 1882 and other Exclusion legislation, Angel Island, each sojourner-bachelor history, Jade Snow Wong, Pearl Buck and Anna May Wong, and, still more immediately, San Francisco's Chinatown as American *tableau vivant*. The novel textually embodies ('Everyone wants to get into the act', witnesses Wittman, p. 276), even as it reports, the quest.

'Fake Book', Kingston has several times explained, refers to a musical or theatre prompt-book as a baseline for improvisation. The novel's authorial voices, accordingly, play off, and compound, the other, typically in each chapter ending:

> Our Wittman is going to work on his play for the rest of the night. If you want to see whether he will get that play up, and how a poor monkey makes a living so he can afford to spend the weekday afternoon drinking coffee and hanging out, go on to the next chapter. (p. 35)

'Tripmaster', likewise, and with its footfall of hallucinogenic LSD, points to yet further doublings. If aspirant 'Chinese' writer-dramatist, with a Berkeley degree in English, Wittman at the same time affects 'American' Bay Area peacenik and Beat. If the committed poet with a trunk full of verse, he also sees his life, and at times suicidal impulses, reflected to a detail in Rilke's anatomy of alienation as given in *The Notebooks of Malte Laurids Brigge*. Either way, and as he avers at the outset, 'No ching-chong Chinaman for me' (p. 23).

One line takes him back into China folklore, Cantonese opera, Confucian thought, Hong Kong movies and, above all, Sun Wu Kong as Monkey ('I am really: the present-day USA incarnation of King of the Monkeys', p. 33). The other speaks to an America of the 1960s, love-ins, hippiedom, pot, Berkeley on the one hand, Vietnam, corporate wealth, the military-industrial complex and nuclear weaponry on the other. He authors, and re-authors, himself, and, anything but unaware of the irony, most of all as would-be pacifist dramatist, or rather re-dramatist, of 'the mightiest war epic of all times' (p. 340), *The War of the Three Kingdoms*. Chinese theatre, in his dramaturgic shaping, is to be transformed into American theatre, Chinese life into American life. But none of it will be at the price of orientalist sell-out or spectacle. Wittman shows his understanding of so wrong a turn in the frequent allusions to life in California, and in both Chinese and non-Chinese America, as seemingly run by 'Central Casting' (pp. 56, 75).

Naming, at the outset, gives positioning terms of reference. Wittman Ah Sing playfully fuses Ah Sin, the stereotypic title-hero of the John Chinaman drama written by Mark Twain and Bret Harte in 1877, the Whitman of 'I Sing America' and, evidently, the word 'wit' itself. It makes quite the aptest of monograms for the Frank Chin-like writer whose ambition is to write America's ultimate China play only to have the imagining of that play mirrored in, and in large measure made over as, *Tripmaster Monkey*. That play Wittman himself intends as a rebuff to China stereotype running from Twain/Harte's *Ah Sin*, and based on Harte's poem 'The Heathen Chinee' (1870), through to a confectionary, and massively popular, Chinatown musical like *The Flowerdrum Song*. How, given these lights, and in theatrical guise, to give the best 'true' theatrical reflection of America's China?

Kingston has Wittman's life wonderfully reel and turn. As a toy salesman, he authors his own firing by having monkeys copulate with Mattel barbie dolls. He inveighs against eye operations which 'un-Asian' Chinese and other Asians by having the lid's 'epicanthic' fold surgically removed. His quips ('Every heroin addict I know is on health foods', p. 92) and euphoric speechifyings against war, stereotype, consumerism, wage slavery, and even modish Asian hair ('their hair was so shiny that you could see why they call the crown of the head the crown. Buddhaheads', p. 59), carry their own missionary zeal. Pratfalls, however, at the same time trip him even as he aspires to rectitude.

Judy Louis, fellow store employee, bores him on the subject of eyes to the point where he fakes being Japanese ('We have the eyes that won the West', runs one of his counters, p. 314). His affair with the China-chic aspirant actress, Nanci Lee, flounders on her obtuseness about his poetry. So acute becomes his sense of self-confinement that he suffers agoraphobia on San Francisco's Market Street. His love-hate of his best friend, Lance Kamiyama, 'successful' Japanese American and new husband, leads to literal physical sparring and combat. His odd-funny family life might almost be a terrace of mistakes, whether his parents Ruby Long Legs (one-time opera star) and Zeppelin Ah Sing, or his blonde wife Taña de Weeze ('Please be the girl I'm in love with', p. 151, he implores her, Wittman the American as much as the Chinaman), or his abandoned but found-again gambler grandmother Po Po. Yet as the liberationist Great Play is finally brought into being, with both the 'cast' of his own family, friends, and to include a white 'Yale Younger Poet' and Employment-office Chicano, and with a melee of Chinatown acrobats, jugglers, musicians, dragon and monkey actors and 'a thousand firecrackers' (p. 301), not to say a huge participant audience, life and theatre once more engagingly refract and join.

Monkey finds his avatar voice in Wittman ('I'm a realist . . . It's the business of a playwright to bring thoughts into reality', p. 240). Wittman finds his own in the novel's overall voice. The novel's trickster telling calls up not only ancient or even modern story but, demonstrably, and in all its performative feints, also the postmodern. The point is given a perfect gloss at the novel's conclusion when, quite expressly, the novel's different companion voices are made to meet:

> Of course, Wittman Ah Sing didn't really burn down the Association house and theater. It was an illusion of fire. Good monkey. He kept control of the explosives, and of his arson's delight in flames. He wasn't crazy; he was a monkey. (p. 305)

Tripmaster Monkey has fairly won plaudits on a number of fronts, among them the intimate China allusion, the observational energy, the reservoirs of humour and satire. But wholly as much to the fore has to be the sustained finesse with which Kingston subjects Wittman's story, Chinese and Chinese American, and with himself as at once actor and actor-manager, to the regime of her own metafictive storytelling.

Theresa Hak Kyung Cha's *DICTEE* increasingly wins canonical status, albeit conferred as though fugitively, almost *in absentia*.[19] The organisational gappings, each conscious show of fracture as word, syntax or visual image, and the interlingualism of English with French, Latin, Korean, Japanese and Chinese, doubtless has been a bar to wider readership. But as Walter K. Lew, Cha's fellow Korean American writer, suggests in his tributary collage *Excerpts from ΔIKTH/DIKTE for DICTEE* (1992):

> Whatever one does, one always rebuilds the monument in his own way. But it is already something gained to have used only the original stones. (p. 11)

Approaches, inevitably, differ. *DICTEE* is to be thought colonial, yet also postcolonial. If it tells several tiers of Korean history – Japanese occupation, divided status, military governance – it finds a coeval prism in the Asiaphobia visited upon Korean American history. If feminist self-history told in the voice of the *diseuse*, the woman speaker, it carries also the history of Hyung Soon Huo, Cha's Manchuria-raised mother, and Yu Guan Soon as early mother-of-the-nation nationalist martyr. Language, and the power behind it, is likened to a sexual filling of the female body ('She allows others. In place of her. Admits others to make full. Makes swarm. All barren cavities to make swollen', p. 3). Yet, as the opening citation from Sappho makes clear ('May I write words more naked than flesh . . .'), this will be a voicing, an 'uttering' (p. 4), in fact to contest all forms of *diktat*, whether imperialist, national, political or male-sexual.

In exploring these 'mother' languages as nominative power, *DICTEE* becomes a subversive language performance in its own right, even a dramatised tractatus of sorts. Components usually meant to give the impression of fixed configuration work at the same time to challenge, and countermand, the hegemony's signifiers be they scriptural or visual. The use of *diseuse* acts as counter-voice to disease, disuse (p. 133), a resistance to unsought invasion of one's own word or body by others. No one language, in fact, and as Cha's fashioning of her text makes clear, suffices to dictate the actual identity of her narrator or the competing histories and geographies which have gone into its formation.

The novel, of necessity, offers an 'open' postmodern text, one which almost explicitly forbids the fixed reading. The French dictation and exercises, and prayers, border on pastiche, rituals exposed to their own unritualising. Portraiture, of Cha's mother among others, carries the accusation of her forced birth and upbringing in China as a teacher. The text, for all that it uses the nine categories of Greek rhetoric (History to Sacred Poetry), can be seen to work uncategorically, collateral alignment more than ranking.

Each component sequence and image acts to create an interplay: the opening Korean wall graffiti for 'home/nation', the Chinese hierarchical calligraphy for Father and Mother and for Man and Woman, the physiological chart for how human phonetics are actually made, and the map of Korea divided at the DMZ. The interstitial narrative likewise runs in parallels and connecting eddies: handwritten letters, an address to her mother in Manchuria ('you speak the tongue the mandatory language like the others . . . The tongue that is forbidden is your mother tongue', p. 45), a Chinese fortune-telling chart and, throughout, fragments of diary and memory.

In all of these constituent threads, Cha's un-dictation of 'dictated' legacy may not make for easiest access. This is a text more than usually still in process of being negotiated for its collagism, its very meaning and impact. But, justly enough, it has come to be thought a rare coup, a landmark of postmodernity in Asian American literary fiction.

VI

Postmodernism, undoubtedly, has been a vexing, even a fighting, term in current literary-cultural production, not least in having been drawn eclectically from language-philosophy, the visual arts, material culture and, to re-invoke Lyotard, cultural critique. But it has posed quite especial challenges in connection with US multicultural texts. For has not its provenance usually been assigned elsewhere, if not exactly to a mainstream American literary vanguard, then something akin? In the fictions of Reed, Vizenor, Castillo, Kingston and Cha, however, one can look to a yet different kind of postmodern literary custodianship, that of multicultural – ethnic – imagining, and whatever opinion otherwise, that of no one's minority.

NOTES

1. Jean-François Lyotard (1983), *The Postmodern Condition: A Report on Knowledge*, Minneapolis, MN: University of Minnesota Press, pp. xxiv, 37. Translated by Geoff Bennington and Brian Massumi. Originally published as *La Condition postmoderne: rapport sur le savoir* (1979), Paris: Les Editions de Minuit.
2. Milan Kundera (1986), *The Art of the Novel*, translated by Linda Asher. New York: Harper and Row, p. 159.
3. bell hooks (1990), 'Postmodern Blackness', *Postmodern Culture*, 1:2, 10.
4. A most useful summary of the literary contours of postmodernism is to be found in Hans Bertens, 'The Return of the Vanished Narrative: Cultural Identity and Postmodern Fiction', in Jaap Lintvelt, Richard Saint-Gelais, Will Verhoeven and Catharine Raffi-Béroud (eds) (1998), *Roman contemporain et identité culturelle en Amérique du Nord/ Contemporary Fiction and Cultural Identity in North America*, Québec: Editions Nota Bene, pp. 245–59.
5. A classic case is that of Richard Wright. I have argued the limits of holding his fiction to this account in A. Robert Lee (1987), 'Richard Wright's Inside Narratives', in Richard Gray (ed.), *American Fiction: New Readings*, London: Vision Press, pp. 200–21.
6. A seminal article, in this respect, is to be found in Anthony Kwame Appiah (1991), 'Is the Post- in Postmodernism the Post- in Postcolonial?' *Critical Inquiry*, 17:2 (Winter), 336–55. Homi Bhabha (1994) links the issue to what he calls 'contramodernity', the postmodern made subject to a postcolonial regimen of 'in-betweenness' and necessary cultural hybridity. See his 'The Postcolonial and the Postmodern: The Question of Agency', in *The Location of Culture*, London: Routledge, pp. 171–97.
7. The original phrase is to be met with in Randolph S. Bourne (1916), 'Trans-National America', *Atlantic Monthly*, 97 (July), reprinted in Randolph S. Bourne (1964), *War and the Intellectuals: Collected Essays, 1915–1919*, New York: Harper & Row.
8. Other accounts of the reception of black modernism and the postmodern are to be found in Charles Johnson (1987), *Being and Race: Black Writing since 1970*, Bloomington and Indianapolis, IN: Indiana University Press, and Madelyn Jablon (1997), *Black Metafiction: Self-Consciousness in African American Literature*, Iowa City, IA: University of Iowa Press.
9. The Silko/Erdrich exchange began with Silko's review of *The Beet Queen*, 'Here's an Odd Artifact for the Fairy-tale Shelf', *Impact Magazine Review of Books, Albuquerque Journal*, 7 October 1986, reprinted in *Studies in Indian American Literature*, 10 (1986), 177–84. For an excellent account of the implications, see Susan Pérez Castillo (1991), 'Postmodernism, Native American Literature and the Real: The Silko–Erdrich Controversy', *The Massachusetts Review*, 32:2 (Summer), 285–94. Elizabeth Cook-Lynn's essay, 'American Indian Intellectualism and the New Indian Story', appears in *American Indian Quarterly*, 20:1 (Winter 1996), 37–76. The phrase 'phantom artifact' appears in Louis Owens (1998), 'Beads and Buckskin: Reading Authenticity in Native American Literature', in *Mixedblood Messages: Literature, Film, Family Place*: Norman, OK: University of Oklahoma Press, p. 17. 'Bankable simulation' appears in Gerald Vizenor (1994), *Manifest Manners: Postindian Warriors of Survivance*, p. 10.
10. The best account of the 'border' ethos is to be found in José David Saldívar (1997), *Border Matters: Remapping American Cultural Studies*, Berkeley, CA: University of California Press. Reference to *This Bridge Called My Back: Writings by Radical Women of Color*, as to other work by Moraga and Anzaldúa, is given in the primary and secondary bibliographies.
11. See the secondary bibliography for the Epifanio San Juan and David Mura references.
12. Charles Johnson (1982), in *Oxherding Tale*, Bloomington, IN: Indiana University Press, speaks to one kind of implication: 'The Negro . . . is the finest student of the White World, the one pupil in the class who watches himself watching others', p. 128.

13. Ishmael Reed (ed.) (1971), *19 Necromancers from Now*, New York: Doubleday, introduction, p. xx.
14. The phrase 'synthetic master-text' is used by Patrick McGee (1997) in *Ishmael Reed and the Ends of Race*, Basingstoke: Macmillan, p. 113.
15. Neal Bowers and Charles Silet (1981), 'An Interview with Gerald Vizenor', MELUS, 8:1, 41–9.
16. Gerald Vizenor (1995), 'Visions, Scares, and Stories', in *Contemporary Authors Autobiography Series*, vol. 22, Detroit, MI: Gale Research Company, p. 3.
17. A greatly influential essay in this regard is William Bevis (1987), 'Native American Novels: Homing in', in Brian Swann and Arnold Krupat (eds), *Recovering the Word*, Berkeley, CA: University of California Press, pp. 580–620.
18. Elizabeth Blair, 'Whodunwhat? The Crime's the Mystery in Gerald Vizenor's *The Heirs of Columbus*', in A. Robert Lee (ed.) (2000), *Loosening the Seams: Interpretations of Gerald Vizenor*, Bowling Green, OH: Bowling Green State University Popular Press, pp. 155–65.
19. In 'Unfaithful to the Original: The Subject of *Dictée*', pp. 35–69, in Elaine H. Kim and Norma Alarcón (eds) (1994), *Writing Self/Writing Nation: A Collection of Essays on DICTEE by Theresa Hak Kyung Cha*, Berkeley, CA: Third Woman Press, Lisa Lowe helpfully summarises as follows: 'An Asian American text, a post-colonial text, and a woman's text, it evokes alternately a girlhood education in French Catholicism, a brief history of Korean nationalism during the Japanese colonial occupation, as well as episodes from the narrator's displaced adulthood as a Korean American immigrant and her return to military-ruled Korea' (pp. 35–6).

CHAPTER TEN

Epilogue

Fictions of Whiteness

Is there a 'black' race, or a Swedish race? There is not, any more than that there is a 'white' race, a 'yellow' race, or a 'red' race. (Ashley Montague)[1]

You can't ask who is 'white' without asking, by association, who is 'American' . . . To principally define yourself as 'white' as the majority of Americans have throughout US history, said nothing about your view of God, man's place on Earth, magic, your ancestors or your history. It has no cultural significance, and is ethnically meaningless.

Of course, there are bona-fide cultures represented in America, the members of which call themselves 'white', Germans, Jews, Irish, Greeks, some Latinos, Russians, Italians, etc. [These] are all 'white Americans'. Many of the cultures in these groups have little in common. These cultures can share little or nothing, yet all their people are identified as 'white'. Why? What is the significance of this ridiculously broad, yet empty term? (Leone Gaiter)[2]

Maybe I'm uncomfortable extolling white culture especially if it replaces other folks's culture, like prayer in the schools and boarding schools for Indian children and English only and the Ku Klux Klan. It seems to me that too much of white culture is built on stamping out culture that isn't white, or culture that isn't white enough, or even culture that doesn't happen to be the correct shade of white. (Bonnie Kae Grover)[3]

I

US ethnicity, and the literary fictions it has engendered, of necessity involves a reckoning with America's pervasive, however often contradictory, codes of whiteness. For the implicit assumption from Atlantic settlement onwards has been that whiteness bears the very DNA of American nationhood, the identifying etiquette of an Americanism derived from, and indeed essentially the remaking of, Europe. But, with the unfolding of the 1960s, a counter-recognition emerges. America is to be seen not only as somehow newly ethnic but in fact, and endemically, as having been ethnic from its very foundation. To the extent that they have long given a frame, a touchstone, the fictions of whiteness within, and about, the making of America invite every consideration.

By whiteness, evidently, a great deal more than mere skin pigmentation comes into play, be it attributed to the Puritans, a pantheon of Revolutionary names, holders of the Presidency, US soldiery, the Daughters of the American Revolution or, eventually, Hollywood's photogenic cowboys and blondes. The true loading lies in the construction of cultural or ideological whiteness, a belief, tacit or otherwise, that America embodies, indeed simply *is*, a white polity and civilisation. The outward show, the individual white face, thereby, gives off a raciality assumed by destiny, 'manifest' or otherwise, to preside. It is that which has come into question, America called upon better, or more self-comprehendingly, to confront itself as a multiculture.

Custom, for the most part, has rested comfortably upon watchwords like melting pot or mixing bowl, however selectively, not to say self-servingly, keyed to the settlement of the country by a white European gallery of, pre-eminently, English, Scots, Scots Irish and Irish, together with Germans, Dutch, Scandinavians, Italians, Polish, Hungarians, and even, despite anti-semitism, different Jewish tiers. Small matter, seemingly, that, at different times, not a few of these, from eastern Europe in the 1920s notably, themselves were made subject to xenophobic quotas.

In *Making Americans: Immigration, Race, and the Origins of Diverse Democracy* (2000), Desmond King is far from the only historian to consider the melting pot 'soaked in racial hierarchy and eugenic arguments' and founded on 'an Anglo-Saxon conception of U.S. identity'. On this measure non-whites, Natives, African Americans, Hispanics, Asians, those of mixed origins, all, in one manner or degree, and at different times, have been assigned outsider or inferiority status. Allowing for intermarriage and other cross-racial relationship, or each political alliance from slavery's Underground Railroad to different civil rights groups, King goes on to observe that to challenge the melting pot means 'challenging the idea, as an empirical fact or as a normative theory, that all these cultures can "melt" into anything other than an Anglo white person'.[4] In an *American Scholar* symposium in 1955, Ralph Ellison offered his own succinct version: 'For a long time if you asked someone what an American was, he would usually describe an Anglo-Saxon of New England background – really one of many types'.[5]

As America became the successor world power to Europe, industrial barons like J. P. Morgan in banking, John D. Rockefeller in oil, Henry Ford in automobiles and William Randolph Hearst in the press, were among the foremost in promoting ideologies of *white* capitalism. Ford, notoriously, drew from Nazi-inspired material in his 1930s letters to Model T and other factory employees in Highland Park, Michigan. His melting-pot films, in which men and women of different ethnicities march into a Wellsian rebirth machine to reappear as white workers, and his virulent anti-semitism in the name of protestant Christianity as expressed in the weekly *Dearborn Independent*, have become classic case-studies of aryan propaganda. Hearst newspapers, likewise, wholly dominant in the interwar period, downplayed the Mexican Revolution on grounds of its worker-campesino, even socialist, implications for the USA and gave support to Hitler through to the late 1930s; not a little startlingly, Germany's *Führer*-to-be, like Mussolini, actually contributed copy.[6]

Woodrow Wilson, born a southerner in Virginia, showed D. W. Griffith's virtuoso but black-phobic *The Birth of a Nation* (1915) to White House staffers as a racial cautionary tale (it was, and is, but not in the sense Wilson intended). America's Second World War military forces, pledged to the defeat of fascism, did not desegregate until 1948 and then only by Truman's Executive Order. Corporation top management in finance, insurance and real estate, sometimes given the acronym FIRE, has almost effortlessly been white whatever the colour mix of its workforce. Ivy League universities, until the 1960s, drew a well-known line against general access by Jews (Brandeis University, founded in 1948, was in part a reaction), along with Blacks and other minorities. White suburbs have notoriously resorted to red-lining or zoning as a policy of refusing loans to ethnic undesirables. In each of these, white America has shown its resolve to remain just that, white.

II

New England. New France. New Spain. Cities like New York or New Orleans. The paradigm, indelibly, links 'new' to one or another redrawn Euro-Atlantic site, the dream – the fiction – of European renewal. Even the ports of entry up and down the Atlantic seaboard could seem Europe's own uniquely destined thresholds into America. Boston grew from colonial beginnings into a hub of European Atlantic trade and migration. Philadelphia and Charleston, likewise, served as throughways for Europe's goods (slaves not least) and would-be settlers. New York's Ellis Island, in the subsequent years of 1892 to 1943, would process arriving Europeans literally in the millions. If, indeed, America was to be a crucible, a New World process of human melt or mix, there could be no mistaking the colour of those predestined, seemingly, for access to political and cultural power.

Tensions in Europe's making-over of America are hardly to be denied. Was New England to become puritan or secular? How to balance Virginia southern gentry with a poor-white lower order? Were north and south, their two systems of economy, their very notions of society, and slaveholding as against abolition, inevitably bound for the fatal division of civil war? What was to be the right balance of federal and state power? Yet about one issue there was little contestation. America, in people as in governance, would be pre-eminently a *white* world, an Anglo and cognately European dispensation of language, institutions, culture and style.

The 1960s, to repeat an emphasis given several times, called time on this version of things. America found itself invited, even compelled, to face the fuller, as against the token, sight and sound of its ethnic plurality. Civil rights and each long hot summer in the cities created one focus. The Vietnam War (1961–75), with its race-loaded incursions against an Asian enemy, created another. Thereafter, and through to the Clinton and Bush Jr presidencies, terms like 'multicultural' and 'ethnic' would take on renewed loading across a span of politics, the academic syllabus, labour practice and the media. Whether African, Native, Latino/a or Asian and Pacific island in origin, or of mixed white and other lineage, or drawn from each further current of Latin American and Third World immigration, the changing demographics were unmistakable, an America ever less likely to be monochrome white.

Few had anticipated this change better than James Baldwin in 'Stranger in the Village' (1953), one of his several landmark diaries of black American exile. Having retreated from Paris after a nervous breakdown to the Swiss home village of his unnamed lover, Lucien Happersberger, he imagines himself in this snow-clad, whitest alpine outpost as the very *figura* of a larger African and African American diaspora. For even as the children, innocently or otherwise, call out 'Neger!' in *Schweizerdeutsch*, he repudiates any notion that his blackness any longer makes him a 'stranger' within the white governing western order. With an eye to all past colonialism, European and American, and arising from it slavery and the black Atlantic, he claims tenure for himself and all human blackness at the very centre of things, neither separate nor apart, nor, in recent parlance, *othered*. His closing sentence memorably offers a blend of diagnosis and prophecy: 'This world is white no longer, and it never will be white again'.[7]

Afro-America, be it under the clergy-centred leadership of Martin Luther King or a whole black-radical cadre for which Malcolm X and Stokely Carmichael were mainstays, gave challenge both to the south's Jim Crow and the north's ghettos. The Civil Rights Act of 1964 and Voting Rights Act of 1965 were but two gestures towards national redress. Native America re-entered the frame both through AIM and in legal suits over land rights, schooling, the return of museum bones and artefacts, and language politics, along with continuance of its long-time sparrings with the BIA and for which the memorial protest surrounding Wounded Knee, South Dakota, in 1973, became a touchstone.

Latino/a America arose as at no time before both from within, and beyond, the *barrio*. Whether César Chávez and the UFW in California and Chicano movements across the southwest, or the activism in Spanish Harlem and island Puerto Rico, or, albeit of a different political stripe, the exile anti-Castroism of 'Cuban' Florida, America witnessed a new politics of *latinidad*. Asian America, from Hawai'i to California to New York, and with histories rooted in the Pacific, likewise laid claim to fuller recognition, the China, Japan, Korea, Philippines, and Vietnam, along with India, Pakistan and other South Asia, not only within America's past and present, but ever more, its future. Other related American ethnicities have increasingly been heard, not least in symptomatic collections like *Ho'omanoa: An Anthology of Contemporary Hawai'ian Literature* (1989), *Hmong Means Free: Life in Laos and America* (1994), *The Butterfly's Way: Voices from the Haitian Dyaspora in the United States* (2001), or, from a tradition, more accurately traditions, notably long under-attended, *Post Gibran: Anthology of New Arab American Writing* (1999).[8]

Here, for many, is, and long has been, an America whose lineages from Africa, Native culture, *Hispanidad*, Asia and the Pacific, and all arising *mestizaje*, not only belong endemically within the national identity but at once interiorise and complicate it in almost every respect of colour, gender, community and history. Yet the overriding version of America as WASP, buttressed by each satellite style of whiteness, has long

been accorded privilege. The 1960s, however, invested ethnicity with a new spirited-
ness, the call to recognition of cultural width and depth well beyond some passing term
for choice of restaurant, or local pottery, or a style of dance or dress. In the same sweep,
white itself, and its best-known permutation as Anglo, came under yet greater
interrogation. Does cultural whiteness accommodate all Euro-Americans, not to
say Latinos/as of lighter hue, or those of mixed genealogy?

Conservative opinion has indeed been quick to speak of balkanisation, ethnic
grievance, ghettoing, pc tyranny, the loss of a one nation or canonical America.[9]
The left, neo-Marxist or not, has indeed been heard to speak of a boutique ethos,
mere pluralist good feeling which avoids issues of capital, hegemony, consumerism,
and labour and migrancy exploitation.[10] For those who persist, however, multiculturalism faces, and disarms, both kinds of objection, the prospect, not to say
relish, of an America of reordered priorities. For under its construing since the 1960s,
as at no time before, it gives the promise of helping usher in what, in 1916, Randolph
S. Bourne brilliantly, and quite prophetically, hypothesised would be Trans-
National America.[11]

Accounts like Ronald T. Takaki's A Different Mirror: A History of Multicultural
America (1993) have helped explain this turn of events. Beyond an evident flair in
chronicling the plethora of American ethnicities, Takaki's work, as that of others,
signals changed rules of engagement. Majority and minority as a familiar binary has
come under serious interrogation, along with notions of mainstream, colour (and
with it the colour-coding of migrancy), and the pre-emptive consensus that the
nation remains in pretty well all essential aspects 'white'.[12] It was in a spirit of this
kind, and almost as if taken unawares, that a Time review of Amy Tan's The Joy Luck
Club drew attention to how literary work was contributing to the change: 'Growing
up ethnic is surely the liveliest theme to appear in the American novel since the
closing of the frontier . . .'[13] It fell to the 1960s, and amid all the era's other energies
of change, to call for an end to the marginalisation of these ethnicities and of the
diverse literary voices arising from them. Each, to put things at their minimum, was
to exert an ancestry of at least co-existence with the WASP and related genealogies
canonically taken for the mainstream.[14]

This is still not to underplay how American nationhood, almost by rote, has been
associated with the lineage begun from the Mayflower's landing at Plymouth Rock in
1620, with the Massachusetts Bay Colony to follow, and from the Jamestown
settlement of Virginia under Christopher Newport in 1607.[15] Whatever else encodes
the founding of the United States, whether New England's Puritan congregations, or
the south's plantations, or independence in 1776 and the constitution, there can,
once again, be little doubt of the prerequisite all were to bequeath: the fiction of
America, and with it Americanism, as whiteness.

III

Northwards, New England was to be the main originating centre of this whiteness.
It has usually been thought to have made its bow in terms of millennial bible

Puritanism, a theocracy of minister, magistrate and congregation. But Anglo-American Puritanism also meant a standard of colour, the Atlantic landfall as white New Jerusalem, Zion or Canaan. Certainly the Pilgrim Fathers, whether John Winthrop (1588–1649) as Massachusetts Bay Company governor and author of *A Model of Christian Charity* (1630), or Increase Mather (1639–1723) and son Cotton Mather (1663–1728) as dynastic Puritan zealots and administrators, or William Bradford (1590–1657) as New England worthy and the historian of *Of Plimmoth Plantation* (1630), could not give a more white-patriarchal, visage to power.

Colonial Massachusetts, and, emerging from it, Connecticut, Rhode Island, Maine, Vermont and New Hampshire, serve as Old England made New. Theirs would be the mission of Protestant Christian belief as white governance over opposition thought of as Red Indian savagism, black witchcraft (or Vodoun) of the kind for which Tituba, Carib-Barbadian slavewoman, underwent trial in Salem in 1692, Judaism as Kabbalah and deicide, and Catholicism as 'scarlet' anti-Christ papistry. Education from grade school to Harvard (founded 1636) and Yale (founded 1701), if adapted to local conditions, still looked to models across the Atlantic from grammar school to Oxford and Cambridge. Each New England township, church, farm, or meeting house, along with city placenames like Boston or Plymouth, however more obliquely with time, thread a remembered England into America.

Similarly, many of New England's calls to arms perpetuate, even as they adapt, Anglocentric origins. Puritan theocracy, if centred in the Atlantic seaboard, looks to the English Reformation and a litany of the King James Bible, Cromwell and Bunyan. The transcendentalism of the 1840s, whatever Emerson's 'spiritual laws' and 'optative' mood, has intimate roots in English Platonism and sermonry. A Connecticut reformer like Josiah Holbrook in 1826 begins America's Lyceum Movement from a pedigree English to a fault. Independence may have meant political severance from Britain but hardly from its white-cultural footfalls. Even as history seemed to move on from New England, it sought to export its cultural style and values into the then frontier, notably through midwest colleges like Antioch, Kenyon, Grinnell or Wooster.

No arena more reflects New England's white voice than abolition. As slavery rises to shadow, and accuse, the New Republic, the answering chord is to be heard in a William Lloyd Garrison, Wendell Phillips or Harriet Beecher Stowe. But if each bears their individual stamp, a fiercely Yankee particularity, they also reflect shared WASP roots and manner. Both Garrison and Phillips were often reluctant to let ex-slaves actually speak at rallies, racist paternalism as it has been called. Stowe, for all her anti-slavery, feared, and condemned, miscegenation. Suffrage, notably in the persons of Susan B. Anthony and Elizabeth Cady Stanton, extends matters into New York and beyond. They, too, though exemplars in the struggle to dismantle male power over women's lives, remained always oddly uninviting of women of colour into the cause and, thereby, into their own privileges of whiteness.

Whether, thus, a Europe to which America's writers, Irving to James, Hawthorne to Wharton, would defer as the very repository of canonicity in culture and thought, or an America freed to 'write its own books' as Emerson said in 'The American Scholar' (1837), the same assumption of ascendancy persisted. With westward expansion, and the changing demography brought on by new immigration, it frequently became nostalgia, defensive Anglo-Saxonism. But its sway cannot be doubted, white, custodial, a cultural seam, a once-mainstream, long thought synonymous with America itself.

Southwards, Virginia, and around it Maryland, the Carolinas, Mississippi, Georgia, Alabama and Louisiana, parlay their respective versions of cultural whiteness into American pastoral. Virginia's own coining, for Elizabeth I as Virgin Queen, calls up unsullied monarchy. The myth becomes cavalierism, a benign white agrarian hierarchy of Jeffersonian planters and yeomen. With the defeat of the Confederacy, and postbellum economic decline and widespread rural poverty, Dixie as Arcadia, paradoxically, takes even greater hold. 'The War', not least through the military leadership of Robert E. Lee, Stonewall Jackson, Jefferson Davis, or the guerilla-spy Colonel John Singleton Mosby, renders the whole into lost but always gloriously white heroic cause.

One apotheosis emerges in *Gone with the Wind*, Margaret Mitchell's 1936 bestseller with Scarlett O'Hara and Rhett Butler as love-crossed belle and beau, Tara as family plantation in cotton Georgia, and with a climax in General William Tecumseh Sherman's vengeful burning of Atlanta. In David O. Selznick's Hollywood version of 1939, starring Clark Gable and Vivien Leigh, the south veers even more into a confection of magnolia, costume, errantry and (Hattie McDaniel's role as the slave Mammy notwithstanding) one of America's greatest formula white romances.

Selective memory, in this version of the south, plays its part, notably over issues of class formation and conflict, colour and gender. Poor whites, white trash, somehow fall conveniently out of view. A slave population, whether of Charleston dockside pen, New Orleans auction block, Georgia cotton or Maryland tobacco labour, transforms into a regimen of acquiescent house or field workers, the purported uncles and mammies of the quarters. Virginia itself, slave-shadowed, and never without its own rural white poor, is elevated into the very ideality of Dixie, Mother of the South or Old Dominion, a timeless world of gentry, manners, derring-do and Palladian architecture.

Dissent did occur. Mark Twain, for one, would have none of it. Raised Samuel Clemens in border-state Hannibal, Missouri, before taking his pseudonym from Mississippi river piloting, he recurrently gave Dixie feudalism a drubbing as sham chivalry. In a celebrated jibe, he once blamed the ruination of the south, as he saw it, on Sir Walter Scott, history tricked out, and hopelessly romanticised, as Highland or Celtic twilight. This same bogus white-gentry he has underwrite the murderous feud between the Shepherdsons and Grangerfords in *Huckleberry Finn* (1884) and the clash of court hierarchy and people in *A Connecticut Yankee at the Court of King Arthur* (1889).

Nevertheless Dixie whiteness, at all levels, managed to endure, and often enough, flourish. Throughout the upper, lower and much of the border south, its best-known rallying cry became Anglo-Saxonism, a writ extended across class lines of landowner, township middle class, and hill and back-country sharecropper. So self-confirming a raciality, of necessity, required an equally racialised counter-face or, more accurately, faces. These have long included black southerners, tribes like Mississippi's Chickasaw and Choctaw or Florida's Creeks and Seminoles, Mexicans and Chicanos (foreign both by their language and Catholicism as well as brownness), Jews and Asians.

The myth of white southern buccaneer finds early embodiment in Captain John Smith. His incarnations are several, whether the prisoner of Powhatan as leader of Virginia's Powhatan confederation, or the supposed object of an interracial love and rescue by Pocahontas, or the author of *The General History of Virginia, New England and the Summer Isles* (1624). Each bequeaths the myth of white hetero-masculinity subsequently to come under challenge from a number of latter-day ethnic, feminist and gay quarters as that of the Dead White Male (DWM) – power conferred by dint of colour and gender. Does not Smith's very name, one of the most ancestral and frequent in English, itself carry more than a visceral link to whiteness?

A connected latter-day controversy arises in the claims by Thomas Jefferson's black descendants to be constituted family through his thirty-year liaison with Sally Hemings, and as given written witness to by Madison, their third son from within a likely progeny of six. This mixed line of descent has largely been edited out of the Monticello story through to the point where black claimants have been excluded from the Jefferson family burial plot. As slavemaster, Jefferson himself knew as well as any the cross-racial genetics of the south. If, in his retirement, he assumed elder statesman pose, a maker of America's independence, he also still refused to free his slaves, kept his silence in the face of popular press slurs of a slave mistress (Monticellian Venus and Black Sal were among attributed names) and offspring, and even tried to work out the generational duration whereby black might become white. Broodingly, he also foresaw race, in which by his own acts of both white and slave fathering he was so personally implicated, as a likely source of American civil war between north and south. Afro-America's own literary fictions, from Frances Ellen Watkins Harper's *Iola Leroy* (1892), written in Woman's Era America, to Barbara Chase-Riboud's *Sally Hemings* (1979), written a century later within the current of Alice Walker's womanism, have had good reason to ponder the Jefferson–Hemings liaison and its multiculturalist challenge to white-national Founding Father iconography.[16]

The Winning of the West contributes its own conquering whiteness of prairie wagons, Indian fighting, homesteading, cavalry, cattle drive and 1850s Gold Rush. This racialised triumphalism pervades the west's early pop culture: the Cody and P. T. Barnum circuses; figures like Kit Carson (1809–68), scout and Indian-killer, and a man who himself could not read transposed from actual to cartoon frontier hero; and a film tradition from D. W. Griffith and the silent era to the Hollywood of Indian-vanquishing US soldiery. Women embody frontier whiteness in a range of ways: wife-mother, schoolma'am, prostitute, preacher's wife, and even figures of gun-culture as in the Ohio-born Annie Oakley (Phoebe Ann Moser) and Deadwood's Calamity Jane (Martha Jane Burke), both to take on whitest screen-fictional lives by a siren Barbara Stanwyck in *Annie Oakley* (1935) and a tomboy Doris Day in *Calamity Jane* (1953).[17]

This same white version of the frontier Ishmael Reed deflates in his Hoodoo comic western, *Yellow Back Radio Broke-Down* (1969), with its spoof radio-script format, its cast of Loop Garoo as trickster black sheriff and Drag Gibson as white rancher-boss, and its virtualised outlaws, chases and stagecoaches.[18]

For the most part the tribes, notably the Plains Comanche, the Dakota, Lakota and Nakota Sioux, the Navajo, the Pawnee and Nez Percé, would feature as impediments and threat to the white frontier. Ex-slave and other black southerners, like those caught up in the Exoduster Movement of the 1870s with its westward migrancy from Mississippi and Louisiana to Kansas, or black cowboy tradition personified in a figure like Nat Tate, become near-invisible. Mexican *vaqueros*, who passed on their horse and herding skills, are subsumed under the white cowboy ethos. The Chinese evaporate into figurines as pigtailed launderer, cook or railroad worker even if, in a state like Montana, by the 1880s they were a tenth of the population.

Each phase of US expansion, moreover, whether the Louisiana Purchase in 1803, the negotiation of Oregon country from Britain in 1846, or the formalisation of Texas and California as American territories in the Treaty of Guadalupe-Hidalgo in 1848, adds to this white nationalist mythology of frontier, America as essentially Euro-America.[19] A symptomatic early version of Manifest Destiny as whiteness is to be heard, for instance, in the 1830s with Sam Houston's plan for making the Mexican province of *Tejas* into the American state of Texas: 'The Anglo-Saxon race must pervade the whole southern extremity of this vast continent. The Mexicans are no better than the Indian and I see no reason why we should not take their land . . .'[20]

The inexorability of the process is also recalled in a 2000 millennial issue of *The Economist*. Looking back to the Lewis and Clark expedition of 1804–6, and its Jeffersonian brief to explore the lands west of the Missouri River, the exchange implications for a Native America which had actually saved the trek from starvation and ruin make for the following summary:

> White America. The Corps of Discovery as the expedition styled itself, arrived half-dead in Indian villages. It was cared for. Its Indian hosts were offered 'the hand of unalterable friendship'; what they got was ruin. By 1900 whole nations had died of smallpox, and those that were left had been cheated or hunted off their ancestral lands. . . . And today's United States was born; no longer a nervous ex-colonial fringe along the Atlantic seaboard, but a continental power.[21]

IV

Even if, overall, American whiteness could ever have been invoked without reference to the familiar, but always hopelessly inadequate, human colour chart of black, red, brown or yellow, it would still carry its own contradictions. For the assumption, not to say the vaunting, of one white standard, Anglo-Saxonism, has always meant ignoring the conflation of peoples in origin diversely Angle, Saxon, Jute, Scot, Irish, Welsh, Manx, Cornish, Scandinavian and Norman, let alone all subsequent European crossovers and mix.[22]

James M. McPherson in *Is Blood Thicker than Water? Crises in Nationalism in the Modern World* (1998) gives further context to Anglocentrism within American history:

> Almost from its founding, the United States was a multi-ethnic nation. Although English language, law, and culture predominated, nearly two-fifths of the white population in 1790 came from non-English stock: Scots, Irish, Germans, French and other European groups. Even if the Scots and Irish are grouped with the English, more than one-fifth of the American white population were non-British. The percentage increased over time, with heavy immigration of non-British peoples, especially after 1840.[23]

It perhaps can little surprise that Whiteness Studies have become a latest academic domain. Is this legitimate study or mere passing cultural fashion? Bizarrely, a few white supremacist cells have even thought that introducing such courses gave proof that college America had finally come round to their way of thinking.[24] Valerie Babb, in *Whiteness Visible: The Meaning of Whiteness in American Literature and Culture* (1998), helpfully re-stresses whiteness as 'a created identity . . . sustained by hegemony, a complex network of cultural relations including, among other things, literature, museums, popular music, and movies'.[25]

Toni Morrison, 1993 Nobel laureate, gives her weight to the ongoing discussion in *Playing in the Dark: Whiteness and the Literary Imagination* (1992), the luminous 1990 Massey lectures she gave at Harvard.[26] She first challenges any, indeed all, assumptions that American culture has been given over principally to whiteness with a few ethnic footnotes added along the cultural pathway. Africanism, especially, and as she takes meticulous care to define it, she insists on as not only inextricable from the very definition of Americanness, but a massive, underwriting presence in nothing other than its assumed white-literary mainstream. Her commentary lays out the contours of an argument as succinct as it is full of discerning:

> until very recently, and regardless of the race of author, the readers of virtually all of American fiction have been positioned as white. I am interested to know what that assumption has meant to the literary imagination. When does racial 'unconsciousness' or awareness of race enrich interpretative language, and when does it impoverish it? What does positing one's writerly self, in the wholly racialized society that is the United States, as unraced and all others as raced entail? What happens to the writerly imagination of a black author who is at some level *always* conscious of representing one's own race to, or in spite of, a race of readers that understands itself to be 'universal' or race-free? In

other words how is 'literary whiteness' and 'literary blackness' made, and what is the consequence of that construction? How do embedded assumptions of racial (not racist) language work in the literary enterprise that hopes and sometimes claims to be 'humanistic'? (pp. xii–xiii)

In this respect, much newspaper space was taken up with Shelley Fisher Fishkin's study *Was Huck Black? Mark Twain and African American Voices* (1991). If Twain indeed had modelled Huck's voice on that of an overheard black child, what ethnic-racial implications arise about the literary genealogy of America's best-loved figure of white boyhood?[27] Morrison herself would give an addendum to the arising issues in a 1998 interview with *Le Monde* when she asks: 'Will I be allowed, finally, to write about black Americans without having to say that they are black just as whites write about white Americans?'[28]

Eric Liu, in his *The Accidental Asian: Notes of a Native Speaker* (1998), the echo in his title clearly calculated to call up James Baldwin's *Notes of a Native Son*, offers another connecting bead. Mindful of the historic workings of Yellow Peril, and of ongoing patronage of Asian Americans as the Model Minority, he observes with some acidity: 'Times have changed, and I suppose you would call it progress that a Chinaman, too, may now aspire to whiteness'.[29]

V

White ethnicity, Irish to Jewish, and all other kinds of European, invites its own historic and cultural understanding, not least given the US 2000 census figures which of a total US population of 281.4 million enumerates the following break-down: Anglo 75.2 per cent, Hispanic 12.5, African American 12.3, Native 1.5, Asian 4.2 and Other Race 6.6 per cent. A shared demographic prediction, on grounds of birthrate and immigration especially from Latin America and Asia, is that by 2050 fewer than one in two Americans will be a Euro-American. Within this one adds, inevitably, the ever-growing tide of *mestizaje*, children born of one or another kind of intermarriage or relationship (for some, misgivingly, called marrying out). California's Lieutenant Governor Cruz Bustamante summarises the implications: 'If there are no majorities, then there are no minorities'.[30]

In the case of the Irish, the ambiguities can rarely have been greater, as a study like Noel Ignatiev's *How the Irish Became White* (1995) conscientiously gives proof.[31] On the one hand, whiteness gave a degree of head start to those seeking from America land, money or political efficacy. On the other, for many of the five million who emigrated in the nineteenth century, it has been a whiteness that, often painfully, also had to be earned. For just as those who left after the Great Famine of 1845–7 would not easily forget starvation, lack of franchise, unfair taxes, or English repression and religious intolerance, so the nearly 45 million Americans who now claim Irish ancestry look back, equally, to a New World catalogue of steerage, then indenture in Appalachia and other rural America, and labourer and maid-servant status in the cities.

Theirs was to be a hard-won struggle against Anglo-America's condescension and resistance, not least each stereotype of white-trash dirt or hill farmer, illiterate, drinker, pedlar, domestic servant, meddling priest, or even conspirator by association of name, as with the Molly Maguires for a secret coalmining union in 1870s Pennsylvania. Paradoxically, the rite-of-passage took place even as many Irish themselves sought cited lace-curtain respectability in a Boston, Philadelphia or San Francisco. White insignia did not come easily.[32]

Paradox, in fact, greatly continues to play its hand. Paul Dever, Governor of Massachusetts from 1949 to 1952, once spoke of John F. Kennedy, Harvard-educated as may have been but also a Catholic born in Brookline, as the 'first Irish Brahmin'. Ronald Reagan, in the 1980s, expediently rediscovered his own distant family Irishness. Safely ensconced in the presidency, he could add to his perceived homeliness an Irish tongue, or charm, the furtherance of his cachet as the Great Communicator. If urban Irish America were to look to its own literary fictions, they would include Peter Finley Dunne's vernacular yet trenchant Mr Dooley columns begun in the Chicago *Evening Post* in 1893, James T. Farrell's naturalist South Side trilogy *Studs Lonigan* (1932–5), Edwin O'Connor's tribute to the old-time Irish politics of New England in *The Last Hurrah* (1956), Mary McCarthy's intimate *Memories of a Catholic Girlhood* (1957), and William Kennedy's *Ironweed* (1983) and the rest of his inspired city cycle of Irish American family and political life since the 1930s in Albany, New York. Few recent autobiographical fictions can have been more affecting, tough, or seriously funny, than Frank McCourt's *Angela's Ashes* (1996), a lived working-class Irishness steering its way through into shared Americanism.[33]

Germans, either from the Bavarian south or Hanseatic north, and with a history which saw nearly seven million immigrants arrive between the centuries, would abandon old divides of region and religion and feed a shared Teutonism into the American way. That could embrace a Lutheran church, a family farm in the midwest of Illinois, Iowa or Indiana, a German-heritaged American first couple like Ike and Mamie Eisenhower, or, in the likes of Bob Haldeman, John Erlichman and Ron Ziegler, White House functionaries and each a Southern Californian and Christian Scientist, who became known as Nixon's Prussian Guard. Even the Second World War, if it interned Japanese Americans, imposed only selective curfews on German Americans suspected of pro-Axis sympathies. For their whiteness as Americans was not in general doubt. In *Slaughterhouse-Five* (1969), Kurt Vonnegut, German American, writes one of the great science-fiction war texts of, among other things, so ambiguous an inheritance: a Germany whose aryanism led it to become a brute scourge and pariah yet a Germany with its own scars of the kind imposed by the Allies in the Dresden bombing.[34]

In this same overall scheme, massive Polish emigration (over two million by the turn of the incoming twentieth century) could look to America both as respite from peasant indigency and old Russo-Polish territorial scars. Yet if there was Chopin, and the *beau idéal* version of Poland, there was also the battery of 'dumb Polack' jokes and slurs; it was another whiteness which needed its negotiation.[35] Scandinavians, in assuming their American credentials, had an easier time (a Bohemian version is to be met with in Willa Cather's *My Antonia* (1918)), stalwart Viking prairie-dwellers as co-runners of a kind with the Anglo stable and whose chronicles include Ole Edvart Rølvaag's *Giants in the Earth: A Saga of the Prairie*, with its South Dakota pioneer setting and first published in Norwegian in 1924–5 and in English in 1927.[36]

But however tough, or easy, could they, or fellow northern European Americans, be expected to share their Ceiling of Europe lightness of skin with darker-aspected Mediterranean Greeks or Italians?[37] The rite of passage whereby Italians, for instance, became white has entailed a near-classic shift from stereotype of peasant, mafioso, pasta chef, Calabrian or Sicilian grandmother into mainline American. In *Another Country* (1962), James Baldwin has one of his protagonists, Vivaldo, Italian American, underline the paradox of this will to be incorporated into white America. The locale is Little Italy in Greenwich Village:

> He walked along McDougal Street. Here were the black and white couples, defiantly white, flamboyantly black; and the Italians watched them, hated them, hating, in fact, all the Villagers, who gave their streets a bad name. The Italians, after all merely wished to be accepted as decent Americans and probably could not be blamed for feeling that they might have had an easier time of it if they had not been afflicted with so many Jews and junkies and drunkards and queers and spades.[38]

As to Italian American fiction itself, Helen Barolini's *Umbertina* (1979), or even Mario Puzo's Mafia romances like *The Godfather* (1969), give their own explorations of the rite-of-passage out of *Italianità* into Americanness. But many have perceived an altogether more figural transformation in play, that of imputed Mediterranean darkness into American whiteness.[39]

Jewish Americans, whiteness of a different colour in a recent phrase, look to their own on-off relation within America's ethnographic story.[40] Whether Askenazi or Sephardic, and against a long history of immigration (German-Jewish from 1820–80, the *pogrom*-inspired two million from East Europe between 1881 and 1924, and with the 1930s flights from Nazism to follow), the anti-semitism they would face drew from ancient myths of usury, swarthiness, sexual rapacity, or supposed alien or double allegiance be it to Zionism, Communism or, eventually, Israel. The Democratic Party candidacy for Vice President, alongside Al Gore, of Connecticut's Senator Joe Lieberman in 2000, Orthodox Jewish and Sabbath-observing, remains a source of comment, surprise, not least his own.

Few better literary accounts exist than Alfred Kazin's three formidably articulate volumes of autobiography, *Starting Out in the Thirties* (1965), *A Walker in the City* (1951) and *New York Jew* (1978), or Irving Howe's *World of Our Fathers* (1976). Each looks to a Jewish urban America which embraces a European past of the *stetl* and Yiddish (not least in the fiction of a vital, enduring writer like I. B. Singer), the haunting legacy of Hitlerism, 1930s Leftism, the rise of a prime American literary intelligentsia in names like Delmore Swartz, Saul Bellow, Bernard Malamud, Philip

Roth and Cynthia Ozick, with ranking house magazines like *Commentary*. Best-known locales include the Lower East Side, Brooklyn or the suburbs of New York's White Plains, Chicago's Skokie or Florida's Miami.[41]

Jewish Americans, moreover, and to add complication, have also, and many times over, been non-white. The several Ethiopian Hebrew Congregations or *falesh* believers in their Harlem synagogues give one evidence. A 1920s bibliophile like the Puerto Rico-raised Arthur A. Schomburg gives another, whether as founder of the Negro Society for Historical Research in 1911, luminary with Alain Locke, Claude McKay, Jean Toomer and others of the 1920s New Negro Movement, or as bequeather of the momentous black manuscript and book archive which bears his name at the 135th Street branch of the New York Library. Jewish authorship also extends to a 1960s Beat figure like Bob Kaufman, born in New Orleans of a Jewish father and African American Catholic mother, and the distinguished *Puertorriqueña* poet Aurora Levins Morales, with her daughter Rosario Morales, the co-authors of *Getting Home Alive* (1986) as an exploration in verse and prose of island–mainland cultural legacy in its eclecticism of site, ethnicity, language and gender.[42]

White nor not, however, the snare of anti-semitism has indeed long exerted its reach, whether in access to the top military, or in housing, or business, or different kinds of sports club and school. One riposte, almost ancestrally, is to be found in Jewish humour from the Marx Brothers to Woody Allen, Jack Benny to Bette Midler, and from the New York *borsht* belt to Las Vegas. Entertainment, even so, from early vaudeville into Hollywood and TV, notably has exacted gentile renamings, whether Al Jolson (Asa Yoelson), Eddie Cantor (Isador Iskado Iskowitch), Sophie Tucker (Sophia Abuza Kalish), Danny Kaye (Daniel David Koninski) or Kirk Douglas (Issur Danielovich). Academia, like most of the professions, from science to the arts to law and as an east-coast educational axis like that of CCNY/Columbia University has vintagely given proof, required its own storming. At another angle, a memoir by Al Hinkle recalls the effort of Allen Ginsberg, Beat poet-bard and Jewish bad boy par excellence, to secure a job on the San Francisco railroad in 1952: 'They wouldn't hire Allen as a brakeman at that time because they wouldn't hire any Jews . . . At that time there was, actually, in the union a clause that you had to be white – and that [didn't] include Jews, too.'[43]

Hassidic-Orthodox, Conservative, Reform, or secular, citied or suburban, traditional or feminist, varieties of Jewish style inevitably have been many. Often overlooked, for instance, and as Rich Cohen's *Tough Jews* (1998) underscores, has been a de-stereotyping line of gangster figures, whether Bugsy Siegel and his Murder Inc. in the 1930s or Meyer Lansky and Arnold Rothstein of contemporary mob, FBI and Cuba lore. Be it Hollywood, the professoriat, medicine, the law, politics (Henry Kissinger offers a perfect recent case-study), New York's garment industry, showbusiness, consumer names like those of Helena Rubenstein, Vidal Sassoon and Calvin Klein, an advice columnist as assiduously consulted as Ann Landers (Esther Friedman Lederer), or even racketeering, Jewish entry into whiteness has involved its own vexed negotiation, anything but automatic rights of admittance.[44]

VI

On a related tack, American whiteness cannot be disengaged from issues of American class-formation: from WASP upper echelons to Middle America to the blue-collar city and rural poor whites. The first is early to be met with in the Virginia dynasties of Jefferson, Madison, Monroe and others, and in the New England presidencies of John and John Quincy Adams with Henry Adams in his celebrated *Education* (1907) as their wistful end-of-legacy memorialist. Later manifestations include the great banking and corporation families of Morgan, Carnegie, Vanderbilt and Rockefeller; a social circuit of Old New York, or fashionable Boston with Rhode Island or Martha's Vineyard for holidaying; the country club; and private school and Ivy League education each, also, part of a marriage brokerage system. Nor is this to deny WASP philanthropy, a civic religion of educational, art and other foundations, of which the Smithsonian established in Washington DC in 1846, or the modern New York Public Library begun from Astor money and the Tilden trust in 1895, would be typical.

Groupings like the Daughters of the American Revolution (DAR), the Daughters of the American Confederacy (DAC), or the First Families of Virginia (FFV), have long embodied the claim to Anglo-American ascendancy. Theirs, in one view, may have been a case of trivial pursuits, with the *Mayflower* and (the actually non-existent) Plymouth Rock, or Jamestown and Appomattox, objects of class fetish and snobbery, together with the workings of the Social Register as a means of keeping up on the debutante season, dynastic marriages, dress and etiquette codes, and wills and transfers of property. WASP-Brahmin mental breakdown, and hospitalisation, his own included along with those of Sylvia Plath and the Nobel mathematician John Forbes Nash Jr (of the book and film *A Beautiful Mind*), would lead Robert Lowell, in his poem 'Waking in the Blue', to speak sardonically of 'Mayflower screwballs'.

One way in which the racial implications of this hierarchy showed their hand was when, in May 1939, and on unadorned racist grounds, the DAR refused their Constitution Hall in Washington DC for a concert by the distinguished black contralto Marian Anderson. A salutary counter-action involved Eleanor Roosevelt, as well-born as any DAR member yet a political liberal and long-time NAACP board member, who helped to arrange in its place a greatly attended recital at the Washington Monument.[45]

Other old-money players include Edith Wharton, born a Jones into the New York family which gave rise to the catchphrase 'keeping up with the Joneses', and whose fiction chronicles Hudson Valley and other major WASP and Anglo-Dutch domains; Henry Luce as advocate in his magazines *Time* (1923), *Fortune* (1930) and *Life* (1936) of an Anglocentric, conservative America, and whose legacy Claire Booth Luce would long continue; or Pamela Harriman, wife to both Randolph Churchill and US ambassador Averell Harriman, as ranking Anglo-American doyenne, DC hostess and pillar of the Democratic Party establishment. If, in the years from Reagan to Clinton to George W. Bush, a new top-wealth cadre has been created through e-commerce, IT and the NASDAQ, and with a best-known name in Microsoft's Bill Gates, it remains overwhelmingly one of white corporate America.

Middle America, almost automatically, calls up the whiteness of suburbia. Once this meant company America, a white-collar salariat with a single wage-earner. But the profile has changed: working wives, two incomes, no longer the 1920s Babbitry pilloried by Sinclair Lewis. 1950s sociology invoked the White Collar Worker and Organization Man (with women socially gendered into homemaker and Mom). With ever wider stockholding, the investment portfolio as against the office, and the home computer, America's very definition of work has changed.

Suburbia as landscape, even so, remains familiar: the two- or three-garage tract home duly lawned and with basketball hoop, the local junior high, high school and PTA, the white churches, the network of masonic and other lodges like the Elks, Lions or Kiwanis, and the mall or plaza as both consumer and youth venue. Golf or tennis have long been its signature sports. Allowing for an increasing black middle-class and Asian presence, and whether older business families or professional and home-based dot.com types, the burbs, in media jargon, continue to remain still more whiteloaf than not. Monied upper-middle America looks to the Washington DC/Maryland of the Beltway, Upper New York's Westchester County, California's Silicon Valley, or affluent Seattle.

Blue-collar white ethnicity has increasingly come to be thought of as an urban-enclave heritage, not least in the rustbelt cities of the northeast and midwest. Even so, Irish Boston, New York or San Francisco vaunt St Patrick's Day parades, shamrock groups, priests and city parochial schools. Chicago or Milwaukee witnesses to Polish and Ukrainian local newspapers, work-clubs and churches. Hell's Kitchen Italian New York retains its family eateries and argot. The Jewish Lower East Side has its continuing rag trade, kosher delicatessens and bagel shops, not to mention the nearby theatre district. Each, typically, still implies the inner city or quarter, and mayorships up from the ranks like those of an 'Irish' Richard Daley of Chicago in the 1960s or 'Italian' Frank Rizzo of Philadelphia in the 1970s.

As to the whiteness of rural America, no region has more won attention than Appalachia, the South of the Cumberland Gap down into deepest Dixie, a world of sharecropper, back-country, hill clan, Bible fundamentalism, and the Klan. The nomenclature has long grown familiar, whether white trash, with trailer trash an update, poor white or redneck, along with hillbilly, honkie and doughface. Film, jokes, cartoons of which Li'l Abner became among the best known, have all added to the insignia, typically in the form of Bubba or Good Old Boy (Jimmy Carter's brother, Billy, became a 1970s version), and whiskey stills, pick-up trucks, fried chicken, grits and six-packs. Its music has been country and western from Jimmie Rodgers through to Tammy Wynette, Bobbie Gentry and Conway Twitty.

Appalachia's demographics look back to both English and Irish or Scots-Irish indenture. The latter, often fiercely anti-English, gave rise to another term of general usage for poor white, namely cracker, originally meaning itinerant horsetrader. Twain's Pap Finn offers a satire of typecast, a muted Irishness of drinking, violence and shiftlessness. The span of a generalised rural whiteness, over time, has enlarged to include, say, German-descended farmer lines in Illinois or Indiana, Scandinavians from the farm and prairie upper midwest of Nebraska, Wisconsin and the Dakotas, or hardscrub migrants from Oklahoma, Okies, caught out by the Dustbowl 1930s and whose westering journey John Steinbeck sought to capture in the Joad family story of *The Grapes of Wrath* (1939).[46]

The paradoxes, again, remain many. One set of origins lies in the plantocracy's fear of slave revolt, from the 1739 Stono Rebellion in South Carolina to those led by Gabriel Prosser in Richmond, Virginia, in 1800, by Nat Turner in Southampton County, Virginia, in 1831, and by Denmark Vesey in Charleston, South Carolina, in 1832. However reluctantly, the planter elites, or bourbons, found themselves obliged to extend their own class-based economic and social whiteness to poor whites. Elevated as for the first time to a place into whiteness as hierarchical power, they quickly enough served as its instruments.

First they took against the blackness of slaves, and after the civil war, of ex-slaves, with whom, and on economic if no other grounds, they might otherwise have made common cause. In 1663, for instance, in Gloucester County, Virginia, indentured white servants and black slaves had joined in common revolt. In the War of 1812, slaves and free blacks fought alongside white Americans (many of the former then found themselves returned to slavery).[47] This class-and-race-fuelled southern phobia has persisted, whether in the 1860s against Yankee soldiery seeking to free the slaves or, a century later, in the 1960s against civil rights workers working for desegregation.

VII

White supremacism, though anything but exclusively southern, has long had its well-known recent southern tableaux: George Wallace's standing in the doorway of the University of Alabama and declaiming 'Segregation Now, Tomorrow and Forever' (1963) or the killing of the three student civil rights workers, Michael Schwerner, James Chaney and Andrew Goodman in 1964. Despite the version given in the film *Mississippi Burning* (1989), it was no Sheriff Anderson (Gene Hackman) turned FBI hero who discovered the truth amid a township of all-too conveniently passive black southerners. Rather, the bodies were discovered in a nearby dam as a result of a $30,000 bribe to Klan members. A reluctant J. Edgar Hoover, forced to take action by Robert Kennedy as Attorney General, had long been more interested in proving Martin Luther King somehow a Communist, whatever his obvious Christianity, rather than devoting the Bureau's manpower and forensics to pursuing any investigation of Klan violence. The grounds were unapologetically racist.

White supremacism, again, has always had a class dimension. Only over time would it be shared downwards by the south's ruling castes. The checklist, inevitably, includes the Ku Klux Klan, on its own styling the Invisible Empire, whose origins lie in the Confederacy's largely Scots-American and officer class. Begun in Pulaski, Tennessee in 1865, the white feudal robes, lynchings, cross-burnings and night rides came to mean racial ascendancy by upper-class *diktat*. Other Reconstruction-era white supremacist groups include the Knights of the White Camelia, the White Brotherhood and the '76 Association, each assured of its aristocracy of blood and race. Its enrolment of lower-order whites was always a concession, the fear of slave insurrection but also the decline of the plantation economy.[48]

The Scottsboro case, of twelve young black men falsely accused of the Alabama boxcar rape of two white women in 1931, acts as a symptomatic case-study: the readiness to attribute bestiality, endemic sexual threat, to all black males. During the Second World War, the Red Cross established segregated blood banks to accommodate a white Dixie soldiery fearful of mongrelisation in the words of Congressman Rankin of Mississippi. White Citizens Councils first began in 1954, supremacist to the core, to many simply the Klan and its sympathisers under another name, and given to camouflaging its ideology under the mantle of state rights.

This kind of white nativism would have an extending compass. It stalks the memory of the 1960s civil rights marches, along with the Klan bombing of the Sixteenth Street Baptist Church in Birmingham, Alabama, and the death of the four girl worshippers in 1983, the Selma March of 1965, and the murder of Martin Luther King in 1968. In 1982, it underwrites the notorious baseball killing of Vincent Chin, Chinese American draughtsman, by two white laid-off Chrysler workers who thought Chin Japanese and so an Asian figure readily scapegoated. Both killers, to Asian community dismay, were let off with relatively light sentences. It remains a source of perceived race-preferential treatment.[49]

In the 1990s, it takes the form of survivalist groups, militia, and skinheads in Doc Marten boots and crew cuts, all committed to whiteness as a millennial vision of offence and defence. Timothy McVeigh, the Oklahoma bomber, is frequently advanced as the very pathology of the lower-class white loner – though the explosion was first widely and stereotypically attributed to 'Muslim terrorists'. In his novel *Civil War II* (1999), Thomas Chittum, Vietnam War veteran, offers an aryan-propagandist vision of the break-up of the Union into separate, and separatist, racial states. White supremacists belonging to the National Alliance, led by William Pierce, vaunt their own CDs and White Power music, a mix of Wagner and rock, under the label of Resistance Records, one of which has a cover of swastikas and Jewish corpses.[50]

The formula is as hierarchical as it has always been abusive: whiteness against non-white periphery. Blacks fall under the historically toxic 'nigger', whatever its black in-house uses or media-sanitisation into 'The N-word', along with nigrah and coon. Natives remain breeds and halfbreeds, Latinos 'greasers' and 'spics', Jews 'hymies' and 'kikes', Chinese 'chinks', Japanese 'japs' and 'nips', Filipinos 'brown monkeys', and Koreans and Vietnamese 'gooks'. How, also in this context, to construe the use of 'whitey', mere or understandable mirror-speak, one more unlovely inflection in the linguistic guerilla warfare of ethnic slur?[51]

A vehement recent controversy arises over the flying of the Confederate Battle Flag over the State Capitol in Columbia, South Carolina. Similar flag issues have arisen in Mississippi, Georgia, Alabama and Arkansas. Is this to flaunt the memory of slaveholding, as the NAACP and local black church and community groups claim (a typical placard reads 'Your Heritage is My Slavery'), or is it to give honour to the legacy of Confederate heroism in the face of federal-Yankee invasion, as its largely lower-class white rural defenders counter-claim? Either way, its class as much as white ethnic dimensions are clearly on view.

To this can be added the events in June 1998 in Jasper, Texas. Three white former convicts, bearing supremacist tattoos and SS lightning bolts, chained a black townsman, James Byrd Jr, to a pick-up truck, and dragged him for miles which led to his decapitation and loss of an arm. During their trial for murder, Darrell Flinn, Irish-descended Imperial Wizard of the Klan in nearby Vidor, Texas, offered a near-classic reaction. He found himself moved to public condemnation of the crime on the brutally exquisite grounds of its having done little or nothing to 'preserve white history and secure a better place for the white race.'

VIII

Religion offers its own styles of institutionalisation to American whiteness. As Anglo-American Puritanism apportions into Congregationalism, Baptism, Methodism, Quakerism, or, in the early nineteenth century, Unitarianism, with, notably, Christian Science, Seventh Day Adventism and Mormonism to follow, it was overwhelmingly assumed that they each meant a white adherence to their systems of belief and liturgy. However given to sectarianism, there was little doubt of a presiding white-protestant God. That, in turn, meant that faiths from Catholic Ireland and Poland, or from Orthodox Greece, Armenia or Russia, or from Jewish Europe, would need to parlay their way into also giving the appearance of having become white-American religions. 'Spanish' or 'brown' Catholic America would wait until very recently, and then selectively, to see top echelons in the hierarchy drawn from its own ranks.[52]

A dramatic example, still within memory, occurred in the case of John F. Kennedy as presidential candidate. It was in 1960, in a Houston TV studio and before selected Protestant clergy, that Kennedy was obliged to affirm his belief in the separation of church and state. Despite a distinguished war record, or a career as Massachusetts Congressman and Senator, he was actually allaying old fears of Irish access to power as a route for Vatican manipulation and, thereby, the legitimacy of his entitlement to mainstream cultural and political whiteness.

Black Baptist Christianity, Mexican Catholicism, Native American belief systems, and, latterly, Asian religions from Buddhism to Hinduism, have regularly been thought discrepant, at least at odds with the visceral notion of white-protestant American godhead. Is not Buddhism, whatever its diverse cultural origins and forms in Asia, merely the fad of a 1960s hippie flower-power generation? How can Hinduism, with its plural deities, be a true one-godhead religion?

Islam, and its American followers, however overwhelmingly peaceful, even conservative in their social practices and politics, fall under a yet more accusing suspicion, its believers to be construed as fanatic, given over only to *jihad*. One manifestation was to be associated with the Black Muslims, founded as the Nation of Islam by Elijah Muhammad in Detroit in 1930. Throughout the 1960s, they were to be thought a threatening spectre whose embodiment lay in the figure of Malcolm X. The fiery pulpitry and rallies of Louis Farrakhan have given continuity.

Yet if they were, and remain, a small minority within America's seven million or so Muslim believers (of whom roughly half are Arab Americans), they have frequently been taken to do duty for all and, along with 'Muslim' international terrorism, to have put whiteness, the white citizenry of America, under permanent siege. In this respect, it remains to be seen how far the World Trade Center attacks in September 2001, despite the diversity of those killed, and however unrepresentative the perpetrators, will again lead to profiling Islam as inimical to the white west.[53]

Few white religions in America have better provided a working touchstone than Mormonism. Its best-known features look to a prophet martyr in Joseph Smith, lost golden tablets containing scripture, the resolute, murderous, and to be sure at times epic journey from New York through Illinois and eventually into Utah, and the Franklin work ethic and fervent capitalism (despite an early flirtation with socialism) which has led to business empires in insurance and investment in Salt Lake City, Ogden and the rest of the state. The emphasis on total genealogy, required missionary work, and at its edges polygamy, has long made it a byword.

On these grounds, it has often been called the classic American religion, white-protestant, patriarchal, family-centred, and always fiercely and conservatively patriotic. Yet until lately, and much to the point, it subscribed to policies of white church governance and racial exclusion of Blacks from the hierarchy, with Natives seen as a lost tribe of Israel.

IX

Popular culture, whatever its supposed democratising impact, has long been complicit in the dissemination of whiteness as norm. Media and film, the body beautiful, music, space-exploration, and inevitably sport, to take a selection of arenas, all afford illustrative examples. Each, too, interconnects and overlaps, a working fabric whereby America, explicitly or subliminally, has projected itself as overwhelmingly a white cultural edifice.

Radio, with film, and then TV in its wake, supplies a first touchstone, most of all the Hollywood of white stardom, male and female, generally to be set against blacks as minstrel entertainers, athletes, house servants, and maids, monosyllabic Indians, the sleepy *campesino* and his 'firecracker' female counterpart, and one or another species of either singsong or conspiratorial-fiend Asian. Two white–black examples from both ends of the the postwar span bear out the point.

The Jack Benny Show from the 1940s onwards held sway as one of America's best-loved comedies of radio and TV. Not the least of its appeal, seemingly, was how Benny found himself outmanoeuvred by Eddie Robinson in the updated Step 'n' Fechit role of the black manservant Rochester. When, however, LeRoi Jones/Amiri Baraka turned the comedy about-face in his play *Jello* (1970) and had Rochester actually murder Benny, it was as if media sacrilege had been committed, a hallowed formula desecrated. Jones/Baraka clearly meant it as riposte, revenge for the one, and with it all, black stereotype. It could be little surprise that as a theatre piece it had a near-impossible time getting either published or performed.

In the 2000s, there has been the phenomenon of Eminem as white rapper, real name Marshall Mathers, profane, street-savvy, for many a misogynist, yet hugely popular. Is he best thought a kind of harlequin, the embodiment of white blackness or, as likely, its reverse? No one, certainly, could doubt the tough-guy lyrics, rap as would-be white ghetto idiom. His song, 'White America', candidly admits the further implication: 'Let's do the math/If I was black I would've sold half'.

Of all screen forms, few have given more immediate figuration to whiteness than the Western, not least through its gallery of heroes, a largely Anglo or Anglo-Irish gallery to include William S. Hart, Roy Rogers, William Boyd in the more than sixty Hopalong Cassidy movies, and, above all, John Wayne as the very incarnation of WASP manhood. His drawl, loping gait, even his large frame, became a Hollywood signature for white, straight, good-guy masculinity, a posture he came to believe he had earned in life as well as art. The line runs from John Ford's classic *Stagecoach* (1939), through each cowboy, cavalryman, US army and frontier marshall role, to late films like *Rooster Cogburn* (1975) and his valedictory to the gunfighter, *The Shootist* (1976).[54]

Yet Wayne, in fact, was born Marion Michael Morrison to Irish American parents in Winterset, Iowa, took his name from a War of Independence hero General Anthony Wayne (with the WASP-aristocratic 'Duke' thrown in), never fought in any war, and became a case of life imitating art in his arch-conservative support for the McCarthyite witch-hunts and address to the 1968 Republican Convention. In 'The Invention of John Wayne', the leading Native novelist and critic Louis Owens perfectly well acknowledges a number of 'great westerns'. But he also insists upon the link between the Wayne persona, whiteness and Indian-killing, not least in *The Searchers* (1956) as one of his more ambiguous white–Native films:

> The truth is that he was indeed the great American cowboy and Indian fighter, throwing his stalking shadow across the continent and beyond. But it is even more true that he made everything up, reinventing himself during an incredible career . . . In the course of more than 150 films, with the Indian as mirroring 'other', Marion Morrison grew into the giant figure America demanded, molding himself to match the nation's pathological craving for an archetypal hero fitted to the great, violent myth of the American West.[55]

That the Western, however, has begun to change in image, locale, and in its presentation of gender, has everything to do with the politics of multiculturalism. Films like *Midnight Cowboy* (1969) and *Taxi Driver* (1976) are routinely associated with Manhattan as white-urban frontier. *Little Big Man* (1970) and *Blazing Saddles* (1974) turn upon pastiche, the white west as misnomer, comedy of errors, selective vision. A modern white-feminist frontier is to be seen in *Thelma and Louise* (1991). John Sayles's *Lone Star* (1996) unravels a multicultural southwest of border lives and histories. Native cinema looks to films like *Smoke Signals* (1998), written by Sherman

Alexie and directed by Chris Eyre (Cheyenne), to counter the Hollywood Indian. Jonathan Wacks's *Powwow Highway* (1989) gave an indication that even mainstream cinema was also beginning to unstereotype the Native image.[56] Both Michael Cimino's ambitious but ill-fated Wyoming epic, *Heaven's Gate* (1980) and Clint Eastwood's sepia-tinted *Unforgiven* (1992) have been thought the backward glance, different kinds of elegy to the traditional Western. They offer counter-myths, the close of masculinist, gun-carrying whiteness as all-triumphant and, with it, the frontier reduced to simple High Noon morality, or tall-in-the-saddle sheriff in pursuit of the outlaw, or the cavalry defeating the tribes.[57]

Hollywood, and the casino and the showtime world of Las Vegas as associated playground, threw up another silhouette in the person of Sammy Davis and his marriage, in 1960, to Mae Britt. In the first instance, they embodied a prohibited iconography, pre-eminent black entertainer and member of Sinatra's Rat Pack with beauteous ultra-white Swedish actress. At the time, interracial marriage was outlawed in no fewer than thirty states. Given Sinatra's connection to John F. Kennedy, the marriage was also postponed until after the Massachusetts Senator, however wafer-thin or likely ballot-rigged his win, was safely ensconced in the presidency. Yet when Sinatra was given charge of the White House celebration gala, Davis found himself asked not to attend for fear of alienating Congressional and other southerners. Whiteness, and its politics as cultural and sexual code, had once again exerted sway.

The American body beautiful, female and male, overwhelmingly until late has meant the white physique: Marilyn Monroe or Clark Cable, Madonna or Robert Redford. The effect was to exoticise even as it objectified any other kind of racial body: Natives as 'Indian' warrior or doe-eyed squaw, Blacks as slave fieldhand pugilist or mulatto mistress, Latinos/as as hoodlum or hot señorita, Asians as martial-arts master or China Doll. Few forums have more institutionalised this beauty-myth than the Miss America contests. Begun in Atlantic City in 1921 as a means of extending the social season, and against a national backdrop of the Red Scare, the organisers spoke of seeking to promote, precisely, 'wholesome American beauty' and 'good values'. It would, however, take until 1945 for a Jewish contestant, Bess Myerson (subsequently a famed panellist on *What's My Line?*), and until 1984 for a black woman, Vanessa Williams, to win. The choreography of these contests, from the start, was assiduously given to projecting beauty as white American womanhood.[58]

As a slight remove, Mattel Toy Company's barbie dolls, launched in 1959 and though eventually to adapt to ethnic diversity, initially were thought of as almost synonymous with either the blonde and blue-eyed norm or the ravishing brunette. In the flurry about whether the pageants demean women, or reduce them to objects of male gaze, issues of ethnicity have been among the last to surface.

In parallel, there has been popular culture's white male standard. Charles Atlas served as 'The World's Most Developed Man', an icon not only of American white male muscularity but, as his name implied, of global aryan strength. Swimming supplied Johnny Weissmuller as the screen's best-known Tarzan, his muscled body situated against savagist male blackness. White-played 'Indian' screen warriordom has been another twist, the masculinity of a Jack Palance or Jeff Chandler. Buster Crabbe, also an ex-athlete, played Flash Gordon and duly saved the earth from Ming the Merciless as a sinophobic variation of Sax Rohmer's Fu Manchu. No whiter man-god has been conceived than Superman, Clark Kent as the weak, bespectacled newspaperman who alternates into the all-powerful fantasy figure. That a latest TV version ('Lois and Clark: The New Adventures of Superman') is played by Dean Cain, who declares himself Japanese American, offers an irony to ponder. In all these reckonings, nonetheless, the perceived standard of American maleness, in not just body but also mind, has been nothing if not white.

Space exploration, allowing for occasional later ethnic or female astronauts, yields another venue as Tom Wolfe's celebrated white tableau of the Right Stuff.[59] This embraces the first moonwalker, Neil Armstrong, Buzz Aldrin, and Senator John Glenn of Ohio as heroic continuity figure between NASA's inaugural Mercury flight in 1962 and the Discovery mission in 1998. Starting from the early Saturn rocketry of a Werner Von Braun spirited out of Hitler's aryan Germany, to the moonlander LEM (Lunar Extra-vehicular Module), to, in the 1990s, the Hubble Telescope, it would be near-impossible to dissociate space technology from its white astronaut élite. Was not each to be construed as the bravest masculine embodiment of white America?

Rock 'n' roll as America's prime white-youth music has found no greater personification than in Elvis Presley. Born of poor origins in Tupelo, Mississippi, he became from the 1950s onwards, and both to teenager pleasure and parental shock, the very stuff of lower-class white-masculine strut and testosterone with his lowered eyes, quiff, lips and gyrating pelvis. Presley may well have grown up on country and western, hillbilly and the Grand Old Opry, sometimes called white blues, along with an early radio star like Jimmie Rodgers or Hank Williams and Carl Perkins (a tradition to lead on to Loretta Lynn, Jerry Lee Lewis, the Everly Brothers and Willie Nelson). But when, in 1956, he appeared on the Ed Sullivan Show to be watched by 82 per cent of all Americans who owned TV sets, he performed songs he had heard in person by black gospel choirs and in the Beale Street of a then still segregated Memphis. To his credit, he personally left no doubt of his black debts and borrowings, whether the records he first made at Sam Phillips's Memphis Sun Studio, or, later for RCA. White as rock 'n' roll was assumed to be, and for sure marketed, it was always in truth a fusion, on the one hand the funk, the inescapable sexuality, of Afro-America's rhythm and blues, and on the other the vernacular sound of white-country.[60]

Sport throws up its own styles of racialisation, the more so given its pre-eminence in American life. Tennis, golf, swimming or ice hockey overwhelmingly have been white, basketball and sprint black. Professional football has grown more mixed although quarterbacks, as playmakers, tend nearly always to be white. Baseball offers a similar refraction. Once rigorously segregated until Jackie Robinson signed for the Brooklyn Dodgers in 1947, it, too, has managed a growing diversity from Roberto Clemente as legendary Latin outfielder for the Pittsburgh Pirates in the 1960s through to Sammy Sosa, Dominican-born slugger for the Chicago Cubs or Hideo Nomo as Japanese pitcher for the LA Dodgers and Ichiro Suzuki as outfielder for the Seattle Mariners. The baseball diamond, the mitt or bat, even so, tends still to be thought of in terms of white nostalgic homage, whether as the insignia of Holden's dead poet-brother in J. D. Salinger's *The Catcher in the Rye* (1951) or as fond, back-to-childhood pastoral in a Kevin Costner film like *Field of Dreams* (1989).

Other racial markers equally have been plentiful. In boxing from Jack Johnson (1871–1938), whose liaisons with white women aroused their own complication, to Muhammad Ali, there has always been talk of a Great White Hope to offset the ring's show of black physical grace or prowess. Is not part of the frisson of golf's Tiger Woods its challenge to the sport's country or suburban club image? His self-designation, furthermore, as Cablinasian (Caucasian, Black, Indian, Asian – his father, Earl, is 'mixed' African American, his mother, Kultida, who calls him 'a universal child', is Thai), gives a new spin to the image of the minority athlete. It suggests a genuine ethnic complexity, a move forward from the stereotyping perception a generation before of Lee Trevino as an upstart Tex-Mex whose volubility was often described as ungenteel or loud. It also helps make less atypical other golfing contemporaries like the Native American Notah Begay III.

Tennis's Williams sisters, raised in tough, inner-city Compton, California, add to this changing ethnic sports profile by their shared conquests of Wimbledon, the US Open and other Grand Slam competitions. Althea Gibson there may have been in the 1950s, Arthur Ashe and Zina Garrison thereafter, but in Venus and Serena Williams there has never been quite the intrusion into sport's almost by definition white middle American terrain. That brings with it a dimension of class as much as ethnicity (jestingly or not, Serena has several times mentioned the distant sound of street gunshots as an unlikely help in keeping focus).[61]

At the 1992 Winter Olympics in Albertville, murmurings arose as to whether Kristi Yamaguchi, ice-skating medalist or not, as Japanese American could be thought a truly representative American. Similar misgivings would attach to her fellow skater, Michelle Kwan, as Chinese American. When she was beaten at the same Olympics by Tara Lipinski, one media website ran a headline under the loaded formula of 'American beats out Kwan'.[62] Where, ran the subtext, were to be found white ice queens in the previous mould of the (Norwegian-born) Sonja Henie or (Irish American) Nancy Kerrigan?

Sport as mirror to diversity can also look to the 1999 Wimbledon headlines made by Alexandra Stevenson, the teenage daughter of a white journalist mother and the legendary Julius Erving, the Dr J of the Philadephia 76ers. She found herself spoken of as half-white, half-black, somehow, even in the 1990s, caught in a racial limbo. Like anyone of mixed origins, in fact, hers was, and remains, an identity perfectly complete on its own terms: a young woman athlete of personality and an appetite for her chosen metier. Blood, skin or any other quantum remain quite the least of it.

X

Endemic to issues of whiteness has long been the controversial proposition that America's language indeed is English Only. Yet another irony attaches to the fact that it was Senator S. I. Hayakawa, linguistician, born Japanese Canadian, and a California politician well to the right of the Republican Party, who proposed in the 1980s that English be made the official language of the United States and founded the organisation *US English* to that end. It drew from a spectrum to embrace not only conservatives like Richard Nixon, Charlton Heston, Newt Gingrich, Pat Buchanan (his 'take back America' a clear enough rhetoric), and Linda Chávez, but also 'liberal' names like Walter Cronkite, Whoopi Goldberg and Julia Child.

In *At War With Diversity: US Language Policy in an Age of Anxiety* (2000) James Crawford chronicles how the movement floundered when a racist memo surfaced in 1986. Written by the co-founder, John Tanton, it spoke with Latino birthrate in mind of 'those with their pants up [getting] caught by those with their pants down'. It asked if white Americans seeing 'power and control over their lives declining [would] go quietly into the night'. Crawford gives the following summary:

> this movement was about more than reaffirming language as a totem of national identity. Its stated aim of ethnic harmony and minority advancement were now hard to sustain, with US English leaders cracking jokes about fast-breeding Mexicans.[63]

To date, even so, twenty-six states have given their ratification. What language politics, actually, have been in play? Is US English language under threat, or not, or is this yet more coded, defensive-aggressive nativism? Uniculturalists, in Ishmael Reed's phrase, have long felt uneasy, if not threatened, not so much by the co-existence but by the public sanction of other US spoken languages, with the implication that recognition, or even continued use, of these languages somehow lessens the speaker's Americanness.

A recent collection like *Multilingual America: Transnationalism, Ethnicity, and the Languages of American Literature* (1998), committed according to its German-born editor Werner Sollors to the ethos not of English Only but English Plus, offers a counter-view. Among other questions it poses is the issue of whether American literature can persist in being regarded as only an English-language tradition. Sollers, along with Marc Shell, has since 1994 also headed Harvard's Longfellow Institute with its project to publish American writings in languages other than English.[64]

If American English has long, and inevitably, drawn from other wellsprings, that, too, has not always been welcomed. In his *A Compendious Dictionary of the English Language* (1806), Noah Webster selectively expunged what he believed to be vulgarisms, like the African-derived 'banjo', even though he included 'opossum' and 'hominy', both of Algonquin origins. The attempt, thereafter, to standardise English has recurred from the famed McGuffey *Readers* (begun in 1838) to many contemporary *ESL* (English as Second Language) texts. Official English, and those who oppose it, can be thought but a latest cultural clash.

American English, as from the start, continues to run alongside, as well as draw from, an irrepressibly polyglot context. It spans each variety of Spanish including Ladino or Judaeo-Spanish, along with Portinglés, New Orleans French and Italian. Chinese looks to Mandarin, Cantonese, Hakka and Teochew. Other American Asia speaks Japanese, Korean and Tagalog. German, and with it Yiddish, still has a community base. Active Native tongues include Navajo, Inuit, Chippewa – the word Mississippi once again a best-known derivation – and in Canada, Cree. There has also been English-within-English, none more controversial than Black English, or Ebonics, as an idiom in its own expressive right.

The movement for English Only, as with Official English, has often been taken to signify Speak White, and thereby to downplay, even outrightly to seek to excise, different language histories. Bilingual education becomes a perceived threat to America as a supposed one-language nation. Yet surveys consistently bear out that few Americans for whom English is a second or coeval language fail to acknowledge its national status, or quibble at acquiring basic ground rules of American English grammar, syntax, spelling or usage.

The commentator Domenico Maceri, himself a foreign-language teacher in California, points to yet further implications in having states like his own or Arizona approve initiatives to eliminate bilingual education. America first of all loses language resources: the shortage of speakers of a vital strategic language like Arabic is a case in point (the comparison is drawn with being able to draw upon the language skills of Japanese Americans, Italian Americans and German Americans during the Second World War). Secondly, 'Monolingualism translates into isolationism'.[65]

Professionals in bilingual education have not been the only ones to point to Switzerland, Belgium or, with acknowledgement of broader political tensions, the Québec of nearby Canada, as cultures able to function multilingually. English clearly will continue to prevail in the USA. But to call for English Only, or to make English the official language, is again, and tacitly as may be, to confirm, even to promote, white as against multicultural history, and to risk forgoing the gains over the losses for the nation at large of not only language but cultural pluralism.[66]

XI

Consideration of whiteness in language leads into the whiteness within critical and literary tradition. Until the 1960s, virtually every standard US literary history simply took it for granted that the commanding reaches of the nation's writing were raceless, an assumption which actually meant a white-cultural canon.

Fred Pattee's once-standard *A History of American Literature* (1896), *tout court*, dispensed with anything but white authorship. More egregiously, *I'll Take My Stand* (1930), Dixie-based and linked to Fugitive-Agrarian ideology, gave a not-so-oblique sanction to segregation.[67] The hugely influential New Criticism to which it gave rise in flagship volumes like Allen Tate's *Reactionary Essays on Poetry and Ideas* (1936), John Crowe Ransom's *The New Criticism* (1941), Cleanth Brooks's *The Well Wrought Urn* (1947) and Cleanth Brooks's and Robert Penn Warren's *Understanding Poetry* (1938) and *Understanding Fiction* (1943) posited a formalism as norm. Literary values lay beyond race, ethnicity or history. Even a classic, if triumphalist, text like F. O. Matthiessen's *The American Renaissance* (1941), for all its proven intelligence, assumed a white-only pantheon of literary achievement.[68]

Occasionally, an early dissenting voice was to be heard. One such belonged to the now forgotten Ernest Boyd in his *Criticism in America: Its Function and Status* (1914). There, in language which retains its smack and whose implications were to linger well beyond his own time, he spoke of nothing other than Ku Klux Kriticism.[69]

Of late, whiteness has also begun to be thought a way of construing American fiction thought simply mainstream, and so ever unethnic or raceless. That has rarely ever been so, not least, and to intriguing effect, in a novel as canonical as Scott Fitzgerald's *The Great Gatsby* (1925), the work of a Jazz Age *Wunderkind* but also of an unforgetful Irish American. The outburst he attributes to Tom Buchanan on ' "The Rise of the Coloured Empires" by this man Goddard' wonderfully takes aims at end-of-civilisation race anxiety. He has Daisy's older-monied husband maunder on about 'scientific stuff', 'the dominant race' and 'This idea that we're Nordics . . . we've produced all the things that go to make civilization – oh, science and art, and all that'. Tom's whiteness, be it 'Nordic' or any other appellation, could hardly better have been made subject to ironic deflation.[70]

Whiteness as cultural ideology, in fact, can be advanced as a route into America's fiction of manners at large. Social caste in the novels of Henry James, William Dean Howells or Edith Wharton offers one bearing. Successor fare in the form of an American upper-crust white professional cadre is to be met with in the work of Louis Auchincloss and James Gould Cozzens. Postwar white suburbia has few more assiduous, or ironic, literary anatomists than John Updike in his Rabbit quartet (1960–90).

Bernard Malamud offers yet another bead in *The Tenants* (1970), with its portrait of two New York writers, Jewish and African American, contending for who can best voice the house of the nation. More latterly, is not metropolitan whiteness at issue in the New York drugs-and-affluence world of Jay McInerney's *Bright Lights, Big City* (1984)? Talk has also been frequent about a new white-rural Appalachia in bestsellers from James Dickey's *Deliverance* (1972), with its hunt format, hill-clan violence and religiosity, through to Charles Frazier's *Cold Mountain* (1997) and its historic re-envisioning of southern landscape. In Allan Gurganus's story-collection, *White People* (1990), the focus settles genially, but always with a nice satirical edge, upon whiteness as middle-class comportment and family.[71]

America's multicultural fictions abundantly supply their own quite alternative or counter-imaging. William Melvin Kelley's *dem* (1967), meaning them or white folks, gives an African American depiction of New York as two alien, near-irreal worlds, Harlem and white suburbia.[72] Scott Momaday's *House Made of Dawn* uses the elusive albino figure as a kind of witch, a distortion, through whom to locate his Native protagonist's view of whiteness.[73] Lorna Dee Cervantes's 'Poem for the Young White

Man Who Asked Me How I, an Intelligent, Well-Read Person, Could Believe in the War Between the Races' (1981) takes aim at white patronage and query.[74] Shawn Wong, to cite again from *Homebase*, personifies whiteness as the blonde teenage California girl who to his Chinese American narrator embodies 'the America that I am not'.[75] As to American creolisation, that has rarely been given keener inside expression than in Aunt Eloise's riff on white and black creoles in Leon Forrest's *Divine Days* ('they didn't need a Mardi Gras; they lived a costume ball, a perpetual masquerade, each and every day of their lives', p. 288).

But if these each take on whiteness as cultural styling, the assumed norm, they also belong to a continuance of controversy. For her part, Bharati Mukherjee, Bengali by birth, a Canadian immigrant, US citizen, and novelist, offers her own species of dissent at being thought ethnic. In 'A Four-Hundred-Year-Old Woman' (1992), she writes:

> I am an American writer, in the American mainstream . . . trying to extend it . . . I am not an Indian writer, not an exile, not an expatriate . . . I look on ghettoization – whether as a Bengali in India or as a hyphenated Indo-American in North America – as a temptation to be surmounted.[76]

In 'Becoming Post-White' (1997), Robert Elliot Fox cites a bumper sticker which reads 'The World's Most Endangered Species: The White Race'. This same white race he unhesitatingly pronounces 'the world's most fictional species'.[77]

The one view again calls up ethnicity as limit, burden even, in claiming access to full mainstream agency. The other looks to an end to any one dominant ethnicity, America as not only a multicultural tenancy but a compact of equals. The issues once more join. How, best, to understand American pluralism, hybridity, the multicultural in all its ramifications? Who speaks for whom? What, above all, are the fictions, literary and beyond, most in play?

Multicultural American Literature: Comparative Black, Native, Latino/a and Asian American Fictions, no less than the treasury of texts out of which it arises, is intended to offer something in the way of an appropriate answer.

NOTES

1. Ashley Montague (1942), *Man's Most Dangerous Myth: The Fallacy of Race*, 6th edn, Walnut Creek, CA. AltaMira Press, p. 45.
2. Leone Gaiter, in *The Los Angeles Times*, 25 October 1997.
3. Bonnie Kae Grover (1994), 'Growing up *White* in America?', reprinted in Donald McQuade and Christine McQuade (eds) (2000), *Seeing and Writing*, New York: Bedford/St Martin's Press, p. 377.
4. Desmond King (2000), *Making Americans: Immigration, Race, and the Origins of Diverse Democracy*, Cambridge, MA: Harvard University Press. A useful conspectus on one of the major components in cross-race demographics is to be found in Werner Sollors (ed.) (2000), *Interracialism: Black–White Intermarriage in American History, Literature, and Law*, New York: Oxford University Press.
5. Ralph Ellison, 'What's Wrong with the American Novel?', *American Scholar* (Autumn

1955), 464–503, reprinted in Maryemma Graham and Amritjit Singh (eds) (1995), *Conversations with Ralph Ellison*, Jackson, MS: University of Mississippi Press, p. 36.

6. A study like Neil Baldwin (2001), *Henry Ford and the Jews: The Mass Production of Hate*, London: Public Affairs, makes the relevant points in considerable detail.

7. James Baldwin, 'Stranger in the Village', republished in (1955) *Notes of a Native Son*, Boston, MA: Beacon Press. An earlier version of this analysis appears in my (1998) *Designs of Blackness: Mappings in the Literature and Culture of Afro-America*, London and Sterling, VA: Pluto Press.

8. Joseph P. Balaz (ed.) (1989), *Ho'onmanoa: An Anthology of Contemporary Hawai'ian Literature*, Honolulu: Ku Pa'la; Sucheng Chan (ed.) (1994), *Hmong Means Free: Life in Laos and America*, Philadelphia, PA: Temple University Press; Edwidge Danticat (ed.) (2001), *The Butterfly's Way: Voices from the Haitian Dyaspora in the United States*, New York: Soho; and Khaled Mattawa and Munir Akash (eds) (1999), *Post Gibran: Anthology of New Arab American Writing*, Syracuse, NY: Josor/Syracuse University Press. See, too, Sam Hamod (ed.) (1988), *Grapeleaves: A Century of Arab-American Poetry*, Salt Lake City, UT: University of Utah Press, and Lisa Suhair Majaj (1996), 'Arab American Literature and the Politics of Memory', in Amritjit Singh, Joseph T. Skerrett Jr and Robert E. Hogan, (eds), *Memory and Cultural Politics: New Approaches to American Ethnic Literatures*, Boston, MA: Northeastern Press, pp. 266–90.

9. Standard versions of this viewpoint are to be found in Roger Kimball (1990), *Tenured Radicals: How Politics has Corrupted Our Higher Education*, New York: Harper and Row, and Dinesh D'Souza (1999), *Illiberal Education: The Politics of Race and Sex on Campus*, New York: Maxwell.

10. Among the better-known accounts can be included Gayatri Chakravorty Spivak (1987), *In Other Worlds: Essays in Cultural Politics*, New York: Methuen, and (1999), *A Critique of Post-Colonial Reason: Towards a History of the Vanishing Present*, Cambridge, MA: Harvard University Press; E. San Juan Jr (1992), *Racial Formations/Critical Transformations: Articulations of Power in Ethnic and Racial Studies in the United States*, Atlantic Highlands, NJ: Humanities Press, (1998a), *Beyond Postcolonial Theory*, New York: St Martin's Press, and (1998b), *From Exile to Diaspora: Versions of the Filipino Experience in the United States*, Boulder, CO: Westview Press.

11. Randolph S. Bourne (1916), 'Trans-National America', *Atlantic Monthly*, 97 (July), reprinted in Randolph S. Bourne (1964), *War and the Intellectuals: Collected Essays, 1915–1919*, New York: Harper & Row.

12. Ronald T. Takaki (1993), *A Different Mirror: A History of Multicultural America*, Boston, MA: Little, Brown. Other relevant accounts include Michael Omi and Howard Winant (1986, 2nd edn 1994), *Racial Formation in the United States*, New York: Routledge and Kegan Paul, and Leonard Dinnerstein, Roger L. Nichols and David M. Reimers (1996), *Natives and Strangers: A Multicultural History of Americans*, New York: Oxford University Press.

13. John Skow, review of *The Joy Luck Club*, *Time*, 27 March 1989.

14. In this connection, see also Reginald Horsman (1981), *Race and Manifest Destiny: The Origins of American Racial Anglo-Saxonism*, Cambridge, MA: Harvard University, and Richard Brookhiser (1991), *The Way of the WASP*, New York: Free Press.

15. In 'American Exceptionalism Reconsidered: Anglo-Saxon Ethnogenesis in the "Universal" Nation, 1776–1850', *Journal of American Studies*, 33:3 (December 1999), 437–57, Eric Kaufman helpfully analyses how WASP ethnicity early became a code, a 'myth-symbol complex', for Americanism. He lists the components of this kind of 'ethnonationalism' as follows: 'a sense of election (Puritan), a myth of exclusive genealogical descent (Anglo-Saxon), a set of cultural boundary markers ("WASP"), a process of dominant-conformity (Anglo-conformity), a life-style representation (Yeoman), and a communal Golden Age (Jefferson's Republic) to which the group seeks to return' (p. 156).

16. Few accounts of Jefferson and Hemings have proved more controversial for their excavation of race and relationship than that of Fawn Brodie (1974), *Thomas Jefferson: An Intimate History*, New York: Norton. More recently, and based on conferences in Virginia in 1999 and 2000, the issues have been re-aired (not least with reference to DNA as much as to Madison Hemings) in Jan Lewis and Peter S. Onuf (eds) (1999), *Sally Hemings and Thomas Jefferson: History, Memory, and Civil Culture*, Charlottesville, VA: University of Virginia Press.

17. *Annie Oakley*, directed by George Stevens, 1935; *Calamity Jane*, directed by David Butler, 1953.

18. For an excellent synopsis, see Larry McMurtry (2000), 'Inventing the West', *The New York Review of Books*, 47:13 (August), 24–8. Ishmael Reed (1969), *Yellow Back Radio Broke-Down*, New York: Doubleday.

19. For the black peopling of the west, see especially Nell Irwin Painter (1977), *Exodusters: Black Migration to Kansas after Reconstruction*, New York: Knopf.

20. *450 Años del Pueblo Chicano/450 Years of Chicano History*, Albuquerque, NM: Chicano Communication Center (1976), p. 25. A spirited update of the whiteness/Chicanismo equation can be found in Angie Chabram-Dernersian (1997), 'On the Social Construction of Whiteness within Selected Chicano/a Discourses', in Ruth Frankenberg (ed.), *Displacing Whiteness: Essays in Social and Cultural Criticism*, Durham, NC and London: Duke University Press, pp. 107–64.

21. *The Economist*, Millennial Special Edition, vol. 353, no. 8151 (31 December 1999), pp. 49–50.

22. In this respect, it is useful to compare evolving accounts of the impact of race and ethnicity on the formation of American national identity. Where, say, an influential study like Sacvan Bercovitch (1975), *The Puritan Origins of the American Self*, New Haven, CT: Yale University Press, invokes a founding discourse of theological mission, and exceptionalism, a more recent account like Jared Gardner (1998), *Master Plot: Race and the Founding of American Literature, 1787–1845*, Baltimore, MD: The Johns Hopkins Press, emphasises early fantasies of 'an American race', both as the 'purification' of the old European population mix and to be set against Afro-America as slavery and Native peoples as savagery.

23. James M. McPherson (1998), *Is Blood Thicker than Water? Crises in Nationalism in the Modern World*, New York: Random House/Vintage, p. 35.

24. Important contributions include Reginald Horsman (1981), *Race and Manifest Destiny: The Origins of American Racial Anglo-Saxonism*, Cambridge, MA: Harvard University Press; R. D. Alba (1990), *Ethnic Identity: The Transformation of White America*, New Haven, CT: Yale University Press; David R. Roediger (1990), *Towards the Abolition of Whiteness: Essays in Race, Politics and Working-Class History*, London and New York: Verso, and (1991) *The Ways of Whiteness: Race and the Making of the American Working Class*, London and New York: Verso; Phyllis Palmer et al. (1993), 'To Deconstruct Race, De-construct Whiteness', *American Quarterly*, 45:2 (June), 281–94; Theodore W. Allen (1994), *The Invention of the White Race, Volume One: Racial Oppression and Social Control*, New York and London: Verso, and (1997) *The Invention of the White Race, Volume Two: The Origins of Racial Oppression in Anglo-America*, New York and London: Verso; M. Novick (1995), *White Lies, White Power*, Monroe, ME: Common Courage Press; Ian F. Haney-López (1996), *White by Law: The Legal Construction of Race*, New York: New York University Press; Ruth Frankenberg (ed.) (1997), *Displacing Whiteness: Essays in Social and Cultural Criticism*, Durham, NC and London: Duke University Press; Mike Hill (ed.) (1997), *Whiteness: A Critical Reader*, New York: New York University Press; Robert Elliot Fox (1997), 'Becoming Post-White', in Ishmael Reed (ed.), *MultiAmerica: Essays on Cultural Wars and Cultural Peace*, New York: Viking Penguin, pp. 6–17 and Pepi Leistnya; (1998), 'White Ethnic Unconsciousness', *Cultural Circles*, 2 (Spring), 33–51.

25. Valerie Babb (1998), *Whiteness Visible: The Meaning of Whiteness in American Literature and Culture*, New York: New York University Press, pp. 4–5.

26. Toni Morrison (1992), *Playing in the Dark: Whiteness and the Literary Imagination*, Cambridge, MA: Harvard University Press.

27. Shelley Fisher Fishkin (1991), *Was Huck Black? Mark Twain and African American Voices*, New York: Oxford University Press.

28. 'Morrison, la guerrière', interview with Josyane Savigneau, *Le Monde: Livres*, 29 May 1998, pp. V–VI (my translation).

29. Eric Liu (1998), *The Accidental Asian: Notes of a Native Speaker*, New York: Random House, p. 35.

30. For an account of America's changing demography based on the 1990 census figures, see Sam Roberts (1993), *Who We Are: A Portrait of America Based on the Latest US Census*, New York: Times Books/Random House, especially Chapter IV, 'Our Changing Complexion', and Chapter V, 'Our National Obsession'.

31. Noel Ignatiev (1995), *How the Irish Became White*, New York: Routledge. Another helpful overview is to be found in Donald Harman Akenson (1998), *The Irish Diaspora: A Primer*, Toronto: P. D. Meany Company, especially Chapters 9 and 18, 'North America'.

32. Since the seventeenth century, an estimated ten million Irish have emigrated to America – an astonishing figure, given so small a country.

33. Peter Finley Dunne, 'Mr Dooley' columns: see Charles Fanning (ed.) (1978), *Peter Finely Dunne and Mr Dooley: The Chicago Years*, Lexington, KY: The University Press of Kentucky; James T. Farrell (1935), *Studs Lonigan: A Trilogy*, New York: Vanguard Press; Edwin O'Connor (1956), *The Last Hurrah*, Boston, MA: Little, Brown; Mary McCarthy (1957), *Memories of a Catholic Girlhood*, New York: Harcourt, Brace; William Kennedy (1983), *Ironweed*, New York: Viking Press; and Frank McCourt (1996), *Angela's Ashes*, New York: Scribner. For overall accounts, see Daniel J. Casey and Robert E. Rhodes (eds) (1979), *Irish-American Fiction: Essays in Criticism*, New York: MS Press; Daniel J. Casey and Robert E. Rhodes (eds) (1989), *Modern Irish American Fiction: A Reader*, Syracuse, NY: Syracuse University Press, and Charles Fanning (1990, 2nd edn 1999), *The Irish Voice in America: 250 Years of Irish-American Fiction*, Lexington, KY: The University Press of Kentucky.

34. Kurt Vonnegut (1969), *Slaughterhouse-Five; or The Children's Crusade, A Duty-Dance with Death*, New York: Delacorte Press. For a timely essay-collection, see Winfried Fluck and Werner Sollors (eds) (2002), *German? American? Literature?: New Directions in German-American Studies*, New York: Peter Lang.

35. A comprehensive account of Polish American literary tradition is offered in Thomas J. Gladsky (1992), *Princes, Peasants and Other Polish Selves: Ethnicity in American Literature*, Amherst, MA: The University of Massachusetts Press.

36. Ole Edvart Rølvaag (1927), *Giants in the Earth: A Saga of the Prairie*, New York: Harper & Brothers. Critical overviews are to be found in Dorothy Burton Skardal (1974), *The Divided Heart: Scandinavian Immigrant Experience through Literary Sources*, Lincoln, NB: University of Nebraska Press, and Orm Overland (1996), *The Western Home: A Literary History of Norwegian America*, Northfield, MN: Norwegian-American Historical Society, reprinted (2002), Champaign, IL: University of Illinois Press.

37. Greek America has been studied in Alexander Karanikas (1981), *Hellenes and Hellions: Greek Characters in American Fiction*, Urbana, IL: Illinois University Press; Yiorgas Kalogeras (1985), 'Greek-American Literature: An Introduction and a Bibliographic Supplement', *Ethnic Forum*, 5, 106–28; and George A. Kourvetaris (1997), *Studies in Greek Americans*, New York: Columbia University Press.

38. James Baldwin (1962), *Another Country*, New York: Dial, p. 297.

39. Helen Barolini (1979), *Umbertina*, New York: Seaview, and Mario Puzo (1969), *The Godfather*, New York: Putnam. Critical accounts include Anthony Julian Tamburri,

Paolo Giordano and Fred L. Gardaphé (eds) (1991), *From the Margin: Writings in Italian Americana*, West Lafayette, IN: Purdue University Press, and Fred L. Gardaphé (1996), *Italian Signs, American Streets: The Evolution of Italian American Literature*, Durham, NC: Duke University Press.

40. Matthew Frye Jacobson (1999), *Whiteness of a Different Color: European Immigrants and the Alchemy of Race*, Cambridge, MA: Harvard University Press. The story is also told in Karen Brodkin (1999), *How Jews Became White Folks and What That Says about Race in America*, New Brunswick, NJ: Rutgers University Press.

41. Alfred Kazin (1951), *A Walker in the City*, New York: Harcourt, Brace, and (1962) *Starting Out in the Thirties*, Boston: Little, Brown, and (1978) *New York Jew*, New York: Knopf; and Irving Howe (1976), *World of Our Fathers*, New York: Harcourt Brace Jovanovich, reprinted as (1976), *The Immigrant Jews of New York*, London: Routledge & Kegan Paul. Standard overall literary accounts include Robert Alter (1969), *After the Tradition: Essays on Modern Jewish Writing*, New York: Dutton; Mark Schechner (1987), *After the Revolution: Studies in Contemporary Jewish-American Imagination*, Bloomington, IN: Indiana University Press; and Sanford Pinsker (1992), *Jewish American Fiction*, New York: Twayne.

42. Aurora Levins Morales and Rosario Morales (1986), *Getting Home Alive*, Houston, TX: Arte Público Press.

43. Barry Gifford and Lawrence Lee (1994), *Jack's Book: An Oral Biography of Jack Kerouac*, New York: St Martin's Press, p. 165.

44. Rich Cohen (1998), *Tough Jews*, New York: Simon & Schuster.

45. A full account of this episode appears in Allan Keiler (2000), *Marian Anderson: A Singer's Journey*, New York: Scribner.

46. Relevant analysis is to be found in Matt Wray and Annalee Newitz (eds) (1997), *White Trash: Race and Class in America*, New York: Routledge.

47. For accounts, see Howard Zinn (1980), *A People's History of the US*, London: Longman, especially p. 36.

48. For an analysis of this legacy, see Andrew Hook (1999), *From Goosecreek to Gandercleugh: Studies in Scottish-American Literary and Cultural History*, East Linton, Scotland: Tuckwell Press, pp. 197–201.

49. The Chin murder, along with the Korean–Black confrontation at the Red Apple Market in Brooklyn, the issue of hiring a non-Asian lead in the Broadway production of *Miss Saigon*, and the Los Angeles Korean–Black confrontations throughout the 1990s, are given sharp scrutiny in Helen Zia (2001), *Asian American Dreams: The Emergence of an American People*, New York: Farrar, Straus and Giroux. See also the film documentary *Who Killed Vincent Chin?*, directed by Renee Tajima, PBS, 1988.

50. Thomas Chittum (1999), *Civil War II*. Show Low, AZ: American Eagle Publications. A vivid account is to be found in James Ridgeway (1990), *Blood in the Face: The KKK, Aryan Nations, Nazi Skinheads and the Rise of a New White Culture*, New York: Thunder's Mouth.

51. For a summary, and genealogy, of the best-known of these terms, see Randall Kennedy (2002), *Nigger: The Strange Case of a Troublesome Word*, New York: Pantheon.

52. Relevant materials are to be found in David Turley (ed.) (1998), *American Religion: Literary Resources and Documents*, Robertsbridge, Sussex: Helm Publications.

53. A useful recent overview is to be found in Jane I. Smith (1999), *Islam in America* New York: Columbia University Press.

54. The scholarship on Wayne is voluminous. But the following are especially helpful: Joan Didion, 'John Wayne: A Love Song', *Saturday Evening Post*, 14 August 1967, pp. 76–9; Maurice Zolotow (1974), *Shooting Star: A Biography of John Wayne*, New York: Simon and Schuster; Randy Roberts and James S. Olson (1995), *John Wayne: An American*, New York: Free Press; Ronald L. Davis (1997), *Duke: The Life and Image of John Wayne*, Norman, OK: University of Oklahoma Press; Gary Wills (1997), *John Wayne's America*, New York: Simon and Schuster.

55. Louis Owens (1998), 'The Invention of John Wayne', *Mixedblood Messages: Literature, Film, Family, Place*, Norman, OK: University of Oklahoma Press, pp. 100–1.
56. In this connection, see Jacquelyn Kilpatrick (1999), *Celluloid Indians: Native Americans and Film*, Lincoln, NB: University of Nebraska Press.
57. This issue has been brilliantly explored in John Cawelti (1998), 'Post(Modern) Westerns', *Paradoxa: Studies in World Literary Genres*, 4:9, 3–18.
58. A comprehensive account is given in Sarah Banet-Weiser (1999), *The Most Beautiful Girl in the World: Beauty Pageants and National Identity*, Berkeley, CA: The University of California Press. Other contextual scholarship includes the following landmarks: Betty Friedan (1963), *The Feminine Mystique*, New York: Norton; Naomi Wolf (1991), *The Beauty Myth*, New York: Morrow; and Camille Paglia (1994), *Vamps and Tramps*, New York: Vintage Books.
59. Tom Wolfe (1979), *The Right Stuff*, New York: Farrar, Straus and Giroux.
60. An excellent analysis of Presley and the 'blackness' of his music is to be found in Michael T. Bertrand (2000), *Race, Rock and Elvis*, Urbana, IL and London: University of Illinois Press. Recalling how, even at the height of his popularity from 1957 into the early 1960s, Presley provoked murmurings about his black debts, he writes as follows: 'at a time when many southern whites persisted in denigrating their black neighbors as inferior, Presley seemed intent on acknowledging his black roots. Many recognized that he had an "unusual" white singing style that was derived from black music. In the words of one startled disk jockey, he sang "hillbilly in R-and-B time. Can you figure that out?" "I got my singing style listening to colored spiritual quartets down South", Presley replied. Similarly, he later told an audience that rock'n'roll "stemmed from gospel music or rhythm and blues and gospel mixed with country and western".' Other relevant accounts include Philip H. Ennis (1992), *The Seventh Stream: The Emergence of Rock 'n' Roll in American Popular Music*, Hanover, NH: Wesleyan University Press, and (1995) *All Shook Up: Mississippi Roots of Popular Music*, Mississippi Department of Archives and History; and James Miller (1999), *Almost Grown: The Rise of Rock*, London: Heinemann.
61. The US Open tennis final in September 2001 carried much of the relevant symbolism: the two Williams sisters, Afro-America's probably most visible female athletes, competing in the Flushing Meadow stadium named after Arthur Ashe as tennis's best-known black player, and (with the exception of family and a number of black notables) before a crowd overwhelmingly representative of white Middle America.
62. A fuller account can be found in Frank H. Wu (2002), *Yellow: Race in America Beyond Black and White*, New York: Basic Books, p. 21.
63. James Crawford (2000), *At War with Diversity: US Language Policy in an Age of Anxiety*, Clevedon England and Buffas, NY: Multilingual Matters, p. 31. For a further airing of the issue, see Roseann Dueñas González and Ildikó Melis (eds) (2000), *Language Ideologies: Critical Perspectives on the Official English Movement*, Urbana, IL: National Council of Teachers of English.
64. Werner Sollors (ed.) (1998), *Multilingual America: Transnationalism, Ethnicity, and the Languages of American Literature*, New York: New York University Press.
65. Domenico Maceri, 'Language Handicap Hurting America', *The Japan Times*, 28 October 2001, p. 19.
66. An excellent summary of the issue is to be found in Wolfgang Pauels (1998), 'Language Diversity and Cultural Identity in the USA – A European View of a Controversy', *ZAA (Zeitschrift für Anglistik und Amerikanistik): A Quarterly of Language, Literature and Culture*, 46:3, 193–203. See also James Crawford (ed.) (1992), *Language Loyalties: A Source Book on the Official English Controversy*, Chicago, IL and London: The University of Chicago Press.
67. Twelve Southerners (1930), *I'll Take My Stand: The South and Agrarian Tradition*, New York: Harper & Brothers.

68. Fred Pattee (1896), *A History of American Literature*, New York: Silver, Burdett and Co. Pattee's other influential, and equally 'white', writings include (1915), *A History of American Literature since 1870*, New York: D. Appleton-Century Co., (1919) *Century Readings for a Course in American Literature*, New York: Century Co., and (1935) *The First Century of American Literature*, New York: D. Appleton-Century Co. See also Allen Tate (1936), *Reactionary Essays on Poetry and Ideas*, New York: C. Scribner's Sons; John Crowe Ransom (1941), *The New Criticism*, Norfolk, CT: New Directions; Cleanth Brooks (1947), *The Well Wrought Urn*, New York: Reynal & Hitchcock; Cleanth Brooks and Robert Penn Warren (1938), *Understanding Poetry*, New York: H. Holt, and (1943) *Understanding Fiction*, New York: F. S. Crofts & Company; and F. O. Matthiessen (1941), *American Renaissance: Art and Expression in the Age of Emerson and Whitman*, New York: Oxford University Press.

69. Ernest Boyd (1924), 'Ku Klux Kriticism', in *Criticism in America: Its Function and Status*, New York: Harcourt, Brace and Co., pp. 309–30. I am most grateful to Dr Joe Lockard for calling my attention to Ernest Boyd's work.

70. Scott Fitzgerald (1925), *The Great Gatsby*, New York: Scribner, pp. 13–14.

71. John Updike (1960), *Rabbit Run*, New York: Knopf, (1971) *Rabbit Redux*, New York: Knopf, (1981) *Rabbit Is Rich*, New York: Knopf, and (1990) *Rabbit at Rest*, New York: Knopf; Bernard Malamud (1971), *The Tenants*, New York: Farrar, Straus and Giroux; Jay McInerney (1984), *Bright Lights, Big City*, New York: Vintage Contemporaries; James Dickey (1997), *Deliverance*, Boston, MA: Houghton Mifflin; Charles Frazier (1997), *Cold Mountain*, New York: Atlantic Monthly Press; and Allan Gurganus (1991), *White People*, New York: Knopf.

72. William Melvin Kelley (1967), *dem*, New York: Doubleday.

73. N. Scott Momaday (1968), *House Made of Dawn*, New York: Harper & Row.

74. Lorna Dee Cervantes (1981), *Emplumada*, Pittsburgh, PA: University of Pittsburgh Press. This poem has a near-companion piece in 'For White Poets Who Would Be Indian' by the Hopi-Miwot poet Wendy Rose. See Wendy Rose (1994), *Bone Dance: New and Selected Poems 1963–1993*, Tucson, AZ: University of Arizona Press.

75. Shawn Wong (1979), *Homebase*, New York: I. Reed Books.

76. Bharati Mukherjee (1980), 'A Four-Hundred-Year-Old-Woman', in Janet Sternburg (ed.), *The Writer on Her Work*, New York: W. W. Norton, pp. 33–8.

77. Robert Elliot Fox (1997), 'Becoming Post-White', in Ishmael Reed (ed.), *MultiAmerica: Essays on Cultural Wars and Cultural Peace*, New York: Viking Penguin, p. 12.

Primary Bibliography

Acosta, Oscar Zeta (1972, reprinted 1989), *The Autobiography of a Brown Buffalo*, San Francisco, CA: Straight Arrow; New York: Vintage Books.
——— (1973, reprinted 1989), *The Revolt of the Cockroach People*, San Francisco, CA: Straight Arrow; New York: Vintage Books.
——— (1996), *Oscar 'Zeta' Acosta: The Uncollected Works*, ed. Ilan Stavans, Houston, TX: Arte Público Press.
Alexander, Meena (1993), *Fault Lines*, New York: The Feminist Press at the City of New York.
——— (1996), *The Shock of Arrival: Reflections on Postcolonial Experience*, Boston, MA: South End Press.
Alexie, Sherman (1993), *The Lone Ranger and Tonto Fistfight in Heaven*, New York: Atlantic Monthly Press.
——— (1995), *Reservation Blues*, New York: Atlantic Monthly Press.
Allen, Paula Gunn (1983), *The Woman Who Owned the Shadows*, San Francisco, CA: Spinsters Ink.
Alurista (1971), *Floricanto en Aztlán*, Los Angeles, CA: UCLA Chicano Studies Center Publications.
Alvarez, Julia (1991), *How the García Girls Lost Their Accents*, Chapel Hill, NC: Algonquin Books of Chapel Hill.
——— (1995), *The Other Side/El Otro Lado*, New York: Dutton.
——— (1997a), *¡Yo!*, New York: Plume.
——— (1997b), *In the Name of Salomé*, Chapel Hill, NC: Algonquin Books of Chapel Hill.
——— (1998, reprinted 1999), *Something to Declare*, Chapel Hill, NC: Algonquin Books of Chapel Hill; New York: Penguin/Plume.
Anaya, Rudolfo (1972), *Bless Me, Ultima*, Berkeley, CA: Quinto Sol Publications.
——— (1979), *Heart of Aztlán*, Berkeley, CA: Editorial Justa Publications.
——— (1986), *A Chicano in China*, Albuquerque, NM: University of New Mexico Press.
——— (1992), *Albuquerque*, Albuquerque, NM: University of New Mexico Press.
——— (1999), *Shaman Winter*, New York: Time Warner.
Andrews, Raymond (1978), *Appalachee Red*, New York: Dial Press.
Angelou, Maya (1969), *I Know Why the Caged Bird Sings*, New York: Random House.
Anzaldúa, Gloria (1987), *Borderlands/La Frontera: The New Mestiza*, San Francisco, CA: Aunt Lute Books.
Apess, William (1829), *A Son of the Forest: The Experience of William Apess, a Native of the Forest*, New York: self-published.
Arias, Ron (1975, reprinted 1978), *The Road to Tamazunchale*, Reno, NV: West Coast Poetry Review; reprinted Albuquerque, NM: Pajarito Publications.
Baca, Jimmy Santiago (1987), *Martín and Meditations on the South Valley*, New York: New Directions.

Baldwin, James (1955), *Notes of a Native Son*, Boston, MA: Beacon Press.
—— (1961), *Nobody Knows My Name: More Notes of a Native Son*, New York: Dial.
—— (1963), *The Fire Next Time*, New York: Dial.
—— (1985), *The Price of the Ticket: Collected Non-Fiction 1948–1985*, New York: St Martin's/ Marek.
Bambara, Toni Cade (1971), *Gorilla, My Love*, New York: Random House.
Baraka *see* Jones
Barolini, Helen (1979), *Umbertina*, New York: Seaview.
Barrio, Raymond (1971, 1984), *The Plum Plum Pickers*, Sunnyvale, CA: Ventura Press; reprinted, with introduction and bibliography, Binghamton, NY: Bilingual Press/Editorial Bilingüe.
Bell, Betty Louise (1994), *Faces in the Moon*, Norman, OK: University of Oklahoma Press.
Black Elk (1932, 1979), *Black Elk Speaks*, Lincoln, NB: University of Nebraska Press.
Bradley, David (1981), *The Chaneyville Incident*, New York: Harper and Row.
Bulosan, Carlos (1946, 1973), *America is in the Heart*, New York: Harcourt, Brace and Company; reprinted Seattle, WA: University of Washington Press.
—— (1978), *The Philippines is in the Heart*, Quezon City: New Day Publishers.
Butler, Octavia (1976), *Patternmaster*, New York: Warner Books.
Campbell, Maria (1973, 1982), *Halfbreed*, New York: Saturday Review Press; reprinted Lincoln, NB: University of Nebraska Press.
Candelaria, Nash (1977, 1985), *Memories of the Alhambra*, Palo Alto, CA: Cibola Press; reprinted Ypsilanti, MI: Bilingual Press/Editorial Bilingüe.
—— (1982), *Not by the Sword*, Ypsilanti, MI: Bilingual Press/Editorial Bilingüe.
—— (1985), *Inheritance of Strangers*, Binghamton, NY: Bilingual Press/Editorial Bilingüe.
Cano, Daniel (1991), *Pepe Rios*, Houston, TX: Arte Público Press.
Cao, Lan (1997), *Monkey Bridge*, New York: Viking.
Cary, Lorene (1991), *Black Ice*, New York: Knopf.
Castellano, Olivia (1993), 'The Comstock Journals', extracted in Tiffany Ana López (ed.), *Growing up Chicano/a*, New York: Morrow.
Castillo, Ana (1986), *The Mixquiahuala Letters*, Binghamton, NY: Bilingual Press/Editorial Bilingüe.
—— (1990), *Sapogonia*, Houston, TX: Bilingual Press/Editorial Bilingüe.
—— (1993), *So Far from God*, New York: W. W. Norton.
—— (1994), *Massacre of the Dreamers: Essays on Xicanisma*, Albuquerque, NM: University of New Mexico Press.
Cha, Theresa Hak Kyung (ed.) (1981), *Apparatus Cinematographic Apparatus: Selected Writings*, New York: Tanam Press.
—— (1982), *DICTEE*, New York: Tanam Press.
Chang, Diana (1956), *The Frontiers of Love*, New York: Random.
Chase-Riboud, Barbara (1979), *Sally Hemings*, New York: Crown.
Chávez, Denise (1986), *The Last of the Menu Girls*, Houston, TX: Arte Público Press.
—— (1994), *Face of an Angel*, New York: Farrar, Straus and Giroux.
Chavez, Linda (1991), *Out of the Barrio: Towards a New Politics of Hispanic Assimilation*, New York: Basic Books.
Chin, Frank (1972), *The Chickencoop Chinaman* and *The Year of the Dragon*, Seattle, WA: University of Washington Press.
—— (1988), *The Chinaman Pacific & Frisco R.R. Co.*, Minneapolis, MN: Coffee House Press.
—— (1991), *Donald Duk*, Minneapolis, MN: Coffee House Press.
Chin, Marilyn (1994), *The Phoenix Gone, the Terrace Empty*, Minneapolis, MN: Milkweed Editions.
Chu, Louis (1961), *Eat a Bowl of Tea*, New York: Lyle Stuart.
Cisneros, Sandra (1983), *The House on Mango Street*, Houston: Arte Público Press.

—— (1991), *Woman Hollering Creek and Other Stories*, New York: Random House.

Cleaver, Eldridge (1968), *Soul on Ice*, New York: McGraw Hill.

Cook-Lynn, Elizabeth (1991), *From the River's Edge*, New York: Arcade.

—— (1996), *Why I Can't Read Wallace Stegner and Other Essays: A Tribal Voice*, Madison, WI: University of Wisconsin Press.

Cumpián, Carlos (1991), *Coyote Sun*, Chicago, IL: MARCH/Abrazo Press.

Danticat, Edwidge (1994), *Breath, Eyes, Memory: A Novel*, New York: Vintage.

—— (1995), *Krik? Krak!*, New York: Soho Press.

Davis, Angela (1974), *An Autobiography*, New York: Random House.

Delany, Samuel R. (1979–87), *Return to Everyon* (series), New York: Bantam; Hanover, NH: University Press of New England.

Deloria, Vine (1969, 1988), *Custer Died for Your Sins: An Indian Manifesto*, New York: Macmillan; reprinted Norman, OK: University of Oklahoma Press.

Demby, William (1965), *The Catacombs*, New York: Pantheon.

Díaz, Junot (1996), *Drown*, New York: Riverhead.

Dinh, Tran Van (1983), *Blue Dragon, White Tiger: A Tet Story*, Philadelphia, PA: Tri-Am Press.

Dixon, Melvin (1989), *Trouble the Water*, Boulder, CO: University of Colorado and Fiction Collective 2.

Douglass, Frederick (1845), *Narrative of the Life of Frederick Douglass, an American Slave, Written by Himself*, Boston, MA: The Anti-Slavery Society.

Eastman, George (1902, 1922), *Indian Boyhood*, Boston, MA: Little, Brown.

Eaton, Edith a. k. a. Sui Sin Far (1912), *Mrs Spring Fragrance*, Chicago, IL: A. C. McClurg.

Eaton, Winnifred aka Onoto Watanna (1899), *Miss Numè of Japan: A Japanese American Romance*, Chicago, IL: Rand McNally.

Ellis, Trey (1988), *Platitudes*, New York: Vintage.

—— (1993), *Home Repairs*, New York: Simon and Schuster.

Ellison, Ralph (1952), *Invisible Man* (Thirtieth Anniversary Edition, 1982), New York: Random House.

—— (1964), *Shadow and Act*, New York: Random House.

—— (1996), *Flying Home and Other Stories*, New York: Random House.

—— (1999), *Juneteenth*, New York: Random House.

Erdrich, Louise (1984, expanded version 1993), *Love Medicine*, New York: Henry Holt and Company.

—— (1986), *The Beet Queen*, New York: Henry Holt and Company.

—— (1988), *Tracks*, New York: Henry Holt and Company.

Fernández, Roberto (1982), *La vida es un especial/Life is a Bargain*, Houston, TX: Arte Público Press.

Flowers, A. R. (1986), *De Mojo Blues: De Quest of Highjohn the Conqueror*, New York: E. P. Dutton.

Forrest, Leon (1973), *There is a Tree More Ancient than Eden*, New York: Random House.

—— (1977), *The Bloodworth Orphans*, New York: Random House.

—— (1984), *Two Wings to Veil My Face*, New York: Random House.

—— (1992), *Divine Days*, Chicago, IL: Another Chicago Press; reprinted (1993) New York: W. W. Norton.

Frazier, Charles (1997), *Cold Mountain*, New York: Atlantic Monthly Press.

Gaines, Ernest (1971), *The Autobiography of Miss Jane Pittman*, New York: Dial.

Garcia, Cristina (1992), *Dreaming in Cuban*, New York: Knopf.

Glancy, Diane (1992), *Claiming Breath*, Lincoln, NB: University of Nebraska Press.

—— (1993), *Firesticks*, Norman, OK: University of Oklahoma Press.

Gómez-Peña, Guillermo (1991), *Border Brujo, Drama Review*, 35: 3, 49–66.

—— (1993), *Warrior for Gringostroika*, St Paul, MN: Graywolf Press.

Gonzalez, Ray (1993), *Memory Fever*, Seattle, WA: Broken Moon Press.

González, Rodolfo (1972), *I am Joaquín/Yo Soy Joaquín*, New York: Bantam Books.

Gurganus, Allan (1991), *White People*, New York: Knopf.

Guy, Rosa (1983), *A Measure of Time*, New York: Holt, Rinehart and Winston.

Hagedorn, Jessica (1990), *Dogeaters*, New York: Random House/Penguin.

Hale, Janet Campbell (1993), *Bloodlines*, New York: Random House.

Harper, Frances E. W. (1892), *Iola Leroy or Shadows Uplifted*, Boston, MA: James H. Earle). Reissued (1987), with introduction by Hazel V. Carby, *Iola Leroy or Shadows Uplifted*, Boston, MA: Beacon Press.

Hijuelos, Oscar (1989), *The Mambo Kings Play Songs of Love*, New York: Farrar, Straus and Giroux.

Hilden, Patricia Penn (1995), *When Nickels Were Indians: An Urban Mixed-Blood Story*, Washington, DC: Smithsonian Institution Press.

Himes, Chester (1957), *For Love of Imabelle*, Greenwich, CT: Fawcett. Republished (1965) as *A Rage in Harlem*, New York: Avon Books.

—— (1972), *The Quality of Hurt*, New York: Doubleday.

—— (1976), *My Life of Absurdity*, New York: Doubleday.

Hinojosa, Rolando (1976), *Klail City y sus alrededores*, Havana, Cuba: Casas de las Americas.

—— (1983), *The Valley*, Ypsilanti, MI: Bilingual Press/Editorial Bilingüe.

—— (1987) *Klail City*, author's English-language translation, Houston, TX: Arte Público Press.

Hogan, Linda (1988), *Savings*, Minneapolis, MN: Coffee House Press.

—— (1990), *Mean Spirit*, New York: Athenaeum.

Hongo, Garrett (1982), *Yellow Light*, Middletown, CT: Wesleyan University Press.

—— (1995a), *Volcano: A Memoir of Hawai'i*, New York: Knopf.

—— (ed.) (1995b), *Under Western Eyes: Personal Essays from Asian America*, New York: Anchor/Doubleday.

Houston, Jeanne Wakatsuki and James D. Houston (1973), *Farewell to Manzanar*, Boston, MA: Houghton Mifflin.

Hughes, Langston (1940), *The Big Sea*, New York: Knopf.

—— (1956), *I Wonder as I Wander*, New York: Rinehart.

—— (1965), *The Best of Simple*, New York: Hill and Wang.

Hurston, Zora Neale (1942), *Dust Tracks on a Road: An Autobiography*, Philadelphia, PA: Lippincott.

Inada, Lawson Fusao (1971), *Before the War: Poems as They Happened*, New York: Morrow.

Islas, Arturo (1984, 1991), *The Rain God*, New York: Avon Books.

Jackson, George (1970), *Soledad Brother: The Prison Letters of George Jackson*, New York: Random House.

Jacobs, Harriet (1861, 1987), ed. Jean Fagan Yellin, *Incidents in the Life of a Slave Girl, Written by Herself*, Cambridge, MA: Harvard University Press.

Jen, Gish (1991), *Typical American*, Boston, MA: Houghton Mifflin/Seymour Lawrence.

Johnson, James Weldon (1912), *The Autobiography of an Ex-Colored Man*, Boston, MA: Sherman French.

—— (1933), *Along This Way: The Autobiography of James Weldon Johnson*, New York: Viking.

Jones, LeRoi/Imamu Baraka, Amiri (1969), *Black Magic: Collected Poetry, 1961–1967*, Indianapolis, IN: Bobbs-Merrill.

—— (1984), *The Autobiography of LeRoi Jones/Amiri Baraka*, New York: Alfred A. Knopf.

Jordan, June (1981), *Civil Wars*, Boston, MA: Beacon.

Kadohata, Cynthia (1989), *The Floating World*, New York: Viking.

Kenan, Randall (1989), *A Visitation of the Spirits*, New York: Grove Press.

Kim, Ronyoung (1986), *Clay Walls*, Sag Harbor, NY: Permanent Press.

King, Thomas (1990, 1997), *Medicine River*, Markham, Ontario and New York: Viking.

—— (1993), *Green Grass, Running Water*, Boston, MA: Houghton Mifflin.

Kingston, Maxine Hong (1977), *The Woman Warrior: Memoirs of a Girlhood among Ghosts*, New York: Vintage Books.

—— (1980), *China Men*, New York: Knopf.

—— (1989), *Trickmaster Monkey: His Fake Book*, New York: Knopf.

Kogawa, Joy (1982), *Obasan*, Boston, MA: David R. Godine.

Larsen, Nella (1929), *Passing*, New York and London: Knopf.

Law-Yone, Wendy (1983), *The Coffin Tree*, New York: Knopf.

Lee, Chang-rae (1995), *Native Speaker*, New York: Riverhead Books.

—— (1999), *A Gesture Life*, New York: Riverhead Books.

Lee, Gus (1991), *China Boy*, New York: Dutton.

Lee, Li-Young (1990), *The City in which I Love You*, New York: BOA.

—— (1995), *The Winged Seed: A Remembrance*, St Paul, MN: Ruminator Books.

Lee, Mary Paik (1985), *Quiet Odyssey: A Pioneer Korean Woman in America*, Seattle, WA: University of Washington Press.

Lee, Sky (1991), *Disappearing Moon Cafe*, Seattle, WA: Seal Press.

Lei-lanilau, Carolyn (1997), *Ono Ono Girl's Hula*, Madison, WI: University of Wisconsin Press.

Lew, Walter K. (1992), *Excerpts from ΔIKTH/DIKTE for DICTEE, Critical Collage*, Seoul: Yeul Eum Sa.

López, Tiffany Ana (ed.) (1993), *Growing up Chicano/a*, New York: Morrow.

Lorde, Audre (1982), *Zami: A New Spelling of My Name*, Watertown, MA: Persephone.

Lowe, Pardee (1943), *Father and Glorious Descendant*, Boston, MA: Little, Brown.

Mailer, Norman (1968), *Miami and the Siege of Chicago*, New York: World Publishing Company.

Major, Clarence (1987), *Such was the Season*, San Francisco, CA: Mercury House.

—— (1988), *Painted Turtle: Woman with a Guitar*, Los Angeles, CA: Sun and Moon Press.

Malcolm X (1965), *The Autobiography of Malcolm X*, New York: Grove.

Martínez, Demetria (1994), *Mother Tongue*, New York: Random House/Ballantine.

McCunn, Ruthanne Lum (1981), *Thousand Pieces of Gold*, San Francisco, CA: Design Enterprises.

McKay, Claude (1928), *Home to Harlem*, New York: Harper.

—— (1937), *A Long Way from Home*, New York: Lee Furman.

McMillan, Terry (1992), *Waiting to Exhale*, New York: Simon and Schuster.

McPherson, James Alan (1969), *Hue and Cry*, Boston, MA: Little, Brown.

—— (1977), *Elbow Room*, Boston, MA: Atlantic-Little, Brown.

Menández, Ana (2001), *In Cuba I was a German Shepherd*, New York: Grove Press.

Méndez, Miguel (1974), *Peregrinos de Aztlán*, Mexico: Ediciones Era.

—— (1992), *Pilgrims in Aztlán*, translated by David William Foster, Tempe, AZ: Bilingual Press/Editorial Bilingüe.

Meriwether, Louise (1970), *Daddy was a Number Runner*, Englewood Cliffs, NJ: Prentice-Hall.

Michener, James (1959), *Hawaii*, New York: Random House.

Miyamoto, Kazuo (1964), *Hawaii: End of the Rainbow*, Rutland, VT and Tokyo: Charles E. Tuttle.

Mohr, Nicholasa (1973), *Nilda: A Novel*, New York: Harper.

Momaday, Scott (1968), *House Made of Dawn*, New York: Harper and Row.

—— (1969), *The Way to Rainy Mountain*, Albuquerque, NM: University of New Mexico Press.

—— (1976), *The Names: A Memoir*, New York: Harper and Row.

—— (1997), *The Man Made of Words: Essays, Stories, Passages*, New York: St Martin's Press.

Moraga, Cherrié (1983), *Loving in the War Years: lo que nunca pasó por sus labios*, Boston, MA: South End Press.

—— (1993), *The Last Generation*, Boston, MA: South End Press.

Moraga, Cherrié and Gloria Anzaldúa (eds), (1981), *This Bridge Called My Back: Writings by Radical Women of Color*, Watertown, MA: Persephone Press.

Morales Alejandro (1975), *Caras viejas y vino nuevo*, Mexico: J. Mortiz.

—— (1998), *Barrio on the Edge/Caras viejas y vino nuevo*, translated by Francisco A. Lomeli, Tempe, AZ: Bilingual Press/Editorial Bilingüe.

Mori, Toshio (1949, 1985), *Yokohama, California*, Caldwell, ID: Caxton Printers; reprinted Seattle, WA: University of Washington Press.

—— (1979), *The Chauvinist and Other Stories*, Los Angeles, CA: Asian American Studies Center, The University of California.

—— (2000), *Unfinished Message: Selected Works of Toshio Mori*, Berkeley, CA: Heyday.

Morrison, Toni (1970), *The Bluest Eye*, New York: Holt, Rinehart, Winston.

—— (1977), *Song of Solomon*, New York: Knopf.

—— (1981), *Tar Baby*, New York: Knopf.

—— (1987), *Beloved*, New York: Knopf.

—— (1992a), *Jazz*, New York: Knopf.

—— (1992b), *Playing in the Dark: Whiteness and the Literary Imagination*, Cambridge, MA: Harvard University Press.

—— (1998), *Paradise*, New York: Alfred A. Knopf.

Mukherjee, Bharati (1989), *Jasmine*, New York: Grove Weidenfeld.

Mura, David (1991), *Turning Japanese: Memoirs of a Sansei*, New York: Atlantic Monthly Press.

—— (1995), *The Colors of Desire*, New York: Anchor/Doubleday.

—— (1996), *A Male Grief: Notes on Pornography and Addiction*, New York: Anchor/Doubleday.

Murayama, Milton (1975), *All I Asking for is My Body*, San Francisco, CA: Supa Press.

Naylor, Gloria (1988), *Mama Day*, New York: Houghton Mifflin.

Ng, Faye Myenne (1993), *Bone*, New York: Hyperion.

Nichols, John (1974), *The Milagro Beanfield War*, New York: Holt, Rinehart.

—— (1978), *The Magic Journey*, New York: Holt, Rinehart.

—— (1981), *The Nirvana Blues*, New York: Holt, Rinehart.

—— (1984), *Mysteries of Winterthurn*, New York: Dutton.

Oates, Joyce Carol (1989), *American Appetites*, New York: Dutton.

Occom, Samuel (1762), 'A Short Narrative of My Life' various reprints.

Ogawa, Joy (1981), *Obasan*, Boston, MA: David Godine.

Okada, John (1957, 1979), *No-No Boy*, Rutherford, VT: Charles Tuttle; reprinted Seattle, WA: University of Washington Press.

Ortiz Cofer, Judith (1989), *The Line of the Sun*, New York: Feminist Press at the City of New York.

—— (1990), *Silent Dancing: A Partial Remembrance of a Puerto Rican Childhood*, Houston, TX: Arte Público Press.

—— (1993), *The Latin Deli: Prose and Poetry*, Athens, GA: University of Georgia Press.

—— (2000), *Woman in Front of the Sun: On Becoming a Writer*, Athens, GA: University of Georgia Press.

Owens, Louis (1991, 1996), *Wolfsong*, Albuquerque, NM: West End Press; reprinted Norman, OK: University of Oklahoma Press.

—— (1992), *The Sharpest Sight*, Norman, OK: University of Oklahoma Press.

—— (1994), *Bone Game*, Norman, OK: University of Oklahoma Press.

—— (1996), *Nightland*, New York: Dutton Signet.

—— (1998), *Mixedblood Messages: Literature, Film, Family, Place*, Norman, OK: University of Oklahoma Press.

—— (1999), *Dark River*, Norman, OK: University of Oklahoma Press.

—— (2001), *I Hear the Train: Reflections, Inventions, Refractions*, Norman, OK: University of Oklahoma Press.

Pak, Gary (1992), *The Watcher of Waipuna and Other Stories*, Honolulu: Bamboo Ridge Press.

—— (1998), *A Ricepaper Airplane*, Honolulu: Bamboo Ridge Press,

Petry, Ann (1946), *The Street*, Boston, MA: Houghton Mifflin.

Pharr, Robert Deane (1971), *SRO*, New York: Doubleday.

Pinckney, Darryl (1992), *High Cotton*, New York: Farrar, Straus and Giroux.

Polite, Carlene Hatcher (1975), *Sister X and the Victims of Foul Play*, New York: Doubleday.

Rechy, John (1963), *City of Night*, New York: Grove Press.

Reed, Ishmael (1967), *The Free-Lance Pallbearers*, Garden City, NY: Doubleday.

——— (1969), *Yellow Back Radio Broke-Down*, Garden City, NY: Doubleday.

——— (1972), *Mumbo Jumbo*, Garden City, NY: Random House.

——— (1974), *The Last Days of Louisiana Red*, New York: Random House.

——— (1976), *Flight to Canada*, New York: Random House.

——— (1978), *Shrovetide in Old New Orleans*, Garden City, NY: Doubleday.

——— (1982), *The Terrible Twos*, New York: St Martin's Press/Marek.

——— (1986), *Reckless Eyeballing*, New York: St Martin's Press.

——— (1988), *Writin' is Fightin': Thirty-Seven Years of Boxing on Paper*, New York: Atheneum.

——— (1989), *The Terrible Threes*, New York: Atheneum.

——— (1993a), *Japanese by Spring*, New York: Atheneum.

——— (1993b), *Airing Dirty Laundry*, Reading, MA: Addison Wesley.

——— (ed.) (1997), *MultiAmerica: Essays on Cultural Wars and Cultural Peace*, New York: Viking Penguin.

Ríos, Isabella (1976), *Victuum*, Ventura, CA: Diana-Ema.

Rivera, Edward (1983), *Family Installments: Memories of Growing up Hispanic*, Harmondsworth and New York: Penguin.

Rivera, Tomás (1971, 1987), '. . . *y no se lo tragó la tierra'/And the Earth did not Part*, Berkeley, CA: Quinto Sol Publications. Reissued (1987) as '. . . *y no lo tragó la tierra'/And the Earth did not Devour Him*, Houston, TX: Arte Público Press, English translation by Evangelina Vigil-Piñon. Also reissued (1985) as *This Migrant Earth* translated by Rolando Hinojosa, Houston, TX: Arte Público Press.

Rodriguez, Richard (1982), *Hunger of Memory: The Education of Richard Rodriguez*, Boston, MA: Codine.

——— (1992), *Days of Obligation: An Argument with My Mexican Father*, New York: Viking Penguin.

Saiki, Jessica Kawasuna (1991), *From the Lanai and other Hawaii Stories*, Minneapolis, MA: New Rivers Press.

——— (1993), *When I was Puerto Rican*, Reading, MA: Addison-Wesley. Spanish version (1994), *Cuando era Puertorriqueña*, New York: Vintage.

Santiago, Esmeralda (1999), *Almost a Woman*, New York: Vintage Books.

Santos, Bienvenido N. (1987), *What the Hell For You Left Your Heart in San Francisco*, Quezon City, Philippines: New Day Publisher.

Sasaki, R. A. (1991), *The Loom and Other Stories*, St Paul, MN: Graywolf Press.

Schuyler, George (1931), *Black No More*, New York: Macauley.

Shell, Ray (1993), *Iced*, New York and London: HarperCollins, Flamingo.

Silko, Leslie Marmon (1977), *Ceremony*, New York: Viking Press.

——— (1981), *Storyteller*, New York: Little, Brown/Arcade, in arrangement with Seaver Books.

——— (1991), *Almanac of the Dead*, New York: Simon and Schuster.

Sone, Monica (1953, 1979), *Nisei Daughter*, Boston, MA: Little, Brown; reprinted Seattle, WA: University of Washington Press.

Standing Bear, Luther (1928, 1975), *My People, the Sioux*, Lincoln, NB: University of Nebraska Press.

——— (1931), *My Indian Boyhood*, New York: Houghton Mifflin.

Styron, William (1968), *The Confessions of Nat Turner: A Meditation on History*, New York: Random House.

Suarez, Virgil (1989), *Latin Jazz*, New York: W. Morrow.

Swann, Brian and Arnold Krupat (eds) (1987), *I Tell You Now: Autobiographical Essays by Native American Writers*, Lincoln, NB: University of Nebraska Press.

Tan, Amy (1989), *The Joy Luck Club*, New York: Random House.

—— (1991), *The Kitchen God's Wife*, New York: Random House.

—— (1995), *The Hundred Secret Senses*, New York: G. P. Putnam's Sons.

—— (2001), *The Bonesetter's Daughter*, New York: G. P. Putnam's Sons.

Thomas, Piri (1967), *Down These Mean Streets*, New York: Knopf.

Thompson, Hunter (1971), *Fear and Loathing in Las Vegas: A Savage Journey to the Heart of the American Dream*, New York: Random House.

Updike, John (1960), *Rabbit Run*, New York: Knopf.

—— (1971), *Rabbit Redux*, New York: Knopf.

—— (1981), *Rabbit is Rich*, New York: Knopf.

—— (1990), *Rabbit at Rest*, New York: Knopf.

Valdez, Luis (1992), *Zoot Suit and Other Plays*, Houston, TX: Arte Público Press.

Vega, Ed (1985), *The Comeback*, Houston, TX: Arte Público Press.

Verdelle, A. J. (1995), *The Good Negress*, Chapel Hill, NC: Algonquin Books.

Villarreal, José Antonio (1959), *Pocho*, New York: Doubleday.

Viramontes, Helena (1985), *The Moths and Other Stories*, Houston, TX: Arte Público Press.

Vizenor, Gerald (1978a, 1990), *Darkness in Saint Louis Bearheart*, Minneapolis, MN: Truck Press; revised as *Bearheart: The Heirship Chronicles*, Minneapolis, MN: University of Minnesota Press.

—— (1978b), *Wordarrows: Indians and Whites in the New Fur Trade*, Minneapolis, MN: University of Minnesota Press.

—— (1981), *Earthdivers: Tribal Narratives on Mixed Descent*, Minneapolis, MN: University of Minnesota Press.

—— (1987, 1990), *Griever: An American Monkey King in China*, Normal, IL: Illinois State University/Fiction Collective; reprinted Minneapolis, MN: University of Minnesota Press.

—— (1988), *The Trickster of Liberty: Tribal Heirs to a Wild Baronage at Petronia*, Minneapolis, MN: University of Minnesota Press.

—— (1990a), *Crossbloods: Bone Courts, Bingo, and Other Reports*, Minneapolis, MN: University of Minnesota Press.

—— (1990b), *Interior Landscapes: Autobiographical Myths and Metaphors*, Minneapolis, MN: University of Minnesota Press.

—— (1991a), *The Heirs of Columbus*, Hanover, NH: Wesleyan University Press/University Press of New England.

—— (1991b), *Landfill Meditation: Crossblood Stories*, Hanover, NH: Wesleyan University Press/University Press of New England.

—— (1992), *Dead Voices: Natural Agonies in the New World*, Norman, OK: University of Oklahoma Press.

—— (1994a), *Manifest Manners: Postindian Warriors of Survivance*, Hanover, NH: Wesleyan University Press/University Press of New England.

—— (1994b), *Shadow Distance: A Gerald Vizenor Reader*, ed. and intro. by A. Robert Lee, Hanover, NH: Wesleyan University Press/University Press of New England.

—— (1997), *Hotline Healers: An Almost Browne Novel*, Hanover, NH: Wesleyan University Press/University Press of New England.

—— (1998), *Fugitive Poses: Native American Indian Scenes of Absence and Presence*, Lincoln, NB: University of Nebraska Press.

—— (2000), *Chancers*, Norman, OK: University of Oklahoma Press.

Vizenor, Gerald and A. Robert Lee (1999), *Postindian Conversations*, Lincoln, NB: University of Nebraska Press.

Walker, Alice (1982), *The Color Purple*, New York: Harcourt Brace Jovanovich.

Watanabe, Sylvia (1992), *Talking to the Dead and Other Stories*, New York: Doubleday.

Welch, James (1974), *Winter in the Blood*, New York: Harper and Row.

—— (1986), *Fools Crow*, New York: Viking.

—— (1990), *The Indian Lawyer*, New York: W. W. Norton.

—— (2000), *The Heartsong of Charging Elk*, New York: Doubleday.

Wideman, John Edgar (1970), *Hurry Home*, New York: Harcourt, Brace, World.

—— (1981), *Damballah*, New York: Random House.

—— (1984), *Brothers and Keepers*, New York: Holt, Rinehart and Winston.

Williams, Sherley Anne (1986), *Dassa Rose*, New York: W. Morrow.

Winnemucca, Sarah (1883, 1969), *Life among the Piutes: Their Wrongs and Claims*, Bishop, CA: Sierra Media, Inc.

Wong, Jade Snow (1945), *Fifth Chinese Daughter*, New York: Harper.

Wong, Shawn (1979), *Homebase*, New York: I. Reed Books.

Wright, Richard (1945a), *Native Son*, New York: Harper.

—— (1945b), *Black Boy*, New York: Harper.

Yamamoto, Hisaye (1988), *Seventeen Syllables and Other Stories*, Latham, NY: Kitchen Table/ Women of Color Press.

Yamanaka, Lois-Ann (1993), *Saturday Night at the Pahala Theatre*, Honolulu: Bamboo Ridge.

—— (1996), *Wild Meat and the Bully Burgers*, New York: Farrar, Straus and Giroux.

—— (1997), *Blu's Hanging*, New York: Farrar, Straus and Giroux.

Yau, John (1995), *Hawaiian Cowboys*, Santa Rosa, CA: Black Sparrow Press.

Selected Secondary Scholarship

Allen, Paula Gunn (1986), *The Sacred Hoop: Recovering the Feminine in American Indian Traditions*, Boston, MA: Beacon Press.

Allen, Theodore (1994), *The Invention of the White Race*, vol. 1: *Racial Oppression and Social Control*, New York and London: Verso.

——— (1997), *The Invention of the White Race: The Origins of Racial Oppression in Anglo-America*, New York and London: Verso.

Anderson, Eric Gary (1999), *American Indian Literature and the Southwest*, Austin, TX: University of Texas Press.

Appiah, Kwame Anthony (1991), 'Is the Post- in Postmodernism the Post- in Postcolonial?', *Critical Inquiry*, 17: 2, 336–55.

——— (1994), *Identity Against Culture: Understandings of Multiculturalism*, Berkeley, CA: Doreen B. Center for the Humanities.

Arteaga, Alfred (ed.) (1994), *An Other Tongue: Nation and Ethnicity in the Linguistic Borderlands*, Durham, NC: Duke University Press.

——— (1997), *Chicano Poetics: Heterotexts and Hybridities*, Cambridge: Cambridge University Press.

Awkward, Michael (1995), *Negotiating Difference: Race, Gender, and the Politics of Personality*, Chicago, IL: University of Chicago Press.

Babb, Valerie (1998), *Whiteness Visible: The Meaning of Whiteness in American Literature and Culture*, New York: New York University Press.

Bak, Hans (ed.) (1993), *Multiculturalism and the Canon of American Literature*, Amsterdam and New York: VU University Press.

Baker, Houston (1980), *The Journey Back: Issues in Black Literature and Criticism*, Chicago, IL: University of Chicago Press.

——— (ed.) (1982), *Three American Literatures: Essays in Chicano, Native American and Asian American Literature for Teachers of American Literature*, New York: Modern Language Association.

——— (1983), *Singers at Daybreak: Studies in Black American Literature*, Washington, DC: Howard University Press.

——— (1987), *Blues, Ideology, and Afro-American Literature: A Vernacular Theory*, Chicago, IL: University of Chicago Press.

Banks, James A. (1991), *Teaching Strategies for Ethnic Studies*, 5th edn, Boston, MA: Allyn and Bacon.

Baudrillard, Jean (1981a, 1983), *Simulations*, translated by Paul Foss, Paul Patton and Phillip Bietchman, New York: Semiotext(e).

——— (1981b), *For a Critique of the Political Economy of the Sign*, translated by Charles Levin, St Louis, MO: Telos.

Bauman, Zygmunt (1992), *Intimations of Postmodernity*, New York and London: Routledge.

Bell, Bernard W. (1987), *The Afro-American Novel and Its Tradition*, Amherst, MA: University of Massachusetts Press.

Benito, Jesús and Ana María Manzanas (eds) (2002), *Literature and Ethnicity in the Cultural Borderlands*, Amsterdam: Rodopi.

Berkhover, Robert F, Jr (1978), *The White Man's Indian: Images of the American Indian from Columbus to the Present*, New York: Knopf.

Beyerman, Keith (1985), *Fingering the Jagged Vein: Tradition and Form in Recent Black Fiction*, Athens, GA: University of Georgia Press.

Bhabha, Homi (ed.) (1990), *Nation and Narration*, London and New York: Routledge.

—— (1994), *The Location of Culture*, London and New York: Routledge.

Bigsby, C. W. E. (1980), *The Second Black Renaissance: Essays in Black Literature*, Westport, CT: Greenwood Press.

Bird, S. Elizabeth (ed.) (1996), *Dressing in Feathers: The Construction of the Indian in American Popular Culture*, Boulder, CO: Westview Press.

Bloom, Allan (1987), *The Closing of the American Mind*, New York: Simon and Schuster.

Boelhower, William (1997), *Through a Glass Darkly: Ethnic Semiosis in American Literature*, New York: Oxford University Press.

Bone, Robert A. (1958, 1965), *The Negro Novel in America*, New Haven, CT: Yale University Press.

Breinig, Helmbrecht, Jürgen Gebhardt and Klaus Lüosch (eds) (2002), *Multiculturalism in Contemporary Societies: Perspectives on Difference and Transdifference*, Erlangen: Univ-Bibliothek.

Brill de Ramírez, Susan Berry (1999), *Contemporary American Indian Literatures and the Oral Tradition*, Tucson, AZ: University of Arizona Press.

Brooker, Andrew (ed.) (1992), *Modernism/Postmodernism*, London: Longman.

Brookhiser, Richard (1991), *The Way of the WASP*, New York: Free Press.

Brown, Julie (ed.) (1999), *Ethnicity and the American Short Story*, Santa Barbara, CA: ABC-CLIO.

Bruce-Novoa, Juan (1982), *Chicano Authors: A Response to Chaos*, Austin, TX: University of Texas Press.

Brumble, H. David, III (1988), *American Indian Autobiography* Berkeley, CA: University of California Press.

Butler, Robert (1988), *Contemporary African American Fiction: The Open Journey*, Teaneck, NJ: Fairleigh Dickinson University Press.

Butler-Evans, Elliott (1989), *Race, Gender, and Desire: Narrative Strategies in the Fiction of Toni Cade Bambara, Toni Morrison, Alice Walker*, Philadelphia, PA: Temple University Press.

Butterfield, Stephen (1974), *Black Autobiography in America*, Amherst, MA: University of Massachusetts Press.

Calderón, Héctor and José David Saldívar (eds) (1991), *Criticism in the Borderlands: Studies in Chicano Literature, Culture, and Ideology*, Durham, NC: Duke University Press.

Callahan, John (1988), *In the African-American Grain: The Pursuit of Voice in Twentieth-Century Black Fiction*, Urbana and Chicago, IL: University of Illinois Press.

Candelaria, Cordelia (ed.) (1989), *Multiethnic Literature of the United States: Critical Introductions and Classroom Resources*, Boulder, CO: Multiethnic Literature Project, University of Colorado.

Carby, Hazel V. (1987), *Reconstructing Womanhood: The Experience of the Afro-American Woman Novelist*, New York: Oxford University Press.

Cazemajou, Jean (1985), *Les Minorités Hispaniques en Amérique du Nord*, Bordeaux: Presses Universitaires de Bordeaux.

Chandrasekhar, S. (ed.) (1992), *From India to America: A Brief History of Immigration*, La Jolla, CA: Population Review Publications.

Chang, Susheng (1991), *Asian Americans: An Interpretive History*, Boston, MA: Twayne.

Cheung, King-Kok (1993), *Articulate Silences: Hisaye Yamamoto, Maxine Hong Kingston, Joy Kogawa*, Ithaca, NY: Cornell University Press.

Chideya, Farai (1999), *The Color of Our Future*, New York: Morrow.

Christian, Barbara (1984), *Black Women Novelists: The Development of a Tradition*, Westport, CT: Greenwood Press.

—— (1985), *Black Feminist Criticism*, New York: Pergamon.

Christian, Karen (1997), *Show and Tell: Identity as Performance in US Latino/a Fiction*, Albuquerque, NM: University of New Mexico Press.

Chu, Patricia P. (1999), *Assimilating Asians: Gendered Strategies of Authorship in Asian America*, Durham, NC: Duke University Press.

Clarke, Graham (ed.) (1990), *The New American Writing: Essays on American Literature since 1970*, London: Vision Press.

Coleman, James W. (1989), *Blackness and Modernism: The Literary Career of John Edgar Wideman*, Jackson, MS: University Press of Mississippi.

Coltelli, Laura (ed.) (1990), *Winged Words: American Indian Writers Speak*, Lincoln, NB: University of Nebraska Press.

Connor, Steve (1989), *Postmodernist Culture*, New York: Basil Blackwell.

Cooke, Michael (1984), *Afro-American Literature in the Twentieth Century: The Achievement of Intimacy*, New Haven, CT: Yale University Press.

Cruse, Harold (1967), *The Crisis of the Negro Intellectual*, New York: Apollo.

Davis, F. James (1991), *Who is Black? One Nation's Definition*, University Park, PA: Pennsylvania State University Press.

Davis, Mike (2000), *Magical Urbanism: Latinos Reinvent the US City*, London: Verso.

Debo, Angie (1970), *A History of the Indians of the United States*, Norman, OK: University of Oklahoma Press.

Delgado, Richard (1995), *The Rodrigo Chronicles: Conversations about America and Race*, New York: New York University Press.

D'haen, Theo and C. C. Barfoot (eds) (1992), *Shades of Empire: Studies in Colonial and Post-Colonial Literatures*, Amsterdam and Atlanta: Rodopi.

Dinnerstein, Leonard, Roger L. Nichols and David M. Reimers (1996), *Natives and Strangers: A Multicultural History of Americans*, New York: Oxford University Press.

D'Sousa, Dinesh (1999), *Illiberal Education: The Politics of Race and Sex on Campus*, New York: Maxwell.

Eddy, Robert (ed.) (1996), *Reflections on Multiculturalism* Yarmouth, ME: Intercultural Press.

Espiritu, Y. L. (1992), *Asian American Panethnicity* Philadelphia, PA: Temple University Press.

—— (1995), *Filipino American Lives*, Philadelphia, PA: Temple University Press.

Evans, Mari (ed.) (1984), *Black Women Writers (1950–1980): A Critical Evaluation*, New York: Doubleday.

Fabre, Geneviève (ed.) (1988), *European Perspectives on Hispanic Literature*, Houston, TX: Arte Público Press.

Fanning, Charles (1990, 1999), *The Irish Voice in America: 250 Years of Irish-American Fiction*, Lexington, KY: University Press of Kentucky.

Feagin, Joe R., Hernán Vera and Pinar Batur (2001), *White Racism*, 2nd edn, New York: Routledge.

Fischer, Michael M. J. (1986), 'Ethnicity and the Post-Modern Arts of Memory', in James Clifford and George E. Marcus (eds), *Writing Culture: The Poetics and Politics of Ethnography*, Berkeley, CA: University of California Press, pp. 194–223.

Fischer-Hornung, Dorothea and Heike Raphael-Hernandez (eds) (2000), *Holding Their Own: Perspectives on the Multi-Ethnic Literatures of the United States*, Tübingen: Stauffenburg Verlag.

Fishkin, Shelley Fisher (1991), *Was Huck Black? Mark Twain and African American Voices*, New York: Oxford University Press.

Fixico, Donald L. (2000), *They Never Told Us . . . The Urban Indian Experience in America*, Albuquerque, NM: University of New Mexico Press.

Flores, Juan (1984), *Divided Borders: Essays on Puerto Rican Identity*, Houston, TX: Arte Público Press.

—— (1988), 'Puerto Rican Literature in the United States: Stages and Perspectives', *ADE Bulletin*, vol. 91, 39–44.

Fox, Robert Elliot (1987), *Conscientious Sorcerers: The Black Postmodernist Fiction of LeRoi Jones/ Amiri Baraka, Ishmael Reed, and Samuel R. Delany*, New York: Greenwood Press.

Frankenberg, Ruth (ed.) (1997), *Displacing Whiteness: Essays in Social and Cultural Criticism*, Durham, NC and London: Duke University Press.

Fusco, Coco (1995), *English is Spoken Here: Notes on Cultural Fusion in the Americas*, New York: The New Press.

Gardaphé, Fred L. (1996), *Italian Signs, American Streets: The Evolution of Italian American Literature*, Durham, NC: Duke University Press.

Gardner, Jared (1998), *Master Plot: Race and the Founding of American Literature, 1787–1845*, Baltimore, MD: The Johns Hopkins University Press.

Gates, Henry Louis, Jr (ed.) (1987), *Figures in Black: Words, Signs and the 'Racial' Self*, New York: Oxford University Press.

—— (1988) *The Signifying Monkey: A Theory of Afro-American Criticism*, New York: Oxford University Press.

—— (1992), *Loose Canons: Notes on the Culture Wars*, New York: Oxford University Press.

Gayle, Addison, Jr (ed.) (1971), *The Black Aesthetic*, New York: Anchor-Doubleday.

—— (1975), *The Way of the New World: The Black Novel in America*, New York: Doubleday.

Gilroy, Paul (1993), *The Black Atlantic: Modernity and Double Consciousness*, Cambridge, MA: Harvard University Press.

Gish, Robert Franklin (1996), *Beyond Bounds: Cross-Cultural Essays on Anglo, American Indian, and Chicano Literature*, Albuquerque, NM: University of New Mexico Press.

Glazer, Nathan (1997), *We are All Multiculturalists Now*, Cambridge, MA: Harvard University Press.

Goldberg, David Theo (ed.) (1994), *Multiculturalism: A Critical Reader*, Oxford: Blackwell.

Gonzalez, Juan (2000), *Harvest of Empire: A History of Latinos in America*, New York: Viking Penguin.

Gonzalez, Lisa Sánchez (2001), *Boricua Literature: A Literary History of the Puerto Rican Diaspora*, New York: New York University Press.

Gordon, Avery and Christopher Newfield (eds) (1996), *Mapping Multiculturalism*, Minneapolis, MN: University of Minnesota Press.

Greene, J. Lee (1996), *Blacks in Eden: The African American Novel's First Century*, Charlottesville, VA: University of Virginia Press.

Grice, Helena (2002), *Negotiating Identities: An Introduction to Asian American Women's Writing*, Manchester: Manchester University Press.

Hall, Stuart (1989), 'Ethnicity: Identity and Difference', *Radical America*, 23: 4, 9–20.

Harvey, David (1989), *The Condition of Postmodernity: An Inquiry into the Origins of Cultural Change*, Cambridge: Blackwell.

Hemenway, Robert (ed.) (1970), *The Black Novelist*, Columbus, OH: Charles E. Merrill Publishing Company.

Hernández, Guillermo (1991), *Chicano Satire: A Study in Literary Culture*, Austin, TX: University of Texas Press.

Herrera-Sobek, María (ed.) (1985), *Beyond Stereotypes: The Critical Analysis of Chicana Literature*, Binghamton, NY: Bilingual Press/Editorial Bilingüe.

Hill, Mike (ed.) (1997), *Whiteness: A Critical Reader*, New York: New York University Press.

Hogue, W. Lawrence (1996), *Race, Modernity, Postmodernity: A Look at the History and the Literatures of People of Color since the 1960s*, Albany, NY: State University of New York Press.

Hollinger, David (1995), *Postethnic America: Beyond Multiculturalism*, New York: Basic Books.

——(1981), *'Ain't I A Woman?': Black Women and Feminism*, Boston, MA: South End Press.

hooks, bell (1990), *Yearning: Race, Gender, and Cultural Politics*, Boston, MA: South End Press.

Horne, Dee (1999), *Contemporary American Indian Writing: Unsettling Literature*, New York: Peter Lang.

Horno-Delgado, Asunción (ed.) (1989, 1996), *Breaking Boundaries: Latina Writing and Critical Readings*, Amherst, MA: University of Massachusetts Press.

Horsman, Reginald (1981), *Race and Manifest Destiny: The Origins of American Racial Anglo-Saxonism*, Cambridge, MA: Harvard University Press.

Hulan, Renée (ed.) (1999), *Native North America: Critical and Cultural Perspectives*, Toronto: ECW Press.

Hutcheon, Linda (1988), *A Poetics of Postmodernism: History, Theory, Fiction*, New York: Routledge.

Ignatiev, Noel (1995), *How the Irish Became White*, New York: Routledge.

Isernhagen, Hartwig (ed.) (1999), *Momaday, Vizenor, Armstrong: Conversations on American Indian Writing*, Norman, OK: University of Oklahoma Press.

Jacobson, Matthew Frye (1999), *Whiteness of a Different Color: European Immigrants and the Alchemy of Race*, Cambridge, MA: Harvard University Press.

Jahner, Elaine A. (2000), 'Trickster Discourse and Postmodern Strategies', in A. Robert Lee (ed.), *Loosening the Seams: Interpretations of Gerald Vizenor*, Bowling Green, OH: Bowling Green State University Press, pp. 38–58.

Jaimes, M. Annette (ed.) (1992), *The State of Native America: Genocide, Colonization, and Resistance*, Boston, MA: South End Press.

Jameson, Fredric (1991), *Postmodernism, or the Cultural Logic of Late Capitalism*, Durham, NC: Duke University Press.

JanMohamed, Abdul and David Lloyd (eds) (1990), *The Nature and Context of Minority Discourse*, Oxford: Oxford University Press.

Jay, Gregory (1997), *American Literature and the Culture Wars*, Ithaca, NY: Cornell University Press.

Jiménez, Francisco (ed.) (1979), *The Identification and Analysis of Chicano Literature*, Binghamton, NY: Bilingual Review Press.

Johnson, Charles (1990), *Being and Race: Black Writing since 1970*, Bloomington and Indianapolis, IN: Indiana University Press.

Jussawalla, Feroza and Reed Way Dasenbrock (eds) (1992), *Interviews with Writers of the Post-Colonial World*, Jackson, MS: University Press of Mississippi.

Kelley, Lionel (ed.) (1994), *Ethnicity and Representation in American Literature*, Modern Language Review/The Yearbook of English Studies, vol. 14.

Kent, George (1972), *Blackness and the Adventure of Western Culture*, Chicago, IL: Third World Press.

Kim, Elaine (1982), *Asian American Literature: An Introduction to the Writings and Their Social Context*, Philadelphia, PA: Temple University Press.

Kim, Elaine H. and Norma Alarcón (eds) (1993), *Writing Self/Writing Nation: A Collection of Essays on DICTEE by Theresa Hak Kyung Cha*, Berkeley, CA: Third Woman Press.

Kimball, Roger (1990), *Tenured Radicals: How Politics has Corrupted Our Higher Education*, New York: Harper and Row.

King, Desmond (2000), *Making Americans: Immigration, Race, and the Origins of Diverse Democracy*, Cambridge, MA: Harvard University Press.

Krupat, Arnold (1985), *For Those who Come After: A Study of Native American Autobiography*, Berkeley, CA: University of California Press.

—— (1989), *The Voice in the Margin: Native American Literature and the Canon*, Berkeley, CA: University of California Press.

—— (ed.) (1993), *New Voices in Native American Literary Criticism*, Washington, DC: Smithsonian Institution.

—— (1996), *The Turn to the Native: Studies in Criticism and Culture*, Lincoln, NB: University of Nebraska Press.

Larson, Charles R. (1978), *American Indian Fiction*, Albuquerque, NM: University of New Mexico Press.

Lattin, Vernon E. (1986), *Contemporary Chicano Fiction: A Critical Survey*, Binghamton, NY: Bilingual Review Press.

Lauter, Paul (ed.) (1983), *Reconstructing American Literature: Courses, Syllabi, Issues*, Old Westbury, NY: Feminist Press.

Lee, A. Robert (ed.) (1980), *Black Fiction: New Studies in the Afro-American Novel since 1945*, London: Vision Press.

—— (1983), *Black American Fiction since Richard Wright*, BAAS Pamphlet, No. 11

—— (1993), 'Self-Inscriptions: James Baldwin, Tomás Rivera, Gerald Vizenor and Amy Tan and the Writing-in of America's Non-European Ethnicities', in A. Robert Lee (ed.), *A Permanent Etcetera: Cross-Cultural Perspectives on Post-War America*, London: Pluto Press.

—— (1994), 'Afro-America: The Before Columbus Foundation and the Literary Multiculturalization of America', *Journal of American Studies*, 28: 3 (December), 433–50.

—— (1998), *Designs of Blackness: Mappings in the Literature and Culture of Afro-America*, London and Sterling, VA: Pluto Press.

—— (ed.) (2000), *Loosening the Seams: Interpretations of Gerald Vizenor*, Bowling Green, OH: Bowling Green State University Popular Press.

—— (2001), *Ethnics Behaving Badly: US Multicultural Narratives*, Pullman, WA: Working Papers Series in Cultural Studies, Ethnicity and Race Relations.

Lee, Rachel C. (1999), *The Americas of Asian American Literature: Gendered Fictions of Nation and Transnation*, Princeton, NJ: Princeton University Press.

Leistnya, Pepi (1998), 'White Ethnic Unconsciousness', *Cultural Circles*, 2, (Spring), 33–51.

Levine, Lawrence W. (1996), *The Opening of the American Mind: Canons, Culture, and History*, Boston, MA: Beacon Press.

Li, David Leiwei (1998), *Imaging the Nation: Asian American Literature and Cultural Consent*, Stanford, CA: Stanford University Press.

Lim, Shirley Geok-lin and Amy Ling (eds) (1992), *Reading the Literatures of Asian America*, Philadelphia, PA: Temple University Press.

Lincoln, Kenneth (1983), *Native American Renaissance*, Berkeley, CA: University of California Press.

Ling, Amy (1990), *Between Worlds: Women Writers of Chinese Ancestry*, New York: Pergamon.

Ling, Jinqi (1998), *Narrating Nationalisms: Ideology and Form in Asian American Literature*, New York: Oxford University Press.

Liu, Eric (1998), *The Accidental Asian: Notes of a Native Speaker*, New York: Random House.

Lowe, John (1996), 'Monkey Kings and Mojo: Postmodern Ethnic Humor in Kingston, Reed and Vizenor', *MELUS*, 21: 4, 103–26.

Lowe, Lisa (1996), *Immigrant Acts: On Asian American Cultural Politics*, Durham, NC and London: Duke University Press.

Lyotard, Jean-François (1979), *La Condition postmoderne: rapport sur le savoir*, Paris: Les Editions de Minuit.

—— (1984), *The Postmodern Condition: A Report on Knowledge*, translated by Geoff Bennington and Brian Massumi, foreword by Fredric Jameson, Minneapolis, MN: University of Minnesota Press.

Madsen, Deborah L. (2000), *Contemporary Chicana Literature*, Columbia, SC: University of South Carolina Press.

Major, Clarence (1974), *The Dark and Feeling: Black American Writers and Their Work*, New York: The Third Press.

Marçais, Dominique, Mark Niemeyer, Bernard Vincent and Cathy Waegner (2002), *Literature on the Move: Comparing Diasporic Ethnicities in Europe and the Americas*, American Studies Monograph Series, vol. 97, Heidelberg: Universitätsverlag C. Winter.

Martin, Calvin (ed.) (1987), *The American Indian and the Problem of History*, New York: Oxford University Press.

McCarus, Ernest (ed.) (1994), *The Development of Arab-American Identity*, Ann Arbor, MI: University of Michigan Press.

McCracken, Ellen (1999), *New Latina Narrative: The Feminine Space of Postmodern Ethnicity*, Tucson, AZ: University of Arizona Press.

McHale, Brian (1987), *Postmodernist Fiction*, New York: Methuen.

McQuade, Donald and Christine McQuade (eds) (2000), *Seeing and Writing*, New York: Bedford/St Martin's Press.

Michaels, Walter Benn (1995), *Our America: Nativism, Modernism and Pluralism*, Durham, NC: Duke University Press.

Mohr, Eugene (1982), *The Nuyorican Experience: Literature of the Puerto Rican Minority*, Westport, CT: Greenwood Press.

Montagu, Ashley (1942ff.), *Man's Most Dangerous Myth: The Fallacy of Race*, New York: Columbia University Press.

Morison, Samuel Eliot (1942), *Admiral of the Ocean Sea: A Life of Christopher Columbus*, Boston, MA: Little, Brown.

Muller, Gilbert (1999), *New Strangers in Paradise: The Immigrant Experience and Contemporary American Fiction*, Lexington, KY: University Press of Kentucky.

Murray, David (1980), *Forked Tongues: Speech, Writing, and Representation in North American Indian Texts*, Bloomington, IN: Indiana University Press.

Naff, Alixa (1985), *Becoming American: The Early Arab Immigrant Experience*, Carbondale, IL: Southern Illinois University Press.

Nielsen, Aldon (1997), *Black Chant: The Languages of African-American Postmodernism*, Cambridge: Cambridge University Press.

Norris, Christopher (1993), *The Truth about Postmodernism*, Oxford: Blackwell.

O'Brien, John (ed.) (1973), *Interviews with Black Writers*, New York: Liveright.

Omi, Michael and Howard Winant (1986, 1994), *Racial Formation in the United States*, New York and London: Routledge.

Owens, Louis (1992), *Other Destinies: Understanding the American Indian Novel*, Norman, OK: University of Oklahoma Press.

——(1998), *Mixedblood Messages: Literature, Film, Family, Place*, Norman, OK: University of Oklahoma Press.

Palumbo-Liu, David (ed.) (1995), *The Ethnic Canon: Histories, Institutions, and Interventions*, Minneapolis, MN: University of Minnesota Press.

Pearce, Roy Harvey (1988), *Savagism and Civilization: A Study of the Indian and the American Mind*, Berkeley, CA: University of California Press.

Peck, David R. (1991), *American Ethnic Literatures: Native American, African American, Chicano/Latino, and Asian American Writers and Their Backgrounds*, Pasadena, CA: Salem Press.

Penn, William S. (ed.) (1997), *As We Are Now: Mixblood Essays on Race and Identity*, Berkeley, CA: University of California Press.

Perez, Louis A. (2000), *On Becoming Cuban*, Chapel Hill, NC: University of North Carolina Press.

Pérez-Firmat, Gustavo (1994), *Life on the Hyphen: The Cuban-American Way*, Austin, TX: University of Texas Press.

Pérez-Torres, Rafael (1990), *Do the Americas Have a Common Literature?*, Durham, NC: Duke University Press.

——— (1998), 'Chicano Ethnicity, Cultural Hybridity, and the Mestizo Voice', *American Literature*, 70: 1, 153–76.

Pryse, Marjorie and Hortense Spillers (1995), (eds) *Conjuring: Black Women, Fiction, and Literary Tradition*, Bloomington, IN: Indiana University Press.

Rebolledo, Tey Diana (1995), *Women Singing in the Snow: A Cultural Analysis of Chicana Literature*, Tucson, AZ: University of Arizona Press.

Ridgeway, James (1990), *Blood in the Face: The KKK, Aryan Nations, Nazi Skinheads and the Rise of a New White Culture*, New York: Thunder's Mouth.

Rivera, Eliana (1994), 'Hispanic Literature in the United States: Self-Image and Conflict', *Revista Chicano-Riqueña*, 13: 2, 526–40.

Roberts, Sam (1993), *Who We Are: A Portrait of America Based on the Latest US Census*, New York: Times Books/Random House.

Rodríguez de Laguna, Asela (ed.) (1987), *Images and Identities: The Puerto Rican in Two World Contexts*, New Brunswick, NJ: Transaction Books.

Roediger, David R. (1990), *Towards the Abolition of Whiteness: Essays in Race, Politics and Working-Class History*, London and New York: Verso.

——— (1991), *The Ways of Whiteness: Race and the Making of the American Working Class*, London and New York: Verso.

Rosenblatt, Roger (1974), *Black Fiction*, Cambridge, MA: Harvard University Press.

Rothenberg, Paula S. (2002), *White Privilege: Essential Readings on the Other Side of Racism*, New York: Ward.

Ruoff, A. Lavonne Brown and Jerry W. Ward (eds) (1990), *Redefining American Literary History*, New York: The Modern Language Association of America.

Ruppert, James (1995), *Mediation in Contemporary Native American Fiction*, Norman, OK: University of Oklahoma Press.

Said, Edward (1978), *Orientalism*, New York: Random House/Vintage Books.

Saldívar, José David (1991), *The Dialectics of Our America: Genealogy, Cultural Critique, and Literary History*, Durham, NC: Duke University Press.

——— (1997), *Border Matters: Remapping American Cultural Studies*, Berkeley, CA: University of California Press.

Saldívar, Ramón (1990), *Chicano Narrative: The Dialectics of Difference*, Madison, WI: University of Wisconsin Press.

Sale, Kirkpatrick (1990), *The Conquest of Paradise: Christopher Columbus and the Columbian Legacy*, New York: Knopf.

San Juan, Epifanio, Jr (1992), *Racial Formations/Critical Transformations: Articulations of Power in Ethnic and Racial Studies in the United States*, Atlantic Highlands, NJ: Humanities Press.

——— (1998a), *Beyond Postcolonial Theory*, New York: St Martin's Press.

——— (1998b), *From Exile to Diaspora: Versions of the Filipino Experience in the United States*, Boulder, CO: Westview Press.

——— (2002), *Racism and Cultural Studies: Critiques of Multiculturalist Ideology and the Politics of Difference*, Durham, NC: Duke University Press.

Saran, Parmata (1985), *The Asian Indian Experience in the United States*, Cambridge, MA: Schnekman.

Schechner, Mark (1987), *After the Revolution: Studies in Contemporary Jewish-American Imagination*, Bloomington, IN: Indiana University Press.

Schirmer, Daniel B. and Stephen Rosskamm Shalom (1987), *The Philippines Reader: A History of Colonialism, NeoColonialism, Dictatorship, and Resistance*, Boston, MA: South End Press.

Schlesinger, Arthur M., Jr (1992), *The Disuniting of America: Reflections on a Multicultural Society*, New York: W. W. Norton.

Schubnell, Matthias (1985), *N. Scott Momaday: The Cultural and Literary Background*, Norman, OK and London: University of Oklahoma Press.

Shanley, Kathryn W. (ed.) (2001), *Native American Literature: Boundaries and Sovereignties*, *Paradoxa: Studies in World Literary Genres*, no. 15.

Shell, Marc (ed.) (2002), *American Babel: Literatures of the United States from Abnaki to Zuni*, Cambridge, MA: Harvard University Press.

Shirley, Carl R. and Paula W. Shirley (1988), *Understanding Chicano Literature*, Columbia, SC: University of South Carolina Press.

Shuffleton, Frank (1993), *A Mixed Race: Ethnicity in Early America*, New York: Oxford University Press.

Singh, Amritjit and Peter Schmidt (eds) (2000), *Postcolonial Theory and the United States: Race, Ethnicity and Literature*, Jackson, MS: University Press of Mississippi.

Singh, Amritjit, Joseph T. Skerrett Jr and Robert E. Hogan (eds) (1994), *Memory, Narrative and Identity: New Essays in Ethnic American Literatures*, Boston, MA: Northeastern Press.

——(eds) (1996), *Memory and Cultural Politics: New Approaches to American Ethnic Literatures*, Boston, MA: Northeastern Press.

Smith, Jeanne Rosier (1997), *Writing Tricksters: Mythic Gambols in American Ethnic Literature*, Berkeley, CA: University of California Press.

Sollors, Werner (1986), *Beyond Ethnicity: Consent and Descent in American Culture*, New York: Oxford University Press.

——(ed.) (1989), *The Invention of Ethnicity*, New York: Oxford University Press.

——(1997), *Neither Black nor White yet Both: Thematic Explorations of Interracial Literature*, New York: Oxford University Press.

——(ed.) (1998), *Multilingual America: Transnationalism, Ethnicity, and the Languages of American Literature*, New York: New York University Press.

——(ed.) (2000), *Interracialism: Black–White Intermarriage in American History, Literature, and Law*, New York: Oxford University Press.

Sommers, Joseph and Tomas Ybarra-Fausto (eds) (1978) *Modern Chicano Writers: A Collection of Critical Essays*, Englewood Cliffs, NJ: Prentice-Hall.

Somners, Doris (1999), *Proceed with Caution, when Engaged by Minority Writing in the Americas*, Cambridge: Cambridge University Press.

Spivak, Gayatri Chakravorty (1987), *In Other Worlds: Essays in Cultural Politics*, New York: Methuen.

——(1999), *A Critique of Post-Colonial Reason: Towards a History of the Vanishing Present*, Cambridge, MA: Harvard University Press.

Stavans, Ilan (1995), *The Hispanic Condition: Reflections on Culture and Identity in America*, New York: HarperCollins.

Stepto, Robert B. (1979), *From Behind the Veil: A Study of Afro-American Narrative*, Urbana, IL: University of Illinois Press.

Sumida, Stephen H. (1991), *And the View from the Shore: Literary Traditions of Hawai'i*, Seattle, WA: University of Washington Press.

Sundquist, Eric (1983), *To Wake the Nations: Race in the Making of American Literature*, Cambridge, MA: Cambridge University Press.

Swann, Brian (1983), *Smoothing the Ground: Essays on Native American Oral Literature*, Berkeley, CA: University of California Press.

Swann, Brian and Arnold Krupat (eds) (1987), *Recovering the Word: Essays on Native American Literature*, Berkeley, CA: University of California Press.

Takaki, Ronald T. (1983), *Strangers from a Different Shore: A History of Asian Americans*, New York: William Morrow.

——(ed.) (1987), *From Different Shores: Perspectives on Race and Ethnicity in America*, New York: Oxford University Press.

——(1990), *Iron Cages: Race and Culture in Nineteenth-Century America*, New York: Oxford University Press.

—— (1993), *A Different Mirror: A History of Multicultural America*, Boston, MA: Little, Brown.

Tatum, Charles (1980), *Chicano Literature*, Boston, MA: Twayne.

—— (2001), *Chicano Popular Culture: Que Hable el Pueblo*, Tucson, AZ: University of Arizona Press.

Trinh, T. Minh-ha (1989), *Woman, Native, Other: Writing Postcoloniality and Feminism*, Bloomington, IN: Indiana University Press.

Turner, Faythe (1978), *US Puerto Rican Writers on the Mainland: The Neoricans*, Amherst, MA: University of Massachusetts Press.

TuSmith, Bonnie (1993), *All My Relatives: Community in Contemporary Ethnic American Literatures*, Ann Arbor, MI: University of Michigan Press.

Ungar, Sandford (1998), *Fresh Blood: The New American Immigrants*, Urbana and Chicago, IL: University of Illinois Press.

Ushida, Yoshiko (1982), *Desert Exile: The Uprooting of a Japanese Family*, Seattle, WA: University of Washington Press.

Velie, Alan (1982), *Four American Indian Literary Masters: N. Scott Momaday, James Welch, Leslie Marmon Silko and Gerald Vizenor*, Norman, OK: University of Oklahoma Press.

Vigil, James Diego (1984), *From Indians to Chicanos: The Dynamics of Mexican American Culture*, Prospect Heights, IL: Waveland Press.

Vizenor, Gerald (ed.) (1989), *Narrative Chance: Postmodern Discourse on Native American Indian Literatures*, Albuquerque, NM: University of New Mexico.

Wall, Cheryl A. (ed.) (1989), *Changing Our Own Words: Essays in Criticism, Theory, and Writing by Black Women*, New Brunswick, NJ: Rutgers University Press.

Weaver, Jace (1997), *That the People Might Live: Native American Literatures and Native American Community*, New York: Oxford University Press.

Weglyn, Michi (1973), *Years of Infamy: The Untold History of America's Concentration Camps*, New York: Morrow and Company.

West, Cornel (1993), *Keeping Faith: Philosophy and Race in America*, New York: Routledge.

—— (1994), *Race Matters*, New York: Vintage.

Wiegman, Robyn, *American Anatomies: Theorizing Race and Gender*, Durham, NC: Duke University Press.

Wilson, Rob (2000), *Reimagining the Pacific: From 'South Pacific' to Bamboo Ridge and Beyond*, Durham, NC: Duke University Press.

Wilson, William Julius (1987), *The Declining Significance of Race: Blacks and Changing American Institutions*, Chicago, IL: Chicago University Press.

Wong, Hertha Dawn (1992), *Sending My Heart Across the Years*, New York: Oxford University Press.

Wong, Sau-ling Cynthia (1993), *Reading Asian American Literature: From Necessity to Extravagance*, Princeton, NJ: Princeton University Press.

Wray, Matt and Annalee Newitz (eds) (1997), *White Trash: Race and Class in America*, New York: Routledge.

Wu, Frank H. (2002), *Yellow: Race in America Beyond Black and White*, New York: Basic Books.

Yates, Frances A. (1966), *The Art of Memory*, London: Routledge and Kegan Paul.

Yin, Xia-huang (2000), *Chinese American Literature since the 1850s*, Urbana and Chicago, IL: University of Illinois Press.

Young, Robert (1990), *White Mythologies: Writing History and the West*, New York: Routledge.

—— (1995), *Colonial Desire: Hybridity in Theory, Culture and Race*, New York: Routledge.

Zia, Helen (2001), *Asian American Dreams: The Emergence of an American People*, New York: Farrar, Straus and Giroux.

Selected Literary Anthologies

GENERAL

Gillan, Maria Mazziotti and Jennifer Gillan (eds) (1999), *Identity Lessons: Contemporary Writing about Learning to be American*, New York: Penguin Putnam.

Haslam, Gerald W. (ed.) (1970), *Forgotten Pages of American Literature*, Boston, MA: Houghton Mifflin.

Lauter, Paul et al (eds) (1999), *The Heath Anthology of American Literature*, Lexington, MA: D. C. Heath.

Moraga, Cherríe and Gloria Anzaldúa (eds) (1983), *This Bridge Called My Back: Writings by Radical Women of Color*, rev. 2nd edn, New York: Kitchen Table, Women of Color Press.

Phillips, J. J., Ishmael Reed, Gundar Strads and Shawn Wong (eds) (1992), *The Before Columbus Foundation Poetry Anthology: Selections from the American Book Awards 1980–1990*, New York and London: W. W. Norton.

Reed, Ishmael, Kathryn Trueblood and Shawn Wong (eds) (1992), *The Before Columbus Foundation Fiction Anthology: Selections from the American Book Awards 1980–1990*, New York and London: W. W. Norton.

AFRICAN AMERICAN

Cade, Toni (ed.) (1970), *The Black Woman: An Anthology*, New York: Signet.

Chapman, Abraham (ed.) (1968), *Black Voices*, New York: New American Library/ Mentor.

—— (ed.) (1972), *New Black Voices*, New York: New American Library/Mentor.

Emanuel, James A. and Theodore Gross (eds) (1968), *Dark Symphony: Negro Literature in America*, New York: Free Press.

Gates, Henry Louis and Nellie Y. McKay (eds) (1997), *The Norton Anthology of African American Literature*, New York: W. W. Norton.

Hill, Patricia Liggins (ed.) (1998), *Call and Response: The Riverside Anthology of the African American Tradition*, Boston, MA: Houghton Mifflin.

Jones, LeRoi and Larry Neal (eds) (1968), *Black Fire: An Anthology of Afro-American Writing*, New York: William Morrow.

Young, Al (ed.) (1995), *African American Literature: A Brief Introduction and Anthology*, The HarperCollins Literary Mosaic Series, New York: HarperCollins.

NATIVE AMERICAN

Glancy, Diane and Mark Nowak (eds) (1999), *Visit Teepee Town: Native Writings After the Detours*, Minneapolis, MN: Coffee House Press.

Harjo, Joy and Gloria Bird (eds) (1997), *Re-Inventing the Enemy's Language: Contemporary Native Women's Writing of North America*, New York: W. W. Norton.

King, Thomas (ed.) (1990), *All My Relations: An Anthology of Contemporary Canadian Native Fiction*, Toronto: McClelland and Stewart; reprinted (1992), Norman, OK: University of Oklahoma Press.

Niatum, Duane (ed.) (1988), *Harper's Anthology of 20th Century Native Poetry*, New York: HarperCollins.

Rosen, Kenneth (ed.) (1974), *The Man to Send Rain Clouds: Contemporary Stories by American Indians*, New York: Viking.

Trafzer, Clifford E. (ed.) (1992), *Earth Song, Sky Spirit: Short Stories of the Contemporary Native American Experience*, New York: Doubleday-Anchor.

Velie, Alan R. (ed.) (1979), *American Indian Literature: An Anthology*, Norman, OK: University of Oklahoma Press (rev. edn 1991).

Vizenor, Gerald (ed.) (1995), *Native American Literature: A Brief Introduction and Anthology*, The HarperCollins Literary Mosaic Series, New York: HarperCollins.

LATINO/A

Augenbraum, Harold and Margarite Fernández Olmos (eds) (1977), *The Latino Reader: An American Literary Tradition from 1542 to the Present*, Boston, MA: Houghton Mifflin.

Augenbraum, Harold and Ilan Stavans (eds) (1993), *Growing up Latino: Memories and Stories*, Boston, MA and New York: Houghton Mifflin/Marc Jaffe.

Babín, Maria Teresa and Stan Steiner (eds) (1974), *Borinquen: An Anthology of Puerto Rican Literature*, New York: Vintage.

Cardenas de Dwyer, Carlotta (ed.) (1975), *Chicano Voices*, Boston, MA: Houghton Mifflin.

Corpi, Lucha (ed.) (1997), *Máscaras*, Berkeley: Third Woman Press.

Fernández, Roberta (ed.) (1995), *In Other Words: Literature by Latinas*, Houston, TX: Arte Público Press.

Flores, Lauro (ed.) (1998), *The Floating Borderlands: Twenty-Five Years of US Hispanic Literature*, Seattle, WA and London: University of Washington Press.

Gómez, Alma, Cherrié Moraga and Mariana Romo-Carmona (eds) (1983), *Cuentos: Stories by Latinas*, New York: Kitchen Table Press.

Gonzalez, Ray (ed.) (1994), *Currents from a Dancing River: Contemporary Latino Fiction, Nonfiction, and Poetry*, San Diego, CA: Harcourt Brace.

Herrera-Sobek, María and Helena María Viramontes (eds) (1996), *Chicana Creativity and Criticism: New Frontiers in American Literature*, Albuquerque, NM: University of New Mexico Press.

Heyck, Denis Lynn Daly (ed.) (1994), *Barrios and Borderlands: Cultures of Latinos and Latinas in the United States*, New York and London: Routledge.

Hospital, Carolina (ed.) (1998), *Los Atrevidos: Cuban American Writers*, Princeton, NJ: Ediciones Ellas/Linden Lane Press.

Kanellos, Nicolas (ed.) (1995), *Hispanic American Literature: A Brief Introduction and Anthology*, The HarperCollins Literary Mosaic Series, New York: HarperCollins.

—— (ed.) (2002), *Herencia: The Anthology of Hispanic Literature of the United States*, New York: Oxford University Press.

Keller, Gary D and Francisco Jiménez (eds) (1980), *Hispanics in the United States: An Anthology of Creative Literature*, Ypsilanti, MI: Bilingual Press/Editorial Bilingüe.

Ludwig, Ed and James Santibañez (eds) (1971), *The Chicanos: Mexican American Voices*, Baltimore, MD: Penguin Books.

Steiner, Stan and Luis Valdez (eds) (1972), *Aztlán: An Anthology of Mexican American Literature*, New York: Knopf.

Turner, Faythe (ed.) (1991), *Puerto Rican Writers at Home in the USA*, Seattle, WA: Open Hand Publishing Company.

Zamora, Bernice (ed.) (1981), *The Best of Chicano Fiction*, Albuquerque, NM: Pajarito Publications.

ASIAN AMERICAN

Asian Women United of California (eds) (1989), *Making Waves: An Anthology by and about Asian American Women*, Boston, MA: Beacon Press.

Chin, Frank, Jeffery Paul Chan, Lawson Fusao Inada and Shawn Wong (eds) (1974), *AIIIEEEEEE! An Anthology of Asian-American Writers*, Washington, DC: Howard University Press.

——(eds) (1991), *The Big Aiiieeeee! An Anthology of Chinese American and Japanese American Literature*, New York: Meridian/Penguin.

Chock, Eric and Darrell H. Y. Lum (eds) (1986), *The Best of Bamboo Ridge: The Hawaii Writers' Quarterly*, Honolulu: Bamboo Ridge Press.

Day, A. Grove and Carl Stroven (eds) (1959), *A Hawaiian Reader*, New York: Appleton-Century-Crofts.

Fenkl, Heinz Insu and Walter K. Lew (eds) (2001), *Koru: The Beacon Anthology of Korean American Fiction*, Boston, MA: Beacon Press.

Francia, Luis H. and Eric Gamalinda (eds) (1997), *Flippin': Filipinos in America*, Seattle, WA: University of Washington Press.

Hagedorn, Jessica (ed.) (1993), *Charlie Chan is Dead: An Anthology of Contemporary Asian American Fiction*, New York: Penguin Books.

Hongo, Garrett (ed.) (1995), *Under Western Eyes: Personal Essays from Asian America*, New York: Anchor-Doubleday.

Kim, Elaine H. and Eui-Young Yi (eds) (1996), *East to America: Korean American Life Stories*, New York: New Press.

Lim, Shirley Geok-lin Lim, Mayumi Tsutukawa and Margarita Donnelly (eds) (1989), *The Forbidden Stitch: An Asian American Women's Anthology*, Corvallis, OR: Calyx Books.

Lum, Darrell H. Y., Joseph Stanton and Estelle Enoki (eds) (2000), *The Quietest Singing: Hawai'i Awards for Literature*, Honolulu: University of Hawai'i Press.

Maira, Sunaima and Rajini Srikanth (eds) (1996), *Contours of the Heart: South Asians Map North America*, New York: The Asian American Writers' Workshop.

Realuyo, Bino A., Rahna Reiko Rizzuto and Kendal Henry (eds) (1999), *The NuyorAsian Anthology: Asian American Writings about New York City*, Philadelphia, PA: Temple University Press.

Rustomji-Kerns, Roshni (ed.) (1999), *Encounters: People of Asian Descent in the Americas*, Lanham, MD: Rowman and Littlefield.

Srikanth, Rajini and Esther Y. Iwanga (eds) (2001), *Bold Words: A Century of Asian American Writing*, New Brunswick, NJ: Rutgers University Press.

Tachiki, Amy et al. (eds) (1971), *Roots: An Asian American Reader*, Los Angeles, CA: Asian American Studies Center, University of California at Los Angeles.

Tran, Barbara, Monique T. D. Truong and Luu Truong Khoi (eds) (1998), *Watermark: Vietnamese American Poetry and Prose*, New York: Asian American Writers' Workshop.

Watanabe, Sylvia and Carol Bruchac (eds) (1990), *Home to Stay: Asian American Women's Fiction*, Greenfield Center, NY: Greenfield Review Press.

———— (eds) (1996), *Into the Fire: Asian-American Prose*, Greenfield Center, NY: Greenfield Review Press.

Wong, Shawn (ed.) (1995), *Asian American Literature: A Brief Introduction and Anthology*, The HarperCollins Literary Mosaic Series, New York: HarperCollins.

OTHER

Danticat, Edwidge (ed.) (2001), *The Butterfly's Way: Voices from the Haitian Dyaspora in the United States*, New York: Soho.

Bibliographic and Reference Studies

General

Di Pietro, Robert and Edward Ifkovic (eds) (1983), *Ethnic Perspectives in American Literature: Selected Essays on the European Contribution, A Sourcebook*, New York: The Modern Language Association of America.

Holte, James Craig (ed.) (1988), *The Ethnic I: A Sourcebook for Ethnic American Autobiography*, Westport, CT: Greenwood Press.

Knippling, Alpana Sharma (ed.) (1996) *New Immigrant Literatures in the United States: A Sourcebook of Our Multicultural Heritage*, Westport, CT: Greenwood Press.

Maitano, John R. and David R. Peck (eds) (1996), *Teaching American Ethnic Literatures*, Albuquerque, NM: University of New Mexico Press.

African American

Andrews, William L., Frances Smith Foster and Trudier Harris (eds) (1997) *The Oxford Companion to African American Literature*, New York: Oxford University Press.

Bruccoli, Matthew and Judith S. Baughman (eds) (1994), *Modern African American Writers*, New York: Facts on File.

Davis, Thadious M. and Trudier Harris (eds) (1994), *Dictionary of Literary Biography. vol. 33: Afro-American Fiction Writers after 1955*, Detroit, MI: Bruccoli Clark/Gale.

Harris, Trudier (ed.) (1987) *Dictionary of Literary Biography. vol. 76: Afro-American Writers 1940–1955*, Detroit, MI: Bruccoli Clark/Gale.

Houston, Helen Ruth (1997), *The Afro-American Novel 1965–1975: A Descriptive Bibliography of Primary and Secondary Materials*, Troy, NY: Whitson.

Inge, M. Thomas M., Maurice Duke and Jackson R. Bryer (eds) (1978), *Black American Writers: Bibliographical Essays*, vols 1 and 2, New York: St Martin's Press.

Turner, Darwin (ed.) (1970), *Afro-American Writers*, New York: Appleton-Century Crofts.

Valade, Roger M., III (ed.) (1996), *The Essential Black Literature Guide*, Detroit, MI: Gale Research/Visible Ink Press, published in association with the Schomberg Center for Research in Black Culture.

Werner, Craig (ed.) (1989), *Black American Women Authors: An Annotated Bibliography*, Pasadena, CA and Englewood Cliffs, NJ: Salem.

Native American

Allen, Paula Gunn (ed.) (1983), *Studies in American Indian Literature: Critical Essays and Course Designs*, New York: The Modern Language Association of America.

Colonnese, Tom and Louis Owens (eds) (1985), *American Indian Novelists: An Annotated Critical Bibliography*, New York: Garland Publishing.

Hoxie, Frederick E. (ed.) (1996), *Encylopedia of North American Indians*, Boston, MA: Houghton Mifflin.

Littlefield, Daniel F. and James W. Parins (eds) (1981), *A Bibliography of Native American Writers, 1772–1924*, Metuchen, NJ: The Scarecrow Press.

—— (1985), *Supplement*, Metuchen, NJ: The Scarecrow Press.

Marken, Jack W. (ed.) (1978), *The American Indian: Language and Literature*, Arlington Heights, VA: AHM Publishing Corporation.

Morrison, Dane (ed.) (1997), *American Indian Studies: An Interdisciplinary Approach to Contemporary Issues*, New York: Peter Lang.

Roemer, Kenneth M. (1997), *Dictionary of Literary Biography, Native American Writers of the United States*, vol. 175, Detroit, MI: Gale Research.

Ruoff, A. Lavonne Brown (1990), *American Indian Literatures: An Introduction, Bibliographic Review, and Selective Bibliography*, New York: The Modern Language Association of America.

Whitson, Kathy J. (1999), *Native American Literatures: An Encyclopedia of Works, Characters, Authors, and Themes*, Santa Barbara, CA: ABC-CLIO.

Wiget, Andrew (ed.) (1985), *Critical Essays on Native American Literature*, Boston, MA: G. K. Hall.

—— (1994), *Dictionary of Native American Literature*, New York: Garland Publishing.

Witalec, Janice (ed.) (1995), *Smoke Rising: The Native North American Literary Companion*, Detroit, MI: Visible Ink Press/Gale.

LATINO/A

Boswell, Thomas D. (1984), *The Cuban-American Experience: Culture, Images, and Perspectives*, Totowa, NJ: Rowman and Allanheld.

Foster, David William (ed.) (1982), *Sourcebook of Hispanic Culture in the United States*, Chicago, IL: American Library Association.

Kanellos, Nicolás (1983), *Puerto Rican Literature: A Bibliography of Secondary Sources*, Westport, CT: Greenwood Press.

—— (ed.) (1989), *Biographical Dictionary of Hispanic Literature in the United States: The Literature of Puerto Ricans, Cuban Americans and Other Hispanic Writers*, New York: Greenwood Press.

—— (ed.) (1994), *Hispanic Almanac: From Columbus to Corporate America*, Visible Ink Press/ Gale Research.

Kanellos, Nicolás and Clandio Esteva-Fabregat (eds) (1994–5), *Handbook of Hispanic Culture in the United States*, vols 1–14, Houston TX: Arte Público Press.

Lomelí, Francisco (ed.) (1983), *The Handbook of Hispanic Cultures in the United States: Literature: and Art*, Houston, TX: Arte Público Press and Instituto de Cooperación Iberoamericana.

Lomelí, Francisco and Carl R. Shirley (eds) (1989), *Dictionary of Literary Biography*, vol. 82: *Chicano Writers*, Detroit, MI: Gale Research.

Lomelí, Francisco and Donaldo W. Uriosto (eds) (1976) *Chicano Perspectives in Literature: A Critical and Annotated Bibliography*, Albuquerque, NM Pajarito Publications.

Martínez, Julio A. and Francisco Lomelí (eds) (1985), *Chicano Literature: A Reference Guide*, Westport, CT: Greenwood Press.

Olivares, Julián (1988), *US Hispanic Autobiography*, Houston, TX: Arte Público Press.

Valk, Barbara G. (ed.) (1988), *Borderline: A Bibliography of the United States–Mexico Borderlines*, Los Angeles, CA: UCLA Latin American Studies Center Publications.

Wagenheim, Karl (1973), *The Puerto Ricans: Documentary History*, New York: Praeger.

Zimmerman, Marc (1992), *US Latino Literature: An Essay and Annotated Bibliography*, Chicago, IL: March/ABRAZO Press.

ASIAN AMERICAN

Cheung, King-Kok (ed.) (1997), *An Interethnic Companion to Asian American Literature*, Cambridge: Cambridge University Press.

Cheung, King-Kok and Stan Yogi (eds) (1988), *Asian American Literature: An Annotated Bibliography*, New York: The Modern Language Association of America.

Kim, Hyung-Chan (ed.) (1986), *Dictionary of Asian American History*, Westport, CT: Greenwood Press.

Nelson, Emmanuel S. (ed.) (2000), *Asian American Novelists: A Bio-Bibliographical Critical Sourcebook*, Westport, CT: Greenwood Press.

Nomura, Gail M., Russell Endo, Stephen H. Sumida and Russell C. Leong (eds) (1989), *Frontiers of Asian American Studies: Writing, Research and Commentary*, Pullman, WA: Washington State University Press.

Trudeau, Lawrence J. (ed.) (1999), *Asian American Literature: Reviews and Criticism by American Writers of Asian Descent*, Detroit, MI: Gale.

Wong, Sau-ling Cynthia and Stephen H. Sumida (eds) (2001), *A Resource Guide to Asian American Literature*, New York: The Modern Language Association of America.

Index